FR
ARABYE
TO
ENGELOND

vi

FROM ARABYE TO ENGELOND

MEDIEVAL STUDIES IN HONOUR OF MAHMOUD MANZALAOUI ON HIS 75TH BIRTHDAY

Edited by

A. E. Christa Canitz
and
Gernot R. Wieland

UNIVERSITY OF OTTAWA PRESS

University of Ottawa Press gratefully acknowledges the support extended to its publishing programme by the Canada Council and the University of Ottawa.

We acknowledge the financial support of the Government of Canada through the Book Publishing Industry Development Program (BPIDP) for our publishing activities.

Canadian Cataloguing in Publication Data

Main entry under title:
    From Arabye to Engelond: medieval studies in honour of Mahmoud Manzalaoui on his 75th birthday

(Actexpress)
Includes bibliographical references.
ISBN 0-7766-0517-8

1. Medieval literature–Arab influences.   2. English literature–Arab influences.
3. English literature–Middle English, 1100-1500.   4. Middle Ages. 5. Middle East.
I. Manzalaoui, Mahmoud. II. Canitz, Auguste Elfriede Christa, 1956-   .
III. Wieland, Gernot R. (Gernot Rudolf), 1946-   .   IV. Series.

PN681.F76 1999   820.9′001   C00-900015-1

UNIVERSITY OF OTTAWA
UNIVERSITÉ D'OTTAWA

Cover illustration: The illumination is taken from a 15th-century manuscript of the *Secretum Secretorum*, a work that purports to be a letter in which Aristotle advises his pupil, King Alexander, on a wide variety of topics. (University College MS. 85, p. 70; reproduced by kind permission of the Master and Fellows of University College, Oxford.)

"Books in the ACTEXPRESS series are published without the University of Ottawa Press's usual editorial intervention. The editorial process for and copy editing of *From Arabye to Engelond: Medieval Studies in Honour of Mahmoud Manzalaoui on His 75th Birthday* have been ensured by the editors and their contributors."

ISBN 0-7766-0517-8
ISSN 1480-4743

© University of Ottawa Press, 1999
542 King Edward, Ottawa, Ont. Canada K1N 6N5
press@uottawa.ca   http://www.uopress.uottawa.ca

Printed and bound in Canada

CONTENTS

ACKNOWLEDGEMENTS

Numerous friends and colleagues have helped in the preparation of this collection, and it is a pleasure to acknowledge the many debts of gratitude we have incurred.

For generously sharing their expertise, we are particularly grateful to Professors Michael Cummings (York University, Toronto), Siân Echard (University of British Columbia), Roberta Frank (University of Toronto), Melissa Furrow (Dalhousie University), Andrew Galloway (Cornell University), Walter Goffart (University of Toronto), Sebastian Günther (University of Toronto), Paul Harvey (Pennsylvania State University), Constance Hieatt (University of Western Ontario), James Noble (University of New Brunswick, Saint John), William Paden (Northwestern University), Marjorie Ratcliffe (University of Western Ontario), Mary Rimmer (University of New Brunswick), Teresa Tavormina (Michigan State University), Andrew Taylor (University of Saskatchewan), and Jane Toswell (University of Western Ontario). Their comments and criticisms helped shape the individual papers.

We also had editorial help from Colin Smith (University of New Brunswick), and from Roger Seamon (University of British Columbia), who helped proofread large parts of this volume and contributed in many other ways too numerous to mention. Jane Foster and Susan Miller, of the Department of English, University of New Brunswick, kindly provided technical assistance.

We also gratefully acknowledge publication grants provided to us by the Vice-President, Academic, and the Dean of Arts at the University of New Brunswick and by the Vice-President, Research, and the Dean of Arts at the University of British Columbia; without these grants this volume could not have been published.

ABBREVIATIONS

CCSL	*Corpus Christianorum Series Latina*
CSEL	*Corpus Scriptorum Ecclesiasticorum Latinorum*
EETS	Early English Text Society
ELH	*English Literary History*
ESC	*English Studies in Canada*
GRLMA	*Grundriß der romanischen Literatur des Mittelalters.* Gen. eds. Hans Robert Jauss and Erich Köhler. Heidelberg: Winter, 1979.
GRM	*Germanisch-Romanische Monatsschrift*
HE	*Historia Ecclesiastica. Bede's Ecclesiastical History of the English People.* Ed. B. Colgrave and R. A. B. Mynors. Oxford: Clarendon, 1969.
MED	*Middle English Dictionary*
MGH	Monumenta Germaniae Historica
OED	*Oxford English Dictionary*
PL	*Patrologiae cursus completus . . . Series Latina*
RES	*Review of English Studies*
ZDA	*Zeitschrift für deutsches Altertum und deutsche Literatur*

A. E. Christa Canitz
Gernot R. Wieland

INTRODUCTION

As both person and scholar, Mahmoud A. Manzalaoui embodies the dialogue between cultures, languages, and traditions that is fundamental to the reality and the ideal of a multicultural civilization. The present collection of essays by colleagues, former students, and academic friends is a tribute to and reflection of the scholarly dimension of his multiculturalism.

Born in London, England, Mahmoud Manzalaoui was educated in Alexandria and in Cairo, at Victoria College, a British public school. He read English literature at the University of Cairo and took his first degree there in 1944, before matriculating at Magdalen College, Oxford, where he–inverting the usual sequence–graduated B.Litt. in 1947, B.A. in 1948, and D.Phil. in 1954. This period at Oxford also saw the gradual maturation of his work on the connections between Arabic and English literature as his primary field of scholarly enquiry. While his B.Litt. thesis, supervised by C. S. Lewis, was concerned with English translations of Arabic literature of the eighteenth and early nineteenth centuries and their influences on nineteenth-century English literature, his D.Phil. dissertation, which he wrote under J. A. W. Bennett's guidance, laid the foundations for his life's work on the pseudo-Aristotelian advice treatise *Secretum Secretorum*. This thesis presented his first findings on the impact of the *Secretum* on English literature and thought.

After almost twenty years' teaching at the University of Alexandria, Professor Manzalaoui followed his two former Oxford mentors, C. S. Lewis and J. A. W. Bennett, to Cambridge. He has remained associated with Cambridge ever since, first as a Visiting Fellow at Clare Hall while also teaching for King's College, and later as an Associate of Clare Hall.

In 1969, he changed countries once again, coming to Canada to accept an appointment at the University of British Columbia, where he taught until

1

his retirement in 1989. During this time, he published numerous articles and reviews, especially on Arabic influences on, and the representation of Arabic culture in, English literature, medieval, Renaissance, and modern. However, the breadth of his publications is best illustrated by his books: his two-volume edition of *Arabic Writing Today* (a collection of translations, including his own, of short fiction and drama), and his monumental EETS edition of the *Secretum Secretorum: Nine English Versions* (presenting nine medieval and early modern versions as parallel texts). Ever since its publication in 1977, the latter work has served as a major resource for medievalists with a wide variety of research interests, from the 'advice to princes' tradition to the application of physiognomical lore in the portraits of Chaucer's pilgrims.

Apart from pursuing his own research, Professor Manzalaoui has always been most generous in sharing his wide-ranging knowledge. There can be few who are more erudite and truly learned and at the same time more self-effacing in letting others benefit from a lifetime of study. For almost three decades, *Medium Ævum* and other journals relied on his expertise for reviews of works concerned with the connection between Arabic and Western European cultures. English departments and Comparative Literature programmes both in Canada and in England similarly depended on him as external examiner of theses in this area. Students of Chaucer everywhere know his paper on "Chaucer and Science" (in Derek Brewer's volume *Chaucer and His Background*, 1974). And students and colleagues in his own department have profited immeasurably from his immense learning, both before and after his retirement. After a conversation with Mahmoud, whether at length over dinner or briefly in the departmental hallways, one comes away with the sense that one has learned something, yet he wears his erudition gracefully. It is a rare experience (and delight!) to have read a book before he has.

Having lived in Egypt, England, and Canada and being fluently trilingual in Arabic, English, and French as well as being thoroughly familiar with the literatures written in these languages, Mahmoud Manzalaoui is a cosmopolitan, transnational scholar, a person genuinely without borders. His edition of the *Secretum*, a work that exists in numerous versions and languages, is an emblem of this cosmopolitanism. Leaving Egypt in the late 1960's was an act of self-imposed exile. More than most of us, he has experienced the makings of modern history: members of his family who had once held imperial Russian titles were sold into slavery, only to rise again to exalted positions in the Egyptian court and aristocracy before becoming connected by marriage to the Manzalaouis, an ancient Egyptian family of landowners with connections to the Sufi mystic order; he himself witnessed the arbitrary imprisonment of friends and students by the dictatorial regime in Egypt during the period of the Six-Day War; and he experienced first-hand the effects of a country's colonization. Yet while others might have perceived living in North America as exile from Arabic and European culture and felt bitter about this experience, Mahmoud Manzalaoui represents the human capacity to assimilate and adopt the best that diverse cultures have to offer, spiritually, culturally, and intellectually. The academic world provided him with the opportunity to cross boundaries of language, culture, ethnicity, and nationality in pursuit of an ideal–the notion of a human universality based on learning, which transcends such boundaries. For others, scholarship might be an add-on; for him, it is at the centre of being, with learning being taken for granted as a good in itself.

But lofty ideals are not all there is to life. Daily experience also has more mundane challenges which are not subject to scholarship–including xerox machines, lawnmowers, and police cars. Before his retirement, Mahmoud could strike terror in the secretaries in the UBC English department, simply by approaching the photocopier, where his knack for pushing the wrong buttons was believed to lead to the complete malfunction and irremediable shut-down of the machinery. Lawnmowers present other problems; when Mahmoud lost a fingertip because he had forgotten to turn off the mower before inspecting the running blades, there ensued a pronounced incongruity between the gesture of his continuously raised (though bandaged) middle finger and Mahmoud's normally much more gentlemanly manner. But the gentleman again triumphed when it came to questions of etiquette in the treatment of a policewoman–is she to be treated as a lady or as a police officer? Mahmoud must be the only person in North America who can get away with opening the driver's door of a police cruiser in order to let the lady take her seat behind the wheel so that she might help him recover his stolen property.

Mahmoud Manzalaoui is loved by his friends and colleagues for his combination of sophistication and unworldliness, and respected for his scholarship, erudition, and fair-mindedness. On the occasion of his seventy-fifth birthday, we all present this volume to him in token of our deep affection and profound respect for him as a scholar, colleague, former supervisor and teacher, and friend.

3

A festschrift, by necessity, reflects the interests of the person being honoured as well as those of the persons wishing to honour him. When all these various interests are brought together between the covers of one book, there will be a great diversity, even though all the papers deal with one aspect or another of the Middle Ages. Within this broad category, some general patterns quickly emerge: Hanna Kassis, Derek Carr, and Chris Turner write on what might be called "Matters Middle Eastern"; Christa Canitz, Murray Evans, Kieran Kealy, Derek Brewer, Laurel Brinton, Beryl Rowland, and Douglas Wurtele write on "Matters Middle English"; and the remaining contributors, Paul Burns, Elisabeth Brewer, Anne Klinck, Patricia Merivale, John Mills, and Gernot Wieland, write on other medieval and medievalist matters ranging "from Arabye to Engelond." In their wide range of topics and diversity of critical approaches, the papers collected in this volume represent an interdisciplinary slice of academe and reflect a major fact about academic commentary today. There is no grand synthesis, no "master narrative." Instead, we encounter a composite picture, held together by the intricate relationships among the parts.

Hanna Kassis' "Images of Europe and Europeans in Some Medieval Arabic Sources" and Derek Carr's "Arabic and Hebrew *auctoritates* in the Works of Enrique de Villena" clearly belong together in that they examine the extent of the knowledge Arabs had of Europeans, and Europeans (or at least Enrique de Villena) had of Arabs. Chris Turner's "The First Patriarchate of Gennadios II Scholarios as Reflected in a Pastoral Letter" also deals to a large extent with the relations of Europeans to Islam, specifically with Gennadios II Scholarios' attempts to find a *modus vivendi* with Sultan Mehmed II, the new ruler of Constantinople after the fall of the city in 1453. Traces of "Matters Middle Eastern" also appear in other essays. Derek Brewer's "The Compulsions of Honour" refers to the "honour systems [which] are clearly evident . . . in Islam, where they are going strong today," and attempts in part to illuminate the honour system apparent in Middle English literature, specifically in *Sir Gawain and the Green Knight*, in Chaucer and in Malory, by means of anthropological studies done on honour systems in Arabic countries. Beryl Rowland's "'Ad restringuendum coytum': How to Cool Lust," another of the "Matters Middle English" essays, mentions the Arab physician Avicenna, whose *Canon of Medicine* strongly influenced European medical writers. Rowland's and Carr's papers thus complement each other in showing Avicenna's influence on European medical writers in general and on Enrique de Villena in particular. Anne Klinck's "The Oldest Folk Poetry? Medieval Woman's Song as 'Popular'

Lyric" also touches on "Matters Middle Eastern" in her discussion of the Mozarabic *kharjas*, which form the conclusions to more elaborate poems in Arabic or Hebrew. Read singly, Hanna Kassis', Chris Turner's, and Derek Carr's papers provide illuminating glances at Arab-European relations; read in conjunction with Derek Brewer's, Beryl Rowland's, and Anne Klinck's papers, they become part of a larger picture hinting at the much more pervasive interaction between the European and Arabic cultures.

Several of the essays focus on "Matters Anglo-Saxon," yet also make connections with the Middle English period. Paul Burns' "The Writings of Hilary of Poitiers in Medieval Britain from c. 700 to c. 1330" explores literary echoes of Hilary's works in the Anglo-Saxon period, and catalogues the manuscripts of the Anglo-Saxon and Middle English periods which contain works of Hilary. Likewise, Laurel Brinton, in her essay "'Whilom, as olde stories tellen us': The Discourse Marker *whilom* in Middle English," moves from the Old to the Middle English period in her examination of this word's semantic and morphological history. Derek Brewer's essay draws on the Cynewulf and Cyneheard episode of the *Anglo-Saxon Chronicle* (entry for the year 757), and traces the concept of honour gleaned from this episode into the Middle English period. Anne Klinck's essay also contains matters Anglo-Saxon, examining the notoriously enigmatic Old English poem "Wulf and Eadwacer" as part of her larger discussion of *Frauenlieder*, and considering it different from the heroic poetry of the time, in being more lyrical. Thematic links appear also between certain passages in Chris Turner's essay and Gernot Wieland's "*Ge mid wige ge mid wisdome*: Alfred's Double-Edged Sword": when Gennadios wondered why Christian Byzantium had been conquered by the "infidels," he could only answer that the conquest must have been a punishment by God for the sins of the Christians. Similarly, in Wieland's paper Alfred the Great comes to the conclusion that the pagan Vikings were sent as punishment to the Christian Anglo-Saxons because they had neglected their search for wisdom. "Matters Anglo-Saxon" are thus interwoven with both "Matters Middle English" and "Matters Middle Eastern" and present illuminating linkages with essays in the other groups.

Among the papers discussing Middle English language and literature, three share a concern in elucidating Chaucer's literary methods. Kieran Kealy's "Voices of the Tabard: The Last Tales of the *Canterbury Tales*," Christa Canitz's "Courtly Hagiomythography and Chaucer's Tripartite Genre Critique in the *Legend of Good Women*," and Douglas Wurtele's "Another Look at an Old 'Science': Chaucer's Pilgrims and Physiognomy" all deal directly and only with Chaucer. Wurtele attempts to determine the extent to which Chaucer was influenced by physiognomical handbooks and draws specifically on Mahmoud Manzalaoui's own edition of the *Secretum Secretorum*; Kealy explores the way in which the last of the *Canterbury Tales* prepare for Chaucer's Retraction; and Canitz examines Chaucer's use and subversion of the genres epic, romance, and hagiography. By also including Malory and the poet of *Sir Gawain and the Green Knight*, D. Brewer's paper expands the focus from Chaucer to Middle English literature generally. Murray Evans' "Coleridge's Sublime and Langland's Subject in the Pardon Scene of *Piers Plowman*," in turn, shifts the focus to Langland. Brinton, concerned with Middle English language, draws among others on the works of Chaucer and Gower for her examples of *whilom*. Beryl Rowland's "'Ad restringuendum coytum': How to Cool Lust" focusses on a Latin text in a Middle English manuscript in order to examine an important aspect of medieval English culture, specifically some of the means to curb forbidden sexuality. John Mills' essay, "The Pageant of the Sins," concentrates on Errour and the Seven Deadly Sins of Spenser's *Fairie Queene*; at the same time it exhibits an interest in medieval preoccupations, best seen in the sections discussing the representation of these same sins in Chaucer's *Parson's Tale*. With seven of the sixteen papers firmly anchored in the Middle English period, and an eighth closely related to it, the essays dealing with Middle English language and literature form the nucleus of this collection, and this is as it should be since their interests overlap most closely with those of the festschrift's honoree.

Two other essays form a sub-group dealing with the continuing appeal the Middle Ages have to later periods, the nineteenth and twentieth centuries respectively. Elisabeth Brewer's "John Ruskin's Medievalism" examines Ruskin's reflections on the Middle Ages, and Patricia Merivale's "*Sub Rosa*: Umberto Eco and the Medievalist Mystery Story" ponders the long shadow Eco's *The Name of the Rose* casts on medievalist mystery writers such as Ellis Peters, Peter Tremayne, and Sharan Newman, and even on the non-medievalist writer Philip Kerr. The phenomenon of "medievalism" cannot be discounted by any medievalist. The fictional efforts of an Ellis Peters or an Umberto Eco resemble the scholarly efforts of a Ruskin, a Tolkien, or a Manzalaoui. Whether through fiction or through scholarly criticism they–in Wordsworth's words–"throw . . . a certain colouring of imagination" over the Middle Ages and in their various ways pursue the common goal of making the medieval past come alive. Essays examining "medievalism" are an essential component of the study of the Middle Ages.

In their interconnectedness these essays form a web as intricate as any created by an Anglo-Saxon interlace. Collectively, they examine the Middle Ages from about the year 700 to its end, explore the ways in which the medieval period has been represented in the nineteenth and twentieth centuries, and cover a geographical area ranging "from Arabye to Engelond." Our hope is that in their rich variety these essays echo, and add to, the interests of Mahmoud Manzalaoui, and are a suitable tribute to an esteemed colleague, a valued teacher, and a generous friend.

Christa Canitz, Fredericton, New Brunswick
Gernot Wieland, Vancouver, British Columbia
March 1999

Hanna E. Kassis

IMAGES OF EUROPE AND EUROPEANS IN SOME MEDIEVAL ARABIC SOURCES

"Europa," or the fair *'Orphah* ("the girl with a full mane") as she was known in some early Semitic languages, was the daughter of the Phoenician king of Tyre (modern Lebanon), who was abducted by Zeus and for whom she bore three sons. Her brother Cadmus was sent by her father to fetch her; but instead of bringing her back, he settled in Thebes, where he taught the Greeks the alphabet of his people, the Phoenicians. 'Orphah's name, adapted to "Europa" as it was unpronounceable to the Greeks, came to be applied first to the Greek mainland and subsequently to the land mass behind it.

Unlike their Greek predecessors and mentors (particularly the second-century [Christian era] Egyptian-born astronomer / geographer Ptolemy, whose writings gained wide currency in Arabic sources), Arabic[1] geographers initially paid little attention to "Europe" (as a continent) and the "Europeans" as such. They tended to focus more attention on regions within the vast Islamic world itself (stretching from Central Asia to the Atlantic Ocean), as well as on parts of Asia and Africa that were outside the "house of Islam." "Europe," by contrast, attracted them less. This may have been due to the fact that there was little in Europe to interest the Muslims and, consequently, Arabic writers. This was certainly different with Byzantium, India, or China, which fascinated them and captured their creative imagination.

Arabic writers had some acquaintance with "Europe"; the toponym appears in the adaptation of Ptolemy's *Geography* by al-Khwārizmī (d. 847),[2] and is mentioned in passing in some other early Arabic geographical works. For example, Ibn Khurdādhbīh (d. 911?) refers to Europe in his geographical work as *arūfá*, and defines it as follows: "The inhabited world has been divided into four parts. One of these is Europe [*arūfá*], which comprises Spain, the habitation of the Slavs, the Romans, and

9

the Franks, as well as Tangier and beyond, as far as the boundary of Egypt" (Ibn Khurdādhbīh 155 [Arabic], 116 [French]).

He may have been followed by the late tenth-century anonymous Persian author of *Hudūd al-'ālam* ("The Regions of the World"), who calls it *urūfā* and defines it as follows: "The third part has on its east the Straits of Constantinople; on its south, the sea of *rūm* [the Mediterranean]; on its west, the Western Ocean; and on its north, the limit of the cultivated land of the north. This part is called *urūfā*, and forms one-quarter of all the cultivated lands of the world" (*Hudūd al-'ālam* 83).

One of the earliest and most detailed references to "Europe" in Arabic writings is to be found in the translation of Paulus Orosius' *Historiae adversum paganos*, which was carried out in Muslim Spain in the course of the tenth century.[3]

Succeeding writers in Arabic copied and elaborated on Orosius' terse account, which is confined to the definition of boundaries and the description of various regions of Europe and some of its cities. They tended to echo the same type of information about Europe, albeit with some variations, calling it by diverse names and defining its boundaries differently. For example, the tenth-century geographer al-Istakhrī called it "the land of the *rūm*" (the "Romans," see below) and defined its boundaries as follows: "The boundaries of the land of the *rūm* ["Romans"] extend from the [Atlantic] ocean to Constantinople, and encompass Galicia, the land of the Franks (*ifranjah*), Rome (*rūmiyah*) and Athens, and reach as far as the land of the Slavs" (al-Istakhrī 8). He set the southern limits of the continent at Cyprus and Sicily, both of which at the time were under Muslim rule, saying that Sicily was "adjacent to *ifranjah*,"[4] and describing the inhabitants of Cyprus as being of the "people of *rūm*" (meaning "Greeks") (al-Istakhrī 70-71).

As their knowledge of Greek geography was enriched by that of pre-Islamic Persia, Arabic writers (a number of whom were of Persian descent) increasingly shifted their emphasis to the different peoples of Europe, and to the lands and cities they inhabited, rather than simply focusing on land masses. This was more in harmony with their latent inclination to emphasize relationships and affiliations of kinship. In other words, as geographers they became more inclined towards human rather than physical geography. But, regardless of which methodological approach was employed, information about Europe and the Europeans in early medieval Arabic sources remained scanty and perfunctory.

This reluctant interest in European lands and peoples was gradually stirred, however, as Latin Christendom and the world of Islam locked in

10

battle. Whether this was at the Battle of Poitiers (in 732), the unsuccessful invasion of Muslim Spain by Charlemagne (in 778), the occupation of the southern coast of France by pirates from Muslim Spain (890-973), the sudden appearance of Vikings on the banks of the Guadalquivir in Muslim Spain (ninth century), the proto-crusade against Barbastro (1064), the fall of Toledo into the hands of Alfonso VI (1085) and its rapid conversion by the Cluniacs into a city with a Christian character, or the Crusades (as of 1096), these and similar events awakened the world of Islam to the reality of Europe and the Europeans. And while it was descriptive of the various peoples and regions of Europe, such information as was assembled, whether drawn from earlier sources, from travel reports–their own or others'–or from a close observation of the conduct of Crusaders and their families, was also indicative of the attitudes the Muslims maintained towards the different peoples of Europe. As Europe was inextricably associated with Christianity, any description of the Europeans inevitably mirrored the image of the Christians of Europe that was held by the Muslims. Such an image was invariably delineated by the prevailing state of relations between the two religious polities.

We should emphasize here that the encounter with Europe was not Islam's first meeting with Christianity and the Christians. From the onset of Islamic history, two Christian communities had played a significant role in the development of Arabic society. The first of these communities were the *nasārá*, the Christians as they appeared in the Qur'ān and in the experience of Muhammad, the Prophet of Islam. Together with the Jews, the Muslims were enjoined to protect them (*ahl al-dhimmah*, "People of the trust") as they were the earlier recipients of Divine revelation (*ahl al-kitāb*, "People of the Book"). Subsequently, the term referred as well to the indigenous Christian population living under Muslim rule and protection. But in spite of this, description of them as a group in Arabic sources is scanty. This may be due to the fact that they were left to manage their religious and civic affairs on their own. One does encounter the occasional reference to individuals among them in biographical dictionaries relating their particular achievements in any of the various areas of learning or service. For example, the biographical dictionaries of Ibn Juljul, and Ibn Abī Usaybi'ah are replete with references to Arabic Christians who excelled in medicine.

The positive attitude towards the indigenous Christians, the *nasārá*, was not relegated to a nostalgic prophetic past. It is noteworthy that at the peak of Crusader domination in the Near East, the Andalusian / North African traveller, Ibn Jubayr (who journeyed to the Near East between 1182 and

11

1185), reserves praise for the indigenous Arabic Christian population. He describes them as being hospitable to Muslim hermits, sharing with them their food. He boldly adds the comment, "If this is the manner in which the *naṣārá* [the indigenous Christians] treat the opponents of their religion, what would you say of the treatment the Muslims give to one another?" (Ibn Jubayr 260-261).

The second group of Christians identified by Arabic writers were the *rūm*, who in comparison with the *naṣārá*, attract more attention in the written sources. Depending on the context, the term refers to the Greeks, the Romans, or even the people of the Holy Roman Empire. However, in its more immediate application, the term refers to the Byzantines, the body politic presided over by an alien ruler, the Byzantine emperor, who was at once an enemy of Islam and a source of supply of some of the craftsmen and artisans of its building programme. The defeat of a contingent of the *rūm* (Byzantines) during the prophetic age merited the Qur'anic reference, "The *rūm* are vanquished,"[5] and was seen as a sign of the divine vindication of Islam and its perpetual triumph over the disbelief (*kufr*) of Christendom represented by the Byzantines. The Caliph in Damascus would have felt justified when he brazenly demanded of the Byzantine Emperor that he dispatch skilled craftsmen for the construction of the Mosque in Damascus in 706, threatening the destruction of the churches at Edessa, Jerusalem and Lydda if the Emperor failed to comply. But although the *rūm* were the enemy, they merited the respect of Muslims in general.

By contrast, European Christians were imprecisely defined in Muslim perception and were generally recognised by what was seen as the ethnic grouping to which they belonged. Such labels included the *'ajam* (non-Arabic speaking, "barbarian"), *saqālibah* (Slavs, and occasionally, Scandinavians), *al-majūs* (originally "Magi," but applied also to peoples of the north of Europe, namely, Scandinavia and the British Isles), *jalāliqah* (the Galicians of north-western Spain), *washkunsh* (the Basques), and *ifranj* or *al-firanj* (Franks). The latter term was generally applied to those encompassed by the Carolingian empire and subsequently to Latin Europe as a whole. As France, by virtue of its geographic location, was in the forefront of the confrontation between Islam and Latin Christendom, the *ifranj* (Franks), without necessarily being limited to France, occupied more attention than other European people in Arabic travel or geographic writing.

The *ifranj* (Franks) were viewed differently from either the *naṣārá* or the *rūm*. Their overall portrayal in Arabic sources was that of a people not dissimilar from other remote barbarians, who lacked sophistication as well

12

as the creativity of either the Byzantines or the indigenous Arabic Christians. The limited curiosity they did arouse was based more on their behaviour and customs than on their creative qualities. This may be explained by the fact that they came into clearer focus, in Muslim perception, only when they appeared as a ferocious enemy in the course of the eleventh century. The inventiveness of monastic centres had no appeal to Muslims as it concentrated mainly on issues of doctrine and included concepts (for example, matters pertaining to Christology) with which Islam and Christianity are at variance.

As a result primarily of reports of travellers, some Arabic writers viewed the *ifranj* and their territory, prior to the eleventh century, as a subject of intellectual curiosity but with little precision. One such early description is the account of Ibrāhīm Ibn Ya'qūb, an Andalusian Jew from Tortosa, who travelled extensively in the land of the *ifranj* as an emissary of the Caliph of Córdoba in 965. Although his account, which constitutes a description of the land and its peoples based on first-hand experience, is regrettably lost, it is quoted by later Muslim geographers such as al-Bakrī, of whom more will be said further on.

The most extensive extant source of information on the *ifranj* from this early period is that of al-Mas'ūdī (d. 957), who has been described by some Western scholars as the "Herodotus of the Arabic world." Speaking of the *ifranj* in his work entitled *Murūj al-Dhahab* ("Meadows of Gold"), Mas'ūdī gives an impression of a settled warrior people inhabiting a vast land. He identifies them as a northern people who were different from the Byzantines (*rūm*), the Slavs (*saqālibah*), or the Basques (*washkunsh*), and paints a picture of them as well-equipped and terrifying in warfare. However, although they were more able fighters than most northern peoples, they remained inferior to the Galicians (*jalāliqah*), one of whom could brave several Franks. They possessed a large number of cities, of which *barīzah* (Paris) was their capital.[6] The *ifranj* were Christians who were very orderly and obedient to their rulers, united in their word, and without partisan divisiveness (al-Mas'ūdī 2: 5-11).

Mas'ūdī's work had a definite influence on subsequent Arabic writers, and on the image of Europe that they portrayed. Some of these writers limited themselves to a rather cursory description of the terrain, others were intrigued as well by the structures of its more important cities, while yet others included an account, at times vivid, of the customs and behaviour of these "foreigners" (as the term *ifranj* has come to mean in modern Arabic). One writer who merits mention in this regard is the eleventh-century

Hispano-Arabic geographer al-Bakrī (d. 1094), who blended together different methodologies and utilized information drawn from both al-Mas'ūdī and Orosius, among other sources. He gives a more expansive description of Europe, which he calls *ifranjah*, and employs the common Biblical view of the origins of diverse ethnic groups: the human race descending from Noah's three sons. He says, in paraphrase, that the people of Europe (the *ifranj*) are Christians of the Catholic (*malkāniyyah*) rite, and are descended from Japheth, son of Noah. They include Franks, Galicians, Slavs, Lombards (*al-nūkbard*), Spanish (*al-ishbān*), Turkic peoples, Khazars, Burgundians (*al-burjān*), Alans (*al-lān*), and Gog and Magog (*Ya'jūj wa-Ma'jūj*).[7] The confines of their land extend southward to the Syrian Sea (another name for the Mediterranean), and northward to the Ocean, requiring the journey of two months in any direction. It is separated on the north and the east from the land of the Slavs by mountains (the Alps) "that project between the two seas." These mountains stretch as far as the land of the Basques as well as the land of *al-amānīsh* (undoubtedly a corruption of the name of the Alemanns), who speak a language different from that of the *ifranj*. Al-Bakrī describes the land of the Slavs as attached to the land of the *majūs* (the Vikings or Norsemen), who are known as the *anqilish* (the Angles). Speaking of its physical characteristics, he writes that Europe suffers from bad weather due to cold temperatures, although its summers are temperate. It is abundant in fruits and rivers and possesses well-planned cities whose walls are well-constructed (al-Bakrī 143).

Occasionally, the description of European cities in Arabic writings goes into considerable detail. The early tenth-century writer Ibn Rustah (writing between 903-913) described the route from Constantinople to Rome; after giving a rather vivid depiction of the Byzantine capital, his narrative leads us through the land of the Bulgars and the Slavs until we reach

> a village called *bunduqīs* [Venice], whose inhabitants live in a flat land resembling a desert. They possess neither cities nor other villages, and their houses are built of carved boards of wood. They are Christians, in whose land you may travel the distance of twenty days, living in their midst, eating their food and provisioning yourself until you reach *rūmiyah* [Rome].
>
> (Ibn Rustah 128)

Ibn Rustah then describes Rome, beginning with the statement that it was administered by a king call *al-bāba* (the Pope). The city, whose dimensions measure forty Roman miles square, is traversed by a river the base and banks of which were paved with brass (bronze). Bridges over the river were

14

also constructed with the same material. Intriguingly enough, Ibn Rustah then concentrates his attention on "the great church which is at the centre of the city." His reference appears to be to St. Peter's Basilica as, according to his account, it contains the burials of two of the Apostles (of Christ) whom he names as Peter and Paul (*sic*), "made of gold, one of which is at the east end of the church while the other is at the west end." He is very impressed by the number of crosses in the church, six hundred by his report. At first glance, this interest might seem surprising, for to a Muslim, such as Ibn Rustah, the cross symbolizes a point of dogmatic disagreement with Christianity in the Qur'anic assertion that Jesus was not crucified.[8] In fact, Ibn Rustah appears to be swayed not so much by doctrinal issues as by the amount of gold and precious stones present in the crosses in this and other churches.

A similar image of Rome, based on information derived from earlier sources but rich in fanstasy, is presented by the twelfth-century Andalusian writer, al-Zuhrī, who writes of the city,

> One of the wonders of this city is the church known as the church of gold. It was thus named because it contains forty columns, twenty of which are made of gold while the other twenty are made of silver. These support arches and domes of coloured glass mosaics. In every panel of these domes, as well as at the top of each column, a magnetic stone was placed. These maintained the chandeliers in place as they hung in the air by leather cords. If the priests wished to say mass (?) on behalf of someone, they chose a windless day and cut the cords holding the chandeliers. These would remain suspended between heaven and earth [the ceiling and the floor], held in place by the magnetic stones, without either adhesive or nails.
>
> (al-Zuhrī 233)

It should be remembered that Ibn Rustah, like other Arabic writers, relied for his depiction of Europe either on earlier sources or on reports of travellers who not infrequently mingled fact with fiction, the real with the imaginary. Consequently, reality is occasionally peppered with fantasy in his and other writers' accounts of places they had not examined in person. For example, Ibn Rustah recounts a practice which, he says, occurred for nine centuries. Every Maundy Thursday, he tells us, the "king" (the Pope) enters the tomb of St. Peter in order to shave the saint's head and beard, and to clip his nails. The relics thus gathered are distributed among the people of his kingdom (Ibn Rustah 129).

15

What appears to be gold to Ibn Rustah is described as brass by al-Bakrī, who adds further details on the matter of the shaved beards of the people of Rome. According to his information, these Romans shave their beards as a symbol of being Christian. Here is how he explains the practice:

> Their learned ones said that the reason for this practice arises from the fact that Simon, the Rock, and other disciples came to them. 'They were poor people, each carrying nothing but a walking stick and a travelling bag. We [the Romans] were kings, wearing silk brocade and sitting on golden chairs. They [the disciples] called us to Christianity, but we did not heed their summons. Instead, we seized and tortured them, we shaved their heads and their beards. Then, when the truth of their message became evident to us, we shaved our beards as an act of contrition.' (al-Bakrī 205-206)

Such details are largely absent from the work of the twelfth-century al-Idrīsī (d. 1165?), whose geographical masterpiece may have been written as a companion commentary to the silver planisphere he had prepared for his patron, Roger II, the Norman king of Sicily (al-Idrīsī 723-807). Idrīsī's work, which is also known as *Kitāb rujjār* ("The Book of Roger"), is noted for its terseness as well as precision in areas with which he had first-hand acquaintance or drew upon reliable sources. While he does not mention "Europe" either by that name or any other, he deals with its different regions and cities, and the distances between them. But in spite of the concise nature of his coverage, some commentary slips in occasionally. For example, speaking of England he says, "The island of *inqiltārah* [England] resembles the head of an ostrich. It has populous cities, high mountains, overflowing streams, level ground, and abundant prosperity. Its people are patient, determined, and resolute. But its weather is that of endless winter" (al-Idrīsī 944). Elsewhere, he writes that that island (England) is separated from the continent by "a rough sea, ugly in colour, very deep, endlessly dark, with huge waves. It is stormy and difficult to traverse. Its western limits are not known. It is rare that people sail across it. Those who do are daring and have knowledge of it . . . . The people who sail on it most are known as the *inkilīsīyīn* [the English]" (al-Idrīsī 859).

In al-Idrīsī's estimation, the English are acutely different from their Irish neighbours, and from the Bretons. Speaking of the land of the Bretons and adjacent areas, he concludes that "these lands are comparable in their characteristics and conditions. Their built-up areas, regions, produce and abundance are all analogous. The inhabitants are characterized by their ignorance and coarse disposition. In summary, it is a land of abundance, comfort, and insensibility" (al-Idrīsī 859).

He cites one of his Arabic sources as saying that Ireland is a big island in which there are three, unnamed, cities. He adds,

> The people who inhabit these cities engaged in trade in amber and coloured stones. Then malevolence broke out among them as one of them wanted to be ruler over them. He and his people fought against them and enmity fell among them. Thus, they annihilated each other, while some of them fled across the sea to the great land mass [Continental Europe]. Thus, their cities were ruined and they perished. (al-Idrīsī 947-948)

Details about the inhabitants of Europe were limited but varied, depending on the author and his sources, as well as on the prevailing circumstances at the time of the construction of the images. We have already pointed out that, in this regard, the eleventh century must be seen as a major turning point. Until then, the prevailing image created of the Europeans by Arabic writers was simple and limited. The prevalent portrayal was that they were descended from Japheth, son of Noah, which placed them in the second category in the hierarchy of peoples (descendants of Shem being the first). They were Christians of the Melkite tradition (Catholic), and very powerful prior to the rise of Islam. Writers such as al-Bakrī included certain historical details about some of them, such as that "their first king was *qulūduyuh* (Clovis), who was Christianized by his wife *ghurṭilah* (Clotilde), and that their king now, in A.H. 332 (AD 944), is *lathurīq ibn qārluh* (Roderick son of Carlos), which names are often used by their kings" (al-Bakrī 139, 141).[9]

By the end of the eleventh century the tide turned. The first Crusade culminated in a series of events in Spain that included the fall of Toledo in 1085, and the victory of Yusuf Ibn Tashfin over Alfonso VI in 1086 at the Battle of Zallāqah and subsequent victories over his Frankish allies, notably at Lisbon in 1094. A Qur'anic verse was inscribed as a legend on the golden coins of the new rulers of Muslim Spain, the Berber Almoravids. It declared, "Whoso seeks a religion other than Islam, it shall not be accepted of him and in the hereafter he shall be among the losers" (*Sūra* 3:79). Because of the shortage of gold and silver in Europe, these coins were in great demand in Europe. While the Qur'anic passage was intended for internal circulation and directed against those Muslims presumed to be digressing from the faith, Christians saw in it a blatant religious assault. Islam in North Africa and Spain was undergoing a major revival, its first attempt at a return to orthodoxy (Kassis 78-110.). But, given the perception of Islam that prevailed in Europe, the revival movement as well as the legend on the golden coins were seen as an indication of yet another frustration by Muslims of God's will. The Cluniacs had designated Spain–all of Spain–as a land belonging of old to St. Peter, and the task now was to bring about its liberation from the infidel as well as its integration into the fold of Christianity. Franks and Castilians joined hands in the attempt to dislodge Islam from the Iberian Peninsula. This turn of events was in harmony with the billowing wind of war against Islam in the Near East. The trumpet was sounded on either side of the battlefield, in the east and the west, for battle for "God's cause."

It is here, therefore, that we begin to see the beginnings of a change in the attitude of Muslim writers towards the *ifranj*, from one of intellectual curiosity to that of an interest rooted in practical necessity. This did not, however, lead to a greater degree of precision in the knowledge that most Arabic writers had of the people or their territory. The *ifranj* remained largely uninteresting to them. One point, however, was certain, namely that they and their Castilian allies were now regarded as the enemies of God and of Islam, with the same intensity that Christian writers saw Islam and Muslims as such an enemy. Henceforth, the *ifranj* are frequently cursed when they are mentioned in the literature, and their lands are considered to be the domain of disbelief (*kufr*). God's power is invoked to destroy them and their cities, including Muslim cities conquered by these "worshippers of the Cross," and is invoked equally to protect Muslim cities from their assault.

In this new atmosphere, however, Arabic writers had the opportunity to observe the *ifranj* in the reality of their religious and daily lives. Alternatively, they were able to draw upon sources that witnessed this reality. Such first-hand observation was based mainly on the encounter with the *ifranj* in the Near East, their newly-conquered habitat. For example, the Andalusian writer al-Zuhrī, who visited Jerusalem, reports an account by al-Ruwayt,[10] who witnessed the following scene:

> On Christmas eve in Jerusalem, when the Christians [*rūm*] were taking communion, I saw one of the patriarchs of the Christians–this title [patriarch] is applied only to the most learned among them–seated on the Rock.[11] He was shaven in head and beard and was wearing a woollen robe decorated with red gold. On his head was a crown of gold embossed with pearls and rubies. His clavicle [clerical collar?] was pierced by a golden ring to which was attached a golden chain three cubits long. At the end of the chain was a golden chalice. [The Patriarch] fills it with baptismal [sanctified] water and baptizes

patriarchs, bishops, priests and monks. Some would give 1000 dinars to drink [from this chalice], others 500; the least amount given would be 100 dinars. Those who have drunk of this water, bring out the communion host (*qurbān*), as it is known by them.[12] He [Ruwayt] asked his companion, 'Who is that?' 'This is the mighty king, in the language of the Franks and the Syrians [the local Christians], and [he is also] the Patriarch . . . . People learn the sciences of the Christians from him.' It is claimed that whosoever drinks from that chalice, no sin shall be recorded against him, for the Patriarch had absolved him of his sins. It is also said that in the Christian religion, neither deacon nor bishop take office until they have been given to drink of that cup and have in turn given it to seven others. (al-Zuhrī 236-237)

Other writers give us detailed impressions of the *ifranj* as they encountered them. What is interesting is the fact that these writers tend to be more factual than propagandistic in their reports. In their observations, they seem to agree that at times the *ifranj* behaved in a manner which, measured against the strictures of Islamic or Islamicised society, appeared startling, if not reprehensible, to Arabic writers. One example of this is the description of the details of a wedding among the *ifranj* in the Near East by the Andalusian traveller Ibn Jubayr (Ibn Jubayr 278, Broadhurst 320).

Such also were the observations of Usāmah Ibn al-Munqidh (1095-1188), a member of a noble Syrian family, who spent a great part of his life in close contact with Crusader society, recurrently engaged in war against them, but equally often in friendly association with them during periods of peace. His impressions of the *ifranj* as he encountered them are preserved in his memoirs entitled *Kitāb al-i'tibār* ("The Book of [my] Point of View"). In this work he remarks that the *ifranj* were a people lacking in sense and rough in their comportment. This was particularly true of new-comers, some of whom, nonetheless, acquired the refinement of the East after settling there. He observed that they lacked jealousy or a sense of propriety in matters pertaining to sexuality. He was astonished at their judicial procedures, of which, for example, he found particularly curious their settlement of disagreements by duels, among other means. But, in spite of these peculiarities, he noted that they possessed curious medical "knowledge" (Ibn al-Munqidh 161-170).

These and similar opinions were occasionally reflected in subsequent writings, maintaining an image of the *ifranj* as being stalwart in battle, vulgar in their demeanour, and lax in matters of sexuality. Such an image is, perhaps, best summed up by the fourteenth-century Arabic writer al-Himyarī (d. 1348):

> The swords of the *ifranj* are superior to those of India. Precious slaves are brought from their land [*ifranjah*] while they import slaves from the land of the Slavs. There is hardly to be found among the *ifranj* an aging or handicapped person. Intercourse with unmarried women is not forbidden to them. If their elders or rulers break their word they are disgraced and are constantly rebuked for this disgrace. Children of their nobility are nursed away from their parents, not knowing them until they [the children] reach maturity, at which time they return home and treat their parents as lords to whom they are but slaves.
>
> (al-Himyarī 50, Lévi-Provençal 32 [French])

In the course of image-making, individuals or groups tend to emphasize or, at times, fabricate negative qualities about the other. Apart from some positive glimpses in secular writings (*Aucassin et Nicolette*, as one example), medieval Latin literature formulated an intensely negative image of Islam and the Muslims, based on little or no real knowledge.[13] Arabic writers, as well, engaged in representing Europe and the Europeans, positing them in the realm of the exotic, but found them less stimulating to their curiosity than the peoples of Asia or parts of Africa. Such impressions of Europe and the Europeans as had initially been based on the reports of others, were subsequently expanded once the two groups encountered each other during the period of the Crusades. Arabic writers such as Usāmah ibn al-Munqidh found it possible to speak of the good qualities of the *ifranj* and to describe them as hardy and industrious, orderly and obedient. But they somehow did not fully meet the standards of what was perceived to be a civilized society. The reasons for this attitude were not religious, in spite of Islam's rejection of certain, but by no means all, of the doctrines of Christianity. These doctrinal differences were the premise for Europe's rejection of the Muslims. Rather, for Arabic writers measuring the Europeans against the refinement of the Persians or the Byzantines, or that of the pre-Islamic peoples of the Near East, the *ifranj*, to whomever the term applied, weighed lightly in the scales. But in balance, neither Latin nor Arabic writers were able or willing to fully explore and discover the rich qualities of the other.

Notes

1. I use the term "Arabic" rather than "Arab" in order to emphasize the philological rather than the "ethnic" (or religious) affiliation of the various writers. Regardless of their regional or "ethnic" background, the writers utilized Arabic, the language of Islam, as their medium of expression. "Arab" as an ethnic term has very little to defend or substantiate it. The components of Arabic society were descendants of the people of the Arabian Peninsula (who identified themselves by reference to their respective tribes, and for whom the term "Arab" simply meant "nomad" rather than "city-dweller"), the semitic-speaking peoples of Syria / Lebanon / Palestine / Iraq, the Egyptians (non-semitic speaking), the Berbers of North Africa, the Romano-Iberians of the Iberian Peninsula, the Persian-speaking peoples of modern Iran, Afghanistan and parts of Central Asia, and–at a later time–Turkic and other peoples.

2. For a biography of this and other Arabic writers in this essay, see the relevant entry in the *Encyclopaedia of Islam: A Dictionary of the Geography, Ethnography and Biography of the Mohammadan Peoples* and the *Encyclopaedia of Islam* (new ed.). A concise identification of these writers may be found in the *"tableau des auteurs"* at the beginning of André Miquel's indispensable work (Miquel 1, xi-l).

3. This was one of two books sent by Romanus, the Byzantine co-emperor with Constantine Porphyrogenitos, to 'Abd al-Rahmān III, the caliph in Córdoba (912-961). The first book was an illuminated copy of the Greek text of Dioscorides' botanical treatise. The second was the Latin text of Paulus Orosius' *Historiae adversum paganos* (trans. as *Ta'rīkh al-'Ālam [History of the World]*). The translation took place during the caliphate of the bibliophile al-Hakam II (961-976), and was carried out by two Arabic Christians in Spain (Mozarabs). The text has been edited by 'Abd al-Rahmān Badawī, *Ta'rīkh al-'Ālam: al-Tarjamah al-'Arabīyah al-Qadīmah*. Beirut, 1982.

4. Generally a reference to the "land of the Franks" (*ifranj*), but as we shall point out, the terms *ifranj* and *ifranjah* refer as well to peoples other than the Franks or their land.

5. *Sūrah* 30 of the Qur'ān, entitled *al-rūm* and translated variably as "The Romans" or "The Greeks."

6. Erroneously transcribed as *bawīrah*. This error in transcription may be better understood if one bears in mind the closeness in form of the consonants w / r / z; short vowels are normally not written in Arabic.

7. The names and details of Gog and Magog are based on Biblical accounts: Genesis 10:2, where they appear as descendants of Japheth, and Ezekiel 38-39, which point to their eschatological role. The Arabic form appears in the Qur'ān (*Sūra* 21:96) and is incorporated in Arabic / Islamic eschatology, not dissimilar from that encountered in the Bible.

8. The dogma is expressed in the Qur'anic passage, "Yet they did not slay him [Jesus], neither crucified him, only a likeness of that was shown to them"; *sūra* 4 ("Women"), vs. 157, in Arberry's translation (Arberry 1955).

9. Al-Bakrī, copied the information from al-Mas'ūdī who reports that he derived his information from a book he saw in Cairo in A.H. 336 (AD 948), written by the Bishop of Gerona, which was then in Christian hands, and presented to the Andalusian caliph in Córdoba (al-Mas'ūdī 2, 7). We have set aside for the time being the discrepancy in the dates in these accounts. Bernard Lewis is of the opinion that this is in reference to Louis IV (936-954), son of Charles III, the Simple (Lewis 8).

10. According to al-Zuhrī, he was a man of learning who was taken prisoner and accompanied a priest to Constantinople and Rome in 1146. He was freed by 1154, when al-Zuhrī met him in Spain in Segura de la Sierra (*shaqūrah*).

11. He refers to the rock under the cupola of the Dome of the Rock, which at that time had been converted into a Crusader church, *Templum Domini*.

12. The inaccuracies contained in the description of the rite are apparent. I presume that al-Ruwayt is describing the rite of communion, with which rite he is not acquainted. The description, therefore, may be that of the presiding celebrant giving communion (both elements) to the assisting administrators, who in turn offer it (one element) to other worshippers within and outside the structure of the "church," the converted Dome of the Rock.

13. This problem has been best treated by the late Norman Daniel in several of his writings, particularly in his *Islam and the West*. See also his essay "Spanish Christian Sources."

Works Cited

Anonymous. *Hudūd al-'ālam: "The Regions of the World." A Persian Geography, 372 A.H. / 982 AD*. Trans. and explained by V. Minorsky. 2nd ed. London: Luzac, 1970.

Arberry, A. J. *The Koran Interpreted*. London: Allen and Unwin, 1955.

al-Bakrī. *Kitāb al-masālik wal-mamālik* [*The Book of Routes and Countries*], section entitled "Jughrāfīyat al-Andalus wa-Ūrūbbā" ["The Geography of al-Andalus and Europe"]. Ed. 'Abd al-Rahmān 'Alī al-Ḥajjī. Beirut: Dār al-Irshād, 1968.

Broadhurst, R. J. C. *see* Ibn Jubayr.

Daniel, Norman. *Islam and the West: The Making of an Image*. Edinburgh: Edinburgh UP, 1960. Rev. ed. Oxford: Oneworld, 1993.

—. "Spanish Christian Sources of Information about Islam." *Al-Qantara: Revista de Estudios Árabes* 15 (1994): 365-384.

Encyclopaedia of Islam: A Dictionary of the Geography, Ethnography and Biography of the Mohammadan Peoples. Leiden: Brill, 1913-1936; and the *Encyclopaedia of Islam*. New edition. Leiden: Brill, 1960-.

al-Ḥimyarī. *Kitāb al-rawd al-mi'tār fī khabar al-aqtār* [*The Fragrant Orchard of Information about Regions*]: *A Geographical Dictionary*. Ed. Ihsān 'Abbās. Beirut, 1975. Partial earlier edition with French translation by E. Lévi-Provençal, *La Pénisule Ibérique au Moyen-Age*. Leiden: Brill, 1938.

Ibn Abī Usaybi'ah. *'Uyūn al-Anbā' fī Tabaqāt al-Atibbā'*. Ed. Nizār Ridā. Beirut: Dār Maktabat al-Hayāt, 1965.

Ibn Jubayr. *Rihlah*. Beirut: Dār Sādir, 1964. English trans. by R. J. C. Broadhurst. *The Travels of Ibn Jubayr*. London: Cape, 1952.

Ibn Juljul. *Tabaqāt al-Atibbā' wal-Hukamā'*. Ed. Fu'ād Sayyid. Cairo: Institut français d'archéologie orientale, 1955.

Ibn Khurdādhbīh. *Kitāb al-masālik wal-mamālik (Liber viarum et regnorum). Bibliotheca Geographorum Arabicorum*. Vol. 6. Ed. M. J. de Goeje. Leiden: Brill, 1889. Rpt. 1967.

Ibn al-Munqidh, Usāmah. *Kitāb al-i'tibār*. Trans. Philip K. Hitti. *An Arab Syrian Gentleman and Warrior in the Period of the Crusades: Memoirs of Usāmah ibn-Munqidh (Kitāb al-i'tibār). Records of Civilization*. Vol. 10. New York: Columbia UP, 1929.

Ibn Rustah (Rosteh). *Kitāb al-a'lāq al-nafīsah (Part VII)*. Ed. M. J. de Goeje. *Bibliotheca Geographorum Arabicorum*. Vol. 7. Leiden: Brill, 1892. Rpt. 1967.

al-Idrīsī. *Kitāb nuzhat al-mushtāq fī ikhtirāq al-āfāq (Opus Geographicum)*. Ed. E. Cerulli, F. Gabrieli, G. Levi Della Vida, L. Petech, G. Tucci, *et al*. 2nd ed. Leiden: Brill, 1972-75.

al-Istakhrī. *Kitāb masālik al-mamālik (Viae regnorum)*. Ed. M. J. de Goeje. Leiden: Brill, 1870. Reissued 1967.

Kassis, H. "Muslim Revival in Spain in the Fifth / Eleventh Century: Causes and Ramifications." *Der Islam* 67:1 (1990): 78-110.

Lévi-Provençal, É. *La Péninsule Ibérique au Moyen-Age*. Leiden: Brill, 1938. (See al-Himyarī).

Lewis, Bernard. "Mas'ūdī on the Kings of the Franks." *al-Mas'ūdī Millenary Commemoration Volume*. Ed. Ahmad S. Maqbul and A. Rahman. Aligarh: Indian Society for the History of Science, 1960.

al-Mas'ūdī. *Murūj al-dhahab [Meadows of Gold]*. 4 vols. Beirut: Dār al-Andalus, 1978.

Miquel, André. *La géographie humaine du monde musulmane jusqu'au milieu du 11ᵉ siècle*. 3 vols. Paris–La Haye: Mouton, 1967-1980.

Orosius, Paulus. *Historiae adversum paganos*. Ed. 'Abd al-Rahmān Badawī. *Ta'rīkh al-'Ālam: al-Tarjamah al-'Arabīyah al-Qadīmah*. Beirut: al-Mu'assasah al-'Arabīyah lil-Dirāsāt wal-Nashr, 1982.

al-Zuhrī. *Kitāb al-Jaghrāfīyah (Mappemonde du calif al-Ma'mūn reproduite par Fazārī (IIIᵉ/IXᵉ s.) rééditée et commentée par Zuhrī (VIᵉ/XIIᵉ s)*. Ed. Mahammad Hadj-Sadok. Damascus: Institut français de Damas. *Bulletin d'études orientales* 21 (1968).

C. J. G. Turner

THE FIRST PATRIARCHATE
OF GENNADIOS II SCHOLARIOS
AS REFLECTED IN A PASTORAL LETTER

George Scholarios was about fifty years old when the City (as Constantinople was known) finally fell to the Turks under the Sultan Mehmed II on 29 May 1453. Three years earlier he had taken the name Gennadios on becoming a monk. Under that name he had continued the campaign of resistance to the Union of the Greek and Roman churches that had been agreed–with his own aid and co-operation–at the Council of Ferrara-Florence (1438-39);[1] and it was as the second of that name that he was shortly to become Patriarch of Constantinople. He was in fact to hold office as Patriarch three times, but it must have been his first tenure of office that was the most important in establishing a *modus vivendi* for the Greek church and nation under the new circumstances whereby the *basileus* was no longer a Christian Emperor but a Turkish Sultan. Gennadios himself likened the situation to that of the pre-Constantinian church of over a thousand years earlier: "At present Christendom is as it was before Constantine, for now, as then, we have no Emperor, no free Church, no freedom of speech" (IV 203.27-29).[2]

The lines just quoted are from a letter to Maximos Sophianos and the monks of Sinai written during his first Patriarchate. Another and longer Pastoral Letter, written apparently in August of 1455, expands on this novel situation and on his own attempts to meet its challenges. As is indicated by its title in the codex Parisinus 1289 ("on the fall of the City and his abdication of the Patriarchate"), he is here "combining the personal with the general" (213.24-25) by treating two topics in particular: how to reconcile the fall of the capital of Christendom with the providence of the Christian God, and why he feels unable to continue as Patriarch of Constantinople. As with most Byzantine letters, it is disappointingly hard to wrest much tangible fact from what was a highly stylized form;[3] but the letter remains Gennadios'

25

most deliberate attempt to review the problems and achievements, the successes and failures, of his first Patriarchate.

It begins by saying that surprise had been expressed by some that he had not yet attempted a formal explanation of the catastrophe that had occurred. Gennadios claims that he has already given his opinion both verbally and in letters, but it is a specific concern of this letter. The City, in spite of its supernatural defenders (Baynes 165-77), had fallen into the hands of the infidel Turks; its people were enslaved, its churches defiled, the Christian Empire was no more; yet the world had not come to an end and many were tempted to apostatize. Gennadios was faced with an immense theological and pastoral problem, worse even than had been faced by Augustine and Orosius a millennium earlier in the West; and, as Patriarch, he could not evade it.

Gennadios' theodicy broadly follows the lines of the "monastic" philosophy of history that he had been developing in the years before the fall: all historical events are to be interpreted theocratically; the defeat of the Christian Empire is therefore to be seen as a disciplinary act of God; what is important is that divine favour should be regained by a spiritual revival. This theodicy is founded on the doctrine of God's good and comprehensive providence, about which he later wrote in his retirement a series of essays that are generally recognized as his theological masterpiece.[4] As there so also here, he adduces some contorted arguments for how God's good providence extends both "to our departed relatives [some of whom had been killed in the siege] and to those of us who are still alive" (223.11-12). God's discipline of us in this "stadium" (Gennadios thrice uses the word στάδιον) must therefore be a chastening and a healing (παιδεία, ἰατρεία). But he wanted at the same time to maintain human free will (214.24-25: "we govern our lives in concert with divine providence"): hence the way that we accept or respond to such chastening is decisive. Occasionally, as in his Panegyric of the Holy Apostles (written in June 1456, after his first abdication; I 172-87), he was capable of drawing an optimistic message from this doctrine (Tomadakes 257-61, 292-95): if his nation underwent a proper ethical reformation, then its fortunes too should recover. But for the most part he was content to recognize that "the whole hope of the wretched remnant of the Greeks had been lost" (220.3-4) and to wallow in the sins of his fellow-countrymen.

But just what sins did he have in mind? It is tempting to adduce first of all the ecclesiastical Union with Rome agreed at Florence and proclaimed in Hagia Sophia in December 1452, practically on the eve of the conquest. But

Gennadios, perhaps sensing that the Union had already become a dead issue, does not explicitly refer to it, unless that is what he had in mind when he wrote that, shortly before the fall, "[we were permitted] to dare to be more shameless in practising the usual evils and boldly to embark on those not yet dared" (216.11-12) and that "the woes we suffered came rather from the direction from which we hoped for rescue" (216.30-31). But when he writes of "the progress of apostasy from the love of Jesus" (219.25-26) and of clergy, as well as laymen, "deserting to the infidels or threatening to desert" (225.35-36), he means conversion to Islam, which, not unknown before the fall, had been considerably encouraged and accelerated by the Ottoman conquest. The Union was, at best, only a very partial answer; more significant, to Gennadios' mind, were the "usual evils."

But here too he was, for the most part, far from specific. He spends several pages railing against pride and ambition, the gratification of the senses and "the slavery of the passions" (221.38), disobedience to the will of God as revealed in Holy Scripture, and failure to repent. Rather surprisingly, he asserts at one point that "a detailed account of our wickedness . . . would not be appropriate at present" (219.29-30). After that, however, he does become a little more specific when he accuses the Greeks of having sold out for temporal and mundane advantage and, moreover, of having sold public and ecclesiastical treasures while preserving private fortunes. Mercenaries and the mere hope of military aid from the West had levied a heavy toll on the Byzantine purse.

One evil that, according to Gennadios, had been growing in the Byzantine church for fifty years (IV 202.9) and that was to continue to grow under the Sultans, was simony, the buying and selling of ecclesiastical office. In 1451, as he tells us in a manuscript note (III 240), Gennadios had sent to the Emperor Constantine a work specifically against simony–and "he was none the better for it"! It was, he claimed, a major reason for God's wrath manifested in the plight of the Empire. Similar views are expressed in a letter (IV 480-81) that he wrote at about the same time. In his Pastoral Letter Gennadios does not refer to simony as such, but, in its autobiographical section, he does make a point of claiming that, as Patriarch, he had "made appointments to ecclesiastical office, which was the main source of income to our shameless contemporaries, without special request, without partiality and without blemish" (225.28-31). He again claims to have given a good example in this respect in his letter to Maximos Sophianos in which he is at the same time surprisingly lenient towards simony under exceptional circumstances (IV 202.16-20). The assertion that appointment to high ecclesiastical office was, presumably in default of civil and military service, the most lucrative source of income for Greeks in the early years of Turkish rule helps to explain the bitter accusations of simony and of improper appointment that were frequent under Gennadios' immediate successors. It is not surprising that simony receives special mention in his pastoral work on the First Service of God (IV 244.15) and that, in a late work, it figures as one of the vices of a degenerate clergy which are partly responsible for the rarity of miracles at the present time (III 385).

All this is fairly heavy reading that is echoed in other writings, such as the Public Prayer (IV 352-55), which is one of the few works that may safely be dated to his first Patriarchate, or the later Lamentation (I 283-94). But its tone is lightened by the occasional stylistic embellishment: the monastic concept of chastening can be buttressed by many Old Testament quotations, such as that from Psalms 81 and 89 with which he opens his subsequent pastoral letter (IV 231.15-18: "Oh that my people had harkened unto me and Israel had walked in my ways! I should soon have subdued their enemies, and turned my hand against their adversaries: but now with rod and whip shall I visit their iniquities"), and the illustration of Jonah and the Ninevites (216.3) is helpful. What, however, purports to be a Pauline quotation (216.21-22: "as it is written, 'Thou hast uncovered their sins in order that Thy judgment may appear'; in such passages the methods of the divine order were proclaimed long ago by Paul") seems not to be a precise quotation but a distillation of the opening chapters of Epistle to the Romans. Metaphor, too, is used occasionally: Gennadios writes, as we have seen, of the stadium of life, and he writes also of "the rose of religion among the thorns" (218.25-26 & 39). More pointed imagery comes when he writes that "Now we perceive the shame of our faces in the mirror of the disasters by which we have been chastened" (221.40-222,1) or asks "with what whitewash shall we cover up the cracks?" (221.32). From this he concludes that "the smoke of our sins has stopped up the source of Thy mercy to us, and the whole scale of justice has tipped against us" (222.8-9). It is remarkable that the "shame of our faces in the mirror of disasters" and the "tipping of the scale of justice," as well as the "stadium of our trials," recur in the Public Prayer (IV 354.33-34; 355.3 & 20). And at least at one point he contrives a pun: "ξένου . . . ξαίνοντες . . . ξαίνουσιν" (220.25-26).

The Pastoral Letter, as indicated above, refers to many of the concerns of Gennadios' later years in general and of his first Patriarchate in particular.

Any consideration of the fall of Constantinople from a religious point of view, for instance, could hardly avoid taking into consideration also the fall of Jerusalem, whether in 587 BC or in 70 AD, and the consequent diaspora of the Jews. And Gennadios duly spends a page or more on such a consideration, quoting Isaiah 19: 14 ("God has mixed / prepared for them a spirit of error / wandering") and comparing the capture and sack of Jerusalem with that of Constantinople, the New Jerusalem. This was a standard argument in Gennadios' anti-Jewish polemic and recurs in the Dialogue (III 251-304) that he wrote in 1464 in refutation of Judaism, in which he emphasizes the contrast rather than the parallel, claiming that the plight of the Jews is much more serious than that of the Christians, since the latter are permitted to practise their religion fully. This is not an indication of Moslem severity towards Judaism but rather a reference to the fact that the Jews are not permitted by their own Law to practise their full rites outside Jerusalem. The dispersion of the Jews and their repeated failure to re-establish their state, the destruction of Jerusalem and the cessation of the Temple observances–all this indicated the wrath of God for the rejection of the Messiah.

The Dialogue in refutation of Judaism also echoes some other concerns tangential to the Pastoral Letter. Oracles, for instance, like prophecy, depend for their validity on a strong doctrine of God's providence and foreknowledge: He knows what the future is to be, and sometimes He lets men know. Hence Gennadios believed implicitly in oracles of three main kinds: those that could be interpreted as foretelling the Christ, those that seemed to foretell the end of the Byzantine Empire, and those that were to be fulfilled before the end of the world. In the Dialogue he spends some time on the first of these classes, regretting the loss of a collection that had been in his possession. In his Pastoral Letter he spends less time on the second class, referring in particular to the oracle about "the poor king" (214.6: τοῦ πένητος ἐκείνου βασιλέως) that was recurrent in Byzantine collections of oracles. The third class mingled with prophecy, especially from the Book of Daniel, to convince him that the world would come to an end before long (Rigo 151-85). At the end of his life he specified 1493 (IV 511-12), when according to the Byzantine reckoning the year 7000 would have been reached; but in his later years, in view of the state of the world as he saw it, he spoke increasingly of the end as nigh, as he does in his Pastoral Letter: "the consummation, which is near" (219.6-7).

Similarly, both the Dialogue (III 287.2-6) and the Pastoral Letter (221.27-31) make brief references to the revival of Hellenic paganism under the influence of Gennadios' great rival, George Gemistos Plethon (whom the Dialogue mentions by name).[5] Plethon was primarily a philosopher in the Neoplatonic tradition. His polytheism, which is expressed most obviously in his *Book of Laws* that became known after his death and is only partially extant, was based on his view of the nature of being (which had been one point in the clash between him and Gennadios in the 1440's about the respective merits of Plato and Aristotle) and on the Neoplatonic chain of being. This philosophy has been described as "un déterminisme à la fois rigoureux et optimiste, polythéiste et moniste" (Masai 217). It was inimical to orthodox Christological doctrine, and led to an etiolated concept of sin and none of salvation. Gennadios' attitude to Plethon was generally ambivalent, often suspicious, and increasingly hostile; his later works are studded with references to the absurdity of Hellenic polytheism. Before the fall of Constantinople he had written a congratulatory letter on the execution of another neo-pagan (IV 476-89); and he bore the responsibility for the burning of Plethon's *Book of Laws* and for determining which parts of it to preserve. While this proscription probably took place when Gennadios was Patriarch, it does not seem to have occurred before 1460 and is therefore attributable to a time when he was Patriarch for a second or third time (Zakythinos 366-67). If, in fact, he did not actually set eyes on the *Book of Laws* until later, some years after the death of Plethon in June of 1452, it is understandable that Gennadios does not treat of this matter at any length in any of the writings preserved from his first Patriarchate. He could scarcely have been satisfied with the refutation of Plethon's determinism (ἡ εἱμαρμένη) written by his pupil Matthew Camariotes in 1455,[6] even if he knew of it (and he never refers to it). Yet recurrent tangential allusions indicate that the attempted revival of Hellenic paganism, even in a refined philosophical form, was an ongoing concern for Gennadios, particularly as Patriarch, since it was liable to lead his flock astray.

I have called the latter part of the Pastoral Letter "its autobiographical section." It is, indeed, much more personal, and it makes rather less use of the kind of nebulous generalizations that render so much of the letter opaque. Gennadios spends much of his time complaining about what he has had to endure on the "unhappy throne" (229.17; the same phrase recurs in his Lamentation [I 292.15]) and weighing up what to do about it. Nevertheless some hard facts emerge that require relatively little supplementation from elsewhere. Taken captive on the day of Constantinople's fall, together with his sister and his beloved nephew, Theodore Sophianos, whose funeral oration he was to give only two years later, Gennadios had been taken to the neighbourhood of Adrianople, where he was well treated: "none of these dreadful barbarians put me in bonds, none abused me, kicked me, left me hungry or to tramp the streets, or ordered me to work as a slave" (224.4-6). His master, a Turkish nobleman, probably heard that the Sultan (who was in Adrianople during the summer of 1453 [Inalcik 412-13]) was looking to re-establish the Patriarchate of Constantinople, which had been vacant since Gregory Mammas had fled to the West in 1451, and certainly learnt that Gennadios was the obvious candidate for such office: "that man is the one who ought to take charge of our souls" (224.19). Consequently, in about September of 1453 Gennadios was taken to Constantinople (Darrouzès 101, 123), where he was put in charge of a monastery, many of whose monks he had to ransom and reassemble. Finally, at the beginning of 1454, "a Synod of many bishops, some from Asia and others from Europe, was summoned and [Gennadios] was made first deacon, then priest, then bishop and Patriarch" (224.38-225.2) on 6 January.

It was the Sultan who had chosen Gennadios as Patriarch. As leader of the opposition to Union, he may have been the obvious candidate; but his prickly sensitivity and his largely traditionalist approach did not fit him too well for the tasks of ecclesiastical administration, of establishing a *modus vivendi* with the new masters of the City and of inspiring unity among a body of clergy that increasingly cherished personal resentments and jealousies. And it was the Sultan (here called *basileus*) who retained him in office against his will (226.34-227.2), in spite of written guarantees of liberty that Gennadios mentions twice (228.36; 229.10). Mehmed apparently needed him for political purposes: he was concerned for the repopulation and defence of Constantinople, and wished to facilitate loyalty, order, and tranquillity among the Greek subjects of his Empire.[7] Gennadios' attitude to Mehmed in his Pastoral Letter is ambivalent: he is pained at being required to remain in office and refers to the "anger" (226.34) that the Sultan had evinced; but he "does not dare to say anything" against him (223.34) and is in fact gratefully surprised by the re-establishment of the Church and its authority (227.14-15). The impression given by all our sources is that relations between Sultan and Patriarch were at least cordial, and in later years Gennadios was to speak warmly of Mehmed's φιλανθρωπία (IV 265-66).

Pseudo-Sphrantzes reports both that the Sultan deliberately imitated the procedure by which the Christian Emperors had installed Patriarchs and that Mehmed handed to Gennadios a *berat* that guaranteed his personal inviolability, immunity from prosecution, exemption from taxation, and security from deposition.[8] How much of this actually occurred and how much is an attribution to this time of what happened in earlier or later periods is still disputed. It is noticeable that Gennadios himself gives few details, although he does refer to some kind of a written guarantee and complains that the liberty laid down in writing had been annulled by the refusal to accept his resignation (228.35-229.3). Similarly doubtful is the question of what judicial authority was vested in Gennadios, who had served the Empire as 'Judge General' until 1447; but the Church at least retained jurisdiction in matters, such as marriage, that had a religious connotation.

Three times (III 468.16) Mehmed visited Gennadios and listened to his exposition of the Christian faith. This took place in a side-chapel of the church of the convent of the Pammacaristos to which the Patriarchal seat had soon been transferred from the church of the Holy Apostles where Gennadios had first been established. Wishful thinking soon gave rise to the rumour that Mehmed, who was accompanied by Moslem theologians, was seriously thinking of converting to Christianity; and this later contributed to the relatively frequent publication (often in truncated or mangled form) of Gennadios' resulting Confession of Faith. But modern scholarship is almost unanimous in declaring that this "act of statesmanship" (Arnakis 237) by Mehmed had primarily political motivation. After the second interview he asked for a written copy of what Gennadios had said; later he requested a shorter version. Both are extant, both are officially entitled The Only Way of Salvation, and both were swiftly translated into Turkish,[9] although the translation seems not to have been completed until after Gennadios' abdication. These works (III 434-58) are an efficient exposition of Orthodox Christianity, without emphasizing differences from Roman doctrine or directly attacking Moslem theology or indicating any undue hope of effecting a conversion. It is noticeable that, towards the end of the first piece, Gennadios shows his continuing concern about the revival of polytheism by pouring scorn on anyone who would now return to the practice of pagan religion. And in both pieces he appeals to Hellenic oracles as evidence for Christ. Both together and separately these writings are essentially an apologetic work by an accomplished theologian in response to a request from his secular master.

One sentence in this latter section of Gennadios' letter (227.10-11: "actions are bound to conform to dispositions, as fruit to the tree as Scripture says") reminds us that, along with Scripture (in this instance the reference is to Matthew 12: 33), his chief authorities were Aristotle and St. Thomas Aquinas; for the terms used here (ἐνέργειαι, ἕξεις) are prominent in both of them and are discussed, for example, in Gennadios' summary of Aquinas' *Summa Theologiae* IᵃIIᵃᵉ 49-54 (VI 51-59), the starting point for which is found in passages of Aristotle's *Categories* and *Metaphysics*. His indebtedness to "the Philosopher," to Western Scholasticism and to Aquinas in particular was great throughout his life and continues to be studied.[10] His summary of the Prima Secundae may have been made, like his summaries of the *Summa contra Gentiles* and the first book of the *Summa Theologiae* (V 2-510), as late as his third Patriarchate (1464-65) and for the same purpose: so that he could the more easily and safely carry them with him wherever the vicissitudes of his life should take him (V 1).

We have only patchy records of Gennadios' administrative work as Patriarch. He appointed his friend, Theodore Agallianos, as Grand Chartophylax and his pupil, Matthew Camariotes, as Grand Rhetor (which implies the revival of the Patriarchal Academy).[11] His Pastoral Letter complains that he lacked the means to cope with the refugee problem caused by the conquest and efforts to repopulate the City (225.20-21). Other letters, of an instructional nature, show that his authority was recognized far beyond the capital: he answered queries, largely about ritual and canon law, from George Branković of Serbia (IV 207-11); and a pair of letters were sent to the monastery on Mt. Sinai (IV 198-207). The first letter to Mt. Sinai is addressed to Maximos Sophianos and the other monks: some of its topics and phraseology link it with the Pastoral Letter; other parts concern ritual or the treatment of Latin (and Armenian) pilgrims to the Holy Land as schismatics rather than as heretics. The second letter is a brief appendix, addressed to the monk Joachim in particular, that accepts priests whose orthodoxy had been suspect in the past if they now make an orthodox confession. These letters are thus relatively lenient towards Rome and the principles of Unionism and imply a policy of οἰκονομία (accommodation) for which there is further evidence. They also contrast with another pastoral letter[12] (of doubtful authenticity) that shows Gennadios as ridiculing the principle of economy and maintaining a hard line towards Latin doctrine and Unionist clergy. At all events the repercussions of the debate about Union remained in the pastoral and administrative problems of how to deal with Latins and of whether to recognize the validity of priests suspected of Unionism (or of simony).

In his letter to Maximos Gennadios went so far as to call anyone who would in these days insist on punctiliousness (ἀκρίβεια) an enemy of Christianity: what was needed was "a little flexibility in order to preserve the whole" (IV 203.5-6). Similarly, in his Pastoral Letter he wrote of being faced with the dilemma of either conniving at breaches of discipline or condemning "almost everyone" (225.31-33). It was, however, this policy of economy that, if it did not cause hostility, gave a pretext to ecclesiastics and officials in Constantinople who wanted to get rid of Gennadios; and, according to the Pastoral Letter, some of them wanted to be rid of him not only from the Patriarchal throne but from this world: "in return for our zeal on their behalf, they pay us back with chicane and deceit, even plotting against this wretched life" (228.25-27), that is, against "me, who would not hurt a flea" (225.36-37)! Theodore Agallianos informs us that the economy recommended by Gennadios in this instance referred primarily to uncanonical marriages (Patrineles 146-50). Theodore provides details about a fourth marriage in which almost everyone involved acted in ignorance, an adulterous marriage caused by the special circumstances of the conquest and the Turkish administration, and an under-age marriage contracted to avoid the *devshirme* (the forcible recruitment of Greek boys to be trained as Janissaries). Perhaps Gennadios feared the danger that some might convert to Islam for the sake of regularizing polygamy.

It is surprising to see this turn towards economy in Gennadios, who was in most respects a punctilious traditionalist. But he clearly saw no alternative, judging that the salvation of the soul through the maintenance of Christian belief was more important than rigid adherence to canon law. It did, however, offer a handle to some who wanted to promote themselves and line their own pockets. And it was their efforts, with the resulting low morale of the Greek Church and the dissension among its bureaucracy, and not any pressure or machinations on the part of the Sultan and his aides (who, on the contrary, pressured him to remain in office), that made Gennadios' life on the Patriarchal throne such a misery that he had "decided to return to private life" (228.29-30). He adds, what was not uncommon in his writings, that his health was not good: he claims to have often been in danger of falling in a faint while taking services (229.12-14). Hence his Pastoral Letter concludes that there was no point in his staying on, that he was unable to be of benefit to anyone, and that he was in fact ready to die.

He appears nevertheless to have been prevailed upon to remain longer in office; but for how long is not clear. The most precise evidence comes from the end of his subsequent pastoral letter, whose opening quotation from the Psalms has been given above:

> We have written to those who, with God, are able to release us from this burden, saying that we can no longer bear it and that they must consider the others so far as they can, for our work is coming to an end. Two months have passed since we gave them this day as our limit. But on their advice we are willing to forego this limit; for they say, with reason, that it makes no difference if, even after two months, I did the same, and the common good would be secured. Today is the beginning of the tenth month; and, if not sooner, the day of Epiphany, which last year gave me the rank of Archbishop, (that is, after a period of not more than one year) shall see us in a private capacity as a humble monk. (IV 233.22-33)

This paragraph fixes Gennadios' election and consecration as Patriarch as having taken place on 6 January (in all probability of 1454). It also gives its own date as the beginning of the tenth month of his Patriarchate, namely, early October. It reports an attempt to resign made two months earlier, with which the longer Pastoral Letter (which is recalled at the beginning of this letter) was probably connected; that is, the Pastoral Letter itself was written around early August. And it announces Gennadios' intention to resign, at the latest, after one whole year in office.

Jugie noted that there are "indices sérieux" that Gennadios remained in office still longer (VIII 30*). His main evidence for this was a note in a manuscript that misled him into thinking that Gennadios was still Patriarch when he visited the monastery of Vatopedi on 12 May 1456. As a result Jugie toyed with the idea that Gennadios did not become Patriarch until 1455. But the note in fact calls him "the former Patriarch" and therefore provides a *terminus ante quem*, not *post quem* (Turner, "Career" 441 n.2). All we can say for sure, then, is that Gennadios intended to step down on 6 January 1455 and that he had done so by May 1456. There is some evidence, however, that he continued past the first of these dates. His successor Isidore, for instance, died in office on 31 March 1462 (Patrineles 118)–the next firm date that we have–and, according to one source, had held office for six years and two months (Laurent 263), which would suggest early 1456 (possibly 6 January) for Gennadios' abdication. Similarly, Gennadios' letters to Sinai, one of which is dated 6 February (IV 206), refer

35

to his difficulties on the Patriarchal throne, and both cite the example that he has set in resisting simoniac ordinations and in accepting priests whose orthodoxy could be suspect. These comments seem very unlikely if he had himself at that point been ordained for only one month; thus, these letters were probably written in February of 1455. There are serious indications, therefore, that Gennadios' first Patriarchate lasted for more than one year and perhaps as long as two years.

Gennadios' first tenure of the Patriarchate is of exceptional interest because it allowed the career of a strong and multifaceted personality to have its climax in the midst of a delicate and developing situation. And yet the Pastoral Letter in which he publicizes his wish to resign amounts to an admission of failure. He had been the acknowledged leader of the antiunionist faction in the Greek Church whose point had been won *de facto* by the Turkish conquest; he believed himself to be a leader in philosophy and theology; he had been picked to be the leader of his Church and nation by the Sultan who admired and perhaps befriended him. He was enabled to re-establish the framework of Church government within which the Greek clergy could begin to play the political and judicial role that was encouraged by the Turkish governmental system, with the Patriarch himself as Ethnarch. But, far from being able to give any real impetus to an educational, ethical and spiritual revival, he found himself unable to command the united support even of the clergy. He did his job, presumably to the satisfaction of his new master, but clearly not to his own satisfaction. He was great enough to recognize his failure, to abdicate of his own free will, and to retire into a monastery. In his retirement Gennadios seems to have attained a greater personal tranquillity after sailing the stormy seas of the Patriarchate; even the complaints about his health become rarer. At the same time, through the vicissitudes of his life, he had achieved a theological maturity that is expressed in several of his late writings; and, to judge at least by the number of works preserved, his pen was more fruitful than ever.

Such a tranquil, wise, healthy, and fruitful retirement is what we wish for our friend, Mahmoud.

Notes

1. See especially Gill, *The Council of Florence*. For Scholarios in general see Turner, "The Career of George-Gennadius Scholarius" and the bibliography cited there.

2. Page references are to the *Oeuvres complètes de Georges-Gennade Scholarios*, ed. L. Petit *et al*. References to the Pastoral Letter (IV 211-31) give page (and line) only; other references add the volume number.

3. For the complexities of Byzantine epistolography see Hatlie's recent survey of modern research in "Redeeming Byzantine Epistolography."

4. So Jugie in Scholarios I: lxi; cf. Beck 151.

5. See especially Masai, *Pléthon*, and Woodhouse, *George Gemistos Plethon*. See also Turner, "An Anomalous Episode" 56-63.

6. *Orationes Duae in Plethonem de Fato*. For the date see also Astruc 260-61.

7. See Laitila 52-57. See also Vryonis, "The Byzantine Patriarchate and Turkish Islam," which was not available to me when this paper was written.

8. Sphrantzes 446-58. Cf. Papadopoulos 73-101; Runciman 170; Laitila 59-61; Vryonis 83-88.

9. See T. Halasi Kun, *Gennadios török hitvallása*. An English translation of the shorter version is given in Papadakis 88-106.

10. For some recent contributions to this topic see Podskalsky, "Rezeption"; Ebbesen and Pinborg, "Gennadios and Western Scholasticism"; Tavardon, "Georges Scholarios, un Thomiste byzantin?"; Barbour, *The Byzantine Thomism*.

11. For Agallianos see Patrineles, Ό Θεόδωρος Άγαλλιανός. For Camariotes see Astruc, "La fin inédite," and Biedl, "Matthaeus Camariotes."

12. Edited by Turner in "Another Anti-Latin Work," 338-42.

Works Cited

Arnakis, G. G. "The Greek Church of Constantinople and the Ottoman Empire." *Journal of Modern History* 24 (1952): 235-50.

Astruc, C. "La fin inédite du *Contra Plethonem* de Matthieu Camariotès." *Scriptorium* 9 (1955): 246-62.

Barbour, H. C. *The Byzantine Thomism of Gennadios Scholarios and his Translation of the Commentary of Armandus de Bellovisu on the "De Ente et Essentia" of Thomas Aquinas*. Studi Tomistici 53. Vatican City: Libreria Editrice Vaticana, 1993.

Baynes, N. H. "The Supernatural Defenders of Constantinople." *Analecta Bollandiana* 67 (1949): 165-77.

Beck, Hildebrand [= Hans-Georg]. *Vorsehung und Vorherbestimmung in der theologischen Literatur der Byzantiner*. Orientalia Christiana Analecta 114. Rome: Pontifical Institute of Oriental Studies, 1937.

Biedl, A. "Matthaeus Camariotes: specimen prosopographiae byzantinae." *Byzantinische Zeitschrift* 35 (1935): 337-39.

Camariotes, Matthew. *Orationes Duae in Plethonem de Fato*. Ed. H. S. Reimer. Leiden: Conrad Wishoff, 1721.

Darrouzès, J. "Lettres de 1453." *Revue des Études Byzantines* 22 (1964): 72-127.

Ebbesen, S., and J. Pinborg. "Gennadios and Western Scholasticism: Radulphus Brito's *Ars Vetus* in Greek Translation." *Classica et Mediaevalia* 33 (1981-82): 263-319.

Gill, Joseph. *The Council of Florence*. Cambridge: Cambridge UP, 1959.

Hatlie, Peter. "Redeeming Byzantine Epistolography." *Byzantine and Modern Greek Studies* 20 (1996): 213-48.

Halasi Kun, T. *Gennadios török hitvallása.* Budapest: Körösi-Csoma Archivum, 1936.

Inalcik, H. "Mehmed the Conqueror (1432-1481) and His Time." *Speculum* 35 (1960): 408-27.

Laitila, T. "Infidel Orthodox? Patriarch Gennadios II (1454-1456) and the Making of the Ecumenical Patriarchate in the Context of Sultan Mehmed's Policy." *Byzantium and the North.* Ed. P. Hohti. Acta Byzantina Fennica IV. Helsinki: Finnish Association for Byzantine Studies, 1989. 51-76.

Laurent, V. "Les premiers patriarches de Constantinople sous domination turque (1454-1476)." *Revue des Études Byzantines* 26 (1968): 229-63.

Masai, François. *Pléthon et le Platonisme de Mistra.* Paris: Société d'édition "Les Belles Lettres," 1956.

Papadakis, A. "Gennadios II and Mehmet the Conqueror." *Byzantion* 42 (1972): 88-106.

Papadopoulos, C. G. *Les Privilèges du Patriarcat Oecuménique (Communauté Grecque Orthodoxe) dans l'Empire ottoman.* Paris: R. Guillon, 1924.

Patrineles, Kh. G. ʹΟ Θεόδωρος ʹΑγαλλιανός καὶ οἱ ἀνέκδοτοι λόγοι αὐτοῦ. Diss. University of Thessalonike. Athens, 1966.

Podskalsky, G. "Die Rezeption der thomistischen Theologie bei Gennadios II. Scholarios." *Theologie und Philosophie* 49 (1974): 305-23.

Rigo, A. "L'anno 7000, la fine del mondo e l'Impero cristiano. Nota su alcuni passi di Giuseppe Briennio, Simone di Tessalonica e Gennadio Scolario." *La Cattura della Fine.* Ed. G. Ruggieri. Genoa: Marietti, 1992. 151-85.

Runciman, Steven. *The Great Church in Captivity.* Cambridge: Cambridge UP, 1968.

Scholarios, George-Gennadios. *Oeuvres complètes de Georges-Gennade Scholarios.* Ed. L. Petit, X. A. Sidéridès, and M. Jugie. 8 vols. Paris: Maison de la Bonne Presse, 1928-36.

Sphrantzes, Georgios. *Memorii 1401-1477.* Ed. V. Grecu. Scriptores Byzantini V. Bucharest: Editura Academiei Republicii Socialiste România, 1966.

Tavardon, P. "Georges Scholarios, un Thomiste byzantin?" *Byzantiaka* 3 (1983): 57-74.

Tomadakes, N. B. "Γεώργιος ὁ Σχολάριος καὶ αἱ πολιτικαί του ἀντιλήψεις." *Ekklesia* 31 (1954): 257-61 & 292-95.

Turner, C. J. G. "An Anomalous Episode in Relations between Scholarius and Plethon." *Byzantine Studies* 3 (1976): 56-63.

—. "Another Anti-Latin Work Attributed to Gennadius Scholarius." *Byzantinische Zeitschrift* 58 (1965): 337-47.

—. "The Career of George-Gennadius Scholarius." *Byzantion* 39 (1969): 420-55.

Vryonis, Speros. "The Byzantine Patriarchate and Turkish Islam." *Byzantinoslavica* 57 (1996): 69-111.

Woodhouse, C. M. *George Gemistos Plethon: The Last of the Hellenes.* Oxford: Clarendon, 1986.

Zakythinos, D. A. *Le Despotat grec de Morée.* Vol. II. Athens: L'Hellénisme contemporain, 1953.

Derek C. Carr

ARABIC AND HEBREW "AUCTORITATES" IN THE WORKS OF ENRIQUE DE VILLENA[1]

Enrique de Villena (c. 1384-1434), scion of the royal houses of Castile and Aragon, was an eccentric polymath, a reputed *magus*, and a significant figure in the "proto-Humanism" of early fifteenth-century Castile, recognized in his own day–though not always appreciated–for his immense learning and knowledge of languages.[2] Translator of the *Divina commedia*, the *Aeneid*, and the *Rhetorica ad Herennium*, he also wrote on cosmology and hermeticism (*Exposición del salmo 'Quoniam videbo coelos tuos'*), popular superstition in the matter of the Evil Eye (*Tratado de la fascinación* or *del aojamiento*), medicine and biblical exegesis (*Tratado de la lepra*), classical mythology (*Los doze trabajos de Hércules* and *Glosas* on *Aeneid* 1-3), court etiquette (*Arte cisoria*), poetics (*Arte de trovar* and *Glosas*) and politics (*Los doze trabajos* and *Glosas*). Most of his works–including some extant letters–are composed in a highly self-conscious latinized style, much indebted to the precepts of formal rhetoric, especially the medieval *artes dictaminis*. Villena's delight in displays of erudition also comes from formal rhetoric, with its emphasis on the *amplificatio rerum*. His works are liberally laced with references to the obligatory canon of *auctoritates*, classical and medieval, as well as–unusual for the place and time–Jewish and Arabic writers.

On the basis of the extensive roster of *auctoritates* cited by Villena, Emilio Cotarelo y Mori attempted to reconstruct the likely contents of Villena's personal library, most of it burned at his death by order of King John II of Castile because of its alleged collection of *libros de malas artes*.[3] Though not without merit, Cotarelo's efforts failed to take into account Villena's use of second-hand citations culled from *florilegia*, other medieval compilations and commentaries, and from the memory of conversations held with some of the *auctoritates* he mentions. Cotarelo also failed to appreciate the fact that the absence of any reference to a given work cannot be regarded as proof that Villena did not know it. Contemporary documentary evidence, for example, shows that in 1418 Villena was known to possess a copy of the *Historiae* of Trogus Pompeius, yet this author is never mentioned in Villena's works, and hence does not appear in Cotarelo's list (see Vendrell Gallostra 69).

In addition to the shortcomings mentioned above, Cotarelo was unable to make a positive identification of many of the non-Latin *auctores* to whom Villena refers, particularly in his "scientific" treatises. The availability of modern editions of Villena's works (many still accessible only in manuscript when Cotarelo was writing in 1896), as well as the advances made in this century in the history of science, now make it possible to resolve most of the problems concerning the identity of Villena's non-Latin / non-Romance sources, though some uncertainties remain.[4] This article will bring together and synthesize the results of recent scholarship in the field (including my own), and will address the issue of Villena's alleged knowledge of Arabic and Hebrew.

Cotarelo's catalogue contains the names of some 146 individual authors, with perhaps twice as many individual works. The list can be divided into three broad categories. Approximately 50% of the authors mentioned fall under the general heading of "medieval writers," a term which I use here to cover patristic literature (in Latin), the Latin literary and scientific works of the Middle Ages, hermetic writings, and a relatively small number of works written in Romance vernaculars. Some 25% of the authors mentioned are representative of the "medieval canon" of Classical Latin, Silver Age, and late-Latin writers.[5] The remaining 25% of the list, made up of Arabic and Jewish authors, is worth examining in some detail as it raises the question of the extent to which Villena might have had sufficient knowledge of Arabic and Hebrew to enable him to read scientific, philosophical and literary works in those languages. From his contemporary, Fernán Pérez de Guzmán, we know that Villena "sabía fablar muchas lenguas" ["knew how to speak many languages"],[6] but we must approach with extreme caution Cotarelo's *amplificatio* of that statement to the effect that Don Enrique "manifiesta entender, no sólo el latín, italiano, lemosín, francés y otros idiomas vulgares, sino también el árabe, griego y hebreo" ["shows evidence of understanding not only Latin, Italian, *limousin*, French and other vernaculars, but also Arabic, Greek and Hebrew"] (Cotarelo 19, and cf. 130 and 137).

Villena's knowledge of Latin is not in doubt, but he was not a professional humanist. His Latin training was medieval, chiefly juridical and ecclesiastical; the classical language of Vergil was less accessible to him, as we know from his translation of the *Aeneid*.[7] If the translation of the *Divina commedia* is anything to go by, his grasp of Italian was probably little more than a reading knowledge based on a rudimentary form of comparative Romance linguistics.[8] Villena's Valencian upbringing and his frequent presence from boyhood in the Aragonese court in Barcelona gave him fluency in Catalan, as well as exposure to Catalan letters and Provençal poetics.[9] Though Villena was not a stranger to the Languedoc, there is no evidence of any knowledge of *langue d'oïl* or of works written therein. Nor is there any evidence that he knew "otros idiomas vulgares." As Cotarelo exhausts virtually all the possibilities in the Romance vernaculars, it is difficult to understand what he implies by such an observation. Knowledge of non-Romance vernaculars (English, for example) is not totally beyond the bounds of possibility, but is at best extremely unlikely. Cotarelo's claim (166, no.80) that Villena knew Homer's *Iliad* in Greek is based on a misapprehension of a reference to that work. In his lengthy gloss on *Aeneid* 2.198, Villena provides a detailed catalogue of Greek leaders and the number of ships they brought to the siege of Troy. The passage is lifted almost verbatim from Guido de Columnis' *Historia destructionis Troiae*, and concludes as follows: "E Omero dixo en su *Yliada* que non fueran más estas naves de mill e çiento e ochenta e seys" ["And Homer said in his *Iliad* that these ships numbered no more than one thousand one hundred and eighty-six"] (ed. Cátedra 1989, 2:96). However, the remark which Cotarelo took to indicate direct knowledge of the *Iliad* is nothing more than a paraphrase of the final sentence of Guido's naval *enumeratio*: "Homero vero dixit in temporibus suis fuisse naves mclxxxvi. . . ."[10]

We come now to the question of Hebrew and Arabic. The fact that some 25% of the authors found in Cotarelo's list are Arabic or Jewish writers would seem to present a *prima facie* case for his contention that Villena was capable of reading those languages. Nevertheless, a closer examination of the list of works in Arabic and Hebrew, and of the contexts in which they are cited, provides no concrete evidence that Villena had any extensive knowledge of either of the languages in question.

Cotarelo mentions thirty-four references to supposed non-Latin and non-Romance writers or texts in Villena's works; fifteen of them occur in his *Tratado de la fascinación* (c. 1425) alone. It may be instructive to examine them in their order of appearance in the treatise. For ease of reference I quote from Pedro M. Cátedra's recent edition of Villena's complete works (Vol. 1,

1994), with appropriate cross-referencing to earlier editions (Soler 1917; Gallina 1978) and Cotarelo's list.

1. Aben Ruis "en el comento *De sopno et vigilia*" (Cátedra 1:329; Soler 184; Gallina 99; Cotarelo 154, no.5). At first sight, this would appear to be Averroes' commentary on Aristotle's *De anima*. However, as Gallina points out (99, note 37), Villena seems to have suffered a *lapsus memoriae* in his identification of the author, and is in fact quoting from Albertus Magnus, *De somno et vigilia* (Lib.2, Tract.I, cap.VI). Another possibility is that the reference and erroneous attribution come from a *florilegium*.

2. Aben Ohaxia "en la *Philahanaptia mayor*" (Cátedra 1:330; Soler 185; Gallina 101; Cotarelo 153, no.2). The name and title are even more garbled in some mss.: "abenexia en la philaha çiaptia mayor" (Madrid, BN 6599, fol.142v); "abene axia en la philaha çiaptica mayor" (Rodríguez-Moñino V-6-64, fol.124v). This is the *Kitāb al-filāha al-nabaṭiyya* attributed to Ibn Waḥshiyya, written in Iraq c. 904. Purporting to be a work on Nabataean agriculture, it is (in Sarton's view) an alleged translation from ancient Babylonian sources, the purpose of which was to extol the "old" civilization before the *hegira* against that of the conquering Arabs, though this was probably not understood during the Middle Ages (Sarton 1:634). A more recent view is that Ibn Waḥshiyya was little more than a compiler or adaptor of earlier material (see Cátedra, *Exégesis* 55, note 129). The work was known in Muslim Spain and was the main literary source of the *Kitāb al-filāha* of Ibn al-ᶜAwwam, written in Seville c. 1200 (Sarton 2.1:425). It is also cited frequently by Maimonides in the *Guide for the Perplexed*, chiefly as a source of examples to expose the folly of idolators. Villena refers to the *Philahanaptia mayor* in several of his works: in the *Arte cisoria*; in the *Tratado de la consolación*; in the *Tratado de la lepra* (in which he states that the title means *Agricultura caldea*), on the effects of drought on olive-trees. He mentions the *Agricultura caldea* twice in the *Glosas a la Eneida* (ed. Cátedra 1989, 2:58 and 205); in the *Exposición del salmo* he attributes it to "Çuçenmi," that is Qutami, the supposed author of the third version of the Babylonian original "translated" by Ibn Waḥshiyya. As Cátedra points out (*Exégesis* 57), the *Agricultura caldea* was known in the West in a Latin version. One of the lost manuscripts of the Escorial library was a *Libro de la agricultura sacado de chaldeo en arávigo y de arávigo en latín*, a translation made

in the court of Alfonso X; the fifteenth-century library of the Counts of Benavente (a collection quite possibly enriched by items salvaged from Villena's book-cases) contained several copies of the *Agricultura caldea mayor* and *Agricultura caldea menor*. Villena's references, whether first or second-hand, must come from a Latin or Castilian text.

3. Caicamet "en los *Anarrizec*" (Cátedra 1:332; Soler 187; Gallina 109; Cotarelo 160, no.40). Manuscript readings vary: "Caumente" (BN 6599, fol.144r; Rodríguez-Moñino V-6-64, fol.125v); "avarizer" (BN 6599), "auarised" (V-6-64). I have been unable to make a positive identification of the author and work. Ciceri (306), citing Thorndike 2:292, suggests Achmet ben Sirin, the author of a book on the interpretation of dreams, and perhaps an astrological treatise, and who is claimed as a source of William of Aragon's *Liber de pronosticationibus sompniorum*. Villena's reference is second-hand; see Item 4 below.

4. Aben Reduán "en el *Gayad Alhaquim*" (Cátedra 1:332; Soler 187-88; Gallina 109; Cotarelo 154, no.4). "Gayat alhaquin" in BN 6599 (fol. 144r), "alhaquim" in V-6-64 (fol.125v). Aben Reduan is the astrologer and physician °Ali ibn Riḍwān (c. 998-c. 1067). As far as I have been able to ascertain, none of his works go by the name *Gayad Alhaquim* (= *Ghāyat al-ḥakīm*, "The Aim of the Wise"), but this was the title of the work which we know (and which Villena knew) in its Alphonsine translation as *Liber Picatrix*, generally attributed by modern scholars to Maslama ibn Aḥmad al-Majrīṭī (b. Madrid, fl. Cordova, d. c. 1007). See Sarton 1:688.

   Speaking of the works of Caicamet / Caumente and Ibn Riḍwān, Villena states: "Non allego los testos d'ello, porque non vi sus libros, si non que lo oí dezir a mis maestros" ["I do not cite the texts on this, because I never saw their books, I only heard it mentioned by my teachers"] (Cátedra 1:332-33). This is not the place to deal with the fascinating question of the identity of Villena's *maestros*. However, the remark is revealing inasmuch as it shows that his information about the two works was acquired second-hand. A similar possibility must be entertained whenever other authors or works are mentioned *en passant* without any direct quotation.

5. Rabí Açac Alizrraelí "en el libro de los *Harazim*" (Cátedra 1:333; Soler 188; Gallina 110; Cotarelo 171, no.116: "Rabí Zag-el-Irrach"). "Rrabi çag el yrraeli en el libro de los harrasim" (BN 6599, fol.144r); "arrasim" (V-6-64, fol.126r). Cotarelo understandably identified "Rrabi Çag" with Isaac Ibn Sid, the chief collaborator of Alfonso X, but the identification

is by no means certain. The title of the book (a "Book of the Wise," "Magi," "Astrologers," "Craftsmen," or "Mysteries"), cited as a source of Jewish charms and incantations against the Evil Eye, does not enable us to be more precise. Gallina (76 and 110, note 106) prefers the reading *Xarasim* (pronounced *Sharasim*) which she interprets as *Liber radicum*. Rabbi Zag is mentioned again in the same context (Cátedra 1:338) in connection with a *Cábala* (*tabla* in the other mss.) whose contents seem to bear no relationship to the Alphonsine *corpus*. Other possibilities include:

(a) the Egyptian Isḥāq al-Isrā'īlī (d. Tunis c. 932), known in the Middle Ages as Isaac Judaeus. A physician and philosopher, he wrote in Arabic many works on medicine which were translated into Latin by Constantinus Africanus in 1087, and later into Hebrew and Castilian. Villena may be referring to Isaac's *Guide of Physicians*, a work on deontology surviving in Hebrew with the title *Mūsar hā-rōfe'īm* (Sarton 1:639-40).

(b) Isaac ben Joseph ben Israel of Toledo, a Judeo-Spanish astronomer who flourished in Toledo c. 1310 and died after 1330. His best-known work was the *Liber Jesod Olam* (*Foundation of the World*), written in Toledo in 1310 at the request of his master Asher ben Jehiel (Rabbi Asher, q.v. *infra*, nº.12). The fifth part of this work consists of tables and their explanations (Sarton 3.1:691-92).

Neither reference in Villena is sufficiently precise to suggest first-hand knowledge of the works in question.

6. Rasech Enod "e el maestro de Girona en su *Cabbala*" (Cátedra 1:333; Soler 188; Gallina 111: "Rrasetruoch, el maestro de Girona, en su *Tabla*"; Cotarelo 171, no.119). "Rrasechenoch el maestro de Gerona en su tabla" (BN 6599, fol.144v); "rrasecenoch" (V-6-64, fol.126r). This appears to be a reference to two authors in the ms. on which Cátedra's edition is based; in the other 15th-century mss. it seems to refer to one author known as "the Master of Gerona." Gallina (82), citing Rodríguez de Castro's *Escritores rabinos españoles de los siglos XI al XVII*, suggests a certain Enoch ben R. Moseh from Gerona, who wrote in Arabic because the Jews of his day did not know classical Hebrew. Villena refers again to "el maestro de Gerona" in his *Tratado de la consolación* (Cátedra 1:228), where it is clear that he is referring to a biblical commentator, perhaps someone from the school of Moses ben Nahman of Gerona, if not Nahmanides himself.[11] Ciceri (302), relying

on the variant manuscript reading "el maestro de Gepona," identifies the latter as St. Augustine of Hippo, *Adnotationes in Job*.

7. Cleopatra, "muger de Marco Antonio, en el *Libro de sus afeites*" ["the wife of Mark Antony in her *Book on Cosmetics*"] (Cátedra 1:334; Soler 189; Gallina 116; Cotarelo 160, no.45). No comment from Cotarelo. A work on cosmetics, attributed to Cleopatra, was certainly known in the time of Galen (Thorndike 1:152). The reference in Villena is clearly second-hand. Thorndike (2:378) also refers to "a work supposed to have been written by Cleopatra to her daughter on the subject of gynecology, and [which] inserts in condensed form John of Spain's translation from the Arabic of the medical portion of the *Secret of Secrets* . . ." (Ciceri 306).

8. Arpoçraçio "en sus *Quiránidas*" (Cátedra 1:334; Soler 189; Gallina 116; Cotarelo 156, no.18). "Aprocaçio" in BN 6599 and V-6-64. Cotarelo was unable to advance an identification. However, "Arpoçraçio" is Harpocration, and the *Quiránidas* is "a work in Latin of uncertain date and authorship, usually called the *Kiranides* of Kiranus, King of Persia" (Thorndike 2:229). Thorndike states (2:229-30) that it purports to be a translation from the Greek version which in its turn was from the Arabic, and that the medieval Latin translator (who describes himself as an *infimus clericus*) speaks of the work as the *Book of Natural Virtues, Complaints and Cures*, adding that it is a compilation from the *Experience of the Kiranides of Kiranus, King of Persia, and the Book of Harpocration of Alexandria to his Daughter*. It is largely a work on charms and incantations.

9. Cancaf el Indiano (Cátedra 1:335; Soler 190; Gallina 118; Cotarelo 159, no.34). Possibly "cantaf" in BN 6599, and "caucaf" in V-6-64. Kankah al-Hindī (also Kankaraf, Kanaka) may have been an astrologer at the court of Hārūn al-Rashīd, but has become the stuff of legend in medieval Arabic science. According to the *Dictionary of Scientific Biography*, "[i]f . . . one is willing to accept the traditions of the ninth and tenth centuries as referring to an historical personage, Kankah emerges as an Indian astrologer who practised his art in Baghdad towards the end of the eighth and in the early ninth centuries but whose works in Arabic fall within the ʿAbbāsid tradition of astrology (derived from Greek and Iranian sources); and the existing fragments appear to display no specifically Indian traits. . . . Later Arab scholars, especially in Spain, constructed elaborate theories regarding the role of Kankah in the history of Science. . . . Finally, pure fancy has produced a fabulous Kankah

al-Hindī in alchemical literature. His fantastic exploits are recounted in pseudo-al-Majrītī's *Ghāyat al-ḥakīm . . ."* (*Dictionary of Scientific Biography* 7:223a-b). Some of Villena's references to Kankah most likely come from the *Liber Picatrix* (the Alphonsine translation of the *Ghāyat al-ḥakīm*), and from the Alphonsine *Libro de las formas e de las imágenes* (Cátedra, *Exégesis* 58), but see Item 11 below.

10. *Mushaf al-camar* "el corto" (Cátedra 1:335; Soler 190; Gallina 118; Cotarelo 168, no.96). In the mss. of Villena's works there is some confusion as to whether "Mushaf al-camar" (or "alzimar") is a book or a person. In the *Fascinación* ("segúnt cuenta Cancaf el Indiano e *Mushaf al-camar* el corto"), Villena appears to be referring to an individual, but the *e* ("and") which precedes the name should probably read *en* ("in"). In *Glosas* (ed. Cátedra 1:242) he ascribes to "Ballianos el Indiano . . . el libro que los arávigos llaman *Muçaf al-camar"* ["the book which the Arabs call *Musaf al-camar"*], and in the *Exposición del salmo* he attributes it to "Cancaf el Indiano" (q.v., *supra,* Item 9). Once again we are dealing with second-hand references (see Item 11 below).

 Ciceri (312) interprets the name as "libro dei talismani lunari" ["book of lunar talismans"], though it could be a garbled version of *Kitāb al-nāmūdār fi al-ā ʿmār* ("Book of the Namudar [Used for Determining the Lengths of] Lives"), one of the works attributed to Kankah (*Dictionary of Scientific Biography* 7:223a).

11. Xarafi viejo de Guadalhajara (Cátedra 1:335; Soler 190; Gallina 118; Cotarelo 174, no.143). "El Xarafi el viejo de Guadalfajara" in BN 6599 and V-6-64. I have not been able to identify this individual. Villena states that Xarafi was a Moorish sage (*un sabidor morisco*) from Guadalajara, and that from him he obtained the information concerning Cancaf el Indiano and *Mushaf al-camar* (see sections 9 and 10 above).

12. El rab Rabí Aser "en la *Cabala* que dexó en Toledo escripta de su mano" ["in the *Cabbala* he left in Toledo, written in his own hand"] (Cátedra 1:335; Soler 191; Gallina 119; Cotarelo 170, no.114). "Acobala" in BN 6599 and V-6-64. Cotarelo (86n) states rather vaguely that "se le menciona como Presidente de la Academia toledana de judíos en el siglo XI o XII" ["he is mentioned as President of the Toledan academy of Jews in the 11th or 12th century"]. He is undoubtedly Asher ben Jehiel who was born in Western Germany c. 1250, studied in Rothenburg and, in 1303, fled from persecutions to Montpellier, Barcelona, and finally Toledo, where he spent some 28 years as Rabbi and Chief Justice. His major work was a code based on the *Halakot* of

Alfasi, a compendium of the legal part of the Talmud (Sarton 2.2:888-89).[12] Villena gives the impression that he had seen the *Cabbala* of Rabbi Asher, but it is more likely that he was given the information by his rabbinical acquaintances mentioned in sections 13 and 15 below.

13. Maestre Hasdai Crescas, "que fue en este tiempo" ["who lived in our time"] (Cátedra 1:335; Soler 191; Gallina 119; Cotarelo 157, no.23). "Maestro Asday Crestas [or Crescas]" in BN 6599 and V-6-64. Cotarelo was unable to make a positive identification. However, this is clearly a reference to Rabbi Hasdai ben Abraham Crescas (or Cresques, in Catalan) with whom Sarton deals at some length (3.2:1446-48).[13] A Judeo-Catalan philosopher, he was born in Barcelona c. 1340 and died in Saragossa c. 1411. He was leader of the Jewish community in Barcelona, and a favourite at the court of John I of Aragon. Later he became Rabbi of Saragossa and, in 1396 or 1398, wrote a refutation of Christianity and *apologia* for Judaism in Castilian which survives only in a Hebrew extract. Villena knew him personally, but shows no knowledge of his writings; the information in the *Tratado de la fascinación* on Jewish methods of diagnosing the Evil Eye was obtained from Rabbi Crescas *viva voce*.

14. Balihanos (Cátedra 1:336; Soler 192; Gallina 121; Cotarelo 158, no.26). "Balihanos" is not the fanciful Persian author "Vali Han" postulated by Gallina (75), but the Belyenus mentioned as the reputed author of Parts V and VI of the Alphonsine *Libro de las formas et de las imágines* (Sarton 2.2:837). He is also referred to in other medieval manuscripts as Belus, Belbenus, Belenus and Belinus, and may be identified tentatively with Apollonius (Thorndike 2:234-35). Villena's reference is almost certainly from a Latin or Romance source, closely connected with the references to Cancaf el Indiano and *Mushaf al-camar* (see sections 9 and 10 above).

15. Rabí Zarahya "a quien dezían En Ferrer, que fue en este tiempo" ["whom they called En Ferrer, who lived in our time"] (Cátedra 1:338; Soler 193; Gallina 124; Cotarelo 171, no.117).[14] "Rabi Zaraya" in BN 6599 and V-6-64; Cotarelo (171) reads *Enferrez* as the title of a work. As in the case of Rabbi Hasdai Crescas, Villena states that Rabbi Zaraya "me contó provara algunas cosas. . ." ["told me he had tried certain things. . ."] as cures for the Evil Eye. Cotarelo was unable to make any identification. "Rabí Zarahya" is Zerahia Halevi, also known as Rabbi Ferrer Saladin, who succeeded Hasdai Crescas as the Chief Rabbi of Saragossa. He was sent by the Jewish community of Saragossa

to participate as principal Jewish speaker in the famous Disputation of Tortosa in 1413-14 (Baer 2:135, 138, 173, 177, 179, 197 ff., *et passim*).

The results of this examination of the apparently non-Latin sources of the *Tratado de la fascinación* may be summarized as follows:

1. Two references apply definitely to works in Latin (Averroes [but really Albertus Magnus] and Harpocration).
2. Four are made on the basis of second-hand information (Caicamet / Caumente, Aben Reduan, Cancaf el Indiano, *Mushaf al-camar*).
3. Three refer to personal contacts which were almost certainly conducted in Castilian or Catalan (Xarafi de Guadalajara, Rabbi Hasdai Crescas, Rabbi Zerahia).
4. Only one title is intended to be Arabic (Aben Ohaxia, *Philahanaptia mayor*), but the work was known in Spain in a Latin translation.
5. One title is definitely Hebrew (Rabbi Zag, *Harazim*), one is probably Hebrew (Rabbi Asher, *Cabala or Acobala*), but the information is almost certainly second-hand.
6. Four are doubtful (Rabbi Zag, *Cabala* or *Tabla*; Rasech Enod, *Cabala* or *Tabla*; Cleopatra, *Libro de afeytes*; Balihanos), but the first two are almost certainly second-hand references, the third comes from a Romance or Latin source, and the fourth, directly or indirectly, from the Alphonsine corpus.

We can see, therefore, that it is not necessary to postulate an extensive or profound use of original non-Latin / non-Romance sources in the composition of the *Tratado de la fascinación*.

A rapid glance at the remaining eighteen non-Latin / non-Romance writers mentioned in Villena's other works suggests similar conclusions.

a) Of the works attributed to the thirteen authors who can be identified positively, only three are given Arabic or Hebrew titles:

1. Aben Hasdra "en el *Çefer atuamin*" (mentioned in the *Tratado de la lepra*, ed. Cátedra 1:120). This is Abraham ben Meïr ibn Ezra, an Hispano-Jewish philosopher, astrologer, translator from Arabic into Hebrew, and one of the greatest medieval biblical commentators. He was born in Toledo c. 1090, travelled extensively throughout Christian Europe, and died in 1167, probably in Calahorra. The Latin translations of his works were very influential in Christendom. The title of the work mentioned by Villena is probably the *Sefer*

ha-'Azamin, one of the biblical commentaries attributed to Ibn Ezra (Ciceri 304).

2. Maestre Muisén de Egipto "en el *Moré*" (cited in *Exposición del salmo*, ed. Cátedra 1:316). This is the *Moreh Nebukim* (*The Guide for the Perplexed*) of Maimonides (Moses ben Maimon). Villena may have known this work in the Castilian version undertaken by the *converso* Pedro de Toledo on behalf of Gómez Suárez de Figueroa, the son of Lorenzo Suárez de Figueroa, former Master of the Military Order of Santiago, and the father-in-law of Íñigo López de Mendoza, Marquis of Santillana, Villena's protégé in poetic matters. The translation of the second part of the *Moreh* was finished by Pedro de Toledo in 1419, the third and final part in 1432. The fact that Villena uses the title *Moreh* cannot be taken as proof that he was acquainted with the Hebrew version; the translator himself refers to it as "el muy altisimo libro del More que fizo el muy famoso sabio maestre Moysen de Egipto, el Cordoui" ["the most exalted book of the More written by the very famous sage Master Moses of Egypt, the Cordovan"].[15] Villena may also have been acquainted with the medieval Latin version; in fact, a brief quotation from the *Moreh* in *Glosas a la Eneida* (ed. Cátedra 89, 2:252) is in Latin.

3. Rabí Moisén de Egipto "en los *Pacuquim* que fizo en los catorze libros" (cited in *Tratado de la lepra*, ed. Cátedra 1:120). The "catorze libros" must refer to the fourteen books of the *Mishnah Torah*, Maimonides' compilation of Jewish law. *Pacuquim* should probably read *paçuquim*, i.e., *ha-Posekim*, an *accessus*, key or commentary. The passage in the *Tratado de la lepra* is concerned with the interpretation of the laws of the Talmud, and the authority of Maimonides is adduced to refute the highly literal interpretations of the Bible as practised by the *carraym* (the Karaite or Qaraite sect) "que comen puerca cuidando lícito sea, pues en la ley que defendió el puerco non lo vieda nin nombra expressamente" ["who eat sow's meat believing it to be lawful, as the law which forbids pig's meat does not expressly forbid or name it"] (1:120). This would seem to be a reminiscence of the *Mishnah Torah*, Book XIV (*The Book of Judges*), Treatise III, Laws Concerning Rebels 2:9, and 3:1-3. (I have consulted the translation by Hershman [New Haven: Yale UP, 1949, 142-44], but the information given by Villena is second-hand, taken from the *Pugio fidei adversus mauros*

et judaeos [c. 1276-78] by the Catalan Dominican Ramón Martí [Cátedra, *Exégesis* 38].)

b) Nine works are given titles in Romance:

1. Alfargano "en sus *Diferençias*" (mentioned in the *Exposición del salmo*, ed. Cátedra 1:308). The author is al-Farghānī, known in Latin as Alfraganus (fl. c. 850), and the reference is to his *Differentie science astrorum*, also called *Liber de aggregationibus*, a twelfth-century Latin translation from Arabic. See Sarton 1:567, and Thorndike 2:74, *et passim*.

2. Avicena "en el segundo del *Canon*" (cited in *Glosas a la Eneida*, ed. Cátedra 1989, 2:205). Avicenna (Ibn Sīnā, 980-1037), medieval Islam's greatest scientist, requires no introduction. The *Canon* (*al-Qānūn fi'al-ṭibb*) is an immense encyclopedia of medicine, a codification of the whole of ancient and Muslim knowledge. It was translated into Latin by Gherardo Cremonese, in which version it was known throughout medieval Europe. Villena's reference is to *Canon* II, ii, 281, but he extracts his information from Juan Gil de Zamora, *Contra venena et animalia venenosa* (see Cátedra 1989, 2:205, note 61). An additional reference to Avicenna, *in sexto Naturalium* (i.e., *De anima*, IV, 4) went unperceived by Cotarelo (see *Glosas*, ed. Cátedra 1989, 2:252).

3. Picatriz "en el *Libro de sus imágenes.*" Villena mentions this Latin work in the *Epístola a Suero de Quiñones* (ed. Cátedra 1:349). See my remarks above on Ibn Riḍwān.

4. Ageber (*aliis* Algebel) "en la *Suma mayor*" (cited in the *Tratado de la lepra*, ed. Cátedra 1:122). This is Jābir ibn Ḥayyān, the alchemist "Geber" of the Middle Ages (fl. c. 776). Geber is known in medieval Europe through twelfth-century Latin translations of works attributed to him, though many are probably apocryphal (see Sarton 1:532-33 and 2.2:43-45).

5. Alaçén "en su *Prespetyva*" (mentioned in *Glosa* 393, on *Aeneid* 2.250-52, ed. Cátedra 1989, 2:120). The author is Ibn al-Haytham, *nomen latinum* Alhazen (c. 965-c. 1039). The treatise is the *Perspectiva*, part of Alhazen's work on optics which, in its Latin translation, exerted considerable influence on scientists such as Roger Bacon and Kepler (Sarton 1:721).

6. Alý Aben Raxel "en sus *Juyzios*" (mentioned in *Glosa* 371, on *Aeneid* 2.114, ed. Cátedra 1989, 2:60). These are the *Juicios astrológicos* (*Praeclarissimus liber completus in judiciis astrorum*)

of Ibn Abi'l-Rijāl, *nomen latinum* Abenragel. A Muslim astrologer, possibly of Spanish birth, he flourished in Tunis between 1016 and 1040. Villena is referring to his main work, translated from Arabic into Castilian in 1256 by Judah ben Moses, and later from Castilian into Latin by Aegidius de Tebaldis and Petrus de Regio (Sarton 1:599-600). Villena was probably familiar with the Castilian version executed in the court of Alfonso X.

7. Eleno "en el libro mayor de sus *Prestigios*" (mentioned in *Glosa* 431, on *Aeneid* 2.471-75, ed. Cátedra 1989, 2:205). Cotarelo (164, no.67) reads "Galeno." Cátedra (*Glosas* 1989, 2:205, note 68) speculates that it may have been one of the Latin versions of Thābit ibn Qurra's *Liber prestigiorum*, or one of the magical works attributed to "Eleno" (Helenus) in medieval catalogues (Thorndike 5:57).

8. Tebid Aben Cora "en el *Libro de sus ymágines*" (mentioned in *Glosa* 470, on *Aeneid* 2.715, ed. Cátedra 1989, 2:301). Thābit ibn Qurra (c. 830-901), physician, mathematician and astronomer. His works were widely diffused in translation in the Middle Ages (Sarton 1:599-600), the *Liber de imaginibus* circulating in two Latin versions, one by Adelard of Bath, the other by John of Seville. Villena's reference is probably second-hand (Cátedra 1989, 2:301, note 401).

9. Sael, "el libro *De las elecçiones*" (mentioned in *Glosa* 380, on *Aeneid* 2.162-75, ed. Cátedra 1989, 2:86). Sahl ibn Bishr (first half of the ninth century), was a Jewish astrologer who wrote in Arabic. Villena refers to the work known in its Latin translation as *De electionibus* (Sarton 1:569).

c) Two authors are mentioned without any reference to a specific work:

1. Abumaxar (mentioned in the *Epístola a Suero de Quiñones*, ed. Cátedra 1:348). Cotarelo (154, no.6) reads incorrectly "Abu-majerar." This is Abū Maʿshar, *nomen latinum* Albumasar, who flourished in Baghdad and died in 886. He is described by Sarton (1:568) as the astrologer more frequently quoted in the West than any other. His many astrological works were very soon translated into Latin and were widely diffused throughout the Middle Ages.

2. Alquinde (mentioned in the *Epístola a Suero de Quiñones*, ed. Cátedra 1:348). Al-Kindī, *nomen latinum* Alkindus, was born in Basra c. 800, flourished in Baghdad, and died c. 873. Known as

51

"the philosopher of the Arabs," he wrote encyclopedic works on mathematics, astrology, physics, music, medicine, pharmacy and geography, many of which were translated into Latin by Gherardo Cremonese (Sarton 1:559). Villena's references, both to Albumasar and Alkindus, are too vague to imply first-hand knowledge of their works, but they are clearly from a Latin or Romance source.

d) The five cases of doubtful identity may be divided as follows:

1. Three second-hand references:

   i) Ceman, mentioned in the *Arte cisoria* (cap.2, ed. Cátedra 1:140) in connection with ancient rhetoric. Brown (308) takes the word to be the name of "a rhetor, probably Arabic, otherwise unidentified." Cátedra (1:140) does not take the word to be a proper name, but provides no gloss. I have not been able to identify the origin of the passage, but it is probably connected with the source for ii) and iii) below.

   ii) Ferreicún, mentioned in the *Arte cisoria* (cap.2, ed. Cátedra 1:139) in connection with the compilation of ancient legal codes, but otherwise unidentified, though it may be a garbled reference to the astronomer/astrologer ʿUmar ibn al-Farrukhān who flourished in Baghdad between 762 and 812 (see *Dictionary of Scientific Biography* 13:538a-39a). Villena cites the *Philahanaptia mayor* (q.v., *supra*) as the source of his information. He also refers to a Cahit in the same context. The name is missing from Cotarelo's list. Cátedra (*Exégesis* 56), quite plausibly, takes it to be a syncope of "Çaherit" identified in the Alphonsine *Lapidario* as a "sabio de la agricultura caldea."

   iii) Ledán, also cited in the *Arte cisoria* (cap.2, ed. Cátedra 1:139) in the same context as Ferreicún. Cátedra (*Exégesis* 56) suspects that the name is a corruption of Ibn al-Adami, one of the authorities cited in the *Agricultura caldea*, and a source of possibly legendary information about Kankah the Indian (*Dictionary of Scientific Biography* 7:223a). In the *Exposición del salmo* (ed. Cátedra 1:312) and the *Tratado de la lepra* (ed. Cátedra 1:126) Villena attributes to Ledán a *Libro de jacinto* (on which, see Cátedra, *Exégesis* 56, 58 and 103); the quotation from this book in the *Tratado de la lepra* is in Latin.

2. One work is referred to without a specific title:
   El Zaharahui "en el tractado que partió por treinta *macalas*" ["in the treatise he divided into thirty *macalas*"], is mentioned parenthetically (and probably at second-hand) in the *Tratado de la lepra* (ed. Cátedra 1:122), in a passage, deriving from the *Philahanaptia mayor* (*q.v.*), on diseases of trees. The author is Abu'l-Qāsim (Khalaf ibn ʿAbbās al-Zahrāwī), *nomina latina* Albucasis and Alsaharavius (with many medieval variants). He was born near Cordova, and was physician to al-Ḥakam II (961-76). Alsaharavius is known chiefly for his vast medical encyclopedia in thirty parts, especially the section on surgery translated into Latin by Gherardo Cremonese (*Liber Azaragui de cirurgia*, 1st. ed., Venice, 1498), and later by others into Provençal and Hebrew (Sarton 1:681). The reading "treinta *macalas*," found only in the ms. on which Cátedra bases his edition (Geneva, Bibliotheca Bodmeriana, Cod. 67), confirms my suspicion (Carr 1972:155) that Villena was attempting to reproduce the Arabic *maqālah*, 'chapter, treatise'. The two other mss. reproduce a *lectio facilior*, the Latinism *máculas* for *manchas* ("stains"), which, in the context of a disquisition on the external symptoms of leprosy, would make more sense to a medieval copyist.

3. One work has a title in Romance:
   Pedro Helías "en su libro *De menascalia*" (mentioned in *Tratado de la lepra*, ed. Cátedra 1:121). Taking into account the name of the author, and the spelling of the work (*Menasclī*) in the manuscript he had consulted, Cotarelo clearly thought he was dealing with a Jewish writer and a Hebrew text. Ciceri (313) rightly rejects Cotarelo's suggestion that the author could have been "Pedro Helías Trautman, traductor de la llamada *Carta de Samuel*, en 27 capítulos, obra de Rabí Samuel Marroquí, sobre materia religiosa" ["Pedro Helias Trautman, translator of the so-called *Letter of Samuel*, in 27 chapters, the work of Rabbi Samuel Marroqui, on religious subject-matter"] (Cotarelo 165, no.74), but her own speculations (Pietro d'Abano and Pierre d'Ailly) are equally fanciful. Nor is he to be confused with the grammarian Pierre Hélie who taught in Paris in the middle of the twelfth century (Sarton 3.1:1003). The readings of Rodríguez-Moñino ms. V-6-64 and Bodmeriana Cod. 67, as well as the context, make it clear that we are dealing with a book on *menescalia* (that is, the care of horses), probably written in Catalan

or Aragonese, as the preferred terminology in Castilian was *mariscalia* or *albeiteria*. I have been unable to identify the author.[16]

It goes without saying that the language in which Villena quotes the title of a work is not necessarily the language of the version with which he was acquainted. But the titles he cites in Latin or Castilian are entirely consistent with the general titles under which these works circulated in their medieval Latin or Romance translations. As Thorndike remarks, "when a late medieval writer cites or pretends to cite an Arabic author, he is doing so from a Latin translation or original" (3:147). Thorndike, of course, is referring to the wider European context, and to the fact that translations from Arabic scientific and alchemical works practically ceased after 1300. His remarks, therefore, may not be entirely valid for the Spain of Villena's day, where Hebrew and Arabic manuscripts were more readily available, and where Arabic at least was still spoken by a substantial part of the population. Nevertheless, in the period 1417-34, to which Villena's literary works belong, bilingualism or trilingualism (Romance-Hebrew-Arabic) was largely a one-sided affair, confined on the whole to *moriscos*, Jews and *conversos*, and probably then in a largely qualified sense. Knowledge of Hebrew and Arabic among "old" Christians was largely limited to certain sections of the clergy, whose interest was religious and polemical, rather than academic.[17]

The indications I have given above strongly suggest that, where we are not dealing with second-hand references or with information acquired *viva voce*, Villena's knowledge of Arabic texts came from medieval Latin (and, occasionally, Castilian) translations. On the basis of the Hebrew words and phrases found in the *Tratado de la fascinación*, a case could be made at first sight for Villena's familiarity with Hebrew. On closer examination, however, this "familiarity" reveals itself to be little more than a superficial acquaintance with some of the superstitious elements of the Cabbala, or Jewish tradition (simple charms, incantations, invocations and the use of phylacteries), much of it acquired by Villena when, as a studious and inquisitive young man, he frequented rabbinical circles in Aragon.

Seen in the context of medieval European science, the vast majority of Villena's references to Arabic works are not particularly remarkable; rather, they are to be expected. Largely as a result of the immense body of translations disseminated by the so-called "Renaissance of the Twelfth Century," these non-Christian sources became the common property of the western scientific and philosophical tradition, regularly referred to and quoted by Christian authors. What is remarkable is that Villena should take such obvious delight in his familiarity with them at a time when the spirit of scientific enquiry in Spain was in a decidedly decadent state, and when the common opinion of the Castilian aristocracy regarded such pursuits as ill-befitting a person of noble rank (see *Glosas*, ed. Cátedra 1989, 1:4, 8-9).

Don Enrique de Villena was a complicated, eccentric, opinionated and probably quite testy individual. Yet in spite of this (or perhaps because of it), and notwithstanding the contempt in which he was held by many of his contemporaries, his is the last notable example of openness to the unfettered pursuit of knowledge, including the esoteric, the heterodox and the proscribed, in the increasingly restricted ideological atmosphere of fifteenth-century Castile. In many ways he represents the last gasp of the Alphonsine tradition in pre-Inquisitorial Spain.

Notes

1. I am happy to acknowledge the gracious assistance I received at the beginning of my work on Enrique de Villena from Professor Mahmoud Manzalaoui, and from our colleague Professor Hanna Kassis, in trying to make sense of fifteenth-century Castilian copyists' attempts to render garbled Arabic and Hebrew words and phrases in the Roman alphabet.
2. The standard biography of Enrique de Villena, still useful as a starting point, though now much superseded by studies quoted elsewhere in this article, is Emilio Cotarelo y Mori, *Don Enrique de Villena. Su vida y obras* (1896), cited as Cotarelo in subsequent references. See also Carr, "Don Enrique de Villena, *El tratado*" 24-67; Gascón Vera, "Nuevo retrato" 107-43; Riera y Sans, "Enric de Villena" 109-32; Cátedra, "Para la biografía"; Carr and Cátedra, "Datos para la biografía"; Brown and Carr, "Don Enrique de Villena."
3. Cotarelo's list is to be found in his *Don Enrique de Villena. Su vida y obras*, Apéndice III, "Biblioteca de D. Enrique de Villena," 151-75. On the destruction of Villena's personal library, see Blanco White, "Quema de la librería"; Menéndez Pelayo, *Biblioteca de traductores españoles* 1:135-37; Puymaigre, "Don Enrique de Villena et sa bibliothèque"; Cotarelo 109-17; Waxman 390-96; Alonso Getino xliv-lxii; Round, "Five Magicians"; Gascón Vera, "La quema de los libros"; Cátedra, "Algunas obras perdidas."
4. The most recent editions are in *Enrique de Villena: Obras completas*, ed. Pedro M. Cátedra. Unless otherwise stated, all references are to this edition. A third volume, containing the translation of *Aeneid* 4-12, the translation of Dante, and general indices, is in preparation. See also, *Traducción y glosas de la 'Eneida'*, ed. Pedro M. Cátedra; *La primera versión castellana de 'La Eneida', de Virgilio: los libros I-III traducidos y comentados por Enrique de Villena (1384-1434)*, ed. Ramón Santiago Lacuesta; *Arte cisoria*, ed. John O'Neill; *Arte cisoria*, ed. Russell V. Brown, Diss. U of Wisconsin-Madison, 1974 (from which my references proceed), subsequently published in Biblioteca Humanitas de Textos Inéditos 3 (Barcelona: Humanitas, 1984); *Tratado de aojamiento*, ed. Anna María Gallina; *Exposición del salmo "Quoniam videbo"*, ed. Pedro

M. Cátedra, 85-123; also ed. Maria Ciceri, in "Per Villena," 319-35; *Tratado de la consolación*, ed. Derek C. Carr. The first complete edition of the *Epístola a Suero de Quiñones*, extensively annotated, can be found in my article "La *Epístola*" 10-18. Eccentric, and of little use to the specialist, is the work of Francisco Almagro and José Fernández Carpintero, *Heurística a Villena*, which reproduces uncritically the text of the *tres tratados* (*Aojamiento, Consolación and Lepra*) as published by J. Soler [R. Foulché-Delbosc] in *Revue Hispanique* 41 (1917): 110-214. The almost certainly apocryphal treatise on astrology can be consulted in *El 'Tratado de astrología' atribuido a Enrique de Villena*, ed. Pedro M. Cátedra, Introduction by Julio Samsó (Madrid: Río Tinto Minera, 1980), and the revised edition in Biblioteca Humanitas de Historia del Pensamiento 1 (Barcelona: Humanitas, 1983). For advances in the history of science, we remain permanently indebted to Lynn Thorndike, *A History of Magic*, and to George Sarton's monumental *Introduction to the History of Science*, now somewhat superseded by the *Dictionary of Scientific Biography*, ed. Charles Coulston Gillespie et al.

5. See Curtius 260-64. The authors mentioned by Villena are Apuleius, Aristotle (in Latin), Aulus Gellius, Boethius (and pseudo-Boethius), Cassiodorus, Cato (*Disticha*), Catullus, Cicero, Claudian, Eutropius, Hippocrates, Homer (second-hand ref.), Horace, Xenophon, Juvenal, Lucan, Macrobius, Ovid, Palladius, Persius, Plato (in Latin), Pliny, Seneca, Statius, Suetonius, Terence, Livy, Valerius, Vegetius, and Vergil.

6. *Generaciones y semblanzas*, ed. R. B. Tate (London: Tamesis, 1965) 33.

7. For comments on the accuracy of the translation, see Menéndez Pelayo, *Biblioteca* 1:148; *Bibliografía hispano-latina* 51:365; Amador de los Ríos, *Historia crítica* 6:49-54; and, subsequently, González de la Calle, "Contribución" *Anales* 3 (1934): 16-17; R. Santiago Lacuesta, Introd. to his ed., 12, 28-30; the notes, *passim*, to Pedro M. Cátedra's edition (1989).

8. See Pascual Rodríguez, *La traducción de la 'Divina Commedia'* 9-22.

9. On Villena's childhood in Valencia, specifically in his grandfather's castle in Gandía, see Carr and Cátedra, "Datos para la biografía." On Villena's knowledge of Provençal poetics, see his *Arte de trobar*. It is significant that Villena's earliest surviving literary work, *Els dotzé treballs d'Hercules* (1417), was written in Catalan.

10. See Guido de Columnis, *Historia destructionis Troiae* 88-90. Cátedra (1989, 2:96, note 82) speculates that "in temporibus" might be an error for "in operibus."

11. Cf. Cátedra: "En este *Tratado* cita . . . Villena el 'maestro de Gerona,' seguramente Moshé ben Nehman [*sic*], quien escribió una exposición del Libro de Job . . . , de la que el nuestro tendría noticias indirectas, pues no se halla el pasaje idéntico dentro de esta obra . . ." ["In this treatise . . . Villena cites the 'Master of Gerona', undoubtedly Moses ben Nahman, who wrote a commentary on the Book of Job . . . , about which our author must have had indirect information, since the identical passage is not to be found in this work . . ."] (1989, 1:38, note 570).

12. See also Baer 1:316-25, 2:192-94, and *passim*.

13. See also Millás Vallicrosa 192-94, and *passim*; Baer 2:21, and *passim*.

14. Catalan 'En,' deriving from Latin *domine*, was a title of respect, equivalent to Castilian 'Don,' used with given names or family names.

15. See Schiff 431.

16. Professor Marcelino Amasuno Sárraga, McGill University, has alerted me to the possibility that "Helías" may be a scribal error for "Días" or "Díaz." The confusion of this surname with "Elías" (subsequently written "Helías") is easily explained by the similarity

of minuscule "d" and "el" in the mss. of the period. The only author of that name I have been able to trace is Villena's contemporary (whom he may have known personally), the Valencian Manuel Díaz or Díez, ambassador to the *Compromiso de Caspe* in 1412 which resulted in the election of Villena's cousin Fernando as king of Aragon, and subsequently *mayordomo* of Fernando's son, Alfonso V of Aragon. However, Manuel's famous *Llibre de manescalia* appears to have been written in 1443 during the Aragonese conquest of Naples, nine years after Villena's death. See Sanz Egaña, *Historia de la veterinaria* 99-107 (I have not been able to consult Sanz Egaña's *Noticias acerca de la medicina de los animales en la España cristiana de la Edad Media* [Madrid, 1935]). Manuel Díaz's work is basically a Catalan translation of the Castilian *Libro de los caballos* (second half of the thirteenth century), which in turn is a translation of the *Practica equorum* of the Italian bishop Teodorico Borgognoni di Lucca, born around 1205; see Sachs, ed., *El libro de los caballos*. The work contains no "capítulo de la lepra de los caballos." The text to which Villena refers could well be one of the many Catalan *llibres de menescalia* found in MS. 68 of the Biblioteca Universitaria de Barcelona, but I have been unable to make a positive identification.

17. On the fate of Arabic in the medical curriculum of Spanish universities in the fifteenth century, see Amasuno Sárraga, *La escuela de medicina* 148-49.

Works Cited

Almagro, Francisco, and José Fernández Carpintero. *Heurística a Villena y los tres tratados*. Biblioteca de Visionarios, Heterodoxos y Marginados 15. Madrid: Editora Nacional, 1977.

Alonso Getino, Luis G. *Vida y obras de Fray Lope de Barrientos*. Anales Salmantinos 1. Salamanca: Calatrava, 1927.

Amador de los Ríos, José. *Historia crítica de la literatura española*. Vol. 6. Madrid, 1864. Madrid: Gredos, 1969.

Amasuno Sárraga, Marcelino V. *La escuela de medicina del estudio salmantino (siglos XIII-XV)*. Acta Salmanticensia, Historia de la Universidad 52. Salamanca: U de Salamanca, 1990.

Baer, Yitzhak. *A History of the Jews in Christian Spain*. Trans. Louis Schoffman. 2 vols. Philadelphia: The Jewish Publication Society of America, 1961-66.

Blanco White, Joseph María. "Quema de la librería del Marqués de Villena." *Variedades, o Mensagero de Londres* 1 (1824): 142-43.

Brown, Russell V. "Enrique de Villena's *Arte cisoria*: A Critical Edition and Study." Diss. U of Wisconsin-Madison, 1974.

—, and Derek C. Carr. "Don Enrique de Villena en Cuenca (con tres cartas inéditas del mismo)." *El Crotalón: Anuario de Filología Española* 2 (1985): 503-17.

Carr, Derek C. "Don Enrique de Villena, *El tratado de la consolación*. A Critical Edition with Introduction and Notes." Diss. U of British Columbia, 1972.

—. "La *Epístola que enbio Don Enrrique de Villena a Suero de Quiñones* y fecha de la *Crónica Sarracina* de Pedro de Corral." *University of British Columbia Hispanic Studies*. Ed. Harold Livermore. London: Tamesis, 1974. 1-18.

—, ed. *Tratado de la consolación.* Clásicos Castellanos 208. Madrid: Espasa-Calpe, 1976 [1979].

—, and Pedro-Manuel Cátedra. "Datos para la biografía de Enrique de Villena." *La corónica* 11.2 (1983): 293-99.

Cátedra, Pedro M. "Para la biografía de don Enrique de Villena." *Estudi General* 1.2 (1981): 29-33.

—. "Algunas obras perdidas de Enrique de Villena con consideraciones sobre su obra y su biblioteca." *El Crotalón: Anuario de Filología Española* 2 (1985): 53-75.

Cotarelo y Mori, Emilio. *Don Enrique de Villena. Su vida y obras.* Madrid: Rivadeneyra, 1896.

Curtius, Ernst Robert. *European Literature and the Latin Middle Ages.* Trans. Willard R. Trask. New York: Harper, 1963.

Dictionary of Scientific Biography. Ed. Charles Coulston Gillespie et al. 18 vols. New York: Scribner's, 1970-90.

Gascón Vera, Elena. "Nuevo retrato histórico de Enrique de Villena." *Boletín de la Real Academia de la Historia* 175 (1978): 107-43.

—. "La quema de los libros de don Enrique de Villena: una maniobra política y antisemítica." *Bulletin of Hispanic Studies* 56 (1979): 317-24.

Gónzalez de la Calle, Urbano. "Contribución al estudio de la primera versión castellana de la *Eneida." Anales de la Universidad de Madrid (Letras)* 2 (1933): 131-57; 259-84; 3 (1934): 1-20.

Guido de Columnis. *Historia destructionis Troiae.* Ed. Nathaniel Edward Griffin. Cambridge, MA: The Mediaeval Academy of America, 1936.

Menéndez Pelayo, Marcelino. *Bibliografía hispano-latina clásica.* Ed. Enrique Sánchez Reyes. 10 vols. Edición Nacional de las Obras Completas de Menéndez Pelayo 44-53. Santander: Aldus; Madrid: Consejo Superior de Investigaciones Científicas, 1950-53.

—. *Biblioteca de traductores españoles.* Ed. Enrique Sánchez Reyes. 4 vols. Edición Nacional de las Obras Completas de Menéndez Pelayo 54-57. Santander: Aldus; Madrid: Consejo Superior de Investigaciones Científicas, 1952-53.

Millás Vallicrosa, José María. *Literatura hebraicoespañola.* Barcelona: Labor, 1967.

Moses Maimonides. *The Code of Maimonides [Mishneh Torah]. Book Fourteen. The Book of Judges.* Trans. Abraham M. Hershman. Yale Judaica Series 3. New Haven: Yale UP, 1949.

Pascual Rodríguez, José Antonio. *La traducción de la 'Divina Commedia' atribuida a D. Enrique de Aragón: estudio y edición del 'Infierno.'* Acta Salmanticensia, Filosofía y Letras 82. Salamanca: U de Salamanca, 1974.

Pérez de Guzmán, Fernán. *Generaciones y semblanzas.* Ed. R. B. Tate. London: Tamesis, 1965.

Puymaigre, Comte Théodore de. "Don Enrique de Villena et sa bibliothèque." *Revue des Questions Historiques* 11 (1872): 526-34.

Riera y Sans, Jaume. "Enric de Villena, mestre de Calatrava." *Estudios históricos y documentos de los Archivos de Protocolos* 7 (1979): 109-32.

Round, Nicholas G. "Five Magicians, or the Uses of Literacy." *Modern Language Review* 64 (1969): 793-805.

Sachs, George, ed. *El libro de los caballos: tratado de albeitería del siglo XIII.* Madrid: Bermejo, 1936.

Sanz Egaña, Cesáreo. *Historia de la veterinaria española.* Madrid: Espasa-Calpe, 1941.

Sarton, George. *Introduction to the History of Science.* 3 vols. Carnegie Institute of Washington Publications 376. Baltimore: Williams & Wilkins, 1927-48.

Schiff, Mario. *La Bibliothèque du Marquis de Santillane.* Paris, 1905. Amsterdam: Van Heusden, 1970.

Thorndike, Lynn. *A History of Magic and Experimental Science.* 8 vols. New York: Macmillan, 1923-58.

Vendrell Gallostra, Francisca. "La corte literaria de Alfonso V de Aragón y tres poetas de la misma." *Boletín de la Real Academia Española* 19 (1932): 85-100; 388-405; 468-84; 584-607; 733-47; 20 (1933): 69-92.

Villena, Enrique de. *Tres tratados.* Ed. J. Soler [R. Foulché-Delbosc], in *Revue Hispanique* 41 (1917): 110-214. [*Tratado de la consolación,* 110-82; *Tratado del aojamiento,* 182-97; *Tratado de la lepra,* 198-214.]

—. *Arte de trobar.* Ed. F. J. Sánchez Cantón. Biblioteca Española de Divulgación Científica 3. Madrid: Suárez, 1923.

—. *Epístola a Suero de Quiñones.* Ed. Derek C. Carr, in "La *Epístola que enbio Don Enrique de Villena a Suero de Quiñones* y la fecha de la *Crónica Sarracina* de Pedro de Corral." *University of British Columbia Hispanic Studies.* Ed. Harold Livermore. London: Tamesis, 1974. 10-18.

—. *Tratado de la consolación.* Ed. Derek C. Carr. Clásicos Castellanos 208. Madrid: Espasa-Calpe, 1976 [1979].

—. *Tratado de aojamiento.* Ed. Anna Maria Gallina. Biblioteca di Filologia Romanza 31. Bari: Adriatica, 1978.

—. *Exposición del salmo "Quoniam videbo."* Ed. Marcella Ciceri, in "Per Villena." *Quaderni di Lingue e Letterature* 3-4 (1978-79): 295-35.

—. *Exposición del salmo "Quoniam videbo."* Ed. Pedro M. Cátedra, in *Exégesis–ciencia–literatura.* Anejos del *Anuario de Filología Española de El Crotalón.* Textos 1. Madrid: El Crotalón, 1985 [1986].

—. *La primera versión castellana de "La Eneida," de Virgilio: los libros I-III traducidos y comentados por Enrique de Villena (1384-1434).* Ed. Ramón Santiago Lacuesta. Anejos del *Boletín de la Real Academia Española* 38. Madrid: Real Academia Española, 1979.

—. *El 'Tratado de astrología' atribuido a Enrique de Villena.* Ed. Pedro M. Cátedra. Introd. Julio Samsó. Madrid: Río Tinto Minera, 1980. Rev. ed. Biblioteca Humanitas de Historia del Pensamiento 1. Barcelona: Humanitas, 1983.

—. *Arte cisoria.* Ed. Russell V. Brown. Biblioteca Humanitas de Textos Inéditos 3. Barcelona: Humanitas, 1984.

—. *Arte cisoria.* Ed. John O'Neill, in *The Text and Concordance of Escorial Manuscript f.IV.1. "Arte Cisoria": Enrique de Villena.* Spanish Series 37. Madison, WI: The Hispanic Seminary of Medieval Studies, 1987.

—. *Traducción y glosas de la "Eneida."* Ed. Pedro M. Cátedra. 2 vols. Salamanca: Biblioteca Española del Siglo XV; Diputación de Salamanca, 1989.

—. *Enrique de Villena: Obras completas.* Ed. Pedro M. Cátedra. Biblioteca Castro. Madrid: Turner, 1994. [Vol. 1: *Los doce trabajos de Hércules,* 3-111; *Tratado de la lepra,* 115-30; *Arte cisoria,* 133-218; *Tratado de la consolación,* 221-99; *Exposición del salmo "Quoniam videbo,"* 303-24; *Tratado de fascinación o de aojamiento,* 327-41; *Epístola a Suero de Quiñones,* 345-50; *Arte de trovar,* 353-70; *Exposición del soneto de Petrarca*, 373-79; *Cartas*, 383-95; *Tratado de astrología*, 399-57. Vol. 2: *Traducción y glosas de la "Eneida", libros I-III*, 5-889.]

Waxman, Samuel M. "Chapters on Magic in Spanish Literature." *Revue Hispanique* 38 (1916): 325-463.

Beryl Rowland

"AD RESTRINGUENDUM COYTUM": HOW TO COOL LUST

In a British Library manuscript, Sloane 2463, is a gynecological text written in Middle English in the early fifteenth century. Because it concludes advice on conception with the phrase "witnesse Trotula," it was formerly thought to be a translation from a Latin work ascribed to the legendary Salernitan healer. But in 1992, Monica Green showed that it was one of many manuscripts more properly called "The Sekenesse of Wymmen," derived primarily from Gilbertus Anglicus' *Compendium Medicinae* (ca. 1240), which itself drew heavily on the *Practica medicinae* of Roger de Baron and on three brief chapters of *Trotula minor* for its gynecological and obstetrical material (Green, "Obstetrical" 72ff.).[1]

Far more widely disseminated in late medieval England than the *Trotula* treatises, the "Sekenesse of Wymmen" exists in two versions. The first is a loose translation and adaptation of some fifteen chapters of Gilbertus Anglicus' *Compendium Medicinae*. It focuses on problems concerning menstruation, pregnancy, and childbirth and offers practical remedies that rely mainly on concoctions of herbs. To its modification of the *Compendium* it brings a sense of organization that the *Compendium* lacks. The second version repeats this material, rearranges and greatly expands it. Its most important addition is from Muscio's *Gynaecia* (ca. 500 AD), which gives obstetrical advice accompanied by sixteen or seventeen illustrations of *fetus-in-utero*. There are also references to learned physicians such as Rhases (865-925) and Avicenna (980-1037) and to testimonies to the success of local healers. Of more concern to us here, however, is the fact that this second version is characterized by occasional lapses into Latin.[2]

The paragraph under discussion, "Ad restringuendum coytum," inserted between sections on the provocation of the menses and on the hardness of the womb, is one of those lapses.

Ad restringuendum coytum: Rx: olei 3 iiii, camphore 3 iii, pulverizata camphora, & misceantur et vnge renes & castitatem seruabit. Item si quis comedit florem salicis vel populi omnem ardorem libidinis in eo refrigerabit bene hoc longo vsu. Item veruena portata vel potata non sinit virgam erigi donec deponatur & si sub seruicali posueris non potest erigi virga vii diebus, quod si probare volueris da gallo mixtam cum furfure & super gallinas non ascendet. [f. 227r] Item herba columbina in testiculo extinguit libidinem. Item inunge corrigiam aliquam cum succo veruene & porta ad carnem & eris effeminatus; & si quam tetigerit erit ineptus ad talia quia cor tangentis emollit. Item lapis sulpicis portata in sinistra manu ereccionem virge tollit. Item testiculi galli cum sanguine suo suppositi lectum coitum iacenti in eo vegitant. Item semen lactuce exsiccat sperma & sedat desiderium coitus et pollucionem. Item lapis topazius generat castitatem & reprimit venerem. Item succus iusquiami testiculos invnge calorem & tumocionem & libidinem extinguit. Item lapis ambri portatus dat castitatem. Item semen salicis sumptum libidinem extinguit. Item eruce, rute, & agni casti sicentur & puluerizentur & simul comedentur tollent pollucionem.

Translated, it reads:

To restrain sexual intercourse: Take 4 drachms of oil, 3 drachms of camphor, crushed camphor; let them be mixed and anoint the kidneys, and the preparation will preserve chastity. Again, if anyone eat the best part of the willow or poplar he will effectively cool all the lust in himself by continued usage. Again, vervain carried or drunk will not permit the penis to go stiff until it is laid aside, and vervain placed under the pillow makes an erection impossible for seven days, which prescription, if you wish to test, give to a cock mixed with bran, and the cock will not mount the hen. Again, the herb columbine extinguishes lust in the testicle. Likewise, anoint the shoelaces with the juice of vervain and wear them against the flesh, and you will be effeminate; and if a man touches anyone he will be inept for such things because it makes the heart of the one who is touching gentle. Again, brimstone carried in the left hand will take away an erection. Likewise, the testicles of a cock with its blood placed under the bed cause a man to suppress intercourse. Similarly, the seed in lettuce dries the sperm, quietens lasciviousness and the desire for intercourse. Likewise, the stone topaz produces chastity and represses lechery. Again, anoint the

> testicles with henbane juice and it extinguishes heat, erection,
> and lust. Similarly, the stone amber, if carried, promotes
> chastity. Again, willow seed taken extinguishes lust. Likewise,
> let colewort, rue, and St.-John's-wort be dried and made into
> powder, and eaten together they put an end to
> lasciviousness. (Rowland, *Medieval* 157-59)

Untranslated, this passage would have been incomprehensible to an unlatinate female audience. Yet the preface asserts that the text is intended specifically for women who, fearing reproof and exposure, are ashamed to acknowledge their illnesses. Says the unknown writer: "This book is being written that one woman may help another in her sickness so that she will not have to disclose her secrets to 'uncurteys men'."

Even if the preface can be taken with a pinch of salt, it underscores the ambiguity about the type of audience present in this passage. At the outset a mixture of oil and camphor is recommended as an ointment for *renes* in order to preserve chastity. In Latin, *renes* (plural) was used by such writers as Celsus and Pliny to refer to the kidneys or loins of either sex. In Middle English the word *reynes* had the same meaning (OF *rens*). In context, however, *reynes / renes* may mean the heart or the penis, commonly associated with "fleshly lustes" (*MED*, s.v. *reine* n[2] 2. Pl [a] [b]). Camphor, according to such medical writers as Arnold of Villanova (1238-1311), John of Gaddesden (1280-1336), and others (Noonan 203, 207-9), either "cut off coitus" or "impeded erection." The second prescription is addressed to "whoever" (Latin: *quis*) and the sex is not defined apart from "in eo." The third remedy, employing vervain, certainly refers exclusively to men.

> Item veruena portata vel potata non sinit virgam erigi donec
> deponatur & si sub servicali posueris non potest erigi virga vii
> diebus.
>
> (Again, vervain carried or drunk will not permit the penis to go
> stiff until it is laid aside, and vervain placed under the pillow
> makes an erection impossible for seven days.)

Several other prescriptions are also male-oriented, although the direction of comments about the efficacy of topaz, amber, and certain herbal combinations remain unclear.

What is the condition in life of the people advised "ad restringuendum coytum": are they married or single? are they clerics or layfolk? The admonition "inunge corrigiam aliquam cum succo veruena & porta ad carnem" (anoint the shoelaces with the juice of vervain and wear them against the flesh) does not indicate gender and maintains the ambiguity since shoestraps were often worn by both sexes in the late medieval centuries.

The doctrinal overtones of some of the Latin words concerning sex suggest a clerical bias. *Libido* is cited twice. Pierre Payer, interpreting the medieval theologians, makes a distinction between *lust*, which he calls *libido* and *luxuria*, which he terms lechery, the idea being that *lust* is an integral part of the composition of fallen humanity whereas lechery is a vice that is freely acquired and for which each individual is morally responsible (*Bridling* 54). *Luxuria* does not appear in this paragraph, although its counterpart *venus, veneris* does. *Castitas* (chastity), cited three times, acts as a synonym for the controlling idea. To most medieval theologians this word meant the control of sex and especially of pleasure deriving from sex. It could apply to either sex.

The term *pollutio*, which occurs twice, seems ambiguous. Pollution or nocturnal emission is a subject that was dealt with by the early canons. It continued in the penitentials and in the confessional manuals. It appeared to have a special attraction for theologians, always, of course, with the premise that all permissible sexual activity was confined to married men and women. Priests used their manuals to help them question their parishioners about their sex lives and even to try to regulate the times and methods of sexual intercourse (Payer, "Confession" 1-31, *Bridling* 77, and *Sex* 52ff.). The nocturnal emissions were a matter which had to be investigated with the utmost delicacy to discover whether the penitent's conduct or that of her husband was involuntary or intentional. In medieval medical literature, pollution is a term that is usually applied to men. Albertus Magnus, however, thought differently (Cadden 74n, Jacquart and Thomasset 68). Rufinus in his *Herball*, composed between 1287 and 1300, implies that it refers to both sexes, and the problem can be cured by drinking the juice of lettuce (163). While the meaning seems unequivocal in the first reference, especially since it is associated in the text with the drying of sperm, the final claim that the use of herbs such as colewort, rue, St.-John's-wort (*agnus casti*) dried, made into powder and eaten at once, are of similar benefit seems to suggest that the word for pollution in context may have the more general meaning of sexual incontinence. But if words such as *pollutio* and *libido* may not identify the sex, we have to conclude that the tenor and other words such as *virga*, *testiculum*, and *semen* make clear that the passage is male-oriented. At one point the reader is even addressed in the second person (*eris effeminatus*).

Herbs cited in our passage are frequently used in medical texts. If theologians were reluctant to specify measures that might result in contraception, damage to the fetus, or abortion, specialists dealing with intercourse often followed the ancient and familiar tradition cited by Avicenna (980-1037) whose Arabic *Canon of Medicine* was translated into Latin early in the next century. Material on sexual matters by Avicenna and others became available to those practising in the European cities. Arnold of Villanova (1238-1311), for example, grouped a number of plants together, chaste tree, garlic, calumet, camphor, hemlock, gourds, lettuce, portulaca, rue, sage, and houseleek, and observed "all these cut off *libido*, prevent impregnation, diminish milk and menses." In our text, these plants cannot be interpreted as contraceptives. Sexual desire is lacking because the herbs affect the semen before intercourse. Noonan says of such herbs that in application they could be regarded "as merely artificial aids to continence." He adds, however, "on the other hand they prevent not only intercourse but the fruits. Their purpose is, artificially and deliberately, to depress the physiological and psychological tendencies toward procreation" (Noonan 203). Similarly, rue (*rute*) which occurs in the last line of the paragraph, is commonly cited as drying up the seed and removing all interest in sex. Albertus Magnus, an expert apparently in such matters, attributed to it the same anaphrodisiac effects as those given earlier by such writers as Avicenna (Noonan 201-4). According to Constantinus Africanus' *De Coitu*, "a bundle of rue, ground up in warm water" extinguished desire (64). The early second-century physician, Soranus, in common with many medical writers since, used it as an abortifacient. Macer, as Riddle points out in *Contraception and Abortion from the Ancient World to the Renaissance*, includes rue in the herbs that are abortifacients (114-5). John Gerard's *Herball* (1597) states that it "quencheth and drieth up the naturall seede of generation" (1076). Many of the herbs cited here were also used for contraceptive purposes, although theologians were usually reluctant to specify them.

Most of the herbs cited are given well-known anaphrodisiac properties. Camphor, the first herb mentioned, was said to cut off coitus. Of course, camphor is not a herb in the sense of a herbaceous plant, but the product of a tree, *Cinnamomum camphora*, the wood or young shoots of which is steam-distilled (Albertus Magnus, *Secrets* 95n). Willow and poplar were also said to be cold and dry and the best part of them (*florem*) should be eaten if a man wished to be devoid of sexual desire. *The Book of Secrets* of Albertus Magnus states that the herbs of the planet Venus, *id est columbaria*, and *verbena*, (vervain) are "of great strength in venereal pastimes, that is, the act of generation" (21-23). However, the editorial note (22n) agrees with the

Middle English Dictionary and the *New English Dictionary*, which cite columbine as *Aquilegia vulgaris* and indicate no sexual connotation. In contrast, the properties of vervain, as we have already seen, are more clearly defined. The herb causes impotence even when carried or drunk in a potion. Sleep on it, our text says, and impotence results. Many authorities, including Pliny, give numerous and various attributions to this herb (xxii:3, xxv:59, xxvii:28). In Hieronymous von Braunschweig's *Distyllacion of Herbes*, published in 1527, vervain "withdryveth very much the lechery" (cxxxcii). On the other hand, in some texts a man has only to hold a sprig of vervain and all women will become infatuated with him. Macer's pre-twelfth century Latin poem, which became very popular in translation in the Middle Ages, gives, sometimes skeptically, most of the qualities ascribed to vervain (169-72). Because of its ancient role in magic and ceremonial rituals, it was given supernatural powers for many centuries: it enabled its possessor to conquer enemies and the elements, to make men laugh at the dinner table, cure headaches, stop dogs from barking or attacking anyone. Usually powdered and taken in wine, it cured fevers, headaches, and the stone. That a man became effeminate if the juice of vervain was put on his shoelaces and then worn against his skin is a recipe that, so far, I have not found elsewhere.

Lettuce (*lactuca*) is also a herb that is commonly cited. Constantinus Africanus states that it is one of the cold foods that impedes, represses, and thickens semen and extinguishes lust. It represses desire for intercourse even more effectively if it is cooked with lentils. If the resulting liquor is drunk, it will "destroy lustful desires" (63). The anaphrodisiac qualities of lettuce are also attested by Hildegard of Bingen (col. 1165), and many others (Noonan 211n).

Among the other herbs is henbane. According to the great herbal pioneer, William Turner, it was called *iusquiamus* by apothecaries, and it contained a narcotic hyoscine and was an anaphrodisiac. On the other hand, like vervain, it could possess aphrodisiac qualities. "It is profitable to them that would do often the act of generation," states the *Book of Secrets* (21). In common with many herbs, henbane is said to be cold and dry. Rufinus adds that it has seeds that are white, red, and black, and the black are deadly (160). The others, taken in wine, are a narcotic; they, with other seeds and such herbs as chaste tree, were said to inhibit carnal desire.

The four non-herbal remedies are clearly intended to restrict lust. Brimstone, which can take away an erection if carried in the left hand, the testicles of a cock with its blood placed under the bed, the stone topaz, and the stone amber. The first of these was commonly associated with divine punishment and many kinds of evil. The gem topaz, used as a type of "excellence" in Job 28:19, Psalms 118:1,2,7 and in medieval lapidaries, was frequently cited as a curb against lust (Evans 19, 106, 122). Amber (*sucinus*) was given a similar property. In the *Book of Minerals* ascribed to Albertus Magnus it is said to make those who wear it chaste (121). The recipe which uses a cock's testicles is less easy to interpret. Although the cock is well known as a symbol of lechery, it does not possess testicles, and its reproductive organs if extracted and put under a bed would have inconspicuous sanguinary results.

We still require an explanation for the change from Middle English to Latin. The desirability for restraint in sex is, of course, a very ancient idea and is one by no means peculiar to Christianity. Nevertheless, theologians went much farther than Constantine in his *De Coitu*, who maintained coition was essential to health but, overdone, it could dissipate "the vital spirit" and even cause death (59-61). It was clear that the Church regarded sexual abstinence as the highest ideal (Payer, *Bridling* 161ff.), even in marriage, provided both partners agreed. The reader, therefore, would understand the use of Latin for a discussion of sexual matters. Within the context of Christian theology, the act which is the subject of the paragraph is highly culpable, generated by lust and the fire of concupiscence as Huguccio and many other writers throughout the centuries insisted (Payer, *Bridling* 125).

Ad restringuendum coytum is one of various passages in Latin introduced in a cluster. In the manuscript these passages start on the last six lines of folio 225 verso and finish on the eighth line of folio 228 verso. Since the treatise begins on folio 194 recto and ends on the eleventh line of folio 232 recto, clearly the redactor has already dealt with the major concerns of his work. The question remains: can we further explain the inclusion of the Latin in a manuscript which is in English?[3]

The evident confusion in the treatise may be in itself the explanation. With few exceptions, as for example, when the writer is following Muscio, he is not clear in his organization. He sets out plans and then abandons them. He introduces material that is extraneous to the topic at hand. He gives the contents for ten chapters (Rowland, *Medieval* 60), but after the fourth chapter, which is concerned with the falling of the uterus, he rearranges the material. He is copying, it seems, from various sources, and the same actions recur with different recipes. The Latin is introduced without explanation. It follows a recipe in English on how to cure the swelling in the legs of pregnant women. Its title, "Ad menstrua prouocanda," is clumsily Englished at the beginning of the work as "The stoppyng of her blode that they shuld haue in her purgacions [*menses*] and be purged off" (Rowland, *Medieval* 60). The Latin is much briefer. It says less about patients. Both versions advocate the use of herbs and herbal plasters, and both include abortifacients. With the exception of the stone, most of the topics in Latin do not appear in the English. The hardening of the womb, various jaundices, the swelling of the testicles, tumour of the breast, pestilence, and what the writer calls "a painful discharge of urine and a hindrance from urination," and a recipe that concerns testing for signs of life are not translated (Rowland, *Medieval* 153-63). One of the briefest recipes is the last named. Leaves of henbane and rue, which are indeed deadly herbs, are made into a plaster and applied to a man's forehead. If he sleeps, the account continues, he will be saved; otherwise he will die. The ending is also abrupt. The writer announces a recipe "for women only," which consists of a phlebotomy under the ankles with a fumigation of the root iris. Then he follows with instructions in English and ends each injunction with a Latin title, the apparent source of the information. The titles are very brief, such as *suffocacione menstruorum* and *mola matricis*.

The confusion continues; in the lengthy Latin passage preceding *Ad restringuendum coytum* the stone in the bladder was cured by a marvellous hemagogue of Master Edmund (which purged the womb of many ailments and even brought out a dead child). Another recipe for the stone in Latin follows the treatment for various jaundices, and the chief items of its potions are artemisia and betony. But the stone is also the subject of later passages in the English text, and while they contain many more ingredients than the Latin recipe, they do not include either artemisia or betony. The general turgid and repetitive style and lack of logical sequence suggest that the redactor did not necessarily understand what he was copying.

His lack of comprehension, or at least absence of concentration, may be further indicated in his attitude towards matters which contradict the Christian piety with which the text is imbued. Success in childbirth will be due to the grace of God and the midwife's skill (Rowland, *Medieval* 168), and the treatment given to women is what they deserve. If a pregnant woman is afflicted by pica and gives way to her urge to consort with men she will give birth to a leper (Rowland, *Medieval* 62), and if not a leper, she will give birth to a child with some other "foule syknes." Illness that is due to a woman's "corupt sede" may be healed by intercourse, but it is better for men and women to have the greatest physical ailments while they live than for them to be healed through a deed of lechery or any other deed against God's commands (Rowland, *Medieval* 90). But despite this high moral tone, the writer includes practices which are condemned by the Church. As Jacquart and Thomasset state (90), at that time there was "a flagrant contradiction between the growing mass of prohibitions laid down by the theologians and the influx of information relating to contraception." Albertus Magnus, the greatest scientific mind of his age, demonstrates the inconsistency. In his theological works he condemns all the practices that would prevent conception or delivery of a child. He shows what Noonan calls a "rigorous separation between morals and medicine" (211). In his scientific works, however, in *De plantis*, for example, he describes processes that would inevitably lead to the abortion of a fetus (Jacquart and Thomasset 91). He even warns women of the fatal consequences of accidentally taking too much rue or coriander. Our author is not as frank as some writers who state "ut mulier non concipit" but he does maintain that it is better for a child to be killed rather than the mother's life be sacrificed, and many of his recipes are designed to bring out a child, "quyk" or "dede." The inconsistency may indicate the writer's confusion or failure to understand the significance of what he was writing. It may be that he intended to translate the Latin later and that the inclusion of these passages is simply indicative of his general frame of mind. The Latin itself may have been clinical notes extracted from a pragmatic and expository medical work.

Alternatively, the redactor may have had another purpose. He probably had heard of the wide circulation of manuscripts attributed to Trotula and of the medical works in monastic and university libraries (Fort 412-19; Green,"Obstetrical" 55; James 60, 62, 339-41, 344-47, 385; Voigts, "Medical Prose" 316). He may have envisioned his own works being copied and read many times, not only by the few educated women who then helped the poor and illiterate, but by the religious in monasteries and hospitals. and by scholars in university libraries (Fort 412-19). The insertion of these Latin paragraphs may have a deliberate purpose. They were in Latin for the *literati*. As Owst shows in his works, there was considerable travelling in the British Isles amongst the religious. Others travelled to Britain from overseas (Ohler 56, 82, 173). Some of them may have acquired an understanding of colloquial English but they may not necessarily have been able to follow the written word. For some their mother tongue was not English or they knew English in a different dialect or had never seen it written down. They were for people who were accustomed to speak, write and read in Latin.

The redactor may have considered his address opportune. He was writing at a time when the church increasingly had specified days and times when there were to be no sexual relations between a husband and his wife, and when the highest ideal, whether the man was in orders or was one of the laity, was to have no sexual relations whatsoever (Rowland, "Prescribing" 210). As Payer states in *The Bridling of Desire*, "cumulatively, the times mentioned in these canons represent a substantial number of days in a year, particularly when the details of the general references to feast days and fast days are expanded" (98). The Church's prohibitions were taken very seriously. The passages that are in Latin must have been on the subjects that the redactor considered most essential for clerics to know. As Gurevich remarks, "The Church did not prohibit the gathering of medicinal herbs if it was done piously while praying the Creed and Paternoster" (83). Our redactor may have hoped that many of the practices that he copied were in an unprohibited category. The advice is personal, and when he approaches the subject of sexual temperance, his style is clear and economical, and comparatively well organised. He evidently does not follow the theologians who preached total abstinence. Instead, his advice appears to be what is to be practised as a necessity on certain occasions. Combining pharmacology and magic in a few blunt sentences, he demonstrates, perhaps not without casuistry, how a priest can practise abstinence on the many days of the year that the Church prescribed.[4]

Notes

1. There are now many excellent writers in the field. In particular I would like to pay tribute to that superb and generous scholar, Monica Green, who, beginning with *Transmission of Ancient Theories of Female Physiology and Disease through the Early Middle Ages*, PhD. dissertation, Princeton, 1985, has provided us with so many indispensable articles. While her main research is on the so-called Trotula texts, because of that research she has become the authority on virtually all the other gynecological literature in medieval Europe. Among the works are: "The *De genecia* Attributed to Constantine the African"; "Obstetrical and Gynecological Texts in Middle English"; "Recent Work on Women's Medicine in Medieval Europe"; "The Development of the Trotula"; "A Handlist of Latin and Vernacular Manuscripts of the So-Called Trotula Texts, Part I: The Latin Manuscripts"; "A Handlist of Latin and Vernacular Manuscripts of the So-Called Trotula Texts, Part II: The Vernacular Translations and Latin Re-Writings"; "'Traitie tout de menconges': The *Secrés des dames*, 'Trotula,' and Attitudes Towards Women's Medicine in 14th- and Early 15th-Century France"; *Women and Literate Medicine: Trota and the Trotula* (forthcoming); *'The Diseases of Women According to Trotula': A Medieval Compendium of Women's Medicine* (forthcoming); and with Tony Hunt, *"Les secrés de femmes": An Anglo-Norman Text on Fertility* (forthcoming). See also Rowland's *Medieval Woman's Guide to Health* and "Prescribing Sex in the Middle Ages."

2. For a bibliographical guide to medical manuscripts mainly in the fourteenth and fifteenth centuries, including polyglot or mixed Latin and Middle English, see Voigts, "Medical Prose" and her "Scientific and Medical Books."

3. For a description of this muddled approach, which continued during the Renaissance, see Edwards, "Observations on the History of Middle English Editing." For another indispensable work, see Hanna, *Pursuing History.*

4. I would like to thank Michael R. Best and Frank H. Brightman, the editors of *The Book of Secrets of Albertus Magnus*, for their extraordinarily interesting and valuable notes.

Works Cited

Africanus, Constantinus. *"De Coitu:* A Translation." Trans. Paul Delany. *Chaucer Review* 4 (1969-70): 55-65.

Albertus Magnus. "De vegetabilibus et plantis." *Opera Omnia.* Vol. VII. Ed. A. Borgnet. 35 vols. Paris: n.p., 1890-1899.

—. *The Book of Minerals.* Trans. Dorothy Wyckoff. Oxford: Clarendon, 1967.

—. [pseud.] *The Book of Secrets of Albertus Magnus.* Ed. Michael R. Best and Frank H. Brightman. Oxford: Clarendon, 1973.

Arber, Agnes. *Herbals, Their Origin and Evolution.* (1913). Facsimile of 2nd ed. Darian, CT: Hefner, 1995.

Arnold of Villanova. *Opera omnia.* Basel: n.p., 1585. Ctd. in John T. Noonan. *Contraception.* Cambridge: Cambridge UP, 1986.

Bullough, Vern L., and James A. Brundage, eds. *Handbook of Medieval Sexuality.* New York and London: Garland, 1996.

Cadden, Joan. *Meanings of Sex Difference in the Middle Ages: Medicine, Science and Culture.* Cambridge: Cambridge UP, 1993.

—. "Western Medicine and Natural Philosophy." Bullough and Brundage 51-80.

Edwards, A. S. G. "Observations on the History of Middle English Editing."*Manuscripts and Texts.* Ed. Derek Pearsall. Cambridge: Brewer, 1985. 34-38.

Evans, Joan, and Mary Sergeantson, eds. *English Medieval Lapidaries.* EETS o.s. 190. London, 1933. Oxford: Oxford UP, 1960.

Fort, George F. *Medical Economy in the Middle Ages.* London: Quaritch, 1883.

Gerard, John. *The Herball, or Generall Historie of Plants.* London: n.p., 1597.

Green, Monica H. "The *De genecia* Attributed to Constantine the African." *Speculum* 62 (1987): 299-323.

—. "The Development of the *Trotula." Revue d'histoire des textes* 26 (1996): 119-203.

—. "A Handlist of Latin and Vernacular Manuscripts of the So-Called *Trotula* Texts, Part I: The Latin Manuscripts." *Scriptorium* 50 (1996): 37-75.

—. "A Handlist of Latin and Vernacular Manuscripts of the So-Called *Trotula* Texts, Part II: The Vernacular Translations and Latin Re-Writings." *Scriptorium* 51 (1997): 80-104.

—. "Obstetrical and Gynecological Texts in Middle English." *Studies in the Age of Chaucer* 14 (1992): 72-82.

—. "Recent Work on Women's Medicine in Medieval Europe." *Society for Ancient Medicine Review* 21 (1993): 132-41.

—. "'Traitie tout de menconges': The *Secrés des dames*, 'Trotula,' and Attitudes Towards Women's Medicine in 14th- and Early 15th-Century France." *Christine de Pizan and the Categories of Difference*. Ed. Marilyn Desmond. Minneapolis: U of Minnesota P, 1997. 146-78.

—. *Women and Literate Medicine: Trota and the 'Trotula.'* Forthcoming. Cambridge: Cambridge UP.

—. *'The Diseases of Women according to Trotula': A Medieval Compendium of Women's Medicine*. Forthcoming.

—, and Tony Hunt. *"Les secrés de femmes": An Anglo-Norman Text on Fertility*. Forthcoming.

Gurevich, Aron. *Medieval Popular Culture: Problems of Belief and Perception*. Trans. J. M. Bak and P. A. Hollingsworth. Cambridge: Cambridge UP, 1988.

Hanna, Ralph, III. *Pursuing History: Middle English Manuscipts and Their Texts*. Stanford, CA: Stanford UP, 1996.

Hildegard of Bingen. *Subtilitatum diversarum naturarum creaturarum I, De plantis 92*. *Patrologia Latina* 197.

The Index of Middle English Prose. General ed. A. S. G. Edwards. Volumes VI, VIII, and X. Cambridge: Brewer, 1989-94.

Jacquart, Danielle, and Claude Thomasset. *Sexuality and Medicine in the Middle Ages*. Trans. Matthew Adamson. Princeton: Princeton UP, 1988.

James, Montague Rhodes. *The Ancient Libraries of Canterbury and Dover: The Catalogues of the Libraries of Christ Church Priory and St. Augustine's Abbey at Canterbury and of St. Martin's Priory at Dover*. Cambridge: Cambridge UP, 1903.

McGlynn, Margaret, and Richard J. Moll. "Chaste Marriage in the Middle Ages: 'It were to Hire a Greet Merite'." Bullough and Brundage 103-22.

'Macer Floridus.' *A Middle English Translation of "Macer Floridus de viribus."* Ed. Gosta Frisk. Uppsala: Almquist, 1949.

Middle English Dictionary Part 2. Ed. Robert Lewis *et al.* Ann Arbor: U of Michigan P, 1985.

Noonan, John T., Jr. *Contraception*. Cambridge, MA: Harvard UP, 1986.

Ohler, Norbert. *The Medieval Traveller*. Trans. Caroline Hillier. Woodbridge, Suffolk: Boydell and Brewer, 1989.

Owst, G. R. *Literature and Pulpit in Medieval England*. Cambridge: Cambridge UP, 1933.

—. *Preaching in Medieval England*. [1926]. Rev. ed. New York: Russell and Russell, 1965.

Payer, Pierre. "Confession and the Study of Sex in the Middle Ages." Bullough and Brundage 3-32.

—. *Sex and the Penitentials: The Development of a Sexual Code, 550-1150*. Toronto: U of Toronto P, 1984.

—. *The Bridling of Desire: Views of Sex in the Later Middle Ages*. Toronto: U of Toronto P, 1993.

Pliny. *Natural History*. Loeb Classical Library. 10 volumes. Trans. H. Rackham *et al.* London: Heinemann, 1949-62.

Riddle, John. M. "Contraception and Early Abortion in the Middle Ages." Bullough and Brundage 261-76.

—. *Contraception and Abortion from the Ancient World to the Renaissance.* Cambridge, MA: Harvard UP, 1992.

Robbins, Rossell Hope. "Medical Manuscripts in Middle English." *Speculum* 45 (1970): 393-415.

Rowland, Beryl. *Medieval Woman's Guide to Health.* Ohio: Kent State UP, 1981.

—. "Prescribing Sex in the Middle Ages." *Florilegium* 14 (1995-96): 205-214.

Rufinus. *The Herbal of Rufinus.* Ed. Lynn Thorndike. New York: U of Chicago P, 1946.

Soranus. *Gynecology.* Trans. Owsei Temkin. Baltimore: Johns Hopkins P, 1956.

Turner, William. *A New Herball, Part 1.* Ed. George T. L. Chapman and Marilyn N. Tweddle. Indexes compiled by Frank McCombie. Cambridge: Cambridge UP, 1989.

Voigts, Linda Ehrsam. "Medical Prose." *Middle English Prose: A Critical Guide to Major Authors and Genres.* Ed. A. S. G. Edwards. New Brunswick, NJ: Rutgers UP, 1984. 315-33.

—. "Scientific and Medical Books." *Book Production and Publishing in Britain 1375-1475.* Ed. Jeremy Griffiths and Derek Pearsall. Cambridge: Cambridge UP, 1989. 345-402.

von Braunschweig, Hieronymous. *Distyllacion of Herbes.* London: n.p., 1527.

Derek Brewer

THE COMPULSIONS OF HONOUR

Professor Mahmoud Manzalaoui is trilingual in English, French, and Arabic, as well as learned in medieval scientific Latin. He is in a particularly strong position to appreciate both the cross-cultural similarities of systems of honour from Islam to Europe, and also the variations that each society creates out of general human impulses. The following notes on the obligations, or compulsions, of honour, though only in selected medieval English texts, are offered as a tribute to the breadth of comprehension of his learning, and his unfailing geniality as a friend for over fifty years.

The complex of feelings, desires, rights, obligations, convictions, with some internal contradictions, that we call honour is known in most societies, especially pre-industrial societies. It is much weaker, and the area over which it operates is much more restricted, in modern Western societies because of our utilitarianism, rationalism, and social fragmentation, so that when we come across its manifestations in other present day cultures like Islam, we are inclined to condemn it. Honour even becomes a crime. Its operation in societies which no longer exist, and in the literature which they produced, is likewise often condemned, or simply not noticed. My present concern, after a general sketch of the nature of honour, is to note some instances in Chaucer, the *Gawain*-poet, and Malory, where the overriding demands of honour make a character do what he, or less often she, does not want to do, or would not do according to natural feeling, and yet feels obliged to do, though in other respects, and often, according to modern Western values, it is a crime. This internal self-contradiction is not especially a clash between a good human nature and a bad social construction. The desire for honour is entirely natural, but also a social desire because we are naturally social creatures. Nor is honour purely an external social concern. It is biologically conditioned and strongly internalised.

75

Honour therefore raises some interesting questions of relative values, or even relativism, of judgment, action, education, and the study of literature. The ultimate dilemma, in the study of historical literature in educational systems like ours, arises from the ethical implications we expect to draw from literature, which have been studied in an admirably judicious and learned article by Lee Patterson in a recent issue of *Exemplaria*.

There is not space to follow through all the implications here. The first task which occupies this paper is to examine texts in their own terms. This is of course by no means simple in so inter-subjective a study as that of literature. As a useful working model I would invoke some aspects of the study of social anthropology. The social anthropologist studies, and to some extent lives, in a culture different from his or her own but tries to empathise with it. He or she has to be inward with the culture that is studied, yet retain some sense of detachment. Henk Driessen, in some anthropological reflections on humour, quotes Laura Bohannan, who comments on the gulf between her values and that of the tribe she studied in the matter of humour, though she would have discovered, had she known about medieval humour, that it much resembled that of her African tribe in its cruelty and the use of laughter against tragedy.[1] Pre-industrial agrarian societies with low technology have much in common. The social anthropologist Ernest Gellner remarks on the futility of preaching across cultures (214). It is even more futile to preach to long dead cultures, but that does not preclude attempts to understand them and extract value from them, nor preclude cultural translation. Gellner also remarks, in a way that might well shock modern literary theorists, that one of the greatest human discoveries is that of culturally transcendent truths (214). In other words, judgment is ultimately to be made. But before that, the capacity for double-think between one culture and another–for a kind of play-acting in understanding another culture, in a word, a recognition of a limited relativism in human motives and virtues–is what we need first to practise when reading literature of any other than our own day, and perhaps even in reading that.

It follows from this that I am not going to attack Chaucer's *Physician's Tale* because of the father's self-indulgent care for his daughter's virginity, as Patterson does (*Chaucer* 369), let alone go on to say that because the tale is fraudulent, the Physician to whom it is allotted is a fraudulent physician and no doubt a bad doctor to call in. Nor am I going to talk about Gawain's failure in *Sir Gawain and the Green Knight*, as so many critics do. Nor am I proposing, like Marion Wynne-Davies, to use gender theory to break down the patriarchal nature of Malory's writing (8); nor argue like Lynch in a generally excellent book that honour is simply a disguise adopted for power, there being a fashion in modern criticism to regard power as always a bad thing, perhaps because academics have so little; nor with Riddy in another otherwise good book am I proposing to condemn King Arthur as a bloody imperialist. On the contrary, my aim is to recreate original meaning, not impose modern morality. I want "to read each work of wit / In the same spirit that the author writ."

The views I am opposing have been put forward by learned and highly intelligent critics in good faith, and are, in a sense, a Pickwickian sense, not wrong. They are, in my view, cross-cultural preaching, anachronistic moral judgments. They apply the standards of late twentieth-century Western fragmented, hi-tech, post-industrial, post-Christian culture, to an ancient agrarian culture that was none of these things.

Honour is not the only cultural system which has changed, but it has particular interest in that it still operates in our own society to some extent today, though much changed even since I was a young man. It was formerly, even in my young days, much more powerful and wide-ranging, very complex, yet taken much for granted. This was even more so in earlier centuries, and in so many different cultures. There are honour-systems in both the Old and the New Testament. For example, according to Ecclesiastes 7:3, "a good name is better than precious ointment and the day of death better than the day of birth." Yet the Gospels, as so often, despite being grounded in the Old Testament, often reject aspects of honour in the Old Testament and in their own contemporary society. It is worth mentioning this now because throughout the Christian period in the West, at least, various aspects of honour have been condemned by contemporaries, usually on religious grounds, just as they are now by modern critics, sometimes on similar, though not Christian, grounds. Honour systems with recognisably and fundamentally similar characteristics, though varying in expression, are clearly evident in Classical Antiquity, in Islam, where they are going strong today, in the great eastern cultures of China and Japan, in Icelandic saga of the twelfth and thirteenth centuries, in Arthurian literature in various languages, especially French, in Mediterranean societies up to today, in Spanish literature especially of the seventeenth century, and of course in medieval and later English literature especially of a secular and courtly kind.[2] There are important cultural differences. A sense of honour is strong amongst Greek shepherds, whereas in France and England it is denied to the peasantry and to the bourgeoisie. Because the sense of honour is so widespread I distinguish honour from European chivalry and chivalric ideals though they are very closely related. Perhaps one may say that chivalry, men fighting on horseback, took honour as their ideal code. In *Ywain and Gawain,* Ywain says that the practice of chivalry is for his and his beloved's honour. For other reasons I distinguish honour from virtue, though again they are very closely related. But the passion for honour is greater than the passion for virtue and when occasionally the two are in conflict, it is almost always honour that carries the day.

The leading characteristic of honour is that it is both a claim to social prestige and the recognition of an obligation to maintain that prestige both socially and internally, as self-esteem. The opposite of honour is shame, and so complex is the system that shame is often the word used to activate the compulsions of honour. The avoidance of shame, either socially or as an internal sentiment, may be said to be the ultimate compulsion of honour. The major work on the notion of honour amongst the ancient Greeks and specifically in Homer takes the Greek word for "shame," *Aidōs*, as its title and leading notion.[3] There is no evidence for a clear division between "shame" and "guilt" cultures, as Cairns very effectively argues, and guilt may well be a part of shame, as innocence may constitute part of the right to claim honour.

While honour has both external and internal implications, it is clear that it requires a society in which to exist. Honour for a man marooned on a desert island would be meaningless. There is always an honour-group and also sub-groups. Generally speaking the honour-group is formed out of the higher level of society. This need not be so, as the Greek shepherds show. Lower levels of society may imitate higher levels, or constitute their own group–"honour among thieves" as the saying has it, and amongst *mafiosi*. Broadly speaking, however, in northern European medieval society, honour is restricted to upper levels. Peasants and bourgeois may have virtue but not honour. In Arthurian romance, but also elsewhere, though not universally, honour depends on having honourable (that is, knightly) parents, or at least a father who is a knight or of higher rank. This is very clear in Malory in the case of Sir Torre, and applies also to women. Chaucer's Miller illustrates absence of a sense of honour in ranks below the gentry when he says he is not worried about his wife's faithfulness; by contrast, amongst an honour-group cuckoldry is regarded as the greatest dishonour, along with cowardice (*CT* I.3158-66).

Within the honour-group there is both hierarchy and a sense of equality, as in a department of a British university there are professors, readers, and lecturers, some being more equal than others, constituting a sort of oligarchy.

Also within the honour-group there is both co-operation, indeed comradeship, and, most notably in Icelandic sagas, competition. All these characteristics are easily observed in Arthurian literature and in Chaucer. Orders of precedence in entering halls and in seating plans at high table in hall are concrete examples that remain in modern life–I have even seen them at Harvard. In Icelandic saga, a quarrel over precedence in the *Saga of Burnt Njal* begins the ultimately tragic feud. The origin of Arthur's Round Table was an attempt to avoid quarrels over precedence. The attempt soon fell into desuetude, and in *Sir Gawain and the Green Knight*, for example, the normal priorities of honour are observed in the seating-plan at Arthur's high table in hall.

The honour-group is held together by the bonds of reciprocity found in all viable societies, which are expressed especially in terms of loyalty, to the leader of the group, and between the individuals composing it. Kinship forms a sub-group of honour, especially the nuclear family, but so also does the affinity, the group of the lord's followers. Reciprocity demands the leader's loyalty to the individuals within the group, children's obedience to their parents, and followers' to their lord. Occasions will arise when the loyalties involved are not compatible with each other, as we see in Malory's *Le Morte Darthur*.

In historical English literature a very striking example of loyalty comes very early on with the story of Cynewulf and Cyneheard in *The Anglo-Saxon Chronicle* for the year 757. This is before the word "honour" exists in English. It may be recalled that Cynewulf, the king of the West Saxons for many years, in the year 757 was visiting his mistress at Merton with a small following. An old enemy called Cyneheard discovered this, took him by surprise in the woman's house, and killed him. His thegns rushed up but were outnumbered and failed to save him. Cyneheard offered them money and lands if they would accept him as king. But they would not, and fought until they were all killed. The next morning, the remaining thegns of the dead king heard about his death and, led by an alderman, came up and, in turn, surrounded Cyneheard in the stockade. He offered them money and lands on the same terms. They refused, but offered to let their kinsmen who were with Cyneheard go free. Those inside said the same offer had been made to their kinsmen who had been with the dead king, but they themselves would pay no attention to it, "any more than did your comrades who were slain along with the king" (Whitelock et al. 31). So they fought to the death, only one being saved, the godson of the avenging alderman. Here we see loyalty to the king

79

overcoming bonds of kinship except in the perhaps accidental case of the godson, though that was a strong relationship.

I quote this because although it is usually and rightly said that reputation and self-esteem are the normal driving forces of honour, it is primarily felt by those who practise it as an overriding moral obligation, which may well go against one's natural inclinations and be to one's personal disadvantage. A belief in life after death may modify but does not affect the issue as far as honour is concerned. *The Battle of Maldon* illustrates the same heroic ideal. As is noted again later in connection with Lancelot in Malory, but which may be seen in many other examples, there is a real self-sacrificing idealism and nobility comprised in the notion of honour, going beyond mere concern for reputation, which is the source of its enduring (until the late twentieth century) appeal to many ordinary people, including myself.

Loyalty and bravery are also found in women's honour, but the nature of our records is less likely to reveal them except in hagiography, where the dominant influence is religious. Another general point to be made is that honour is primarily secular. It is true that in later periods it is part of an honourable man's obligation to pay honour to God, as in Arthurian romance and in everyday life, and Christian virtues become part of the quality of an honourable man, but when the obligations of honour and religion diverge, honour usually predominates. Even when religion dominates, as at the end of Lancelot's life, the obligations of honour are still observed, as in *Le Morte Darthur*. When I wrote about this thirty years ago, I exaggerated the difference between sanctity and honour in Malory's work, as I did the difference between shame and guilt (Brewer, "Tragedy" 32); what happens is that some characteristics and aims of honour, which is an active drive, are slightly changed, but not, I now believe, fundamentally altered.

So far the characteristics of honour that I have listed are common, *mutatis mutandis*, to men and women, or rather, to knights and ladies. But now we must observe differences between what I deliberately call sexes, not using the grammatical term "genders." The reason is that while I accept that much that we feel to be natural is "socially constructed" (though that is a question-begging term), there are also general and different innate biological biases in male and female, as I believe anybody with any acquaintance with children will readily agree. It is upon these natural biases which vary in intensity in individuals, that social constructions, dependent on other social, economic and political factors, are based.

Pre-industrial societies in particular tend to differentiate the activities of the two sexes, and we find this in a sharp division between men and women in respect of honour. A man's chief claim to honour is courage and success in fighting. To be defeated in a fight is shameful; this is where honour may seem in short supply since one man's gain is another man's loss. In some cases, however, honour lost in fighting may be regained by later fighting. Also, a brave death may save a man's reputation, and honourable men may have a care for posthumous reputation with the right people. Everything springs from a man's bravery, and his disdain for death, not only his own, but other people's. Closely associated are his loyalty and readiness to keep his word.

A woman must be brave too, since courage is necessary to maintain any other honourable quality, and must be loyal and faithful, but for a woman the essence of honour is her chastity, that is, virginity before marriage, faithfulness to her husband, which is loyalty, after it. Chastity is sometimes demanded of knights, as with Gawain in *Sir Gawain and the Green Knight* or Galahad, but is not usually essential to a man's honour. What is essential to him is the chastity of the women for whom he is responsible, in particular, his wife, sister, or daughter. It seems that the Icelandic sagas, according to Miller, are less concerned with virginity (see note 2), but he would be a bold man who seduced an Icelandic farmer's wife. The Spanish, by contrast, especially in the sixteenth and seventeenth centuries, were obsessed with family honour, and Somerset Maugham in the short story "The Point of Honour" even places such dramas in the early twentieth century. Maugham's treatment in this short story neatly encapsulates both the Spanish compulsion to maintain family honour and the modern Anglo-Saxon repulsion it causes, though Maugham refrains from the moral condemnation expressed by some modern critics of Chaucer and Malory working to a political agenda. In most of these cases the social aspect of honour, a man's reputation in his honour-group, is as strong as his inner self-esteem, and both drive him on to do what he does not naturally want to do. Somerset Maugham and the social anthropologists make the same point–you have to accept that this is how certain societies and people are.

There has always been a minority view which condemns honour. The Gospels have already been noted. Boethius in *The Consolation of Philosophy* is another example, and such opposition is summed up in the medieval Latin proverb, "There are four things that make a fool of a man–wine, women, old age, and honour," subject of a poem by Lydgate (Skeat l-li, 297). This minority view is worth bearing in mind because occasionally it feeds into a complex literary work: but equally it may not. And the clergy are a special case, which there is no space to discuss here.

We may now turn to the texts; first, *Sir Gawain and the Green Knight*. Honour in the poem has been the subject of subtle and perceptive essays by John Burrow and Derek Pearsall.[4] It should be noted that all Gawain's actions from the first are driven by honour. He takes up the Green Knight's challenge on behalf of King Arthur and his court, and then must keep his word to fulfil an obligation, keep his promise, to go apparently to his death, which requires courage of a high order, and he must despise death. Arthur's courtiers take a modern view and blame Arthur for letting Gawain go, but that only emphasises the compulsion Gawain is under. When he is in Sir Bertilak's castle and tempted by the Lady, one of the honourable compulsions is not to be a traitor to his host by cuckolding him, though he is also more profoundly under the compulsion of his personal chastity. The inner quality of honour is well illustrated by his rejection of the guide's suggestion that he should just slip away, and no one would know.

A most interesting aspect of the poem is the total dishonourableness of Bertilak and his wife. Bertilak sends his wife to seduce Gawain. That is grossly dishonourable on both their parts. To act as pander to one's own wife and to be cuckolded are universally regarded as utterly shameful, equal to being defeated or proved a coward; to offer her body is equally the greatest shame for a woman. That they should be so presented illustrates how ancillary they are as personalised characters in the story to Gawain. As I argued many years ago they are, so to say, fantasy-figures in Gawain's own imagination, not characters, realised in their own right. Their absence of honour is an absence of identity. Nor surprisingly do we even know whether Sir Bertilak is really green or really normal.[5]

I turn to Chaucer. As I argued many years ago, honour is profoundly important in many of Chaucer's stories, though he also tells stories about those without honour like the Miller, and translates Boethius's condemnation of worldly honour (Brewer, "Honour" 89-109). Chaucer fully accepts the importance of brave and successful fighting as the basis of male honour, and of chastity as the basis of female honour from *The Book of the Duchess* onwards. But he is not interested in fighting. He is more interested in women's honour and family honour. Women's honour is fully treated in the person of Criseyde, and also in the person of Dorigen in *The Franklin's Tale*, where the husband is involved, and where the agonising compulsions and inner contradictions of the whole concept of honour are most interestingly explored. Honour, in keeping her marital promise to obey, is implicitly part of the reason for Griselda's action. Here I deal in more detail with another aspect of family honour, that between father and daughter, in

The Physician's Tale, which in the past I have touched on only lightly, but has now been so swingeingly attacked by Lee Patterson in his very influential prize-winning book *Chaucer and the Subject of History*, which I can only whole-heartedly admire and sometimes profoundly disagree with.

The story of Virginia is a folktale regarded by Livy as history.

> Over characters as diverse as John Webster and Macaulay, Alfieri and Lessing, the story of Verginia has exercised a curious fascination. That fascination is in large measure due to the skill and poignancy with which L[ivy] has constructed what is one of the noblest episodes in his narrative. Virginia was for him a supreme example of the virtue of *pudicitia*, a supreme condemnation of *libido*. The moral lesson might be conventional but the telling of it was enhanced by all the art which L[ivy] could bring to bear. (Ogilvie 476-77)

Thus the latest commentator on this episode in Livy's history *De urbe condita*. But after two thousand years the nobility and the moral are denied. Modern critics reading the story in Chaucer unite in condemning it as "fraudulent"or false, revealing the false and fraudulent character of the Physician to whom it is attributed.

To recall very briefly the essence of the story: Appius, an unjust judge, becomes enamoured of the beautiful fourteen-year-old Virginia, daughter of Virginius, and arranges for one of his men to claim her as his escaped slave, in order that she may be abducted, enslaved, and raped by Appius. Appius gives Virginia's father no opportunity to save her. Virginius returns home, makes an impassioned speech to Virginia about his love for her, calls her "gemme of chastitee" (VI.223) and says there is no alternative for her but either "deeth or shame" (VI.214). Chaucer wrings out every drop of pathos from the girl's response, but in the end makes her say

> 'Blissed be God that I shal dye a mayde!
> Yif me my deeth, er that I have a shame;
> Dooth with youre child youre wyl, a Goddes name!'
> (VI.248-50)

In her plea she refers to the story of Jephtha (Judges 11:1-40), who was sacrificed by her father, in parallel but not the same circumstances. Other critics who agree with Patterson's general condemnation, say that Virginius is overhasty. Since the people rally to him after Virginia's death, he could have rallied them before. The main answer to that is that that is not the story, well known in the Middle Ages, as told by Jean de Meun, Gower, and Boccaccio among others, though none I think with such an edge as Chaucer gives it.

He has taken the very core of a known story, which he regards as historical, going out of his way to say so: "this is no fable / But knowen for historial thyng notable" (VI.155-56). For all that, Chaucer, as is common with traditional writers, feels free to add detail and change emphasis. The importance of virginity for women was emphasised greatly in the later Middle Ages, as the work of Cadden and others has illustrated.[6] Chaucer especially emphasises virginity in various works, not least in *The Parson's Tale*, where there is a long passage on lechery and it is described, in a curious example of how contemporary religious thought took over many of the notions of honour, as in itself dishonourable, to both men and women, which was not the old view. There are several recent examples of contemporary honour-killings in Islam of daughters by fathers, in one famous case because the daughter merely walked home from school with a boy. This is described as a "crime of honour" by a modern feminist writer, and one can sympathise, but if we are all "socially constructed," what right have we to such preaching?[7]

Chaucer thus makes Virginia die rejoicing that she is a virgin, while by the code of honour Virginius rightly kills her to protect his own honour as well as her virginity, because they are the same thing. Modern critics object that, like Jephthah (Judges 11:30-40), Virginius says in effect, "How terrible for me" not "how terrible for you, Virginia," but that is the logic of the story. One might also note that by insisting on the historical nature of the story and, by implication, placing it in pagan times, Chaucer distances the story. Pagan history has another instance of a father sacrificing a daughter, for example, Agamennon's daughter, Iphigenia, though honour is only indirectly involved. In any case there is no reason to doubt the love and consequent agony of Virginius, as he follows the compulsion, or obligation, of honour for both his daughter and himself.[8]

As my last example I take Malory's *Le Morte Darthur*. Yvonne Robreau has shown in painstaking detail how the thirteenth-century French Arthurian romances are shot through with the concepts of compulsions of honour, and Malory largely takes these over. They are in general what has been sketched earlier in this paper.

Malory's work has suffered a curious fate in the history of English literature. Except in the late seventeenth and in the eighteenth century, *Le Morte Darthur* has always been reasonably popular with ordinary readers "uncorrupted by literary prejudice." Readers as disparate as Spenser, Southey, Tennyson, T. E. Lawrence, and T. H. White have enjoyed it. But ever since its condemnation by puritanical Humanism in the person of Roger

Ascham in Cambridge in the sixteenth century (1570), *Le Morte Darthur* has been neglected or patronisingly misunderstood by the academic critics, in whose keeping lies the canon of English literature.[9] Only since Vinaver's great, if idiosyncratic, edition in 1947 has it received serious attention, and the structure of honour still deserves more study than there is space for here.[10]

Not only the critics and until recently the scholars have ignored Malory; the lexicographers also have paid *Le Morte Darthur* little attention.[11] Yet *Le Morte Darthur* uses the words for and the concept of honour more extensively and concentratedly than any other work of fiction in English. A glance at the lexicography of honour in *Le Morte Darthur* reveals something of Malory's concept.

Two words are used in *Le Morte Darthur* to denote honour; one is "honour" itself, with its grammatically associated forms as noun, verb, adverb, including "dishonour"; the other is "worship" with all similarly associated forms, including "disworship." Here it should be noted that the word "honour" in its earliest occurrences in Old and Middle French, and its late Latin form, *honos*, both primarily meant "possession and control of land" and, thus, "high status."[12] In the course of the French Arthurian romances the meaning became idealised to indicate primarily high status and consequently renown. On the very first page of *Le Morte Darthur* Malory uses it in "idealised" form, when the Duke of Cornwall and Ygrayne, his wife, hurriedly leave King Uther Pendragon's court because Uther is in love with the wife, and as Ygrayne says, "I suppose that we were sente for that I shold be dishonoured" (*Works* 7/15-16). Here "honour" is invoked as the chastity of a faithful wife. Uther is not dishonoured by his wish to seduce the wife of one of his lords, but the lady and her husband would be if she succumbed. She and her husband act under the compulsion of honour in the form of shame, to the point of rebelling against their king. The next use in *Le Morte Darthur* is again the word "honour," this time spoken by Merlin, who promises to fulfil Uther's desire in such a way as shall be to his "honour and profite" (*Works* 8/21), in fact by ensuring that her husband is dead when Uther, disguised as him, sleeps with Ygrayne and begets Arthur. Honour and morality may here be thought to have a somewhat strained relationship, but the honour of both Uther and Ygrayne is saved and we must be satisfied. Merlin promises that the child thus conceived will be to Uther's "worship," that is, to his credit and renown. This is the first occurrence of the word "worship" in Malory, and it is obviously used in the same sense as "honour" earlier. The difference between the two words in English is barely perceptible. The use of "honour" to mean "the domain of a feudal lord" is found in English in the fourteenth century (*MED*, s.v. 6) but is rare and never occurs in Chaucer, who uses the word frequently, or in Malory. The sense of "worthy of respect," "paying respect to," "nobleness of character," and associated forms all occur in the fourteenth century.

The word "worship" derives from Old English, where it has no relation to ownership or command over land, and, from the ninth and tenth centuries, it means "being held in esteem," "having dignity or high rank," "paying respect," "homage." It implies the possession of an inner quality of worth at least from the thirteenth century. To be able to "win worship" (i.e., gain honour) is attested from 1200, and the phrase "a man of worship," which implies the possession of inner worth as well as dignity and renown is first attested from 1340, and is also found in Chaucer's *Franklin's Tale* when Arveragus goes off "To seke in armes worshipe and honour" (V.811), which illustrates both how closely the senses of the two words coincided and also the primary way–by fighting–of acquiring "worship and honour," for Chaucer as for Malory. The religious sense of reverence to a divine being is incidental to the general sense of "doing honour to" and derives its religious implication only from its context, which is occasional, from about 1300. The first record of the meaning of "worship" as "a woman's chastity" dates from the end of the fourteenth century. Chaucer uses it of "goode faire White" in *The Book of the Duchess* (1263, when it contrasts with "shame," 1017 and 1264) to indicate her chastity.

The interesting thing about Malory is that despite the use of forms of the word "honour" as already quoted, he far more frequently uses "worship" and its associates, though one would not realise this from quotations in dictionaries. Malory uses the actual word "honour" in various spellings and associated forms 53 times, while he uses "worship" and its associates 282 times. "Honour" collocates with "worship" only 3 times. "Dishonour" as noun and verb (including the past participle) occurs 37 times, all but one of them in speech. "Disworship" occurs 5 times, only once in narrative. A notable instance is when Merlin says that not to bring adventures to a proper end will be "disworship" to Arthur and the feast he is holding (*Works* 103/15). This further example of the compulsion of honour activated by the fear of shame also illustrates the positive ideal of disinterested service which is as strong as the care for reputation in the desire for honour. The one example of "disworship" not in conversation occurs in Malory the author's (the concept of "the narrator" being self-defeating in reading Malory with understanding) earnest address to the reader about paying honour to God, and having true love for one's lady (*Works* 1119/20). It would seem that "disworship" has a note of particularly strong personal spoken conviction for Malory. In the passage referred to he is condemning lack of "stabylite" in love, which is also lack of "wysedome" and "fyeblenes of nature and grete disworshyp." It thus refers more to the obligation to keep one's word, even to one's own disadvantage and even if no one knows, which is part of the general concept of loyalty, which is in turn the inward aspect of honour, rather than the need to maintain reputation.

"Dishonour" and "disworship" mean "shame," and the various forms incorporating the word "shame" occur 329 times in Malory. "Shame" is by origin an English word but it seems exactly to match in range of meanings the French *honte*. The total occurrences of the words for "honour" and "worship" together amount to 335, those for "dishonour," "disworship," and "shame" to 371. This arithmetical comparison is very crude, but suggests that the concept of "shame" is marginally more powerful than that of "honour." It is very hard to discern any pattern, which could only be subconscious with Malory, in the varying uses of the two words "honour" and "worship." There is perhaps a bias towards using the word "honour" where God and women are concerned, as for example in the passage just referred to, where Malory says, "But firste reserve the honoure to God, and secundely thy quarell muste com of thy lady. And such love I calle vertuouse love" (*Works* 1119/28-30). But this sentence is preceded by two uses of "worshypfull" applied to man and woman, concluding "and worshyp in armys may never be foyled." Though the external social aspects of honour are important, and further extended by the use of concepts such as "name" meaning "renown," Malory's preference for the word "worship," together with its associations with "worthynes," seem to me to suggest a strong sense of the importance in *Le Morte Darthur* of inner worth, as opposed to outward show. There is a clear example of this preference in the case of Balin: "manhode, and worship [ys hyd] within a mannes person" (Works 63/25), though he may be poor and of poor outward appearance. The compulsion of honour is particularly strong for Balin; after the latest of many warnings he says, "I maye not torne now ageyne for shame" (*Works* 89/2).

Andrew Lynch in an original and subtle chapter of his excellent book argues that Balin fails precisely because he lacks the external attributes of honour, which "the narrative" (a somewhat disembodied concept) denies him. Balin's difficulty is rather wider, though it is related to honour in that he fails to realise the importance of making appearance coincide with reality. The outstanding example is when he exchanges his shield, which his brother would have recognised, for another, supposedly better one, offered to him apparently in good faith and accepted by him in the same spirit. Although a lady warns him about this, there is a wilfulness and a death-wish in Balin which compounds his lack of understanding of the meanings of things (*Works* 88/18-39). As in the case of the marvellous spear he snatches up, he does not fully understand what he is doing (*Works* 85/1-30). His tragedy is as much as anything a tragedy of incomprehension, though he is a fully honourable man, and in his deeds is driven by the compulsions of (especially) internal honour.[13]

Lancelot offers the supreme example of the compulsions of honour. Although Lancelot, at the beginning of the section devoted to him, is already supreme "in worship and honoure" (*Works* 253/12-13), and although he does many deeds of arms for Queen Guinevere and will save her from the fire "thorow his noble chevalry" (*Works* 253/19), he is nevertheless eager to "preve" himself further in "straunge adventures" (*Works* 253/21). There is a real nobility and idealism in the notion of honour that compels good knights to seek strange adventures, as already suggested above. It is this idealism, which is a form of altruism and self-sacrifice, as well as a natural desire for an interesting and exciting life, which has rightly appealed to so many generations before our own, despite the rational contemptuous moralisation of Ascham and many later literary critics.

Yet this idealism leads to disaster, because it is either too much or too little, and with Lancelot in particular, at the end, becomes impossibly paradoxical. The most powerful compulsions of honour are those felt by Lancelot, Gawain, and Arthur, and, as I remarked many years ago, it is honour that destroys the honourable society. Lancelot is bound in honour to rescue the Queen from burning, and all his affinity ("my kyn and my fryndis") unanimously tell him that "hit ys more youre worshyp that ye rescow the quene. . . ." He replies, "I wolde be lothe to do that thynge that shulde dishonour you or my bloode" (*Works* 1172/4-24), though he foresees that he will do great damage. So he must fight in the end against Arthur, though when Sir Bors would have killed Arthur, Lancelot prevents him: "For I woll never se that moste noble kynge that made me knyght nother slayne nor shamed" (*Works* 1192/17-19). These episodes sum up the tragic paradox to which Lancelot is driven. The words "worship," "honour," "shame" echo through the final episodes of Arthur's reign, as well expounded by David Benson (231-34). Benson points out that honour is transformed into a deeper sense of responsibility, but one should not forget that honour always included a sense of reciprocity and responsibility for oneself and others. What has changed is the orientation of desire and, one might argue, a truer sense of honour–true devotion to King Arthur, to fellowship. While it is the case that a man is not dishonoured if he cuckolds another, to cuckold one's king, who made one knight, is an act of supreme treachery, of disloyalty, hence of dishonour, and it is Lancelot himself who commits this supreme act of dishonour against Arthur. Once he has done it, he is then compelled to compound the dishonour by the compulsion of honour to stand by his mistress. Though it was Gawain's loyalty to kinship that drove him to seek vengeance, Gawain was right to call Lancelot a traitor knight (*Works* 1221/11). The initial shame was committed by Lancelot and Guinevere, as they both come to realise. In Guinevere's words, "Thorow thys same man and me hath all thys warre be wrought, and the deth of the moste nobelest knyghtes of the worlde; for thorow oure love that we have loved togydir ys my moste noble lorde slayne" (*Works* 1252/8-11). Well might Lancelot and Guinevere repent. Benson argues and seems to deplore the fact that their religious devotion still has the cast of honour, and is still fundamentally secular, but it is difficult to see what else they could do when one considers the harshness of their self-imposed penance. Benson regards the religion expressed as sentimental in having Arthur and Guinevere buried side by side, but this is rather the final assertion of the compulsion of marital honour, that Arthur and Guinevere should be united, if in death. It is the reciprocity required by honour, the repayment of a debt of honour, that characterises the penitence of Lancelot, a final compulsion of honour in another mould. Benson rightly insists on the secular element, but seems to condemn it, implicitly invoking a total otherworldliness for Christianity, denying all secular experience, where not all may wish to follow him. Lancelot had been either too honourable (in trying to combine two incompatible loyalties), or not honourable enough to Arthur. He not only sinned, but he dishonoured Arthur, and his repentance is equally compulsive and necessary within the honour-system. The famous anchoress Julian of Norwich (1343 to some time after 1413) remarks that after proper repentance, earthly sins may be heavenly honours, and that, we may hope, would be the final judgment on Lancelot, Guinevere, and many another.

The best, if unintentional, commentary on Lancelot's and Guinevere's repentance is to be found in Julian of Norwich's writings on God's continuous love, and on repentance and penitence as achieving heaven. In the short text of her "showings" she is concerned to show that sin, which cannot be avoided, may even be turned to good:

> Also god schewed me that syn is na schame, but wirschippe
> to mann . . . [examples of David etc.] howe thaye er knawenn in
> the kyrke of erth with thare synnes to thayre wirschippe. And it
> is to thamm no schame that thay hafe synned–na mare it is in
> the blysse of heven–for thare the takenynge of synne is tourned
> into wirschippe. . . . Synn is the scharpyste scourge . . . .
>
> (I, Ch. xvii, 255-6)

And again, in the long text:

> And god shewed that synne shalle be no shame, but wurshype
> to man . . . . Ryght as dyuerse synnes by ponysschyd with dyuers
> paynes / after that it be greuous, ryght so shalle they be
> rewardyd with dyvers joyes in hevyn for theyr victories, after as
> the synne haue ben paynfulle and sorowfulle to the soule in erth.
>
> (II, Ch. xxxviii, 445)

She later refers to the benefit of "the lownesse and mekenesse that we shall get by the syght of / oure fallyng, for therby we shall hyely be reysyd in hevyn" (II, Ch. 61, 603-4). For Julian the compulsion of shame at sin makes sin itself a sign of honour, as we may well think was the case with Gawain in *Sir Gawain and the Green Knight*.[14]

Notes

1. See Driessen, "Humour," and Bohannan [Bowen], *Return to Laughter*.
2. For the general social anthropological background, see Peristiany, ed., *Honour and Shame*; Peristiany and Pitt-Rivers, eds., *Honor and Grace*; Stewart, *Honor*, who also refers extensively to Islam. For the ancient Greeks see Cairns, *Aidōs*; for Icelandic sagas of the thirteenth century I rely on Miller, *Bloodtaking*; see also Miller, *Humiliation*; for Arthurian literature, see Robreau's study of thirteenth-century French prose romances, *L'honneur*; for English drama of the sixteenth to seventeeth centuries, see C. Barber, *The Theme of Honour's Tongue*; for Chaucer, see Brewer, *Symbolic Stories*; for Malory, see Brewer, "Tragedy." For China and Japan I have relied on general impressions.
3. Cairns, *Aidōs*.
4. Burrow, "Honour and Shame," and Pearsall, "Courtesy and Chivalry."
5. Brewer, *Symbolic Stories* 72-91; Brewer, "The Colour Green."
6. Cadden, *Meanings of Sex Differences*; and Cooper, *The Virgin and the Bride*.
7. Abu-Odeh, "Crimes of Honour."
8. For further comment on "The Physician's Tale" especially and honour generally in Chaucer, see Brewer, *A New Introduction*.
9. On the reception of Malory's *Morte Darthur*, see Edwards, "Reception"; also Brewer, Introduction, *Aspects of Malory*.
10. The first discussion is in Brewer, "Tragedy." See further Lambert, *Malory*; Barber, "Chivalry"; and especially C. David Benson, "Ending" 231-38.

11. The same lexicographical neglect has been noted by Archibald in her valuable "Malory's Ideal of Fellowship."
12. Reynolds (48) notes the general acceptance of inequality, hierarchy, and kingship.
13. Lynch, *Malory's Book of Arms.*
14. Colledge and Walsh, eds. *A Book of Showings.*

Works Cited

Abu-Odeh, Lama. "Crimes of Honour and the Construction of Gender in Arab Societies." Ed. Mai Yamani. *Feminism and Islam: Legal and Literary Perspectives.* New York: New York University P, 1996. 141-94.

Archibald, Elizabeth. "Malory's Ideal of Fellowship." *RES* n.s. 43 (1992): 311-28.

— and A. S. G. Edwards, eds. *A Companion to Malory.* Cambridge: Brewer, 1996.

Barber, C. *The Theme of Honour's Tongue.* Gothenburg Studies in English 58. Göteborg: Acta Universitatis Gothoburgensis, 1985.

Barber, Richard. "Chivalry in the *Morte Darthur.*" Archibald and Edwards 19-35.

Benson, C. David. "The Ending of the *Morte Darthur.*" Archibald and Edwards 221-38.

Bowen, Elenore Smith [Laura Bohannan]. *Return to Laughter.* Garden City, NY: Doubleday, 1964.

Brewer, Derek S. "The Colour Green." *A Companion to the "Gawain"-Poet.* Ed. Derek Brewer and Jonathan Gibson. Cambridge: Brewer, 1997. 181-90.

—. Introduction. *Aspects of Malory.* Ed. J. Takamiya and D. S. Brewer. Cambridge: Brewer, 1981. 1-8.

—. "Honour in Chaucer." *Essays and Studies* 26 (1973): 1-19.

—. *A New Introduction to Chaucer.* London: Longman, 1998.

—. *Symbolic Stories.* Cambridge: Brewer, 1980.

—, ed. "The Tragedy of the Honourable Society." Introduction. *Malory: The Morte Darthur, Parts Seven and Eight.* York Medieval Texts. London: Arnold, 1968. 23-35.

Burrow, J. A. "Honour and Shame in *Sir Gawain and the Green Knight.*" *Essays on Medieval Literature.* Oxford: Clarendon, 1984. 117-31.

Cadden, Joan. *Meanings of Sex Differences in the Middle Ages: Medicine, Science and Culture.* Cambridge: Cambridge UP, 1993.

Cairns, Douglas L. *Aidōs: The Psychology and Ethics of Honour and Shame in Ancient Greek Literature.* Oxford: Clarendon, 1993.

Chaucer, Geoffrey. *The Riverside Chaucer.* Ed. Larry D. Benson. 3rd ed. Boston: Houghton Mifflin, 1987.

Colledge, Edmund, and James Walsh, eds. *A Book of Showings to the Anchoress Julian of Norwich.* 2 vols. Toronto: Pontifical Institute of Medieval Studies, 1978.

Cooper, Kate. *The Virgin and the Bride: Idealized Womanhood in Late Antiquity.* Cambridge, MA: Harvard UP, 1996.

Driessen, Henk. "Humour, Laughter and the Field: Reflections from Anthopology." *A Cultural History of Humour: From Antiquity to the Present Day.* Ed. Jan N. Bremmer and Herman Roodenburg. Cambridge, MA: Polity Press, 1997. 222-41.

Edwards, A. S. G. "The Reception of Malory's *Morte Darthur.*" Archibald and Edwards 241-52.

Gellner, Ernest. *Conditions of Liberty: Civil Society and Its Rivals.* New York: Allan Lane, 1994.

Lambert, Mark. *Malory: Style and Vision in "Le Morte Darthur."* New Haven: Yale UP, 1975.

Lynch, Andrew. *Malory's Book of Arms: The Narrative of Combat in "Le Morte D'Arthur."* Cambridge: Brewer, 1997.

Miller, William I. *Bloodtaking and Peacemaking: Feud, Law and Society in Saga Iceland.* Chicago: U of Chicago P, 1990.

—. *Humiliation: And Other Essays on Honor, Social Discomfort, and Violence.* Ithaca: Cornell UP, 1993.

Ogilvie, R. M. *A Commentary on Livy, Books 1-5.* Oxford: Clarendon, 1965.

Patterson, Lee. "The Disenchanted Classroom." *Exemplaria* 8 (1997): 513-45.

—. *Chaucer and the Subject of History.* Madison: U of Wisconsin P, 1991.

Pearsall, Derek. "Courtesy and Chivalry in *Sir Gawain and the Green Knight*: The Order of Shame and the Invention of Embarrassment." *A Companion to the "Gawain"-Poet.* Ed. Derek Brewer and Jonathan Gibson. Cambridge: Brewer, 1997. 351-62.

Peristiany, Jean G., ed. *Honour and Shame: The Values of Mediterranean Society.* London: Weidenfield and Nicolson, 1965.

—, and Julian Pitt-Rivers, eds. *Honor and Grace in Anthropology.* Cambridge: Cambridge UP, 1991.

Reynolds, Susan. *Fiefs and Vassals: The Medieval Evidence Reinterpreted.* Oxford: Oxford UP, 1994.

Riddy, Felicity. *Sir Thomas Malory.* Leiden: Brill, 1987.

Robreau, Yvonne. *L'honneur et la honte: leur expression dans les romans en prose du Lancelot - Graal (XIIe - XIIIe siècles).* Publications Romanes et Françaises 157. Genève: Droz, 1981.

Skeat, W. W., ed. *Chaucerian and Other Pieces.* Oxford: Clarendon, 1897.

Stewart, Frank Henderson. *Honor.* Chicago: U of Chicago P, 1994.

Vinaver, Eugène, ed. *The Works of Sir Thomas Malory.* 1947. 3rd ed., rev. P. J. C. Field. 3 vols. Oxford: Clarendon, 1990.

Whitelock, Dorothy, David C. Douglas, and Susie I. Tucker, eds. *The Anglo-Saxon Chronicle: A Revised Translation.* London: Eyre and Spottiswoode, 1961.

Wynne-Davies, Marion. *Women and Arthurian Literature: Seizing the Sword.* London: Macmillan; New York: St. Martin's, 1996.

Ywain and Gawain. Ed. Albert B. Friedman and Norman T. Harrington. EETS o.s. 254 (London: Oxford UP, 1964).

Douglas Wurtele

ANOTHER LOOK AT AN OLD "SCIENCE": CHAUCER'S PILGRIMS AND PHYSIOGNOMY

The treatises dating from Geoffrey Chaucer's era that deal with the pseudo-science of physiognomy are usually contained in versions of the long-popular *Secreta Secretorum*, compendiums of practical wisdom that claimed to provide instruction in rulership taught by Aristotle to Alexander. The practical nature of this pseudo-science has been called "the art of interpreting character from physique," an art with close relationships to theories of medicine and the practice of rhetoric (Evans 5). The treatises, some of them extremely detailed, could offer guidance not only to governors at levels from the exalted to the modest but also, as later turned out, to poets in the effective use of the rhetorical device of *effictio*.

If Chaucer did choose, to cite Walter Clyde Curry, "to employ physiognomical principles in the presentation of some of his characters, the main question is not whether he himself believed in physiognomy, but whether his use of it gave greater verisimilitude to the characters in the eyes of his audience" (xvi). Regardless of the poet's own skepticism about the objective validity of these principles, the fact that he could count on physiognomical credence on the part of his audience is shown by the widespread diffusion of the manuals before and during his lifetime.

In Curry's time the sections on physiognomy in the Middle English *Secreta* manuscripts were most readily available in Robert Steele's three-text EETS edition of 1898. The discussion of physiognomy in the first of these, *Secrete of Secretes*, translated from the French, occupies only some 50 lines and for our purposes has little value. *The Governance of Lordschipes* (cited hereafter as *Lordschipes*), translated from the Latin soon after 1400, has a more substantial physiognomical section of nearly 200 lines. The third and best known, the one cited extensively in Curry's study, is *The Governaunce of Prynces* or *Pryvete of Pryveteis* (hereafter *Prynces*), with a physiognomy

93

of some 600 lines, much of it repetitive; it was translated from the French around 1422. Thus, both *Lordschipes* and *Prynces* in their original forms lie plausibly within Chaucer's range of learning.

Were these the only physiognomies accessible to most Chaucer students, there might not be much to add to Curry's analysis of the evidence in the *Canterbury Tales*. Fortunately, however, the far more extensive nine-text 1977 EETS edition by Professor Mahmoud Manzalaoui greatly enlarges the evidence pertaining to Chaucer's use of the pseudo-science in his ironic depiction of the pilgrims and their narratives. Of these nine manuscripts, the second, third, fourth, and eighth have sections on physiognomy. The second, in fact, bears the explicit title *Certeyne Rewles of Phisonomy* and is in a fourteenth-century hand; though very brief, about 160 lines, it adds a few fresh variants on the data in Steele's edition and it too is referred to here (as *Rewles*). Manzalaoui's fourth version, *Þe Priuyté of Priuyteis*, late fifteenth-century, and his eighth, *The Secrete of Secretes*, early sixteenth century, have brief physiognomy sections, but seem to be too late in origin for this study. It is the third version in Manzalaoui's collection that is of prime importance. The "Ashmole" version (so-called from Bodleian MS. Ashmole 396) of *The Secrete of Secretes* contains a remarkably detailed physiognomy section of nearly 800 lines in a mid-fifteenth-century version of an augmented Latin recension. No other available Middle English physiognomical tract provides as much meticulous observation on what Evans has called "the connection between a man's appearance and his inner character" (5) as does this one, where, for example, 300 lines are devoted to the significances detectable in the colour and shape of the eyes, as against only twenty in *Prynces*, the other long version.

There seems little reason to doubt the extensive interest this pseudo-science had for Chaucer's age. As Curry observes, among the pilgrims the "gentlefolk" themselves are "doubtless well acquainted with the current physiognomical lore" (65), an acquaintance that may well account for their unease when the Pardoner is suddenly called upon by the Host. Certainly by their time, circa 1390, there was an abundance of *Secreta* manuscripts, the survivors estimated by Manzalaoui at no less than 500 dating from the twelfth century (ix). Whether known to Chaucer in contemporaneous Middle English translations or in French or in recensions of Latin originals, those singled out above give a probable idea of what he studied. Whatever his own views on their ethical and psychological validity, it seems likely that the physiognomical details inserted in the *General Prologue*, later to resonate ironically with the pilgrim-narrators' own disclosures, come not from random and folklorish "wisdom" but from the authority of several *physiognomica*, including, perhaps, the Peripatetic prototype.[1]

Because to a certain degree the predictions about human behaviour so confidently asserted in page after page of the physiognomies' analyses, for instance, of certain shades and textures of hair or of bodily movements and shapes draw on analogy with the observed characteristics and behaviour of animals, it is useful to supplement the treatises with the Bestiaries such as *Physiologus*.[2] Conversely, some illustrations of aberrant human behaviour in the *Canterbury Tales* are better analyzed through a different kind of science, that of medical theory as set out in the treatises of such medieval physicians as Arnaldus of Villanova and Bernadus of Gordon. These suggest that the facial and bodily contortions exhibited by Arcite when bereft of the sight of Emilie (I.1355-79) indicate less an inborn attribute of character than a sudden attack of *erotomania* or *malattia d'amore*.[3] Palamon's self-diagnosis explains the distinction: "I was hurt right now thurghout myn ye / Into myn herte, that wol my bane be" (I.1096-97).

So numerous are the specific facial and bodily details in the *General Prologue* and so closely do they correspond to details in the *physiognomica* that Chaucer's use of the latter as a reference point seems unmistakable. Moreover, his technique is not merely to add verisimilitude of character, as Curry pointed out, but more important, to achieve compelling ironic effects. To draw some theoretical conclusions about these effects it is helpful to divide the pilgrim-narrators into groups, not necessarily corresponding either to the order of *General Prologue* depiction or to the order of narration. The assumption being made is that there is a planned correspondence between narrator and self-disclosure and narration, itself an element in the "sentence and solaas" competition. There are, of course, other valid ways of reading Chaucer's *book*, as Donald Howard calls it;[4] the one adopted here seems best suited for applying to the *Canterbury Tales* the physiognomical evidence published in Manzalaoui's and Steele's editions.

The interesting question emerging from this evidence is not whether Chaucer's knowledge shows he had any faith in the pseudo-science or merely a skeptical cognizance, but whether he resorted to it to achieve a kind of early psychological realism.[5] His knowledge evinces itself notably in the descriptions of the Miller, Reeve, and Pardoner, sometimes in tones merely satirical, sometimes more condemning: but is that all? Is less obvious evidence to be found in other examples?

To scrutinize such indirect evidence, when in fact it exists, and to apply it to the direct evidence offered by the narrators themselves, I propose to begin with the few members of the First Estate, followed by the Religious of the Second Estate, and then to move on to more analytical groupings.

For the Knight nothing facially pertinent is given; the details of his attire may have symbolic but not physiognomical import. The facial evidence of the protagonists in his exemplum on Providential governance is explained by *erotomania*, not physiognomy. His son, the Squire, however, is described in terms of his hair, a much analyzed feature in the physiognomies. He has "lokkes crulle as they were leyd in presse" (I.81), an ambiguous observation–does his hair curl naturally or not? While the treatises say much about the colour, texture, and quantity of hair, they are silent on its waviness. "Ashmole" prefaces its "significacions" by declaring, "Understand of heres the most sure signes ben, that ben with man at his burth" (92); possibly, then, the Knight's son has been vain enough to resort to curling tongs. His "moderate height" (I.83), however, is clearly a good sign. *Lordschipes* affirms that a man with "body of right and euen stature" is evenly attempered: "hym haue þou with þe" (114); and again: a man of good mind "ys noght mekyll long, ne mekyll short" (117). *Prynces* finds a man of short, small stature to be cowardly, but one of even, average stature to be kind (224). Indeed, the Squire seems neither cowardly nor unkind. What can be gathered from his unfinished tale supports the idea of kindness in matters of love, perhaps more truly than the treatment of "courtly" love by any of his companions. As for the Yeoman, "A not heed hadde he, with a broun visage" (I.109), that is, he is close-cropped and dark hewed. "Ashmole" has much to say about the significations of the "nodell," the top or back of the skull, but the Yeoman's is not well described. Even if the physiognomies singled out "closely-cropped" hair for comment, it would signify little in this case: a literalist might well point out that a forester could scarcely look otherwise and in daily life would hardly occupy a position of significant trust; moreover, no evidential prologue or narrative is assigned to him. Yet the important question of "trust," the fundamental ethical basis of judgement in the physiognomical treatises, is clearly relevant to the very purpose of the pilgrimage. That the competitors in the Host's "game" are entrusted with passing on to each other worthwhile "sentence" is no mean responsibility.

This duty the next four pilgrims, the "Regulars" of the second estate, might be expected to take seriously. The first of them, the Prioress, is thought by some critics to do so. All in this group, save the Second Nun, who is given no physical details, are subject to some degree of satire.

Physiognomical evidence for these three is ample. In quick succession the Prioress's nose, eyes, mouth, and forehead are described. If the reference to her well-formed or "tretys" nose (I.152) means that it is small and delicate or, as *Rewles* has it, "sotyl and smalle," this is a feature indicating wrathfulness and anger (12), not as inapposite a trait as might seem in one who weeps when a dog is struck or a mouse killed, for her Marian miracle legend centres on the implacable wrath of the provost of the "greet citee" in "Asye" (VII.488) when he orders torture and death for the Jews accused of killing the "litel clergeon, seven yeer of age" (VII.502): the Prioress had available to her less wrathful endings in similar miracle legends. In *Prynces* the evidence on the Prioress's pretty nose is not far different: if sharp and small it betokens wrathfulness, reading "sotyl" for "sharp." The nose that is "beste to Prayse" is "meenly longe and menly brode" (233-34).

As noted, the physiognomists give extensive attention to eyes, and not merely to colour. What is meant by "greye as glas" (I.152) is not certain, nor are the Prioress's eyes described specifically–unlike, for example, the person with wide open, glistening eyes, who is deemed to be shameless (*Prynces* 223). Eyes "redy to wepe" betoken one who is compassionate and merciful–an ironic reflection on the Prioress. One with eyes of average size, "blake or grey," is of "Parceuynge vndyrstondynge, courteyse and trewe" (233), a comment supports those who take a favourable view of this pilgrim. "Ashmole" draws much from animal analogies, but focusses on details other than "gray" or "blue": eyes with "dropis of shynyng liquour" betoken one with "blissed and soft maners" (98). *Rewles* finds in one with eyes "of heuenli colour," possibly blue, a quick understanding, "curius and trewe" (11).

The *Prologue* describes the Prioress's mouth as very small and soft, red and elegant (I.153). Because the physiognomies are wholly concerned with male behaviour traits, they offer little help here. "Ashmole" brands a man with a small mouth as "womannysh, and his cheres and inwit accordeth with them" (105). Evidence on the Prioress's best known beauty mark, her broad forehead (I.154-55), yields suggestions at odds with those drawn from her eye colour. In *Prynces* one with a "longe forhede ouer mesure" (and the Prioress's is seven to nine inches in width!) has "a slow witte" (228). "Ashmole" proves contradictory: one with a "litell forhede" is "a foole," but a "spaciose forhede sheweth slow engyne [skillfulness]" and a large one "signifieþ slouth" (94). None of these derogatory epithets would be inapposite for the Prioress, if one takes an adverse view of her tale.

The physiognomy of the next member of this group, the Monk, may give stronger evidence. His head is bald and shining, his face also shines "as he hadde been enoynt," he is fat but in good condition, his complexion is *not* pale, hence, perhaps, ruddy; and his bulging, gleaming eyes are "stepe, and rollynge in his heed, / That stemed as a forneys of a leed" (I.201-202). A man with "great eyes" is said to be "Enuyous & with-outen shame, sleuthful, and vnobeyssant" (*Lordschipes* 115). The tokens of a shameless man are "opyn eighyn and glysinynge" (*Prynces* 223) and those of a lecherous man "fatte heyghen, and rollynge Swyftly in syght like a wode man" (*Prynces* 225). On the evidence of eyes the physiognomists linger avidly: "Whos eyen be grete, he is slowe, shamfast, envious, inobedient" ("Ashmole" 95). "Bolnyng eyen and sanguinolent [dronkelewe], a man it sheweth. . . . Whose eyen outward shynen, he is shameles, a clatterer and a foole" ("Ashmole" 97).

Not all the "tokenes" are consistent. If, indeed, the Monk's face is "ruddy of colure as sanguyne," that can mean he is "honeste and shamefast" (223), yet "Tho that bene rede colure bene hasty and egre" (229), a trait at odds with the slothfulness indicated by his eyes. *Rewles* adds to the complexity: one who is "fleschy and right fat on face" is "litel wyse" (12). Confirmation is offered by "Ashmole": "Whos face is flesshly, he is not wise" (108). A monk "ful fat and in good poynt" (I.200) with a shiny face and an appetite for fat roast swan seems to fit the description of men "that bene moche and have moisti flesh"; these are of slow understanding (*Prynces* 231). If it is fair to regard the Monk's belly as fat, *Rewles* would deem him "indiscrete, foltisch, proude, and lufyng liccheri" (13). "Ashmole" uses almost identical terms: "Who so hath a grete wombe, he is like to be vndiscrete, folissh and proude, and lovyng venerie" (112).

Many of these adverse traits are illustrated in the Monk's behaviour and performance. Inobedience is asserted in his disregard for the "reule of Seint Maure or of Seint Beneit" and in the near-direct speech of "What should he studie and make hymselven wood" poring over books in the cloister's library (I.173, 184). The slothfulness also implied in these admissions and predicted by the physiognomies leads to the failure of his fallacious attempts to draw "sentence" from the misunderstood "tragedies" in his aborted tale.[6] He indeed reveals himself as one who is "litel wyse," but whether he is also to be branded as "lufyng liccheri" is not certain. Nevertheless, the *Prologue*'s innuendoes in the "venerie" and "prikyng" puns are echoed in the Host's sexual taunts (VII.1940-48). As for being "vndiscrete," the Monk's earlier admissions seem now to haunt him, for the self-confidence and defiance have turned to gloom and ill-nature.

Probably no more moral but far less indiscreet, the third member of this group, Friar Huberd, has fewer significant physiognomical signs than the Monk. He has a white neck, a lisping voice, and eyes that twinkle like "the sterres in the frosty nyght" (I.268). But while all four physiognomies note the size and shape of the neck, its shade is not considered. His affectation of a lisp to make "his Englissh sweete upon his tonge" (I.265) is significant. *Prynces*, with much to say on voice, calls a man of very sweet voice "enuyous and suspicious," and "ful grete swetnesse" betokens "foly and vncvnnynge [stupidity, lack of 'cunning']" (234). *Rewles* also deems the sweet-voiced man "envyous and suspicious" (13) and then points to the particular mannerism of the Friar: "And scornyng, lispyng, stameryng, and gamen at harme schewes a right wicked and deceytus man" (14). Chaucer's evocative metaphor for the Friar's twinkling eyes is ambivalent: the twinkling itself may suggest good humour, but the dark frosty night evokes an image of coldness. When a man's eyes are "shifty" that clearly is a bad sign, but this the Friar's are not. His may not even be fairly deemed like those "Whose eyghne meues swiftely and his sight es scharpe, he es gylus, vnfaithfull and theuysch" (*Rewles* 12), even though thievishness was certainly not an uncommon criticism of friars. "Ashmole," the main authority on eyes, is more helpful: "Eyen glysteryng as yse, and shynyng, sheweth a gilefull man, bolde, playn, a waker, a gatter of þynges by malice" (98). Extensive warnings are given about "laughteryng eyen" and those that "twynkell," a sign that can indicate wisdom and gladness but also suggests "wikked þoughtis" and "joye after a wikkednesse done." How are these ambiguous signs to be read? Huberd's well-planned malicious attack on summoners in general and the pilgrim Summoner in particular and his gratuitous gibe at the Wife may reveal a state of mind befitting the physiognomists' warnings, but the most important correlation may lie in the *Prologue*'s account of his thievish depredations on the village housewives whom he pretends to absolve with easy or pleasant penances:

> Ful swetely herede he confessioun,
> And pleasaunt was his absolucion:
> He was an esy man to yeve penaunce,
> Ther as he wiste to have a good pitaunce.
> (I.221-24)

This malpractice Chaucer reiterates in the later comment that Huberd's sweetly lisping voice makes him so congenial a confessor that "thogh a wydwe hadd noght a sho" he would still get from her a "ferthyng er he wente" (I.253-55). In these words lies no mild satire. The Friar is coldly uncaring about the harm he is doing souls. Some of the other pilgrims and certainly many in Chaucer's real audience would be aware of the danger of inadequate penance and absolution so flatly condemned in the *Golden Legend* by Jacobus de Voragine, the widely-read thirteenth-century Dominican. The fires of purgatory, he warns, await those whose contrition is insufficient, unlike those who undergo real sorrow and mortification but die before the completion of their penance. What of those "who indeed have completed the satisfaction imposed upon them, but that satisfaction was not sufficient, due to the ignorance or carelessness of the priest, who imposed it" (II.281)? God, Jacobus warns, "who knows how to match punishments to sins in right proportion, adds a sufficient penalty lest some sin go unpunished" (II.281), in cases where the penance enjoined by the priest is insufficient. The serious point here is not simply that Huberd's penances are "easy" and hence possibly insufficient, but that a licensed friar so knowledgable about *intentio* and so deliberate in his methods can hardly plead either ignorance or carelessness. For the sake of greed, he is practising wilful guile, to use the physiognomists' term, and thus may be as baneful as the Pardoner, whose signs point explicitly to treachery–or even more so, since the Friar's victims can confidently expect him to administer rightful absolution, whereas the Pardoner's ought to know better.

Most of the pilgrims technically belong to the third Estate, though this division of society was already outdated in the late fourteenth century. For some of these, notably the truly lower class members, ample physiognomical evidence is given; for others, the well-to-do members, the opposite is true. To this group belong the Sergeant of the Law, the Physician, the Merchant, and, of course, the five guildsmen, to whom no narratives are assigned; the Franklin, not an easy pilgrim to categorize, will be dealt with later. But for the first three members physiognomy is ignored in the descriptions: all we have is the Merchant's forked beard, and while this may have tempting symbolic associations, it is not a physiognomical feature. Perhaps in reflection of their Graeco-Roman antecedents, none of the four treatises dealt with here mentions the not uncommon facial hair of the Middle Ages.

For the pilgrim churls of the Third Estate, the evidence is spotty. The Plowman has neither features nor tale; the Manciple has a narrative but no description; the Cook has only an aborted tale and a very specific physical feature to which Benson devotes a lengthy note in his edition: "a species of dry scabbed ulcer, gangrenous rather than cancerous" on his shin (814). In the *Secreta* versions, strictly medical peculiarities are, logically enough, not contemplated. The *General Prologue* mentions the Shipman's beard as well as his complexion: "The hoote somer hadde maad his hewe al broun" (I.374), but this is dubious evidence; what is due to weather is hardly to be seen as an inherent character determinant.

Something similar might be said about the Miller's features: would a sack-toting miller *not* be strongly muscled and big-boned, with thick, broad shoulders (I.546-51)? When coupled with a mouth as large "as a greet forneys" and "wyde" nostrils (I.557-59), however, these physiognomical details deserve attention, as Curry's extensive scrutiny warrants. *Lordschipes* teaches that "Broodnesse of brest, and greetnesse of sholdres and bak, bytokyns prowesse, and hardynesse, with witholdynge [keeping, retaining] of wyt, and vndyrstondynge" (116). This judgement "Ashmole" at first confirms: thick shoulders and back and a broad breast show "worthynesse, hardynesse and retencion of vnderstandyng and of sapience"(110). But then "Ashmole" adds: "Of shuldres, the strength and multitude of flessh vpon them founednesse [foolishness] they declaren" (111). Whatever one may think of Robin's rough but not ill-humoured scoffing at the Knight's treatment of "courtly" love, he hardly seems to be acting foolishly. The inconsistencies multiply in *Prynces*, for whom "Grete shuldres and large" betoken an irascible man (224). But it is Oswald, the Miller's antagonist, who displays ire. Yet *Prynces* also finds in "opyn noosethurlls" the very token of wrath (223). In *Rewles* a pair of wide "noseholes" denote lechery (12), again not a specified trait of Robin the Miller. His seemingly simple nature becomes more complex when "Ashmole" is consulted. His "grete and grosse" nostrils indicate a man of "full litell sapience," yet the same physiognomist credits "sapience" to the man with thick shoulders. The man with "brode" nostrils is "lecherous," yet "open" ones signify "fredome [generosity]" and "strength" (105). The signs indicated by his mouth, as wide as a "greet forneys," are less inconsistent: he is "glutonous and bold," "batellous and hardy" (105), traits displayed memorably in his altercation with the Host.

The Miller's bristly beard, and the Reeve's beardlessness, offer no physiognomical signs, nor does the Reeve's docked crown, an adventitious feature. But the Reeve's "sclendre" body and long thin legs "ylak and staf" (I.587-92) afford some clues. "Ashmole," for once, is cursory, but in *Prynces* these legs betoken the "luchrous" man, the actual definition being "smale legges and synnowy" (226). The man "lene of body" should by nature be "coleric" (220), a rare instance of verbal agreement, with "longe legges"

signifying an "ille complexioun" (223). All these signs fit the Reeve well: his
ill nature and choleric disposition are revealed not only in his quarrel with
Robin the Miller but more maliciously in the revenge inflicted on the Miller
in his tale. "Luchrous" he must once have been, as his lament about the
"hoor heed" and the "grene tayl" (I.3878) suggests.

A small but notorious group consists of Church auxiliaries, the
Summoner and the Pardoner. The physiognomical evidence given for both is
extensive, but with an important distinction. The Summoner's facial ugliness
reflects symptoms of self-imposed sickness rather than inborn traits whose
signs, in the Pardoner's case, betoken treachery and deceit. The Summoner's
fiery red, pimpled, swollen face, his narrow eyes and swollen eyelids, his
"scalled" brows, his "piled" beard betray a life of sexual disorder,
exacerbated by his diet. That the hairs of his beard have fallen out is
explained neither by physiognomy nor, as with the beardlessness of the
Pardoner, by animal analogy. That his brows are infected with the scall, a
skin disease, also finds no interpretation by the physiognomists; all four of
our treatises refer to eyebrows as evidence of internal character traits, but
only in respect to their shape, colour, length, and so forth. Those, for
instance, with brows that are not too thick and of even length are of "good
vndyrstondynge" (*Prynces* 233); those with brows "departyd yn and
shortnesse" are of "light vnderstondyng" (*Lordschipes* 115); those with
brows going straight to the temples are "envious" (*Rewles* 12). "Ashmole"
may come nearer the Summoner's eyebrows: "Fewe, thynne and redissh,
sikenesse of inwit it shewith, and hastying to age" and "browes that full oft
and contynuelly closeth and openyth, so the eyen ben smale and litell, he is
feynt and full bad, suffryng a siknesse" (104). The conclusions are not
ill-suited to the Summoner, but the underlying causes make them dubious in
value.

Similarly, the evidence on this unsavory pilgrim's eyes is a mixture of
the physiognomical and the medical. Which science explains his swollen
eyelids? The tokens of a shameless man, as this one certainly is, are
"eighliddes full of blode and grete and shorte" (*Prynces* 223); those with
"reede ey-liddys lowyth comynly wel wyn, and ben gret drynkeres" (*Prynces*
229), an obvious diagnosis for one addicted to "strong wyn, reed as blood"
(I.635). "Ashmole" offers detailed descriptions of eyelids, ending with the
significant statement: "The lidde, and þat þat sheweth, and þat þat lieth
vndre the eye, more swollen þan full aboue, sheweth, vpon, þe slomeryssh
man and a violent" (95). And indeed, the reaction of the Summoner to the
Friar's malice is violent: "Upon this Frere his herte was so wood / That lyk

an aspen leef he quook for ire" (III.1666-67). On the redness of a man's face, the physiognomists are understandably ambiguous. Those who are "red, bene Parcuynge and trechurus" (*Prynces* 229), a character flaw emphasized both in the Friar's taunting and in the Summoner's outraged response. The man with "grete ruddy weynes" around the neck and temples is "wrothy and hugely angry" (*Prynces* 220), to which "Ashmole" adds pointedly, "Whos colour is as a flame of fire, he is vnstable and suffreth manyacy" (91).

Disturbing as the Summoner's physiognomical signs are, those of that deeply scrutinized pilgrim, the Pardoner, are far more complex: hair, eyes, voice are closely described in the *Prologue* and given equally close general interpretations in the treatises.[7] His hair hangs down as smoothly as a hank of flax, then for emphasis is said to hang "by ounces" and again "by colpons oon and oon": yellow, soft, and very thin (I.675-79). His eyes are as "glarynge . . . as an hare" (I.684). He has a voice "as smal as hath a goot" (I.688). His beardlessness ("No berd hadde he, ne nevere sholde have"[I.689]) may not be a physiognomical detail in itself, but it combines with the other signs to produce an unmistakable picture of effeminacy that, combined with animal imagery, points to medieval anti-feminist prejudice at its worst–the taint of treachery, deceitfulness. Regardless of the implications concerning his much-discussed sexuality as eunuch, sodomite, or hermaphrodite, certain damning ethical assumptions derive from the physiognomical evidence by itself. In *Prynces* soft or "nesshe" hair denotes timidity on analogy with sheep and rabbits, and hence is a sign of a cowardly man (221-22). The judgement in "Ashmole" is that "Heres nessh, and passyng thynne and rede, þurgh lakkyng of blode, it sheweth womans witt. . . . Heres yelow and whitissh vntechable and wild maners þei shewen. Heres vnderyelow, thyn and depressed, it sheweth good maners" (92). But which applies? Does the Pardoner in fact have wild manners or good ones? In his self-revelations he makes it clear that when unconstrained he can be wild indeed, but when it suits him he can turn hypocritically good. As for the texture of his hair, long and thin, spreading over his shoulders, the warning in "Ashmole" hits the target: "The thynner þe heeres ben, the more gilefull, sharp, ferefull, and of wynnyng covetous, it sheweth" (92).

With its fullness on ocular signs, "Ashmole" again speaks appositely, if "glaring" and "staring" mean the same: "Staryng eyen, shynyng and lightly intendyng, as tham þat be contumacied and askyng grace it sheweth" (100). The arrogance, willfulness, and rebelliousness suggested by these terms are echoed all too clearly in the Pardoner's self-revelations. It is equally so with his small or goatlike voice, a feature singled out by all the physiognomists.

That kind of man is "dronkelew, enuyous, and lyer" (*Lordschipes* 116), "feynte or cowardly," having "lytill of manhode, and i-likenyd to women" if his voice is also "hei, smale, and swete" (*Prynces* 221, 231). The small voice is a sign of "foly and wommanhede" in *Rewles* (13), and in "Ashmole" it brands him as "vnworthy, founed [foolish], importune, and a lyer" (106). It would be hard to identify more precisely a pilgrim's behaviour with physiognomical judgements than in the Pardoner's case.

If there is one point on which Chaucerians agree, it is the uniqueness of the Wife of Bath. Not only is her prologue far longer than that of any other pilgrim, but it is also closely matched with the *General Prologue* account and, of major importance, with the tale that she adds to her own life story: in every way she can she shapes–or distorts[8]–her narrative to reflect back on the misogyny she has experienced in her own life and which she concedes can be traced back to the time of the "cardinal, that highte Seint Jerome" and beyond (III.674). But a reservation must be made about her physiognomical signs in the *General Prologue*: they are sparse and interpretation is drawn only from the male aspect. Alisoun's notorious defect, being "somdel deef" (446) may, from a Robertsonian bias, symbolize her deafness to the truth of Scripture, but it is no physiognomical token. On her convivial trait–"In felaweshipe wel koude she laughe and carpe" (I.474)–the physiognomists are interested in volume, speed, and tone of voice rather than chattering and laughing, though some negative evidence comes from *Lordschipes*, where one of the "tokenynges of good kynde" is "lytill laghynge, and of lityll bourdyng, & of noon fantome" (117-18). Alisoun may well be in the habit of jesting and deriding. The significance of laughter points to one of the inconsistences of the pseudo-science, for "Ashmole" calls "benygne" who is "laughyng moch," while "all men dedis displesith" the man "who laugheth litell" (107). "Ashmole" also has a little to say about teeth, none of it favourable (106), but on the not-unfamiliar sight of teeth being set wide apart "Ashmole" is silent. According to Robinson, it denoted an amorous nature and a love of travel, as well as boldness, falseness, gluttony, and lasciviousness (663). The Wife's red-hewed complexion, a major feature, has to be set beside the male-centered judgements in *Prynces*. Regarded as "sanguyne," a ruddy face betokens an honest man (223) but also an angry one (224). These are not inappropriate qualities to apply to the Wife's account of herself, but on the whole physiognomy offers little help in understanding her personality.

The four remaining pilgrims are in some ways the most interesting.[9] But they say so little about themselves that nearly all our facts come from the

General Prologue, where unfortunately the physiognomical details are sparse, if not wholly wanting. What gives them their special importance is the exemplary seriousness of mood–which need not mean solemnity–in which they take on the duty of providing "best sentence." The first two in the group, the Parson and the Nun's Priest, are secular members of the second estate. The next two, the Franklin and the Clerk, do not fit well into any of the three estates. The landowner is not of the first but hardly of the third, and the middle class, where his descendants will no doubt prosper, was only then emerging. The Oxford scholar should perhaps by now have joined the second estate, but "hadde geten hym yet no benefice" (I.291).

"Sentence," indeed, is what the Parson, the last speaker on the pilgrimage, provides totally and unremittingly. He scorns the telling of "fables and swich wrecchednesse" (X.34); his "tale" is an orally delivered treatise on penitence, designed with great structural complexity and infused with an extreme rigorist view on sexual matters. So stern is his response when the Host first addresses him disrespectfully,

"Sire preest," quod he, "artow a vicary?
Or arte a person? Sey sooth, by my fey!"

that the Host hastily switches to a more polite form of address:

"Sire preest," quod he, "now faire yow bifalle!
"Telleth," quod he, "youre meditacioun."
(X.22-23, 68-69)

From this exchange and from the Parson's earlier rebuking of the Host's blasphemy (II.1170-71), and above all from the unequivocally severe tone of his address to the pilgrims, we get an impression of a man stern to the point of dourness that is somewhat at odds with the reiterated epithet "benynge" in the *General Prologue* sketch, where something of a contradiction seems to lurk: though "Ne of his speche daungerous ne digne," the Parson will "snybben sharply" one of high or low estate deemed "obstinat" (I.517, 523). But there is not a single physiognomical clue, except perhaps in the twice uttered "benynge." The "Ashmole" physiognomist, as noted earlier, asserts confidently that "Who, laughing moch, is benynge, in all thynge he shall be convenient, for nothynge to moche hevieth neþer besieth hym. Who laugheth litell, he is contrary to hym, for all men dedis displesith hym" (107). Laughter to any degree is hard to associate with the Parson, who, to go by his fulminations, finds much in the deeds of men to displease him.

The Nun's priest, about whom the *General Prologue* says nothing, could hardly be of a more different temperament. He responds cheerfully to the Host's impoliteness–neither before nor after the narration does the Host switch from the familiar pronoun–and relates what may fairly be called, in the true sense of the term, the merriest tale in the competition. Only on its conclusion are we given some observations about the teller's stature, neck, chest, eyes and complexion, thanks to some breezy comments that verge on the vulgar:

> "See, whiche braunes hath this gentil preest,
> So gret a nekke, and swich a large breest!
> He loketh lyk a sperhauk with his yen;
> Hym nedeth nat his colour for to dyen
> With brasile ne with greyn of Portyngale."
> (VII.3455-59)

The Host's pleasantries offer the last and perhaps best example of his tendency to make only superficial judgements. The Nun's Priest's physical signs may well suggest potential or actual sexual prowess, but their physiognomical values are more important. In stature this "sweete preest, this goodly man, sir John" (VII.2820) is muscular and brawny. These are, however, signs not without contradiction. *Lordschipes* teaches that "greetnesse of sholdres and bak, bytokyns prowesse, and hardynesse, with witholdynge of wyt, and vndyrstondynge" (116), terms that may fit the Miller but hardly the Nun's Priest. *Prynces* notes that among the tokens of "a great-hearted man" are "grete stature of bonys and rybbes" and "grete braons and massy" (222), a close approximation of the Host's terms, which are reiterated in the verdict on men with "synnowes and braons apperynge": they are "hardy aftyr the propyrteis of the male" (227). "Ashmole" makes what seem like appropriately favourable judgements: "The thiknesse of the sholdres and of the bak, with a brode brest, shewith worthynesse, hardynesse and retencion of vnderstandyng, and of sapience. The brede of sholdres shewith ay good witte" (110).

The Host's reference to the Nun's Priest's "gret . . . nek" is also ambiguous. Again, a token of a great-hearted man in *Prynces* is a "Synnevey neke and grete, and noght myche fatte" (222). But a neck "ouerchargid wyth flesshe" betokens an evil complexion, while "grette nekkis" betoken a sluggard (223, 225). By "gret" the Host may not mean "fat." A more pertinent definition soon follows: "Tho men whych haue the neke wel dystyncted by his yontes, and wel delyuerit, they bene of good witte and good vndyrstondyng, for that tokenyth good vndyrstondynge and delyuernesse of witte, and that thay Parcewyth lyghtly the mevynges of witte" (227). But "Ashmole" is also ambiguous on "great": "Who hath a grete nekke, he is founyssh and a grete eter. And who hath a grete hard nek, he is stronge,

106

angry, and hasty" (109). The priest's "large breest" no doubt means "stout" rather than "fat." The unfavourable signs in *Lordschipes* on "greetnesse of sholdres," as noted above, also apply to "broodnesse of brest" (116). Yet in *Prynces* another token of a great-hearted man is a "grete breste and brode, vprerid and Sumwhate fatte" (222); conversely, those with "flesshly and fatte brestis bene nesshe men" (226), perhaps a distincion between a stout chest and fat mammary glands. *Rewles* gives an agreeably apt interpretation: "Brede of breste . . . signyfies worthynes, gentilnes, hardynes, beuenes of vnderstondyng and of wisdom" (13). "Ashmole" confirms this, more or less: "The brede and grossenesse of sholdres, and of baak the worthynesse, shewen hardynesse, with retencion of witte and of wisedome. . . . Mediocrité, sothly, of bak and of brest is a sure and a proved signe of vnderstandyng and of good counseill" (111-12).

The Nun's Priest's bright, rosy complexion (which needs no "brasile" and "greyn of Portyngale" for extra colouring [VII.3459]) is a physiognomical feature noted for other pilgrims too, even though the Host has chosen a remarkable metaphor to praise it. The less extravagant likening of the Nun's Priest's eyes to those of a sparrow-hawk possibly refers to their clear and penetrating gaze. If so, *Lordschipes* makes a damaging judgement: "He þat his eghen steryn swyftly, and haues a sharpe sighte, sweche oon is trechour, thef, & vntrewe" (115). If the Host's comparison denotes firmness of gaze, as it well might, *Prynces* makes an interesting observation: "Tho that in lokynge or in rewardynge ficchyth hare syght and hit holdyth stabill, they bene studyous and of good vndyrstondynge" (230-31). The "Ashmole" physiognomist, who prefaces his lengthy discussion by declaring that "Of þe signes and tokens of þe eyen is gretly affermed in the sentence of phisonomy, and here is all auctorité constitut" (95). He reflects that "bright and clere" eyes are a good sign, comparing them to those of the Emperor Hadrian: "humble, egre, grete of light, and full" (98). A man with "sharply beholdyng" eyes is "grevous," although moistness is a sign he is "redy and not noyous" (98). The intense scrutiny of eyes in "Ashmole" yields mostly unfavourable judgements, as in the case of eyes that "lightly moveth and the sight is sharp, that shewith a man fraudelent, a begiler, vntrew, slye and a thef" (101). In this scrutiny animal analogies are numerous, referring to the eyes of cats, rats, snakes, apes, and foxes, but not those of sparrow hawks.

To describe the Franklin, the *General Prologue* says only that his beard is white and his face ruddy or "sangwyn" (I.332-33). While nothing on beards is found in the treatises, its whiteness should offer a clue: a white beard must be matched by a white head. But though this feature may be symbolic of a Nestor-like wisdom, it is of no interest to the physiognomists, perhaps for two reasons. First, their concern is with thickness and thinness, crispness and limpness, shape and parting, and with black, brown, red, yellow (but not white), all to help gauge the trustworthiness of a prospective councillor–and who will employ a white-haired henchman? Secondly, "Ashmole's" confidence in hair as an inherent sign rests on its being established "at his burth" (92)–and who is born with white hair?[10] More can be learned from the Franklin's "sangwyn" complexion. "The sangyne by kynde shold lowe Ioye and laghynge, and company of women, and moche Slepe and syngynge: he shal be hardy y-nowe, of good will and wythout malice" (*Prynces* 219-20), most of these traits being seen in the *General Prologue* and in his address to the Squire and to the pilgrims, along with the added qualities of "fre and lyberall" emphasized in the *Prologue* almost to the point of irony. Malice indeed is absent from the Franklin himself and from his narration–but for all that how much of true wisdom does he purvey? His tale celebrates true love in marriage, free from "maistrie" (V.747), but when the crux comes in the Arveragus-Dorigen arrangement, the wife is commanded by the husband to perform an abhorrent act of adultery based on a promise she did not mean seriously and which itself sprang from a yearning to ensure her husband's return–the command designed to gratify the husband's personal sense of honour, yet with the warning that if the act is made known, he will put her to death. But evidently for the Franklin here is no "maistrie." Nevertheless, much as critical views may diverge on the propriety of Arveragus's insistence, the Franklin's intention certainly is one of "good will and wythout malice."

The Franklin's attempt at purveying "best sentence" does not have to be taken too seriously, but that is not the case with the problematic exemplum delivered by the Clerk of Oxenford, the best educated pilgrim, the *savant* acquainted with the work of Petrarch and immersed in the philosophy of Aristotle. Unsurpassed is the encomium in the *Prologue*: "And gladly wolde he lerne and gladly teche" (I.308). But what has he in fact learned that is of value to the pilgrims and how effectively is it taught? In a perfectly appropriate genre, the Clerk embodies his "sentence" in a kind of secular allegory, narrated far more elegantly than the Sergeant's allegory but much more difficult to interpret. If it is seen as depicting divine testing, then Walter has to be read as God, in a kind of Job-like parallel, or at least as Providence. This is intolerable, as no doubt the Clerk himself would agree–but that may not be the simplistic equivalence he intends. The *General Prologue* clues, not based upon physiognomical lore, point to a love of abstract learning to the point of obsession, by one who is not so worldly as to have "office" or benefice (I.291), who is immersed in philosophy, not life. From his point of view, it is possible to read the allegory in a logical way. Walter himself does not matter; Griselda hardly does. It is the *happenings* that matter and the uncomplaining response. These reflect the things that befall human beings–unexpected, unexplained, undeserved disasters that in the heroic soul do not weaken faith. But even the Clerk has to concretize the inevitability of human sorrow, with no qualms about depicting the anguish of a mother whose children are torn from her by sudden death, the "ugly sergeant" (IV.673), and of a wife whose husband inexplicably and unjustly withdraws his love. Herein lies his unperceived difficulty. Human feeling has to be evoked but only to be consumed in a kind of anagogical ascent beyond transitory human sorrow and pain, and the Clerk seems to expect that his pilgrim-audience can make this ascent by readily extinguishing the literal. Expectations so ill-conceived reveal a grave deficiency: the absence of ordinary human experience.

In matters of such complex character analysis as this, Chaucer's recourse to physiognomical evidence could hardly yield much fruit. It is not that a few typical details are not given. The Clerk's horse is "leene" and so, it is implied, is the rider; in fact, he looks emaciated as well as grave and serious (I.287-89). *Lordschipes* offers a superficial account: "And he þat hauys a lene vysage, ys wys yn his werkys, & of sotyll vndirstondynge" (115). Equally straightforward is *Prynces*: "A lean visage tokenyth study and besynes" (228). Somewhat more thought provoking is the "Ashmole" judgement: "Who hath a sclender face, he is bifore-seen in his werkes and sotill of intellect. Who hath a sotill face, he is of many thoughtis" (108). If the Clerk's sober, serious face is on the pale side, *Prynces* advises that a man of "Pale coloure and saad [serious]" is one to "enchu, for he is disposyd to ille tecchis" (232). For all that the Clerk's teaching may be too detached from his life, it can hardly be called "bad," except from a valid but no doubt anachronistic viewpoint. Whether his voice is loud or soft, weak or strong, sweet or rough–all matters of concern to the physiognomists, especially in *Prynces*–the *Prologue* does not say, but the brevity and the pithiness of his utterance receives praise of rare extent and warmth. When the Clerk's turn to address the pilgrims comes, the Host teases him by calling his demeanour "coy" and "stille" (IV.1-2), psychological rather than physical attributes, but which in general confirm the physiognomies: he is called quiet and modest, reserved and reticent, gentle and peaceable, but also, in a sense perhaps beyond the Host's ken, there is an implication of things hidden, covert, secret. This sense would be consistent with his performance, for he may well serenely realize that the inner meaning of his subtle allegory will remain hidden from an audience like this–as the Merchant's instantaneous and outraged response makes only too plain.

This brief examination has sought to enquire how far Chaucer's interest in the pseudo-science of physiognomy extends in his treatment of character psychology in the *Canterbury Tales*. A few generalizations are possible. The evidence is sufficiently pervasive that one can assert Chaucer knew how to make flexible, imaginative, and far from mechanical use of the physiognomists' teaching. The overtones of satire and irony to which many of the pilgrims are subjected are sharpened when these sub-textual ironies are added to the surface appearance presented by the pilgrims' descriptions and self-revelations. Moreover, while the physiognomies are strictly focussed on the signs revealed in *male* appearance, Chaucer's complex development of the Wife of Bath and the Prioress show an awareness that the pseudo-science can serve in the artistic creation of the female psyche no less than the male. Finally, the examination reconfirms the well-known appreciation of Chaucer's unfailing powers of variation and surprise. The absence of physiognomical clues for the Nun's Priest in the *General Prologue* is remedied unexpectedly by those unwittingly provided by the Host in his ribald address to the most successful player in his competition, that "goodly man sir John."

Notes

1. Evans discusses the establishment of the pseudo-science in the period of Aristotle and his immediate successors. In his introduction, Manzalaoui discusses the Arabic texts from which the Latin *Secretorum* was translated.
2. Animal imagery is especially important for supplementary material on the Pardoner. See *Physiologus*; see also Rowland, *Animals with Human Faces*.
3. See Ciavolella, *La "Malattia D'Amore"* and "Mediaeval Medicine."
4. Such views are, for instance, those of Pearsall, *The Canterbury Tales*, and, conversely, Robertson, *A Preface to Chaucer*. For the *Canterbury Tales* as a unified work, see Howard, *The Idea of the Canterbury Tales*.
5. See Wurtele, "Some Uses."
6. For a fuller discussion, see Wurtele, "Chaucer's Monk."
7. For further details on the Pardoner, see Wurtele, "Some Uses" and "The Concept of Healing."
8. For a treatment of this question, see Wurtele, "Chaucer's Wife of Bath."

9. The Canon's Yeoman and his master who join the pilgrimage at the eleventh hour are, of course, not given *General Prologue* portraits.

10. The reference in the marginal gloss on p.229 of *Prynces* to "white hair" seems to be an error, for the section deals only with facial colour.

Works Cited

Chaucer, Geoffrey. *The Riverside Chaucer*. Ed. Larry D. Benson. 3rd ed. Boston: Houghton Mifflin, 1987.

Ciavolella, Massimo. *La "Malattia D'Amore" dall'Antichità al Medioevo*. Roma: Bulzoni editore, 1976.

—. "Mediaeval Medicine and Arcite's Love Sickness." *Florileguim* 1 (1979): 222-41.

Curry, Walter Clyde. *Chaucer and the Mediaeval Sciences*. 2nd. ed. rev. New York: Barnes and Noble, 1960.

Evans, Elizabeth. *Physiognomics in the Ancient World*. Philadelphia: American Philosophical Society, 1969.

Howard, Donald R. *The Idea of the Canterbury Tales*. Berkeley: U of California P, 1976.

Jacobus de Voragine. *The Golden Legend: Readings on the Saints*. 2 vols. Trans. William Granger Ryan. Princeton, NJ: Princeton UP, 1993.

Manzalaoui, M. A., ed. *Secretum Secretorum: Nine English Versions*. Vol. I: Text. EETS o.s. 276. Oxford: Oxford UP, 1977.

Pearsall, Derek. *The Canterbury Tales*. London: Allen & Unwin, 1985.

Physiologus. Trans. Michael J. Curley. Austin: U of Texas P, 1979.

Robertson, D. W., Jr. *A Preface to Chaucer*. Princeton, NJ: Princeton UP, 1963.

Rowland, Beryl. *Animals with Human Faces*. Knoxville: U of Tennessee P, 1973.

Steele, Robert, ed. *Three Prose Versions of the Secreta Secretorum*. Vol. 1. EETS e.s. 74. London: Kegan Paul, 1898.

Wurtele, Douglas. "Chaucer's Monk: An Errant Exegete." *Journal of Literature & Theology* 1 (1987): 191-209.

—. "Chaucer's Wife of Bath and Her Distorted Arthurian Motifs." *Arthurian Interpretations* 2 (1987): 47-62.

—. "The Concept of Healing in Chaucer's *Pardoner's Tale*." *American Benedictine Review* 41 (1990): 59-79.

—. "Some Uses of Physiognomical Lore in Chaucer's *Canterbury Tales*." *Chaucer Review* 17 (1982): 130-41.

J. Kieran Kealy

VOICES OF THE TABARD:
THE LAST TALES
OF THE "CANTERBURY TALES"[1]

Prologue

He sits in a corner of the pub watching the sundry company, noting their eccentricities. Soon, he will agree to become a part of this motley assembly's pilgrimage to Canterbury, deciding along the way to provide a chronicle of this journey and, more significantly, of the tales told to pass the time on the road to Canterbury. And then, curiously perhaps, as this pilgrimage draws to an end, this thick-waisted "popet" will question the ultimate validity of this spiritual journey and the value of the tales that these pilgrims have provided, particularly those that are clearly secular in nature. Have any truly been able to provide the "sentence" that his age so desperately craves? Should his own life, his very profession be reexamined? Recanted? He sits in the corner of the pub watching the sundry company, little realizing that he soon will be questioning his very validity as a secular artist. He motions to the barmaid: "One more, for the road."

And thus one faces the dilemma that Chaucer's readers and critics have eternally faced when confronting his *Canterbury Tales*: what is one to make of the apparent recantation of a lifetime's work, this retraction? Has Chaucer, in a moment of spiritual enlightenment, discovered the worthlessness of all secular art or is this speaker simply a literary creation–that "elvyssh popet" sitting in the pub? Whoever our speaker, the questions asked are quite serious. Has this journey ultimately been a fruitless one? For both pilgrim and reader? More importantly, have the tales told on this pilgrimage served as little more than an elaborate prelude to the examination of conscience orchestrated by the Parson? Has this entire narrative been nothing more than a devilishly seductive confessional manual?

Yet, before answering such questions, one should recognize that this narrator's retraction is not, in fact, a spontaneous response to the Parson's enticing call for confession. Rather, it is the culmination of a serious examination of the secular tradition that pervades the tales that make up the final moments of this pilgrimage, one that begins with the Second Nun's nihilistic portrait of the follies of man and culminates in the Manciple's repudiation of all tale-telling. The *Retraction* is not an epiphany, but the culminating moment in the progressive disillusionment that this rather confused observer experiences as the very foundations of his profession are questioned. The last tales provide a journey to recantation, both for the poet and, potentially, for the reader, one which systematically confronts persistent medieval beliefs regarding where one seeks the harbingers of truth. And one's response to these final tales is drastically influenced by their dramatic interrelationship, particularly by what directly precedes. Thus our response, and more significantly the narrator's response, to the *Parson's Tale* is a direct result of the "baggage" accumulated in these last moments, in particular, the overriding portrait of a world incapable of discerning truth in anything but the most straightforward of sermons.

Simply put, our narrator will become intoxicated with doubt, one drink at a time, wondering finally if he should have ever left the safe confines of the Tabard. But is the reader meant to be similarly inebriated?

The Second Nun's Tale

Her prologue and tale are not overtly linked to any previous tale. One brief passage in the *General Prologue* represents all we initially know of her: she is the travelling companion of the Prioress, "Another Nonne" (I:163). And yet she tells one of the very few tales Chaucer does not retract, being among those "legendes of seintes" (X:1088) deemed worthy of being preserved. Perhaps this is so because it demands a re-examination of the overall purpose of this entire pilgrimage, thereby anticipating not just the *Parson's Tale*, but the pilgrim-poet's *Retraction* as well. She announces that the time has come to think of this life and the next in an entirely new context and to realize how dangerous it is to trust in the secular heroes and heroines that have previously been encountered on this pilgrimage and the transient world they epitomize.

The *Second Nun's Prologue* is quite different from those that introduce earlier tales. In fact, her three-part montage seems disjointed and rather tangential. It begins by discussing the value of "leveful bisynesse" (5) and the deadly dangers of that "norice unto vices," "Ydelnesse" (1-2). Unlike the Nun's Priest, her travelling companion and the teller of the tale that most manuscripts suggest precedes hers, she does not believe that her audience, like Chaunticleer, can learn from experience, that they can recognize and correct their follies. But the Second Nun does offer a solution for humanity's addiction to the "roten slogardye" (17) that idleness begets: constant perseverance. With this in mind, she offers her tale, her "feithful bisynesse" (24). Before beginning the actual legend, however, the Second Nun has a bit more to say, not only on why she chose such a tale, but on how it should be read and interpreted.

Her discussion begins with an *Invocacio ad Mariam* that concludes with a description of the human condition, describing how her soul is weighed down by the "contagioun" of a body that is insatiably drawn to both earthly lust and false affection, necessitating a new type of hero or heroine, one who actively assists man in his battle to combat the sinful urges of the body, one who can help free his imprisoned soul, a Cecilia. In this context, the Second Nun sees herself as an unworthy son of Eve, a "flemed wrecche, in this desert of galle" (58). And her request of the Virgin is quite specific: give me the wit and space "to werken" (65). Faith alone will not suffice, she argues, for "feith is deed withouten werkis" (64). The Prioress, the Nun's superior, in the invocation that precedes her tale, asks Mary to "[get] us the lyght, of thy preyere, / To gyden us unto thy Sone so deere" (VII:479-80). The Second Nun asks Mary to bring light to a soul in prison, a soul troubled "by the contagioun / Of [its] body" (72-73) and weighed down by "the wighte / Of erthely lust and fals affeccioun" (74).

The Second Nun concludes her prologue by providing a five-stanza exploration of the possible interpretations of Cecilia's name, based primarily not on a sophisticated etymological investigation but on her belief that all texts are meant to be read allegorically, thereby discovering the Christian *sentence* that even a name can evoke. Once again, her method differs significantly from that of the Nun's Priest. The Nun's Priest asks us to look carefully at life, to learn from experience and from tales that depict life's experiences. The Second Nun demands that we recognize the allegorical significance that even a name might imply, thereby providing a method for reading not just Cecilia's legend but all literature and, ultimately, all experience.

Not surprisingly, the Second Nun's heroine is also a figure who overtly confronts the Nun's Priest's views on teaching. She does not tell her audience to learn from experience, as he does, that is, to look at life and not "[wynk]

115

whan he sholde see" (VII:3431). Rather she asks that they learn to smell the "soote savour" (247) of unseen crowns. Common sense is not enough, she argues; one also needs the active assistance of supernatural forces, be they grace or simply the inspiration of legends such as that of Cecilia. Thus when her husband's brother verbalizes his fear of becoming a Christian and thereby risking martyrdom, Cecilia reminds him that life in this world is of little consequence when compared to life in that "oother place" (323). And he is assured of the existence of this "oother place" by being reminded that God's son, while on earth, "By word and by myracle" (330) declared "That ther was oother lyf ther men may wone" (332). It is, of course, precisely this approach to teaching, by word and by miracle, that Cecilia herself employs. For her, teachers do not simply preach; they must also be able to perform miracles. They must be among the chosen.

Soon, inevitably, the time comes for Cecilia to receive the palm of martyrdom. It occurs when she is brought to Almachius, the prefect, and asked to accept his false pagan idols. She responds by questioning his political power, suggesting that his "myght" (437) is "lyk a bladdre ful of wynd" (439) which, once punctured by a "nedles poynt," "is blowe" (440). And Cecilia carries such a "nedles poynt," the wisdom of her faith. She further illustrates the absurdity of his demands by suggesting that his eyes alone–his common sense, if you will–should tell him that these idols are but stone. Though her comments are remarkably similar to those previously made by the Nun's Priest when he argues the value of keeping one's eyes open, the Second Nun is not as confident as her companion that one can learn such a lesson. In fact, she clearly has doubts about one's ability to discern the obvious, a point she clearly suggests when Almachius, rather than believe his eyes and denounce his false idols, becomes enraged, demanding Cecilia's immediate death.

The Second Nun's tale of Cecilia introduces the pilgrims and the reader to many of the themes that will dominate the final tales. Above all, the Second Nun demands that one should recognize just what tales one should tell on the pilgrimage of life and to what tales one should respond. Because she sees man as depraved, materialistic, carnal, and insatiably drawn to idleness, she calls upon Christians to be active, to be ever at their "leveful bisyness." Even their tales, she argues, should draw man not to idleness but to "bisyness," for man must constantly work to save his soul. Above all, the Second Nun points out what must be recognized in these last hours of this pilgrimage: only the chosen can truly teach corrupt and fallible humankind.

The Canon's Yeoman's Tale

There is no epilogue to the *Second Nun's Tale* nor does the prologue of the next tale, that of the Canon's Yeoman, make any mention either of the teller of the previous tale or of the audience's reaction to this pious saint's legend, but it simply says that "ended was the lyf of Seinte Cecile" (554). Suddenly, however, two riders, on horses covered in grime and sweat, appear: a Canon and his Yeoman. At first, Harry is somewhat impressed by the Canon, calling him a "worthy man" (568), yet he cannot help but note that his "forheed dropped as a stillatorie / Were ful of plantayne and of paritorie" (580-81). The reason for this condition is clear: in his frenzy to join the company, the Canon "hadde ay priked lik as he were wood" (576). The association of the Canon with madness, innocuous as it may initially appear, will soon become a serious concern as the pilgrims are asked to consider whether this man's madness might not, in fact, be allied with the sinful idleness the Second Nun has just so confidently condemned.

Our first concrete suggestion that the Canon may, in fact, be inclined to such "ydelnesse" and thus, in the Second Nun's eyes, be truly "wode," is provided when his Yeoman suggests why his master has ridden so hard to join this company: it is "For his desport" (592), for he loves "daliaunce" (592). Earlier such a reason would not have been questioned; in fact, even now, the Host joyfully welcomes the addition of such a jolly man, who might "telle a myrie tale or tweye, / With which he glade may this compaignye" (597-98). Perhaps not all of the pilgrims have been convinced by the Second Nun's call for more serious tales, for sombre tomes of Christian "bisynesse." Certainly Harry has reservations and welcomes a change, a return perhaps to tales which provide a bit more "solaas."

The Canon's Yeoman quickly assures Harry that his master is just such a man, but he also feels compelled to provide a full description of just what kind of "werke" (604) this man does. At first, the Yeoman's description of his Canon's vocation is somewhat vague. He seems a kind of jack-of-all-trades, one who can offer profitable advice on "many a greet emprise" (605). But then the Yeoman, prodded by Harry, begins to provide more specific information on the Canon's "wirkyng" (622): he is an alchemist. Harry, however, is unimpressed by the Canon's credentials and begins to wonder aloud why a man with such remarkable powers should be dressed "so sluttissh" (636). The Yeoman, though initially hesitant, finally admits that his master may be "to wys, in feith" (644) for his own good, for his experiments do not always "preeve / Aright" (645-46). His profession may, in fact, be "as clerkes seyn . . . a vice" (646). The Yeoman then goes on to provide full documentation of his master's continued failures–"For evere we lakken oure conclusioun" (672). Inevitably, all their hopes and aspirations are doomed; as the Yeoman regretfully admits, "it wole us maken beggers atte laste" (683).

The Canon, now realizing that his Yeoman will "telle his pryvetee" (701), flees. When the Yeoman vengefully bids adieu to his fleeing master, hoping that "the foule feend" may "hym quelle" (705), he may well be prophesying not just his Canon's fate but that of all his fellow alchemists should they continue their pursuits. The Prologue ends with the Yeoman's promise to tell, as best he can, "al that longeth to that art" (716), that art that has destroyed both his life and that of his newly departed Canon. Significantly, the dismissal of the Canon is presented in an overtly dramatic context. Both the pilgrims and the audience of Chaucer's text witness, in a clear sequential manner, the type of logical investigation that will expose the ludicrousness of the Canon's profession. And other such professions, too, as the text will soon clearly suggest.

The *Canon's Yeoman's Tale* continues this condemnation of the alchemical art (both what it represents and what it symbolizes), specifically focussing on the temptations it offers for the so easily deceived pilgrims who form the audience of these tales. The Canon's Yeoman begins by providing a quasi-historical account of his seven years with his now departed master, summarizing what he has learned from his apprenticeship. Once, he tells the pilgrims, he was "fressh and gay" (724) in array and "fressh and reed" (727) in colour. Now, however, he wears a "hose" (726) on his head and his complexion is "wan and of a leden hewe" (728). Such, it seems, are the fruits of his science! He further admits that his work–his "swynk" (730)–has blinded him, both physically and spiritually, concluding by saying that such is the "avantage . . . to multiplie" (731). The specific references to work and blindness inevitably link his remarks to the Second Nun's legend of Cecilia, that ever working bringer of light to the blind, and thereby further emphasize the depraved spiritual state that his physical appearance mirrors. As opposed to the golden city and great feast won by the martyrs of the *Second Nun's Tale*, the Yeoman's quest for gold has brought only debt, deprivation, and the promise, at least symbolically, of a hellish fate. The Yeoman fully realizes that his quest has been but "madnesse and folye" (742). The relationships suggested here are fairly obvious: alchemy is a false philosophy, and its adherents, false teachers.

Finally, and most significantly, the Yeoman insists that no one can truly learn this lore, for "Al is in veyn, and parde, muchel moore. / To lerne a lewed man this subtiltee" (843-4). The Yeoman further suggests that such a quest may well result in eternal damnation, for the very terms of alchemy are enough to "reyse a feend" (861). There are two roads to damnation, he argues: reading books on alchemy and listening to teachers who try "To lerne a lewed man this subtiltee" (844). And, he concludes, "they faillen bothe two" (851).

The Yeoman concludes his discussion by turning his attention to the goal of all alchemists, the philosopher's stone, admitting that the quest for it is a fruitless one and concluding by noting what philosophers say about this quest. The philosophers chosen, Arnold of New Town and Plato, however, consider far more than just alchemy, providing an appraisal that could well be extended to include the entire art of teaching and thus all the tales that have thus far been told and heard. First, quoting from Arnold, the Yeoman suggests that no one should dabble in the alchemist's craft "But if that he th'entencioun and speche / Of philosophres understonde kan" (1443-44). If he does not, Arnold continues, he will never understand this "art," for "this science and this konnyng . . . / Is of the secree of secretes" (1446-47). Simply put, few have the proper qualifications to practice this art.

Is this then true of all art? Should we listen only to those few who possess the proper background? The Yeoman's second philosopher, Plato, offers a similar suggestion. When asked by a disciple to tell of the "roote" of "that water [magnasia]" (1461-62), Plato tells him that philosophers have sworn that they will never reveal their wisdom, for, ultimately, Christ alone will decide "where it liketh to his deitee / Men for t'enspire" (1469-70). The sin that the alchemists commit is now clear: they desire to know that which God alone has the right to know. The Yeoman concludes by suggesting that since God does not wish man to "come unto this stoon, / . . . lete it goon" (1474-75), for, by seeking it, he risks making God his "adversarie" (1476) and "for to werken any thyng in contrarie / Of his [God's] wil, certes, never shal he thryve" (1477-78). Man, he argues, is incapable of ever succeeding in gaining the wisdom the philosopher's stone represents; instead he can only ask God for "boote of his bale" (1481).

Few are meant to teach, to be philosophers, the Yeoman suggests, and those few are those inspired by God, like Cecilia. So, despite the obvious contrast established in Fragment VIII between the "bisynesse" of Cecilia and the "werke" associated with alchemy, the tales conclude by positing the same teacher, the inspired mediator of God.

The *Canon's Yeoman's Tale*, then, looks both forward and backward. Initially, it forces us to reexamine the value of the Second Nun's "leveful busyness" by presenting a type of business that leads only to chaos. In doing so, it wonders aloud about the value of any earthly endeavour. Perhaps all should be let go and man should be content simply to pray for help in this world of suffering. The stone idol of the *Second Nun's Tale* becomes the philosopher's stone of the *Canon's Yeoman's Tale*, and both are clearly false gods. But the most telling contrast between the two tales is between Cecilia, the Second Nun's heroine, and the various alchemists that the Yeoman describes. The ever clean, ever bright Cecilia with her crowns of "soote savour" is replaced by the physically blackened figure of the Canon and his "stynkyng" craft, a man both literally and allegorically doomed.

The Nun's Priest admonishes those who waste their lives in silly debates, refusing to take responsibility for their own existence, refusing to admit what life teaches. The Second Nun and the Canon's Yeoman, on the other hand, aware of man's predilection for evil, tell man to leave behind *all* things of this world–they are ultimately worthless. Instead man must await the truth provided for God's chosen and the mercy promised by God's son. Ultimately, like the tale that precedes it, the *Canon's Yeoman's Tale* appears to be considering the value of all secular literature, of all such false teachings, suggesting that it may well be providing a false road to salvation, as enticing and as morally harmful as the alchemist's demonic craft. Many are the pagan idols and pagan rites that must be exorcised.

The *Canon's Yeoman's Tale* clearly posits the alchemist as a kind of anti-Christ, epitomizing the false doctrine and false quests that lead man away from his "feithful bisynesse." He may also represent false artists who delve into areas best left untouched. Rather than transmute metals into gold, perhaps artists should be transmuting their sinful state, thereby preparing for the only destination worth achieving,

The Manciple's Tale

The *Manciple's Prologue* provides what may well be the darkest moment of the Canterbury pilgrimage, perhaps even of Chaucer's literary pilgrimage, a moment that virtually demands the Parson's entrance to redirect man and redefine a pilgrimage which seems destined not for Canterbury, but for Hell itself. The confrontation between the drunken Cook and the Manciple suggests just how far man has fallen, how depraved he may be. And the Manciple's suggestion that truth should be silenced neatly summarizes the problem that the medieval artist inevitably confronted when dealing with an audience difficult if not impossible to teach, one which virtually refused to accept truth.

Earlier in the *Canterbury Tales*, the Cook makes his first appearance on the pilgrimage when he responds to the Reeve's bitter tale of cuckoldry. The Host, as the self-appointed spokesman for the pilgrims, agrees to the Cook's suggestion, hoping, however, that the Cook's tale is a bit better than his cooking, which has been known to evoke "Cristes curs" (I:4349) from many a pilgrim. Quickly realizing that his remarks might cause the same kind of "quyting" that dominated the Reeve's recently concluded attack on the Miller, Harry tells the Cook not to be angry: "be nat wroth for game; / A man may seye ful sooth in game and pley" (I:4354-55).

The importance of this earlier debate on the value of "playful truth" becomes more obvious when the two participants return to centre stage as the pilgrimage draws to a close. The Cook is still drunk, and the topic is still the possibility of discerning truth in tales of game and play. In his earlier appearance, the Cook did manage to provide at least a fragment of a tale. Now, however, he can only babble incoherently. Nonetheless, despite the Cook's obvious drunken state, Harry calls upon him to tell a tale, even if "it be nat worth a botel hey" (IX:14). Once again, in isolation, such a request would not seem terribly significant. Perhaps Harry is just getting tired of this game and will be none too sad when his entourage finally reaches its destination. But given the recent discussions by both the Second Nun and the Canon's Yeoman on true and false business, as well as on true and false teachers, the Host's role becomes more problematic. He is, after all, calling for a tale from a man who is a reminder of just how blind, misdirected and foolish a man can be, one who exists "Oonly to slepe, and for to ete and drynke, / And to devouren al that othere swynke" (VIII:20-21). Harry's moral and literary judgments are clearly becoming more and more questionable as he himself becomes the most obvious example of just how difficult it is to teach fallen man. He has learned virtually nothing from either the Second Nun or the Canon's Yeoman, his decision to call on the Cook being a blatant rejection of what both tales suggest about the value of such men and their words.

But Harry's imprudent call is rejected; the Cook says he would rather sleep than have to deal with such "hevynesse" (IX:22). The Manciple, at this point growing weary of both Harry and the Cook, interrupts, suggesting that the Cook, in his present state, is in no condition to tell such a tale. His description of the Cook, with its references to both his "eyen [that] daswen"

(31) and his breath that "ful soure stynketh" (32)–salient details in earlier descriptions of both Almachius and the Canon–establishes him not simply as a comic figure, some bumbling, happy-go-lucky drunk, but as the epitome of man at his most depraved, the worst possible teacher that the pilgrims could hope to find. Even the Manciple, not the most Christian of men by any means, senses this unsuitability, proclaiming that "the devel of helle" (38) should set his foot in this mouth of this "stynkyng swyn" (40). Clearly, this is is not meant to be seen as a serious moral appraisal of the Cook; in fact, the Manciple is rather amused by him. But again, given the context so meticulously established by the *Second Nun's Tale* and *Canon's Yeoman's Tale*, such details suggest that the Cook should ultimately be seen for what he truly is: an emissary of the devil whose cursed teaching could infect and destroy all mankind.

Harry, however, is far more worried about the immediate repercussions of the Manciple's rather imprudent remarks than any cosmic implications, suggesting to the Manciple that he be wary of condemning another too hastily, particularly if one's own "rekenynges" (74) are not completely honest. The Manciple agrees, and offers the Cook "a draghte of wyn" (83), which the Cook quickly accepts. Such is the power of "good drynke" (96), Harry exclaims; it can "turne rancour and disese / T'acord and love, and many a wrong apese" (97-98). Harry then concludes his celebration of the power of drink with an invocation to Bacchus himself.

As is the case of much of the *Manciple's Prologue*, Harry's prayer to Bacchus, under different circumstances, would be judged as relatively harmless. But the context of the *Manciple's Tale* does not allow such easy dismissals. The previous two tales have warned the pilgrims quite specifically about the dangers of not taking this game seriously, of not realizing how serious life's "bisynesse" is. Thus, when Harry turns over the pilgrimage to a god who symbolizes idleness, the contrary of "bisynesse," he suggests just how unsuited he has come to be as this pilgrimage's moderator and how necessary it may be for someone like the Parson to assume his role. But Bacchus's reign does at least bring a transitory peace to the pilgrimage, enough for the Manciple to begin his story of Apollo and his tell-tale bird, one of the most enigmatic tales of the entire pilgrimage.

The Manciple's portrait of Phoebus Apollo, the god of poetry, as a jealous husband and unrepentant murderer, must surely be a comment on art as well as on the artist's role in society, or why choose such a protagonist? It begins with a brief description of Apollo's skill as both archer and musician, concluding by celebrating him as "the mooste lusty bachiler / In all this world" (107-08), one "fulfild of gentillesse, / Of honour, and of parfit worthynesse" (123-24). And yet it will soon become clear that the particular episode that will be focussed upon does not present him at his most "free" and chivalrous, but instead chronicles the brutal murder of his unfaithful wife. The focus of the tale, however, will not be on his culpability, but on the part his pet bird, a caged crow, plays in the tragedy.

The initial description of this caged bird is one of the most suggestive in all of Chaucer. Here is a bird taught by Apollo to speak "as men teche a jay" (132) and thus to "countrefete the speche of every man" (134) when "he sholde telle a tale" (135). Clearly, this crow can be compared to a certain type of artist, or tale-teller, if you will. He is the prized and beloved pet of the god of music and poetry, and his songs (his tales), are such that "no nyghtyngale" (136) sings "so wonder myrily and weel" (138). Here then is the poet restricted by his sources, one who does not interpret the "speche" of man but merely parrots it.

The Manciple provides no suggestion as to how to interpret his description of the crow (though he does refer to the songs as tales), choosing instead to move directly to the action of his story. Phoebus, it appears, has a wife whom he loves "moore than his lyf" (140), but his love is a typically possessive one, requiring him to keep her constantly guarded, "For hym were looth byjaped for to be" (145). The scene is a familiar one, certainly for this pilgrimage; the Miller and Merchant, in particular, have made very clear what fate has in store for such jealous husbands. But, like all of the final tales, this is not to be a merry tale. Unlike earlier fabliaux, the focus is not to be on the cleverness of the young lovers but on the inherently deceptive nature of this wife and, in fact, of all humankind.

This change in tone is nowhere more obvious than in the Manciple's analysis of just how unsuccessful any attempt to cage a wife is doomed to be. The old clerks all agree, he says, that "To spille labour for to kepe wyves" (153) is but a "verray nycetee" (152). This, of course, Phoebus will soon find out, for his unnamed wife, despite his "manhede" and "governaunce" (158), desires to be free, "a thyng which that nature / Hath natureelly set in a creature" (161-62). This discussion of his wife's natural desires is then overtly related to Apollo's caged bird (and to what it symbolizes); indeed, the Manciple concludes his comparison by suggesting that however generously one provides the caged bird (or wife) with multiple "deyntees" (166), and however splendidly one adorns their golden cages, each would rather "in a forest that is rude and coold / Goon ete wormes and swich wrecchednesse" (170-71). He concludes with what he proposes as a universal maxim on such matters: "For evere this brid wol doon his bisynesse / To escape out of his cage, yif he may" (172-73).

The references to art latent within this passage are delightfully evocative. All artists, the Manciple seems to be suggesting, by their very nature, wish to free themselves from the golden cage of tradition, be it that of rhetorical structure or the necessity for doctrine or truth. They yearn to mix with and talk of other things, of common man and his experiences, to live in cold forests and eat worms and "swich wrecchednesse." If one associates the crow with this type of artist–and the possibility is quite tantalizing–the salient point potentially being made by the Manciple is that the artist, above all else, desires to escape from artistic fetters, to move beyond being able to merely parrot the songs of Apollo.

But does this mean that the only other choice is to grovel in a cold forest amidst wretchedness? The question is an obvious one: if the artist is free, can he write only of wretchedness? Of course not, the Nun's Priest answers, providing just such a tale. Though his hero may literally "ete wormes," Chaunticleer's tale is certainly not one of wretchedness. He is a bird-*cum*-man who can learn from his experiences and, by doing so, provide a comic view of man's capacity to survive. The Manciple, however, rejects such hopeless optimism; his view of humankind is akin to that promulgated throughout the final tales, one which sees bestial man as hopelessly drawn to sin and his own damnation. Not surprisingly, then, the Manciple turns to the animal world when he decides to elaborate upon his views on how "worm-eating" man is dominated by his appetite.

However one may pamper a cat, he says, let it see a mouse and it abandons all: "Lo, heere hath lust his dominacioun, / And appetit fleemeth discrecioun" (181-82). He then describes how a she-wolf inevitably chooses "The lewedeste wolf that she may fynde" (184), the one of least reputation, for her mate. But this is not an instinct confined to women, the Manciple quickly adds, "For men han evere a likerous appetit / On lower thyng to parfourne hire delit" (189-90). He then goes on to provide one final, damning conclusion in his sermon on the power appetite wields over "lewed" and "nyce" man by suggesting that "Flessh is so newefangel, with meschaunce, / That we ne konne in nothyng han plesaunce / That sowneth into vertu any while" (193-95). Nothing that gives any pleasure, the Manciple asserts, can be associated with virtue. Thus all pleasures of this world must be avoided, including, it would follow, all secular literature. That the poet pilgrim chooses to echo the Manciple's "sownen unto virtue" in his retraction is not, then, coincidental, for should one accept the view of art espoused by the

Manciple, the poet inevitably must retract all that he has created that may be deemed pleasurable, all that, as Geffrey's *Retraction* states, "sownen into synne" (X:1086).

The Manciple's nihilistic appraisal of man now complete, he returns to his story, recounting how, while Phoebus was absent, his wife, as was inevitable, took a lover. Unfortunately, this betrayal–"hire werk" (241)–is viewed by the crow and when Phoebus returns, the bird immediately begins to reveal her treachery. Apollo's reaction is immediate: he slays his wife. There is no confrontation, no discussion, only death. Apollo's regret for his act of rashness is just as sudden as the murder itself: he breaks his arrows, his bow, and all of his musical instruments. His songs will no longer be sung. Then he turns to the crow and blames him for what was "wroght" (273). The kind of song Apollo sings, the kind of tale he tells, it appears, cannot stand the test of reality, the suggestion being that man does not really wish to know of the evil within both himself and his world. Thus, observers of man's (and woman's) foibles had best learn to keep quiet or also risk being called traitors.

At first, Apollo does appear to accept at least some responsibility for his act of rashness, warning all listeners to beware of such "ire recchelees" (279). Ultimately, however, he decides that he was not wrong, just ill advised. It is, he concludes, the crow who is responsible for bringing him "in the mire" (290). Thus, Apollo denies any responsibility for his action, refusing finally even to admit that his wife was unfaithful. It is the crow, he decides, who must be punished. And what better punishment than to take away his song, his "sweete noyse" (300)? The portrait of the god of poetry decreeing that all emissaries of truth will, from that day forward, be seen as evil and demonic, with voices harsh and grating, is disturbing, if not frightening. One can, it appears, counterfeit the songs of Apollo, but one should be wary of telling the truth about the world as one sees it. Such is the dilemma of the medieval artist!

The contrast between the *Nun's Priest's Tale* and *Manciple's Tale* becomes even more apparent when Apollo wreaks his vengeance on the defenceless, guiltless crow. Unlike the tale of Chaunticleer, in which the hero does take responsibility for his fall and, learning from his experience, escapes his antagonist, the hero of the Manciple's fable learns nothing from his experience.

And the Manciple wholly accepts Phoebus' rationalization, a fact which becomes obvious when, his fable complete, the Manciple provides his explanation of what his tale teaches. On the surface, the moral he provides is similar to that which the Nun's Priest finds in his tale, both suggesting the value of holding one's tongue. But here the similarities cease, for whereas the Nun's Priest advocates silence as a way of ensuring that man clearly perceive the truth (not winking when he should see), the Manciple suggests that one should close both eyes and mouth, for the evils in this world are not meant to be examined so carefully.

Telling the truth only causes anger, the Manciple suggests; even Solomon realized this. But his most valuable source of wisdom on the subject is his own mother, whose words of truth make up the last forty-five lines of the tale. Her thesis is a simple one: "My sone, thenk on the crowe . . . / . . . keep wel thy tonge, and keep thy freend" (318-19). Her final warning, however, is even more all encompassing: "My sone, be war, and be noon auctour newe / Of tidynges, wheither they been false or trewe" (359-60). Ultimately it matters not whether one tells the truth or lies. Rather, one must beware of all tidings "newe" and of any "auctour" who suggests otherwise. Such is the Manciple's view of the value of truth in art: one should confine one's tongue to "speke of God, in honour and preyere" (331). Should one hear any author with new approaches and innovative subject matter, the mother's advice would be similar to that which she provides her son regarding the advisability of listening to "jangleres": "Dissimule as thou were deef, if that thou heere / A janglere speke of perilous mateere" (347-48). To the Nun's Priest's advice to listen to life and keep one's eyes open to its lessons, the Manciple's answer is simple: keep your eyes and ears closed and your mouth sealed. If this be true, there is no audience for the secular artist who speaks of "perilous mateere." Thus those two birds, Chaunticleer and the crow, provide quite different views of how an artist should communicate.

On the surface, the *Manciple's Tale* may do nothing more than protect its teller from possible retaliation by the Cook. The Host has forced him to realize that there is much about his own life that he would prefer to remain unexamined, so he repents his attack on the Cook and advises all to avoid such verbal onslaughts; they only cause trouble. But far more is being questioned in this tale, most obviously the value of secular art (that art that does not "speke of God"), particularly art that tries to portray this world realistically and honestly. Should, then, the secular artist be content to stay in his golden cage, well fed and well taken care of, imitating the words of his muse, of his Apollo?

The Baggage One Carries

The Manciple's view of art not only rejects that of the Nun's Priest but also foreshadows the need for the words of another priest, who speaks not of cocks and hens but of God "in honour and preyere" (331). Thus, the *Manciple's Tale*, alongside the tales that immediately precede it, seems to offer artists relatively limited scope in which to create. They can either create with the blurred eye of the alchemist, seeking truth where mere man should not look, or tell the truth, as the crow does, and bear the consequences. Or perhaps they can be among the chosen and preach only of God and the next world, as Cecilia does. Whatever their choice, the role of the secular artist has become severely limited.

In addition, the final tales suggest that the artist faces an audience who would prefer not to hear the truth, would prefer that all held their tongues. Why not let Bacchus govern this earthly pilgrimage? Throughout these final tales, then, there is a gradual movement away from the Nun's Priest's comic, satiric resolution of the "sentence / solaas" dilemma. The portrait of man becomes increasingly more pessimistic and perhaps even nihilistic. The artist, it seems, faces a "lewed" and "nyce" audience who both refuse to listen to the truth and are unable to perceive it when it is provided. In addition, both the Second Nun's and Canon's Yeoman's tales suggest that the secular artist may be leading man to idleness, not "leveful bisynesse," seeking truth in this world when his eyes should be directed to the next. Perhaps only prose, only a direct call for man to examine his sinful state, is appropriate. The questions raised by such a surrender to prose and a literature solely devoted to sentence and doctrine are, of course, of extreme importance to any secular artist.

So, is there a place for song, for singing, outside the Church? Is there a place for comedy? For satire? Can the poet ever hope to portray experience accurately enough to truly teach man, particularly a man who prefers not to look at any experience that might hint of his innate sinfulness? Must we all finally "[take] the fruyt, and lat the chaf be stille" (VII:3443)? Must we turn only to "sentence" rather than the merging of "sentence" and "solaas" that the Host argues for in the *General Prologue*? Must we accept the *Parson's Tale* as the only proper and possible way of teaching fallible, fallen man? If we accept Apollo's and the Manciple's condemnation of this tell-tale bird, there may be no more tales to tell. Thus, as suggested earlier, the *Manciple's Tale*, ultimately neither fable nor fabliau, may well provide the darkest moment in all of Chaucerian fiction. It may also be the salient reason why the pilgrim poet retracts a lifetime of secular art. And whether we must also recant is the question the *Canterbury Tales* ultimately poses.

Epilogue

We are now in our own pub, the every day of everyday experiences. We have listened to and heard the voices of this "elvyssh" poet's pilgrims. Their final tales seem to argue that this "experience"–this confronation with the tales that make up the Canterbury journey–has been a potentially dangerous one, one that may well lead to our potential damnation. Only the Parson, it appears, can provide the road to true salvation.

But one must never forget that this journey has been an experiential one. And that we are ultimately left with the voices of not one, but two priests: the Nun's Priest, who argues for the validity of experience and the comic voice; and the Parson, who summarizes the fears and apprehensions of nuns, and manciples, and would-be alchemists. And we are left with the brief reference to Paul (Rom. 15:4) that both the Nun's Priest and our pilgrim poet suggest is the basis of their literary beliefs: "Al that is writen is writen for our doctrine" (X:1083).

Does this doctrine allow for the babblings of millers and wives as well as the pious utterances of parsons? Geffrey's final recantation seems to reject such secular ravings. But Chaucer, the poet, provides no such definitive solution.

And we inevitably begin to gravitate into those small groups, those discussion groups that will consider such matters–when the Tabard opens once again.

Note

1. My focus on these tales does not attempt to provide a comprehensive overview of the valuable suggestions that critics have made in regard to how one responds to these tales. Particularly noteworthy in this regard is the work of Donald Howard on the final tales, as well as more recent examinations of Chaucer's attitude regarding the value of secular art by Alastair Minnis and Melissa Furrow. In fact, the only direct influences on my analysis are derived from the lectures given by Del Kolve long ago when I was his student at Stanford. Rather, my analysis seeks only to chronicle a subjective response to the journey of self-doubt that these final tales provide.

Works Cited

Chaucer, Geoffrey. *The Riverside Chaucer.* Ed. Larry D. Benson. 3rd. ed. Boston: Houghton Mifflin, 1987.

Howard, Donald R. *The Idea of the "Canterbury Tales."* Berkeley: U of California P, 1976.

—. *Chaucer: His Life, His Works, His World.* New York: Dutton, 1987.

Minnis, Alastair J. *Medieval Theory of Authorship: Scholastic Literary Attitudes in the Later Middle Ages.* 2nd ed. Aldershot: Wildwood, 1988.

Furrow, Melissa. "The Author and Damnation: Chaucer, Writing, and Penitence." *Forum for Modern Language Studies* 33 (1997): 245-57.

A. E. Christa Canitz

COURTLY HAGIOMYTHOGRAPHY
AND CHAUCER'S TRIPARTITE GENRE CRITIQUE
IN THE "LEGEND OF GOOD WOMEN"

From the very beginning of the Prologue, the *Legend of Good Women* takes a critical stance towards authority *per se*: not even St. Bernard saw all of heaven and hell, and hence the authoritative account of these realms purportedly provided by "olde bokes" must be questionable. Yet in the absence of direct experiential knowledge, the written tradition is the only possible authority: "Wel oughte us thanne on olde bokes leve, / There as there is non other assay by preve" (G 27-28). And again:

> But wherfore that I spak, to yeve credence
> To bokes olde and don hem reverence,
> Is for men shulde autoritees beleve,
> There as there lyth non other assay by preve.
> (G 81-84)

In other areas of knowledge, however, where direct experience is possible, a written tradition based on merely human authority is open to question. Thus, after once more emphasizing the authority of the written word in areas outside human experience, the narrator explicitly gives his audience leave to give credence to the authority of books or to withhold belief when it comes to strictly human concerns:

> men shulde autoritees beleve,
> There as lyth non other assay by preve.
> For myn entent is, or I fro yow fare,
> The naked text in English to declare
> Of many a story, or elles of many a geste,
> As autours seyn; leveth hem if yow leste!
> (G 83-88)

In matters where it is impossible to obtain first-hand experience, it may well be necessary to depend on reliable written sources–"olde bokes" again, which are "of remembrance the keye" (G 26). However, in matters "Of holynesse, of regnes, of victoryes, / Of love, of hate, of othere sondry thynges" (G 21-23), this is not the case: in the realm of *human* experience, especially when there is a diversity of "autours" (G 88) or sources, authoritative tradition may not even be a reliable guide. In the individual legends, Chaucer explores this issue of the reliability of authoritative writing. The questioning of authority is specifically applied to particular *types* of written authority and authoritative models of writing, especially the literary genres of hagiography, epic myth, and romance as referred to in "olde aproved storyes / Of holynesse, of regnes, of victoryes, / Of love, of hate, of othere sondry thynges" (G 21-23). The narrator's own situation makes him an especially good arbiter with regard to the issue of authority versus experience: inexperienced in matters of love and even uninvolved in the debate concerning the flower and the leaf, he presents himself as an unbiased observer, neither dependent on any type of written authority nor predisposed against it on the basis of personal experience. The narrator thus serves as a front for Chaucer's exploration of the ways in which certain literary genres conventionally represent love relationships and especially the female characters involved in them. This investigation quickly turns into a critique of the restrictive conventions and the essentializing nature of traditional narrative forms. The *Legend*, I would suggest, demonstrates that any literary mode, including the courtly one, becomes too rigid and too restrictive if it relies on prescriptive conventions which suppress and ultimately deny the complexity of experience.[1] Such highly conventionalized genres are in the final analysis unworkable.

Ostensibly written as a penance for the antifeminism perceived in the translation of the *Roman de la rose* and in the portrayal of "fickle" Criseyde in the *Troilus*, the *Legend of Good Women* with its re-application of hagiographic conventions and its ironic glorification of female martyrdom in the service of fleeting male gratification is, I would argue, a critique of the monolithic misogynous implications of the idealizing courtly conventions, which propose an unattainable ideal, both setting women up for an inevitable fall and reducing women to "woman," and then proceed to silence her. Nor do the legends even allow for any pathos which might result from revisioning male heroic myths from a female point of view. This implies that Chaucer is not simply exchanging an inadequate view for a "correct" one but questioning the univocal authority of any single generic perspective.[2] Thus, none of the literary models specifically identified by the narrator is truly authoritative, with the conventions being contradictory and misleading.

Critique of Heroic Myth

For the narrator and his allegorical patrons Cupid and Alceste, the most important types of authoritative guides are, of course, literary models, specifically the accepted literary genres of heroic myth, of courtly romance, and of hagiography, with their time-honoured conventions governing all aspects from plot outline and characterization to point of view, intrinsic values, and even diction and other linguistic and rhetorical conventions. The narrator attempts to relate tales of female victims loyally and courageously suffering for the cause of love, but the first problem arises as soon as the narrator considers his sources. While Ovid's *"Epistels"* (1465) portray the female characters as victims of male callousness and cruelty, other sources, unacknowledged by the narrator, represent the male perpetrators of these crimes against women in a very different light. There the male characters are the heroes of their own myths, celebrated and glorified, with the female characters–the prototypes of the *Legend*'s heroines–relegated to secondary roles and usually instrumental in bringing about the hero's success. They can function, for example, as means of the hero's tempering, as does Dido in the *Aeneid*, or, like Medea, they can possess the specific knowledge or magic which will allow the hero to succeed in a particular trial or overcome an obstacle impeding the accomplishment of a task. Female characters thus tend to figure in very circumscribed episodes within the extended myth narrating the male hero's progress. In the *Legend*, however, the focus generally shifts in such a way that these limited episodes become the centre of the narrative and the action is seen from the point of view of the woman, who consequently becomes the focus of attention. By retelling (in the manner of Ovid's *Heroides*) the myths of great epic heroes from the perspective of the heroes' female victims, individual legends within the *Legend of Good Women* both negate the heroic quality of the male characters and imply that the authority of such well-known myths is deceptive. The redistribution of relative emphasis also serves as a strategy for subverting the authority of a genre, supplemented by other techniques including omission or substitution of significant details, and occasionally intentional narratorial obfuscation which pointedly begs the question.[3]

The original male-oriented form outlined above is still prominent in the "Legend of Hypsipyle and Medea." The two heroines in this legend have little to do with each other, except that they both figure in episodes in the myth of Jason and the Argonauts. In this myth, Jason falls in love with Hypsipyle, but then is obliged to leave her in order to continue the quest for the Golden Fleece; in other words, she provides a way station until a higher purpose propels the hero to his ultimate destination, but within the Jason myth, Hypsipyle herself is ultimately unimportant. Similarly, Medea's purpose is first to provide the means by which Jason can gain the Golden Fleece, and later she becomes the instrument of Jason's ruin, but the myth remains firmly centred on Jason. Yet in the two parts of the "Legend of Hypsipyle and Medea," the focus is on the female characters and *their* perception of the individual episodes. The two episodes thus become the central parts of the narrative, with the rest of the Jason myth providing only the frame for the two major love stories. This shift in focus occurs gradually, with the first third of the legend occupied with a summary of Jason's progress prior to his arrival at Lemnos, indicating that this legend is really about Jason rather than about the two women whose stories are connected only by the fact that both are victimized by the same man. Yet even in this initial prologue to the "Legend of Hypsipyle and Medea," Jason is already transformed from the hero of his own myth into the villain of the two womens' legend, and Hercules later shrinks in stature from a demi-god to Jason's pander as they frivolously conspire to deceive Hypsipyle. Hypsipyle and Medea, on the other hand, are presented as perfectly innocent and unsuspecting victims, a transformation which can be achieved only through the exclusion of other particulars in their own, much shorter myths.[4] Anything that would show the two women as forceful characters or that would detract from their victim-status is omitted or vaguely glossed over.

A similar but more thorough re-focusing can also be observed in the "Legend of Dido," where the material of Books I and IV of the *Aeneid* moves to the centre, with the rest omitted, even though the narrator professes that he will follow Virgil closely:

> Glorye and honour, Virgil Mantoan,
> Be to thy name! and I shal, as I can,
> Folwe thy lanterne, as thow gost byforn.
> (924-26)

Again, the result of the re-focusing is that Aeneas appears not as ancestral hero but as villain, specifically as seducer, liar, and promise-breaker. Significantly, Aeneas's dream, in which Mercury appears to him in order to convey the gods' command that he break away from Dido and fulfil his destiny, is here reported not by the narrator (as in the *Aeneid*) but by Aeneas himself, and therefore no longer appears oracular but simply as a threadbare excuse for Aeneas's sudden departure after he has become tired of the affair. As a result, Dido here is a mere diversion to Aeneas, whereas in the *Aeneid* she serves as a means in the tempering of the hero, who is called upon to sever yet another emotional bond before proceeding to the final parts of his destined mission. Like Jason, Aeneas in the *Legend* loses his status as a heroic figure and becomes an opportunistic philanderer. In both legends, women thus are not the instruments in the implementation of a divine plan but victims of an individual villain's deceptive and exploitative whim.

In the "Legend of Ariadne" this technique is developed even further in the representation of Theseus, where the reperspectivizing is partly achieved by means of subtle changes to and omissions of traditional content. In the "Knight's Tale," presumably written long before the bulk of the *Canterbury Tales*, we still see the older Theseus who is depicted as a hero instituting his own brand of order wherever he goes, not only in Athens but also in Hippolyta's "regne of Femenye" (*KnT* 866, 877) and in Thebes, on a detour on his way home as it were. In the "Legend of Ariadne," however, a similar process occurs as outlined above. Theseus is not portrayed as the heroic figure freeing Athens, with Ariadne's crucial assistance, from its appalling obligation to pay a tribute of maidens and youths to be fed to the Minotaur, but as a self-centred, pleasure-seeking perjurer who will readily discard the woman who saved his life, and abscond with her sister. Theseus's son Demophon, the villain in the "Legend of Phyllis," is similarly deprived of any heroic stature, and the mention of the destruction of Troy serves merely as a time reference (2404). From Phyllis's point of view, he simply appears as a treacherous lover who has broken his promise of marriage and thus despoiled her of her honour. If even the great heroes of classical myth cannot retain their status, heroic men of ancient history certainly have no chance at such an accomplishment. As summed up by Sheila Delany, Antony in Chaucer's version is "a rebel, adulterer, traitor, and bigamist beside" (*Naked Text* 189). Here love, even of the courtly variety, is clearly not ennobling but instead contributes to both Antony's and Cleopatra's undoing.

In all these cases, the isolation of the specific episode from the rest of the respective myth, and the retelling of the episode from the private and personal point of view of the injured woman lead to the subversion of well-known heroic myths. In these counter-versions, supposedly heroic action becomes exploitative of the individuals who are instrumental in bringing about the success of the hero, and the grand heroic gesture is undermined by a focus on the detailed losses of those who serve as stepping stones for the former hero. As a result, the hero figures themselves come across as utterly unheroic and even base in their ethical failures and their need to derive strength from the forced submission of their victims. Thus, the re-telling is not only explicitly critical of the behaviour of heroes but also raises the question of narrative validity as heroic myth appears as just one possible version of any particular story, with no more authority than any other version.

Critique of Courtly Romance

Not only well-known heroic myths are of questionable authority. The *Legend* also demonstrates the hollowness of the conventional stances and idiom of *amour courtois*. The male characters offer their "service" and beg for the lady's "mercy," and the lady–true to her prescribed role–eventually "rewards" the suitor after some initial hesitation (and when the reward is not forthcoming, the suitor simply helps himself: Tarquin rapes Lucrece), but whereas courtly romance would normally end at the point where the suitor's reward is within sight, the legends generally continue and then explore what is left out by conventional courtly romance, what happens when the valorous knight and the debonair lady actually have to deal with the consequences of the successful suit, or what are the results of the lady's having desires too. The effect is always far from the idealized image presented in conventional courtly romance.

The *Legend*, of course, is not the first work in which Chaucer is critical of the generic requirements of courtly romance. In the *Book of the Duchess*, he played the code of courtly love for all its sentimental potential, making the Black Knight younger than his real-life counterpart and giving the lady quasi-sainthood by removing her from the transitory and mutable world of the living into the permanence beyond life and time. In the *Parliament of Fowls*, Cupid's corner seems utterly unattractive in its emphasis on pain, deceit, and suffering, and Venus's temple similarly is depicted as a hotbed of sexual passion, lacking any emotional dimension and allowing no space for a beloved. *Troilus and Criseyde* can be regarded as an anti-romance, allowing the audience to see Criseyde's perspective and depicting her as a woman who is blamed for scheming and opportunism largely because she takes charge of her own situation while her lover ineffectually pines away. Chaucer's ostensible penance for this trespass, the *Legend of Good Women*, serves as a magnifying lens to analyze the constituent parts of the conventions of courtly romance, and hence to discredit them.

The individual legends use, but simultaneously subvert, the language and the stereotypical poses of courtly love. Pyramus, for example, although believing Tisbe to have been killed by the lioness, absurdly wonders "'How shulde I axe mercy of Tisbe'" (835), reproaching himself for having acted in a most uncourtly manner and having neglected his duty by exposing his lady to deadly peril instead of protecting her as he should have done as a true knight. But since both Pyramus and Tisbe come from a bourgeois background–their families live in adjoining city houses with "but a ston-wal hem betweene" (713)–their middle-class failure at courtly love is almost a foregone conclusion.[5] Furthermore, the "Legend of Hypsipyle and Medea" presents the usual emphasis on the need for secrecy, but the implications are sinister rather than honourable. Like Troilus, Jason is

> agast
> To love, and for to speke shamfast.
> He hadde lever hymself to morder, and dye,
> Than that men shulde a lovere hym espye.
> (1534-37)

Here Jason is not concerned with preventing any gossip from besmirching the good name of his lady, but he is worried that word about his liaison with Hypsipyle might cramp his future style. Also, as in the *Troilus* or in the "Knight's Tale," the hero's military prowess and honour are extremely important. Antony, having lost his "worshipe" (659) in the naval battle at Actium, "for dispeyr out of his wit he sterte, / And rof hymself anon thourghout the herte" (660-61), acting properly as Roman knight, but not as lover–unable to live with the shame of defeat he gives no thought to Cleopatra. In the "Legend of Dido," the narrator even comments on the falsity of Aeneas's courtship manouvres (1264-76), embedding them in a long passage introduced by the exclamation

> O sely wemen, ful of innocence,
> Ful of pite, of trouthe and conscience,
> What maketh yow to men to truste so?
> Have ye swych routhe upon hyre feyned wo,
> And han swich olde ensaumples yow beforn?
> (1254-58)

Only after this introduction is Aeneas's love service detailed, with the individual moves now necessarily appearing studied and false:

> This Troyan, that so wel hire plesen can,
> That feyneth hym so trewe and obeysynge,
> So gentil, and so privy of his doinge,
> And can so wel don alle his obeysaunces,
> And wayten hire at festes and at daunces,
>
> . . . .

And fasten til he hath his lady seyn,

. . . .

Now herkneth how he shal his lady serve!

(1264-76)

Even Tarquin is filled with "dispayr" (1754) at seeing Lucrece's beauty while knowing that his desires must be rejected, and, like a true lover, he recalls all the details of her beauty and demeanour:

Thus lay hire her, and thus fresh was hyre hewe;

Thus sat, thus spak, thus span; this was hire chere;

Thus fayr she was, and this was hire manere.

(1761-63)

In this context, it is significant that in the *Legend of Good Women* it is the female, not the male characters who are most concerned with honourable behaviour and integrity, with "trouthe," with being thought of as "trewe" and with living up to that concept. Cleopatra, for example, vows "'And thilke covenant whil me lasteth breth / I wol fulfille; and that shal ben wel sene, / Was nevere unto hire love a trewer quene'" (693-95). The cliché usually associated with male discourse is here given to a female speaker, but while the reference to "trouthe" normally serves to vaguely characterize the male character, the women in the *Legend* act upon it, ready to sacrifice all in its pursuit. By being re-applied in this manner, the codified terminology and postures of courtly romance are subverted.[6]

Another type of subversion is seen in the attributes displayed by the characters. Of course, the heroines have all the standard "lady-like" traits: we hear of Dido's "grete honour" (1008), her "gentillesse, . . . fredom, . . . beaute" (1010), and her "goodenesse, . . . womanhod, . . . semelynesse" (1040-41) as well as her "routhe and wo" at Aeneas's fate (1063 & 1078-85). But frequently, female characters also take on conventionally male attributes and patterns of behaviour. Both Cleopatra and Tisbe, for example, take the usually male trope of dying for love literally, both being unwilling to outlive their lovers. Similarly, Dido suffers the insomnia typical of unrequited male lovers (1164-67), makes her sister her sole confidante, and feels that her life depends on Aeneas's love: "In hym lyth al, to do me live or deye" (1181); again enacting the conventionally male pose, Dido kneels to Aeneas and offers to be his thrall if he will only stay, and "Have mercy" (1311-16), literally re-assigning control of her kingdom to him. Meanwhile, in the "Legend of Ariadne," Theseus takes on a conventionally female pose, having to rely on Ariadne and Phaedra to rescue him from being devoured by the monster. Such role reversals challenge the usual immobilized supremacy

138

of the lady in the courtly love relationship, but also indicate the reversal of the real power relationship between many of the women and men in the *Legend*–between Queen Dido, the independent ruler of a sovereign state, and Aeneas, the shipwrecked refugee of a destroyed nation, and between Cleopatra, Queen of Egypt, and Antony, the renegade Roman triumvir who has just been defeated by his own compatriots. In each case, love has made the independent woman renounce her self-reliance and become psychologically and emotionally dependent on a less powerful man. Even if the political and societal power relationship is not reversed, many of the male characters are dependent on the heroines for physical survival: Dido, Hypsipyle, Medea, Ariadne and Phaedra, Phyllis, and Hypermnestra all save the lives of the men who eventually victimize them.

While these women become active, however briefly, courtly love generally idealizes passive women, and female characters who try to be active or even initiatory in shaping their own fates sufficiently deviate from the ideal to be spurned. This is exactly Criseyde's problem: when she becomes active in taking her fate into her own hands, she becomes suspect and is rejected as a lady or even as a worthy recipient of reader sympathy, because the codified conventions governing the representation of women in courtly romance simply do not allow for a lady who initiates action guided by pragmatism. The "religion of love" is part of the same problem: woman is to be meek, and active only in granting "mercy," that is, ultimately her body. But the giving of the woman's body is taken to the extreme in the *Legend*: man can do with this object whatever he pleases–adore it, use it, violate it, mutilate it, reject or abandon it, and ultimately allow it to be destroyed. The *Legend* exposes the results of this code of passivity by parodying the code: like the opportunistic Diomede in *Troilus and Criseyde*, men in the *Legend* take advantage of the idiom and stances of the courtly lover to exploit appropriately "merciful" women.

Critique of Courtly Love as Hagiography

However, it is not only classical heroic myth and courtly romance which appear intolerably restrictive in terms of their unchanging lack of differentiation in the depiction of female characters; the feminine model provided by hagiographic writing is shown to be equally uniform and thus equally questionable. Just as epic myth diminishes female characters as purely instrumental in the mythological glorification of men, so courtly romance idealizes and simultaneously reifies female characters while also demanding that women display the patience of saints. Yet the unheroic nature of the heroes in Chaucer's *Legend* makes self-sacrifice pointless for the apparently saintlike women in the *Legend*. The legends critique the concept of the saintlike female in courtly-love relationships by demonstrating that the transfer of concepts from hagiography to earthly love relationships is based on a false analogy and is therefore inapplicable. In the series of mock saints' lives, the rhetoric of courtly love conflicts with the requirements of the hagiographic tradition, where one type of saint is that of the savagely mutilated female martyr, a *topos* also found in the *Legend of Good Women*. In saints' lives, this type of martyrdom is inscribed with positive values since it leads to the ultimate good of sainthood, but in courtly love, martyrdom clearly is *not* a desideratum. On the other hand, the requirement of female passivity common in portrayals of courtly-love relationships is not supported by hagiographic conventions; rather than being passively accepting, female saints tend to be active, even aggressive, participants in the process that leads to their martyrdom, largely because death implies victory and promises union with their lord. And even those saints who are not martyred for their faith are actively involved in shaping their lives and respond to changing circumstances. In the *Legend*, however, the death of a female character is generally not a form of victory but the final step in her victimization. Unlike in the Christian context, suffering here has no redemptive capacity and does not bring union with the beloved. On the contrary, while the heroines are expected to take upon themselves "so strong a peyne for love" (F 569), it is explicitly stipulated that the male characters shall be "false men that hem bytraien" (F 486), who gratuitously "al hir lyf ne don nat but assayen / How many women they may doon a shame" (F 487-88).

The *Legend* examines the role of a "good woman" according to the definition laid down by the patristic, largely misogynist tradition, and shows the inadequacy of the hagiographic genre as a model, which the narrator simply cannot follow with any success. In the *Legend*, the tales of martyrdom invariably break away from the parameters of the genre that stipulate self-negation and mutilation as desirables, and turn into contemplations of mutual but tragic, because socially uncountenanced love, into examinations of the conditions under which the demand for perfect female chastity can or cannot be upheld, or into any number of other poetic modes, but none ultimately fulfills the requirements of triumphant martyrdom. This undermining of the hagiographic genre as a literary model questions its fundamental assumption that martyrdom in fact constitutes triumph, and subverts the assumption that hagiographic conventions are indeed transferable to courtly contexts in the guise of the "religion of love." Certainly, most of the women in the *Legend* hardly make a conscious choice to undergo suffering.

Like the ladies of courtly romance, female saints typically are virtuous (usually virgins), beautiful, and of noble, often royal rank. With some of the martyr saints, it is precisely their physical beauty which first draws attention to them and then invites particularly harsh punishment by apparently mocking their judges and their tormentors, who proceed to destroy it by mutilating the woman's body. Similarly, for the women in the *Legend*, beauty proves their undoing by causing their unworthy lovers to desire them in the first place. Unlike the celestial bridegroom to whom the saints have dedicated themselves and to whose glory they are eager to sacrifice their bodies, for the female victims in the *Legend of Good Women* the beloved often becomes the torturer–physically or psychologically–rather than the absolutely loyal and reliable bridegroom to be expected on the basis of the correspondence with saints' lives. In earthly love, the self-negating dedication to the "lord" is thus shown to be at least imprudent and often destructive, without, of course, there being any promise of other-worldly reward; even the expected earthly paradise of the garden of love turns out to be a desert island. Consequently, the authority of the literary code which exalts Cupid as supreme deity is just as questionable as that of pagan heroic myth, and as that of hagiography as applied to earthly love.

Despite some of the superficial correspondences between the romance lady and the saint, other aspects of the two genres make their fusion in the *Legend of Good Women* unworkable. Unlike the usually silent ladies of romance, female saints are often highly educated, generally extremely outspoken, and absolutely sure of themselves and their goals. Naturally, all female saints are perfectly devoted to their heavenly bridegroom or spouse, and ready to suffer unflinchingly and die in his service, being utterly confident of their eternal reward, the "crown of martyrdom" and entry into the heavenly kingdom. During their trial or imprisonment, female martyrs often face the further challenge of having to face demons or devils, in addition to their human adversaries. Nonetheless, they triumph over all challenges to their faith and virtue, defeat their adversaries in argument (or in sheer stubbornness), and emerge victorious in suffering and death, permitting or even actively seeking their physical destruction. Strikingly, numerous female saints are not only perfectly confident of the rightness of their position, but defend it with a certainty which gives them an air of arrogance, contributing further to the severity of the punishment. It goes without saying that there is never a moment's doubt that the heavenly reward might be withheld and that they might find themselves disappointed in their expectations for the hereafter by having their celestial bridegroom turn away from them. Once the saint has bestowed her love, she is ready to lay down her life for this love. But while the saints devote themselves unwaveringly to their celestial lover as his worshippers, the lover is also their lord as well as their spouse and saviour, whereas in romance the relationship is reversed: the prescribed role of the male lover is not that of lord but of the lady's servant in love. Since marriage is too mundane to intrude into romance, he never or only barely becomes her lord. The fundamental difference is, of course, that the martyr saints sacrifice their bodies for the sake of their souls, and that their marriage with their heavenly spouse is of an entirely spiritual nature, with the image of marriage being merely a metaphor for the close union they are striving for.

In contrast, in the *Legend of Good Women* no distinction is made between physical and spiritual aspects, and the simultaneous application of the conflicting conventions of both courtly romance and hagiography causes the women in the *Legend* to fall short of the standards expected in either genre. Both the love relationships and the marriages in the *Legend* are very much of a physical nature, but the stereotypical romance conventions are broken in that in most cases a marriage or troth-plight actually takes place and is consummated immediately.[7] Thus, Jason and Medea enter a formal marriage agreement and then consummate their marriage, giving the contract legal force; Demophon and Phyllis also make a formal troth-plight, although they do not appear to consummate it before he leaves for Athens. Similarly, Ariadne suggests marriage to Theseus and then leaves with him for Athens regarding herself as his wife, and Hypsipyle remains "trewe to Jason . . . al hire lyf, / And evere kepte hire chast, as for his wif" (1576-77) when he deserts her after having two children with her.[8] In those legends where the stereotypical love relationship of romance is carried further, the lover quickly ceases to be the lady's servant and becomes her less than noble lord who, far from being a saviour, leads his wife or bride to her death. Lyno, for instance, abandons Hypermnestra to certain death during their escape, so that she involuntarily becomes the substitute victim after she has saved his life. In contrast, while martyr saints also sacrifice themselves for their lord, they willingly choose to submit to their physical destruction rather than being exposed to it against their will or expectations. Their heavenly bridegroom has already undergone comparable physical suffering himself, thus not exacting from his bride anything that he would be unwilling to suffer himself;

rather, he led the way by active example, voluntarily seeking physical destruction rather than merely falling victim to it.

Furthermore, in actual saints' lives it is not their lord himself who inflicts the saints' suffering; in contrast, for some of the women in the *Legend*, their spouse or bridegroom is also their torturer: Theseus abandons Ariadne to being torn apart by wild beasts on a desert island, and Tereus rapes, mutilates, and then abandons his sister-in-law Philomene. The extreme is represented by Jason in the "Legend of Hypsipyle and Medea." The imagery here clearly indicates that Jason, far from being the saviour of any of his three wives, is thought of as a fiend, a "sly devourere" (1369) who uses his "lures" (1371) to entangle his victims, yet who "can . . . have no pes" (1585) himself as he is driven to seduce ever more women while being ultimately condemned to misery since he cannot share the "better . . . chere" (1386) of true lovers. His deceit is all the more diabolic since he presents himself as a Christ-figure, "mekely and stylle" (1491) and "coy as is a mayde" (1548), but in the end he has paradoxically "abought love ful dere" (1387). Here the imagery even questions some of the deepest assumptions embedded in the transference of concepts from hagiography to courtly love.

But while saints often aggressively, even arrogantly argue with the authorities and become active participants in their own martyrdom, some of the heroines of the *Legend of Good Women* are, as Carolyn Dinshaw points out, extremely passive; they "quake, shake, tremble for dread," but take no active role in preventing their undoing (75). Hypermnestra simply sits down on the ground even though her passive waiting to be arrested means certain death and can bring no reprieve for the fleeing Lyno. As ladies they must be passive, and as saints they must embrace their martyrdom, but clearly the mingling of both roles here leads to disaster. Significantly, only two of the martyr-heroines in the *Legend* gain any kind of other-worldly reward: Lucrece is immortalized in the Roman calendar for providing the cause for Tarquin's expulsion, and Ariadne's wedding crown is mythologically translated into the heavenly regions, becoming part of the constellation Taurus (2223-24), a dim reflection of the saint's crown of martyrdom.

Not only does the "martyrdom" of the mock-saints in the *Legend* generally go unrewarded, but their deaths also appear utterly futile and of no consequence to anyone. While the women in the *Legend* suffer and even die in part as a result of their former lovers' callousness or at least carelessness, they can hardly be said to lay down their lives for the sake of love, since their devotion is in many cases clearly no longer wanted. For Aeneas, for example, Dido serves as a diversion and a source of wealth, and her suicide is irrelevant to him as he departs for Italy and marriage to Lavinia; likewise, Hypsipyle is pining away till death while her husband Jason is plighting his troth to Medea, only to desert her too in favour of a (here unnamed) third wife; nor does Demophon (in Chaucer's version) seem to know or care about Phyllis's suicide after he has "piked of hire al the good he myghte" (2467) and then failed to return to pick her up for their agreed-upon wedding in Athens. Moreover, the saint's absolute submission to the perceived will of her heavenly lover and lord is not always seen in the women of the *Legend* either; some of the heroines justly upbraid their lovers after the betrayal, thus responding more like the saints in relation to their earthly judges and torturers, whom they often reproach and even taunt. In their recriminations, the heroines in the *Legend of Good Women*, however, fail to conform to the image of the gracious but also demure or even meek lady of romance, who is patiently waiting for her plighted lover's return to her bower and never breathes a word of reproach no matter how many years have gone by since she last heard from him. Again, the diverse conventions of the different genres make it impossible for the heroines of the *Legend of Good Women* to satisfactorily respond to the demands of either genre, and thus the characters are doomed to either inertia or futile action, and a genuine resolution of the built-in conflict is pre-empted. Thus, Chaucer draws attention to the incompatible demands which the combination of these narrative forms places on characters. The inefficaciousness of the characters' residual action or at times even the characters' physical destruction becomes a correlative for the debilitating stagnation in the literary forms whose conventions impose this inertia.

"Good Women's" Questionable Goodness

Apart from exploring the contradictory requirements made of female characters in the respective genres, the *Legend* also demonstrates that the various feminine ideals are untenable in themselves. Although most of the heroines conform to some of the terms specified in the Prologue, that does not make them "good" by any standards independent of the specific ideology which demands suffering as a *sine qua non* of "goodness." Collectively referred to as "goode women, maydenes and wyves" (G 474), the heroines must also be measured by the more specific standards rehearsed earlier: "to hyre love were they so trewe / That, rathere than they wolde take a newe, / They chose to be ded in sondry wyse" (G 288-90). By means of the pre-eminence accorded to Alceste, such goodness is implicitly defined as self-sacrifice. Alceste, the women's queen, gains her status among the heroines of the *Legend of Good Women* on the basis of her "grete goodnesse" (G 499), which is shown in her self-negating death in exchange for her husband's life: "She that for hire husbonde ches to dye, / And ek to gon to helle rather than he" (G 501-502). Christ-like in choosing death to permit life, Alceste is set forth as *the* exemplar, a "kalendar . . . / To any woman that wol lover bee" (F 542-43), but taken in series, the legends show this ideal to be, finally, self-defeating.

At first glance, it may appear as if Lucrece fulfilled the criterion of selflessly choosing death for the sake of her husband, or more specifically for the sake of her husband's honour, but this is largely the result of narratorial obfuscation.[9] Whereas Lucrece may have achieved saint-like status in the Roman world as seen through a medieval lens, her status among Christian commentators is more ambivalent. Early in her legend, the narrator refers to Augustine's compassion for Lucrece's suicide: "The grete Austyn hath gret compassioun / Of this Lucresse, that starf at Rome toun" (1690-91). However, it is actually Jerome who approves of suicide after rape, whereas Augustine condemns it. Using Lucrece's case as a well known example, Augustine argues that in killing herself, a rape victim murders an innocent person for the crime of another, and moreover, in the particular case of Lucrece Augustine condemns the suicide because it is motivated by the desire to avoid shame, and thus by pride.[10] By speaking of Augustine's sympathy, the narrator clearly reverses the facts, thus drawing further attention to them. Not only is her suicide questionable from a Christian point of view, but Lucrece willfully persists in her intention, thus denying the patriarchial authority of her husband and her father, both of whom have already pronounced her blameless and do not require any form of exculpation. Paraphrasing Augustine's argument, Jean de Meun lets Lucrece appear almost as an example of stereotypically female stubbornness rather than of exemplary chastity:

> They urged her strongly to let go her sorrow; they gave her persuasive reasons; and her husband particularly comforted her with compassion . . . and studied to find lively arguments to prove to her that her body had not sinned when her heart did not wish the sin (for the body cannot be a sinner if the heart does not consent to it). But . . . she answered them without shame:
>
> 'Fair lords, no matter who may pardon me for the filthy sin that weighs on me so heavily, no matter how I am pardoned, I do not pardon myself of the penance for that sin.'
>
> (*Roman de la rose* 8608-37)

Augustine's assessment also re-echoes in another legend, that of Phyllis, who, after being abandoned by Demophon, reproaches herself for having been too liberal in bestowing her love: "But I wot why ye come nat, . . . / For I was of my love to yow to fre" (2520-21); and having recognized and acknowledged her folly in being too trusting (2525), she commits suicide out of "dispeyr" (2557). Here the narrator does everything he can to separate the heroine from any suggestion of martyrdom and sainthood on the basis of the Christian hagiographic analogy. From the Christian perspective, her suicide resulting from despair is the ultimate and the only unforgivable sin since it irrevocably denies the divine promise of grace. Moreover, Phyllis's acknowledgement of her folly invites a blame-the-victim attitude, illogically implying that if Phyllis had shrewdly refused to sleep with Demophon, he would have returned to her. Thus, these legends examine–and deny–the spiritual foundations of the heroines' status as saints and martyrs. Far from being an indication of the depth and purity of the heroines' devotion, these suicides are depicted as sinful–as well as plain foolish.

Another strategy to subvert the application of Christian concepts occurs in the "Legend of Dido." Dido is continually referred to in imagery otherwise characteristic of Mary, heaven's queen, queen of grace, and mother and maid–roles successively assigned to Dido. Initially, Dido is depicted as a gracious queen whose neighbouring lords come to her court "of hire socour to beseke" (1053); when Aeneas arrives, she is in the temple in the midst of her devotions (in a scene found neither in the *Aeneid* nor in the *Heroides*), but immediately "hire herte hath pite of his wo" (1078) and she promises to "save" his ships and men (1089). As a result of her intercession, Aeneas feels on entering her palace as if he "is come to paradys / Out of the swolow of helle" and now lives "in joye" (1103-1104). Dido surpasses everyone in "fredom" (1127) and is accompanied by "an huge route" of women (1197). Eventually, Aeneas, like Joseph, is commanded in a divinely inspired dream to leave the country of his temporary abode in order fulfill destiny, but in Aeneas's case there can be no question of taking his betrothed wife, the now pregnant Dido, with him. The transvaluation, in which an initially quasi-Marian Dido allows her religious fervour to be replaced by erotic love, culminates in her suicide, when she makes a burnt offering of herself as she leaps onto the burning altar (1350) and kills herself with Aeneas's sword. Formerly a model of purity, fortitude, and wifely devotion, Dido has become guilty of the ultimate sin of suicide as a result of her acknowledging her sexuality and desire–exactly what is suppressed and often symbolically removed, especially in those saints whose martyrdom includes the excision of their breasts. Contrary to the explicit rhetorical purpose of the *Legend* to depict "good women," Dido is nothing of the kind: sexual desire makes her break her vow of chaste widowhood, and the frustration of this desire causes her suicide. The echo of the Christian wedding formula during Dido and Aeneas's "wedding" in the cave scene–on bended knee, Aeneas "swore so depe to hire to be trewe / For wel or wo" that Dido "tok hym for husbonde and becom his wyf / For everemo, whil that hem laste lyf" (1234-39)–only emphasises Dido's departure from the role of virtuous women, who "keped . . . here maydenhede, / Or elles wedlok, or here widewehede / . . . / . . . for verray vertu and clennesse" (G 294-97).

Indeed, if even Lucrece fails to qualify as a "good woman" (Dido clearly is a much less promising candidate), it appears that the very premises underlying the *Legend*'s particular ideal of feminine goodness are questionable. Insisting on a single criterion regardless of circumstances, this ideal stipulates far too restrictive a mould, enforcing infinite repetition without allowing for any variation and thus preventing complexity and flattening any story into two-dimensionality, with the result that the tales included in the *Legend* continually escape the given pattern. In fact, by the definition typified by Alceste, none of the heroines of the individual legends satisfies the criteria for being a "good woman," with the possible exception of Hypsipyle, who provides rest and comfort to Jason on his arduous journey but later simply pines away after being deserted. Objectively speaking, all other women fail. Cleopatra is married to a known bigamist, Tisbe makes her "clennesse" and "maydenhede" (G 294, 297) suspect by being overeager to be united with her lover, Dido and Phyllis commit suicide out of despair, Medea fornicates with an adulterer, Lucrece wilfully commits suicide out of shame (which in Augustine's argument is another form of pride), Ariadne saves and then marries Theseus in order to gain status, Philomene becomes her brother-in-law's victim in an incestuous rape but certainly does not choose to sacrifice herself for him, and Hypermnestra commits incest (though the narrator does his best to explain it away). Yet despite the sometimes appalling details, all of the female characters in the *Legend* are categorized as "good women." In other words, a convention, once established, becomes a compulsion, imposing a superficial conformity on the narrative regardless of the deeper incongruities.

Nor are the purportedly "good women" of the *Legend* necessarily "good" in any terms independent of those defined in the Prologue. None of the heroines is redeemed by behaviour which would objectively make her "good" in an ethical, political, or social sense. Cleopatra and Dido both abandon their political and societal responsibilities as sovereign rulers, exposing their respective countries to social disorder and to the very palpable danger of annexation by other rulers as they themselves withdraw into the private sphere before eventually abandoning their kingdoms altogether by committing suicide. Dido, moreover, drains the economic resources of her newly founded city by enriching Aeneas, who clearly has neither the means nor the intention to reciprocate. Even within the private, moral sphere, Dido's immoderate devotion to Aeneas is highly questionable since it entails the breach of her vow of chastity to her dead husband Sychaeus in favour of the gratification of her sensual desire for a man whom Chaucer depicts more as an opportunistic vagabond than as the epic founder of Rome. As she admits to her sister Anna, she was attracted by his striking masculinity and his foreign, exotic appeal:

> This newe Troyan is so in my thought,
> For that me thynketh he is so wel ywrought,
> And ek so likly for to ben a man,
>
> . . . .
> Have ye nat herd him telle his aventure?
>   (1172-77)

And the narrator similarly comments, "for he was a straunger, somwhat she Likede hym the bet . . ." (1075-76).

While the narrator emphasizes that he is following Virgil and Ovid in presenting the story of Dido and Aeneas, including Dido's betrayal of her vow to her dead husband, Sheila Delany argues that Chaucer almost certainly was aware of a very different tradition "sustained by various grammarians, Virgil commentators, and medieval authors including Servius, Macrobius, Priscian, Petrarch, and early Dante commentators" as well as Boccaccio's *De claris mulieribus* (*Naked Text* 194-95) and briefly mentioned in Augustine's *Confessions* and John of Salisbury's *Policraticus* (Desmond 161); in this tradition Dido never comes in contact with Aeneas but remains the model of wifely piety. Jerome, whose work Chaucer certainly knew well, likewise depicts Dido as a model wife, who sacrifices herself on Sychaeus's funeral pyre, preferring literally "to burn rather than to marry" (*Adversus Jovinianum* I.43, qtd. in Blamires 69). By electing to follow Virgil rather than the alternative tradition, Chaucer chooses to depict Dido as faithless as well as economically and politically irresponsible, not to mention blinded by the sin of lust. In his rejection of the tradition which represents Dido as good because chaste, Chaucer brazenly takes the inversion of normal values to an extreme. The demand that female characters be depicted as "good" simply because they have come to grief in a love relationship here leads to the absurd situation where a tradition which constructs the character as genuinely virtuous is ignored in favour of another which makes the heroine's claim to self-sacrificing virtue in love unsustainable but is more affecting because of its touching sentimentality. The "Legend of Dido" thus is a parody of the basic concept governing the *Legend*–but a parody that is invited by the very terms in which that concept is articulated.

However, Dido is certainly not alone among the women in the *Legend* in betraying family loyalties. While Tisbe simply acts against the wishes of her parents (with disastrous consequences), Ariadne and Phaedra actively and knowingly betray their father Minos, finding a model in their father's betrayal of Nisus's daughter Scylla after she had betrayed *her* father and city for Minos's sake, as the narrator emphasizes by reviewing Minos's history at the beginning of the "Legend of Ariadne." Worse, Ariadne and Phaedra seem to be motivated neither by compassion for Theseus as he is to enter the Labyrinth nor by romantic devotion to him, but by an ambition to raise their social status. After Theseus has consented to Ariadne's suggestion of marriage (though under duress as he still needs their help to have any hope of escaping death in the Labyrinth), Ariadne quietly gloats to her sister,

'Now, syster myn, . . .
Now be we duchesses, bothe I and ye,
And sekered to the regals of Athenes,
And bothe hereafter likly to ben quenes.'
(2126-29)

In an unanticipated reversal, however, Ariadne soon finds herself outmanoeuvred by her sister, who becomes first Theseus's accomplice in Ariadne's desertion as they leave hand in hand (2172-73) and later becomes his wife. What Chaucer omits is the rest of Phaedra's story of incest with Theseus's son Hippolytus. Omitted, too, is the story of Ariadne and Phaedra's mother Pasiphaë, whose copulation with the bull brought about the Minotaur, thus necessitating Theseus's arrival in Crete in the first place. Ariadne, socially ambitious in the most unladylike manner, thus falls victim to her own manipulation of Theseus's problem as much as to the sexually and morally skewed family environment; what the narrator says of Theseus's son Demophon in the "Legend of Phyllis," namely, that "wiked fruit cometh of a wiked tre" (2395), applies equally to Ariadne and Phaedra. As can be observed, once the pattern is established by which any female character is classified as "good" simply because her love relationship has failed in a spectacular fashion, the convention becomes self-perpetuating, regardless of its incongruity, and the series of legends only serves to demonstrate the reductiveness and rigidity of any pattern that is applied generically.

Nor do the other heroines necessarily conform to the image of a "good woman," however such goodness may be defined. Medea is a case in point. Her legend focuses on her abandonment by Jason and her difficult life as a single parent, and only a brief reference to her having "saved hym his lyf and his honour" (1648) glosses over and revalorizes her betrayal of her father and her murder and dismemberment of her brother, but her gruesome vengeance on Jason's new bride and her killing of her two children by Jason are silently excluded altogether. Although the narrator portrays Jason as the devil incarnate, Medea would clearly appear as his equal if all of her myth were retold. Her status as victim in love can be achieved only by the silent exclusion of the greater part of her myth. But as usual, such an omission only serves to foreground the excised parts of the well-known narrative, thus precisely raising the questions which it purports to negate. In comparison with the events in other legends, Hypermnestra's incestuous marriage to her cousin Lyno seems positively innocent. Yet as is so often the case in Chaucer, the narrator makes an effort to excuse the incest ("For thilke tyme was spared no lynage," 2602), thereby only drawing attention to it.

To write of such "good women," then, is just as reductivist as to ask, "What is woman?" and to answer, "Man's undoing" (*Life of Secundus*, qtd. in Blamires 100). Such type-casting of female characters according to a single mould enforces the singular, forever fixed and deprived of multiplicity, complexity, and diversity. The individual legends enact the reductive agenda set forth in the Prologue, where the narrator is required to write

> a gloryous legende
> Of goode women, maydenes and wyves,
> That were trewe in lovynge al here lyves;
> And telle of false men that hem betrayen,
> That al here lyf ne don nat but assayen
> How manye wemen they may don a shame.
> (G 473-78)

This agenda is also part of romance and hagiography, both of which genres allow for essentially only one type of woman respectively. The *Legend of Good Women* shows that suffering for love does not necessarily make women good. In literature, there must be room for Criseyde with all her complexity. At the same time, the *Legend* refuses to allow for easy mental categorizing of "good women" as demanded in the Prologue. The work does not even allow for closure; the apparently fragmentary end of the "Legend of Hypermnestra" and the absence of any kind of final summation, not to mention the failure to execute the entire plan set out in the Prologue, keep the *Legend* open-ended, as if any number of additional variations on the same idea might be added–*ad infinitum.*

All three genres–epic myth, courtly romance, and hagiography–are here brought into conjunction with each other, with the result that the authority of each genre breaks down as each is stripped to the bone. The "naked [sub-]text" of each of the three genres is shown to be reductivist in its totalizing tendencies. In the one, women must serve as an unquestioning instrument, temporarily used (and abused) to bring about the hero's success in his epic struggle; in the second, each woman must be a beautiful and passive goddess-like ornament, yet also the ultimate judge of her worshipper, with her own body becoming the trophy which she is ultimately expected to bestow; and in the third, women must be devoted to the point of self-sacrifice in their extreme and self-negating submission to their Lord. Clearly, all three genres allow for only one pattern respectively, and their attempted conflation demonstrates the flaws in each.

To take female characters from classical mythology and then give them the attributes of courtly ladies while also requiring them to behave like saints . . . is to write "courtly hagiomythography," a monstrous hybrid that is doomed from the start.

Notes

1. Although concentrating on the function and role of the poet as artist in the two Prologues and only briefly glancing at the individual legends, Baker made the same point in general terms when he remarked that "The final rejection of the court of love is, I think, here in this poem" (5); the *Legend* deals with a tradition which is "Artistically and philosophically sterile" (18).

2. Allen makes a related point when he argues that as readers we must "reject the narrator's authority in favour of our own experience of reading. . . . we must learn to make our own judgments about women and men and about our relationship, as readers, to Chaucer's narrator. . . . , reading the poem as one which validates Chaucer's poetry and his female characters–particularly Criseyde–and which encourages the reader to be self-conscious, independent, and affirmative" (420).

3. Fyler surveys the manipulation of the Ovidian sources, especially the suppression of details, in *Chaucer and Ovid* 96-120.

4. Commenting on this exclusion of clearly well-known details, Meale observes, "Chaucer's Medea, by comparison [with Boccaccio's], is characterised by absence. Her legend is, in itself, brief (it consists of ninety-nine lines), and its impact is lessened by the fact that it is bracketed with another, that of Hypsipyle" (61). As Meale shows, Medea's story undergoes a similar reshaping, though for different ends, by Chaucer's near-contemporaries Boccaccio and Christine de Pizan.

5. However, an appropriately courtly environment by no means guarantees success in courtly love. In the "Legend of Dido," much emphasis is placed on the depiction of a glittering aristocratic lifestyle, complete with jousting, elaborately prepared hunting and hawking, feasting, music and dancing, and distribution of largesse in the form of coins and lavish gifts (1114-24, 1189-1211).

6. Such subversions are already prefigured in the reversal of gender roles concerning Cupid and Alceste in the Prologue. As Sheila Delany remarks, this role reversal "gives us a male deity who is narrowminded, selfish and temperamental, with a female adviser who is balanced, objective and controlled" ("Rewriting" 79).

7. Similarly observing that almost all of the legends contain references to marriage or at least troth-plight, Minnis concludes that Chaucer playfully replaces conventional misogyny and misogamy with the narrator's "gynocentric and gamocentric" outlook (169).

8. Examining the details of the male characters' oaths, R. F. Green asserts the legality of the marriages in the *Legend* under both canon law and English customary law, and concludes that "all the heroines we are considering might properly regard themselves as married to the men who betray them" (15).

9. LaHood seems mistaken when he asserts that "Chaucer begins and ends [the 'Legend of Lucrece'] with clear-cut examples of Christianization" (274) and that "In Ovid Lucretia's virtue is natural, whereas in Chaucer it is supernatural" (276).

10. Galloway surveys the views of late medieval, including fourteenth-century English, commentators concerning Lucretia's rape and suicide, especially with regard to the Roman cultural and ideological context. Certain details of Chaucer's non-Ovidian phrasing and his emphasis on the cultural forces which make suicide the most desirable option are, Galloway argues, indebted to these views.

Works Cited

Allen, Peter L. "Reading Chaucer's Good Women." *Chaucer Review* 21 (1987): 419-34.

Baker, Donald C. "Dreamer and Critic: The Poet in the *Legend of Good Women*." *University of Colorado Studies in Language and Literature* 9 (1963): 4-18.

Blamires, Alcuin, ed. *Woman Defamed and Woman Defended: An Anthology of Medieval Texts.* Oxford: Oxford UP, 1992.

Chaucer, Geoffrey. *The Riverside Chaucer.* Ed. Larry D. Benson. 3rd ed. Boston: Houghton Mifflin, 1987.

Dahlberg, Charles, trans. *The Romance of the Rose by Guillaume de Lorris and Jean de Meun.* Princeton: Princeton UP, 1971.

Delany, Sheila. *The Naked Text: Chaucer's Legend of Good Women.* Berkeley: U of California P, 1994.

—. "Rewriting Woman Good: Gender and the Anxiety of Influence in Two Late-Medieval Texts." *Medieval Literary Politics: Shapes of Ideology*. Manchester: Manchester UP, 1990. 74-87.

Desmond, Marilynn. *Reading Dido: Gender, Textuality, and the Medieval Aeneid*. Minneapolis: U of Minnesota P, 1994.

Dinshaw, Carolyn. *Chaucer's Sexual Poetics*. Madison: U of Wisconsin P, 1989.

Frank, Robert Worth, Jr. *Chaucer and the Legend of Good Women*. Cambridge, MA: Harvard UP, 1972.

Fyler, John M. *Chaucer and Ovid*. New Haven: Yale UP, 1979.

Galloway, Andrew. "Chaucer's *Legend of Lucrece* and the Critique of Ideology in Fourteenth-Century England." *ELH* 60 (1993): 813-32.

Green, Richard Firth. "Chaucer's Victimized Women." *Studies in the Age of Chaucer* 10 (1988): 3-21.

LaHood, Marvin J. "Chaucer's 'The Legend of Lucrece'." *Philological Quarterly* 43 (1964): 274-76.

Meale, Carol M. "Legends of Good Women in the European Middle Ages." *Archiv für das Studium der Neueren Sprachen und Literaturen* 229 (1992): 55-70.

Minnis, Alastair J. "Repainting the Lion: Chaucer's Profeminist Narratives." Ed. Roy Eriksen. *Contexts of Pre-Novel Narrative: The European Tradition*. Berlin and New York: Mouton de Gruyter, 1994. 153-77.

Murray J. Evans

COLERIDGE'S SUBLIME AND LANGLAND'S SUBJECT
IN THE PARDON SCENE
OF "PIERS PLOWMAN"

Much has been written on the pardon scene in Passus 7 of the B-text of
Piers Plowman. Not only is the passage an important one, the climax of the
first section of the poem or *Visio* according to some of its manuscript
traditions; but the interpretation of the episode has also been one of the chief
controversies in Langland criticism. Useful surveys of the controversy
already exist (e.g., Pearsall, *Bibliography* 200-06). I am instead interested
in how frequent characterizations of the poem as sublime raise questions
about the subject in Passus 7 and the larger poem.[1] In a recent essay, which
surveys theories of the sublime in relation to criticism of the poem, I have
suggested a contrast between the views of Samuel Taylor Coleridge, eminent
theorist on the subject and the sublime, and those of Freud and Lacan
(Evans 437). I do not dispute that there is value in psychoanalytic readings
of medieval texts. I am concerned, however, that familiar repetition can
transform this one hermeneutic model into fossilized presupposition: for
"cultural schema, taking on material weight with the names they assume, not
only expose or describe actions and allow us to identify them . . . but also
preclude alternative perceptions of the same scene." It is thus all too easy to
allow "the unnamed and the unmarked to merge undifferentiated into the
background" (Stanbury 262). As a counterpoint to the limits, and sometimes
fossilization, of a neo-Freudian hermeneutic, this essay provides a reading
of Passus 7 according to Coleridge's views of the subject and the sublime.
    I begin with a definition of the psychoanalytic sublime and its presence
in the work of Anne Middleton on *Piers Plowman*. Then, in contrast, I
discuss the Coleridgean sublime and show how it informs Piers's literal
departure from the poem in the pardon scene. Here the relevance of Patricia
Yaeger's notions of the female sublime leads me to consider, in turn, two
curious moments in the pardon scene: Will's gaze at the pardon over Piers's

155

and the priest's shoulders, and Will's musing upon waking, "ful pencif in herte," on Piers. These two moments in the passus raise questions about the construction, distinctness, and stability of the subject, questions to which Coleridge provides alternative answers to those of modern psychoanalytic theory. After noting a theoretical gap, which defers my consideration of the gendering of Langland's subject, I finally relate my Coleridgean analysis to the problematic status of Will's making poetry (challenged by Imaginatif in Passus 12) and the nature of "doing well" in the poem.

Thomas Weiskel's *Romantic Sublime* is a major modern Freudian reading of the sublime, i.e., the sense and articulation of what "transcend[s] the human" (3). Weiskel proposes three stages in human experience of the sublime: an initial and "habitual[,] . . . unconscious" relation between mind and object; a breakdown of this relationship by which "[e]ither mind or object is suddenly in excess"; and finally, the recovery of balance when the mind establishes a new relationship between subject and object, taking the eruption of the second stage "as symbolizing the mind's relation to a transcendent order" (23-24). Neil Hertz underlines that Weiskel's characterization of the experience of the sublime is Oedipal, involving the resolution of "the Oedipal moment" or "moment of blockage" into "a one-to-one confrontation" (Hertz 53) between the Kantian imagination and its symbolic father, Kant's reason, as well as the self-sacrificing identification of the former with the latter (Hertz 51, citing Weiskel 92ff.). In this paper, I will use "Oedipal" in this sense of conflict and forceful resolution.

One *Piers Plowman* scholar who adapts such a view of the sublime in eloquent and illuminating essays on the poem is Anne Middleton.[2] She argues that a recurring kind of episode–the dispute or combat, without clear resolution–is paradigmatic to Langland's poem ("Narration" 95-97). Typically, one combatant stands for "natural knowledge" from "personal experience," and the other for "authoritative, . . . systematic, universal" knowledge (106). Middleton's Freudian terminology is evident in her focus on this recurring narrative dynamic as a manifestation of "'the unconscious of the work,'" an "enabling gesture" not confined to any one character, and a "free-floating combative animus" often disproportionate to the event (100-01, citing Macherey 92): "The self as a fictive narrative center for the work appears as an abashed interloper in a stern pantheon of serious genres and clerical modes of discourse" (110-11). According to Middleton, moreover, the pardon scene–in which Piers disputes with the priest and then disappears from the literal narrative of the poem–"offers a paradigm of [this] basic conflict and its outcome throughout the poem" (109). By the end of the scene, Piers shifts from "present authority to absent object of desire" in "the almost erotic intensity of the subject's longing for him," "a human image held in the memory as the Other" (109). Middleton does not pursue the potentially feminist implications of her diction which, in the discourse of projected male desire, are also specifically Lacanian.

An Oedipal / combative note returns in Middleton's subsequent characterization of the discourse of *Piers Plowman* as that of the "life" or "ideal . . . form of living," comprising "individual exercises of lay piety," "*oppositional* practices in action, speech, and writing." This Oedipal note assumes a political dimension, in the shift in discourse in Langland's period from the "totalizing expository array of 'orders' or 'estates'" and monastic spirituality to the "life," deriving from fraternal or mendicant forms of spirituality ("Langland's Lives" 229, 231-32). Accordingly, after the pardon scene, "[b]oth Piers and the supplanted discourses that had called him into action are . . . irrecoverable as social institutions," able to "be repossessed only in subjective reiteration, relived in memory and re-enacted through the language of self-modelling: one can never again *find* Piers, still less seat him securely in a position of leadership, but rather only *remember* and desire him" (233). In the larger narrative, Piers and Will are "deconstructed" (237) by this "built-in principle of degeneration in late-medieval spiritual discourses," as the poem culminates in Conscience's defeat by the friars when "both the defender and the destroyer of Unity are patently the literary creatures of mendicant ethical discourse" (233). Middleton also suggests that Langland realizes a similar deconstruction awaits his own authorship ("Kynde Name" 76), signing himself as "maker" at numerous points of crisis for Will in the poem. Underwriting these unmakings of Piers, Will, and Langland as poet, then, is the discourse of the life that constitutes them and that they are subject to. Thus, in assuming the constitution of the unconscious subject by ideology, Middleton draws on Althusser, who, as Terry Eagleton (171) reminds us, applies the psychoanalytic theory of Freud and Lacan to society.

Middleton's extended analysis of Piers, Will, and William Langland as subjects in the poem is a compelling combination of historical scholarship, close reading, and more recent literary theory. Her discussions also mingle with or imply a discourse of the sublime, for example, in terms of the excess beyond the current boundaries of knowledge in "Langland's enterprise–the wholly *gratuitous* and virtually inexplicable aspect of the lifelong imperative to write, and the uncategorizable nature of the result" ("Langland's Lives"

238 and Evans 432-33). Since I have elsewhere discussed at length Middleton's use of the sublime (Evans 432-35), I would here like to propose a Coleridgean psychological reading of the sublime in the pardon scene, which casts into relief some aspects of the poem that psychoanalytic readings of the poem may not. In this connection, it is significant that Coleridge's is the first recorded usage, in 1800, of "unconscious" as "Not realized or known as existing in oneself" (*OED* A.3).

First, it is noteworthy that Coleridge eschews a combative context for the sublime. In contrast to Immanuel Kant, and Weiskel's own Freudian analysis of the Kantian sublime mentioned above, Raimondo Modiano discerns in Coleridge's sublime no mention of the "mind's rupture from sensible forms" and "flight into the supersensible realm of ideas," as there is in Kant; no "threat of being engulfed" by a violent and chaotic natural world as a prelude to self-aggrandizement; no antecedent "crisis or collapse" of the imagination, "[n]either pain nor bafflement" ("Coleridge and the Sublime" 116-17). Lacking "the rhetoric of power" of much eighteenth-century theory of the sublime (*Coleridge and the Concept of Nature* 121-22), Coleridge's "form of transcendence occurs gradually . . . through an intense engagement with the objects of sense" ("Coleridge and the Sublime" 117). Steven Knapp makes a similar point in defining Coleridge's association of "a metaphysic and psychology of reconciliation with [Edmund Burke's] aesthetic of terror and discontinuity" (10). The difference relates to Coleridge's handling of contradictions, what Elinor Shaffer calls "his characteristically moderate, semi-dialectical method of progressive redefinition: by multiplying slighter gradations between the two terms, they are made to approach each other" ("Revolution" 214). So, in the words of *Biographia Literaria* concerning the "deception" of "telling the half of a fact, and omitting the other half," the "mutual counteraction and neutralization" of both halves leads to the "*whole* truth," a "tertium aliquid different from either" (Engell and Bate I.44, qtd. in Knapp 29). That Coleridge's "tertium aliquid . . ." or "third something else" may at least initially have the aspect of "the vast Terra Incognita of Knowledge" is no impediment: "[o]ur Ignorance with all the intermediates of obscurity [between the known and the ultimate] is the *condition* of our ever-increasing Knowledge" (Coburn, III 3825, cited in Taylor, *Coleridge's Writings* 18-19).

A classic enunciation of this view of the sublime as it relates to literary texts occurs in Coleridge's lecture of December 9, 1811, to the London Philosophical Society, on Shakespeare's *Romeo and Juliet* (Collier 64-66, qtd. in Knapp 8):

I can understand and allow for an effort of the mind, when it would describe what it cannot satisfy itself with the description of, to reconcile opposites and qualify contradictions, leaving a middle state of mind more strictly appropriate to the imagination than any other, when it is, as it were, hovering between images.

Coleridge then quotes the description of Death in Milton's *Paradise Lost*, a commonplace of eighteenth-century discussions of the sublime (Knapp 52):

> The other shape,
> If shape it might be call'd, that shape had none
> Distinguishable in member, joint, or limb,
> Or substance might be call'd, that shadow seem'd,
> For each seem'd either: black it stood as night.
> (II. 666-70)

Then Coleridge concludes,

The grandest efforts of poetry are where the imagination is called forth, not to produce a distinct form, but a strong working of the mind, still offering what is still repelled, and again creating what is again rejected; the result being what the poet wishes to impress, namely, the substitution of a sublime feeling of the unimaginable for a mere image.

My suggestion is that "a middle state of mind . . . when it is, as it were, hovering between images" is a useful model to take to reading *Piers Plowman*, and that the effect of the poem for some of us readers, historically situated this side of Coleridge's sublime, is "the substitution of a sublime feeling of the unimaginable for a mere image." In the memorable phrase of Morton Bloomfield, the poem so often seems to us "a commentary on an unknown text" (32). Indeed, Lee Rust Brown reminds us that the notion of the poem not written, as sustaining the existing fragments of a poem, is a Romantic legacy for modern readers (245).

Such "hovering" is evident in much critical discourse on the pardon scene in Langland's poem, as when the pardon is neither a pardon nor not-a-pardon, but some "tertium aliquid." John Burrow, for example, cites with approval R. W. Frank's assertion that the tearing of the pardon is a "clash between form and content"; when Piers tears the pardon, he rejects pardons as a form, and not his pardon's content (Burrow 223, citing Frank 322-23). I am presently interested, though, in one context where we may experience "the substitution of a sublime feeling of the unimaginable for a mere image": when after the priest's unsuccessful attempt to interpret the pardon (Schmidt B.7.105-14), Piers "for pure tene" tears the pardon and announces a change of life (7.115-30). Burrow points out that the allegory of the dream narrative is here broken. Langland does not *show* us what Piers will be doing if not "pardon-mongering" (224). What will Piers's doing well–i.e., following the injunction of the pardon–look like, at this point and in the continuing allegory of the poem? What Piers says, before he disappears, is somewhat clearer. After citing Psalm 22:4, "(For) though I should walk in the midst of the shadow of death, I will fear no evils: for thou art with me" (Schmidt 7.116-17n), he announces his plans:

> "I shal cessen of my sowyng," quod Piers, "and swynke noght
> so harde,
> Ne aboute my bely joye so bisy be na moore;
> Of preieres and of penaunce my plough shal ben herafter,
> And wepen whan I sholde slepe, though whete breed me faille."
> (7.118-21)

His speech continues with allusions to sorrowful penance (Psalm 41:4) and the parable of God's provision for the "foweles in the feld," against human worry for sustenance (Luke 12:22). On the one hand, yes, there is the combativeness of Piers's anger at the priest's problem with the pardon:

> "Peter!" quod the preest thoo, "I kan no pardon fynde
> But 'Do wel and have wel, and God shal have thi soule,'
> And 'Do yvel and have yvel, and hope thow noon oother
> That after thi deeth day the devel shal have thi soule!'"
> (7.111-14)

The priest and Piers's dispute, apparently about his right to expound scripture, follows. On the other hand, there is much in the passage that is not combative. Steven Knapp's study of Coleridge's theories of the sublime and of allegory discusses his notion of conversions, in a way that illuminates Piers's own, as "moments of simultaneous self-discovery and self-loss": the "self they temporarily disclose can easily become the object of nostalgia. But . . . the exhilaration of conversion derives from the ease with which earlier selves . . . are discarded" (47). The puzzling gap opened up after the "pure tene" of Piers's tearing of the pardon is this sublimely non-combative ease of his change of life–this, and the quickness and duration of his vanishing from the poem.

I would like to pursue this non-combative sublime with reference to Patricia Yaeger's notions of the female sublime, which she contrasts with the "oedipal" or "conventional sublime" of those visionary encounters with nature in Shelley or Wordsworth: "the sublime of one-on-one confrontation that aspires to the recuperation of identity through the sudden overcoming of what blocks or constrains" (Edelman 215). While Yaeger cites Weiskel in her argument, her ideological preference is for the "female sublime," comprising different kinds of visionary empowerment. Her models are surprisingly illuminating of Piers's actions and Will's desire.

Yaeger stipulates that Wordsworth, like other nineteenth-century male writers, discovers "the sublime as a mode allowing trespass and appropriation of 'forbidden and illicit forces'" (199, citing Wolf 205); thus he becomes a poetic genius. In comparison, Piers in the pardon episode also desires apparently forbidden powers, the authority to publicly explicate texts and teach Christian truth. Ridiculed by the priest for attempting to do so (7.135-36), he leaves the narrative as literal ploughman. According to Yaeger, the Wordsworthian experience of the masculine sublime also entails an appropriation of energy "so as to strengthen the ego" (210). In contrast, Piers is denied any share in the charism of preaching, and the boundaries of his "ego" as virtuous ploughman dissolve in the poem, at Will's waking at the end of passus 7. Thus the pardon episode resembles Yaeger's "failed sublime," in which visionary and enabling power is "snatched away–often by a masculine counter-sublime," here the priest speaking for the office of the lettered and male clergy. This episode, moreover, is illuminated by Yaeger's "sovereign sublime," in which the subject "expends or spills whatever power the sublime moment–in its structure of crisis, confrontation, and renewed domination, has promised to hoard" (201-04). The argument breaks off, unresolved; Piers "expends" whatever moral suasion he has had as reforming ploughman and drops, as such, out of the poem. I think these notions of the feminine sublime do illuminate, to some extent, what is happening in the episode. My point is that the resemblance between Piers's actions and Yaeger's "failed" and "sovereign" sublimes underline non-Oedipal dimensions to Piers as subject. To stress the combative aspects of the scene would miss this other side of the picture.[3]

Expansion of this picture leads to what I find to be two curious moments in the episode. The first moment is Will's gaze, behind Piers and the priest, at the pardon: "And Piers at his preiere the pardon unfoldeth– / And I bihynde hem bothe biheld al the bulle" (7.107-08). In a way reminiscent of Yaeger's words, the "self . . . is not obliterated, nor is the object swallowed up by the subject that has perceived it, but the moment of self-structuring is revealed in its doubleness" (207). If we mean to examine Langland's subject as a *tertium aliquid* in terms of the Coleridgean sublime, the tableau of this gaze would suggest that Will's subjectivity cannot be understood apart from Piers and the priest–and the pardon.

What kind of *tertium aliquid* is this subjectivity, then, and how is it sublime? What kind of subjectivity is being enacted in the dynamics of the gaze? First, there is the direction of this gaze. (I will discuss the gaze as it comes to focus on Piers shortly.) Will and, I would suggest, we as readers look at the pardon over the shoulders of Piers and the priest. While this graphic moment may not be a breakdown of allegory such as E. Talbot Donaldson (79) identifies in Passus 20 when Will meets Need outside his dream (20.4), it does transgress one expected boundary for the subject by Will's entering "his own dream in a way that he has not hitherto done" (Bennett 222, line 109n). My use of "trangression" has, of course, a post-structuralist ring. But the argument "employing Kant's use of the parergon [border or frame] to move the boundaries and to call in question the clarity of the distinction between the intrinsic and the extrinsic" was first made, not by Derrida in *La Vérité en peinture* (1978), but by Coleridge in 1825 in *Aids to Reflection* (Shaffer, "Illusion and Imagination" 147). I take this tableau of Will's inserted gaze to interrogate the boundaries between Will, Piers, and the pardon as they bear on subjectivity. The means of this interrogation, for Kant and for Coleridge, is the sublime, "a way of making and figuring distinctions" (Cheetham 359): in Shaffer's terms quoted above, "by multiplying slighter gradations between" two apparently contradictory terms, "they are made to approach each other" ("Revolution" 214), from which proximity arises a *tertium aliquid.* Langland's, and Coleridge's, subject thus bears some resemblance to the "destabilising of the category of the centred person" prevalent in psychoanalytic and post-structuralist theory (Kay and Rubin 3).

Second, the focus of this subjectivity is on an act, in this case the act of beholding, as well as on its object, the pardon. The tableau would suggest that to be a subject involves acting according, not to a logical premise, but to a logically contradictory pardon. Such a pardon, for example, apparently pardons nothing, and should not, logically, be torn up by Piers, Truth's servant, since it is from Truth (Pearsall, *Piers Plowman* 174, line 291n). This is also a pardon whose content governs not just the individual's eternal outcome, but according to the early long section of the passus (7.9-104), all social relations: "Do wel and have wel, and God shal have thi soule . . . ." Those who do well in their various social stations, this opening section repeatedly says, will also receive the benefits of Piers's pardon. I agree with those readers of the poem who have desisted from trying to correlate the successive triads of Dowel, Dobet, and Dobest in the poem, which taken together, are no more communicative on a logical level than the pardon. But the tableau of the gaze would suggest that subjectivity involves contemplating an act–the injunction of the pardon–that must become an act in deed, and that this act of doing well, in answer to prayers for grace, is its own justification "after oure deth day . . . / At the day of dome" (7.196-201).

Steven Cole has recently elaborated such a view of act, contemplated mentally and enacted socially–what he calls Coleridge's "social production of agency" in the subject. This view hinges on Coleridge's definition of "Will" as "a power of *originating* an act or state" (Beer 268 and Cole 91).[4] The will is to be directed to an "ultimate end" that enables "powers of self-construction" (Cole 99). The end Coleridge mentions in his "Essay on Faith," Cole continues, is the Golden Rule, doing to others as you would have done to you (Cole 104-5). (The analogy with Langland's Dowel is close enough.) A subject's consciousness of the Golden Rule is of "a shared human identity" with other subjects (105), the argument continues; accordingly, unless one chooses to treat neighbour as thing and not person, "my treatment of others is that which constitutes my own self" (106). For Coleridge, though, the act of will does not begin in the outer world with the neighbour. "[E]ven the very first step, . . . the Initiative, of this Process," what Coleridge calls "the becoming conscious of a Conscience," itself "partakes of the nature of an *Act*" (Jackson and Jackson 836) and thus "emerges out of consciousness" (Cole 107). This act, according to this end of loving neighbour as self, establishes "I" and "Thou" as equal, since each has a will, yet also different, since subjects use their wills differently (109). Finally, "Unlike a multitude of Tygers, a million of men is far other from a million times one man. Each man in a numerous society is not simply co-existent but virtually co-organized with and into the multitude, of which he is an integral Part. His *idem* is modified by the *alter*" many times over (Jackson and Jackson 841-42). The tableau of the triple gaze at Piers's pardon, in this light, while it cannot do well, can sublimely figure the condition of Dowel's emergence, the possibility of its enactment, the prior act of "becoming conscious of a conscience." According to this Coleridgean reading, moreover, while all three subjects are equal in face of the enigmatic pardon to do well, their difference is also evident in their reactions to it.

But how distinct are these subjects in the longer run of the poem? The priest and Piers we last see disputing. Will's subsequent musings will, with some meandering, come round to the truth in dreams (7.168) and to the relative unreliability of pardons for the soul, in comparison with Dowel (7.180-81). In the course of these reflections, my second curious moment appears, when after awaking, Will muses on his dream in the language of love-melancholy (Schmidt 325 line 146n), "for Piers the Plowman ful pencif in herte" (7.146); and like a courtly lover he will swoon "al for pure joye" at the future mention of Piers' name (16.18-20).

This is a significant moment for the gendering of the subject in the poem, which a gap in current gender theory allows me only to mark but not pursue in this essay. I have already cited Middleton's comment on Piers's leaving the poem in Passus 7, concerning "the almost erotic intensity of the subject's longing for him." She continues: "He becomes the absent beloved, always sought and never recovered[,]. . . Langland's Beatrice, a human image held in the memory as the Other" ("Narration" 109). Both Middleton and David Lawton repeatedly compare Will's "new" subjectivity (Lawton 28) with Margery Kempe's (Lawton 23, 26-28; Middleton, "Narration" 109, 121, and "Kynde Name" 74, 75, 78). What these comments significantly overlook, as do my own so far in applying the female sublime to Piers above, is the fact that Will's desire for Piers is the desire of one male figure for another. Unfortunately, while the Lacanian male gaze of projected desire onto the female body is so ubiquitous as to have become an unexamined commonplace in much literary theory and criticism, the pre-Renaissance gaze is a desideratum in medieval studies, as Sarah Stanbury also points out (262-63). What is more, theory of the male gaze on another male is another gap, this time in gender theory at large.[5] Explorations of medieval masculinities are beginning to appear: in *Interscripta*'s hypertext article, "Medieval Masculinities: Heroism, Sanctity, and Gender" (www.georgetown.edu/labyrinth/e-center/interscripta/mm.html), for example, and in two anthologies, Clare Lees's *Medieval Masculinities*, and Jeffrey Cohen and Bonnie Wheeler's *Becoming Male in the Middle Ages*. But much work remains to be done, for example, in response to this salutary question from Stanbury's essay: "how can we formulate the gaze in a system of representation whose central spectacular body is the body of a man"–the body of Christ (266)? Stanbury's own contribution to addressing this question concerns late medieval devotional art and literature. In her examination of the dynamics of gazes at and from the crucified Christ, she notes that gender is both fluid and not necessarily primary in the desires of such gazes (Stanbury 268); Michael Camille similarly comments on "an eroticised, gender-bending and penetrable body [of Christ] open to flows and fluid desires that signalled danger in other, lesser bodies" in some medieval art (77). For the most part, medieval studies otherwise await more extended research on and theorizing of the homoerotic gaze in a pre-Renaissance context.

Major issues concerning the distinction among subjects in the poem nevertheless remain open to immediate analysis. If, as Burrow says, we do not soon see Piers doing well after his abrupt departure from the poem in the pardon scene, are there ways in which Will as distinct from Piers is presented as doing well in succeeding passus of the poem?

Middleton asserts that those passages following Passus 7 that suggest in particular Will's "literacy and literary pretensions . . . expose him to the same kinds of questioning that Piers received from the priest" ("Narration" 110). After noting Will's rebukes by Lewtee and Reason in Passus 11.84-106 and 375-402 (113), Middleton compares the priest's rebuke of Piers with Imaginatif's rebuke of Will in Passus 12 (112). Just as Piers was drawn from his naturally authoritative experience to the risky handling of "authoritative written instruments," so Will now challenges Imaginatif, "an authorized version of what Will as visionary and maker aspires to do, to integrate what books and experience can show" (112). On this argument Will-as-subject's gaze, along with the priest's and Piers's, at the pardon, and Will's subsequent longing for Piers upon waking, also prefigure his own position with Imaginatif in Passus 12. On the one hand, Middleton adds that Will does not entirely concede to Imaginatif's argument that his poetry wastes time from prayer and duplicates the already numerous books on Dowel. Will can "at least tell his own story of his effort to locate [Dowel] in his own time, interposing this process into the traditional display of encyclopedic and universal knowledge of faith and reason" (119). But in later articles, as I have outlined above, Middleton comes to regard Will and Langland as nonetheless unmade, as Piers is, by mendicant discourses. Middleton's later argument concedes to Langland only the originality of realizing the non-originality of those discourses ("Langland's Lives" 238-39). There is nothing new under the sun.

My Coleridgean reading provides a counterpoint to this view, arguing that the subject in the poem is more than a rehearsal of the same prepossessing discourses, more even than a poet who recognizes this in Althusserian fashion while most around him cannot. It is significant that Psalm 22 figures in both Piers's leavetaking in Passus 7 and Imaginatif's rebuke of Will in Passus 12. In the first context, Piers cites verse 4, "(For) though I should walk in the midst of the shadow of death, I will fear no evils: for thou art with me" (Schmidt 7.116-17n), apparently as a sign of trust in God's "sustenance both spiritual and physical" (Overstreet 289). In Passus 12, Imaginatif cites the latter half of the same verse, "Thy rod and thy staff: they have comforted me" (Schmidt 12.13a note), but here the rod and staff are interpreted as amending blows to the soul in Will's middle age, to get him to "mynne on thyn ende" (12.14-15, 7, 4). While these parallel quotations from the same psalm link Will's subjectivity with Piers, as does his love-longing in Passus 7, Overstreet makes the telling point that the passus is concerned not only doctrinally with salvation, but also with "whether certain occupations are viable in the light of Christian truth" (284). By implication, can Piers be saved as ploughman? He apparently decides that he cannot, in lines already cited above, and gives up sowing in favour of prayer and penance. Overstreet contextualizes his point by establishing how the long proem to the pardon scene in Passus 7 reviews the professions and stations of life as to whether those who occupy them can there be saved (284-87). Merchants (7.18-38), lawyers (7.39-59), and beggars (7.64-104) are three doubtful cases.

In Passus 12, Imaginatif is also attacking Will's profession of making poetry instead of saying his psalter and praying (12.16-17). Will replies that "if ther were any wight that wolde me telle / What were Dowel and Dobet and Dobest at the laste" (12.25-26), he would never work but only pray in church. This is, as has been noted, an "extraordinary" view of the originality of the author for the Middle Ages: that the fact that learned authorities offer "him true and already discovered answers to his questions does not dispense him from his own inquiry" (Kirk and Anderson 12.28 n. 7). Will's comments amount to a defense of poetry "as an irreplaceable way of recovering truth" (Simpson 139). While Imaginatif does repeatedly criticize Will for his dismissals of learning (e.g., 12.97-112), he does not defeat Will's claim. Indeed, Imaginatif notes several cases that clerks and clergy cannot answer (12.235, 268-69). In a crucial last exchange in which Will says that clerks deny that anyone outside Christendom can be saved, Imaginatif counters that the "trewe God" will not reject those who have lived according to truth (12.285-88), and cites, again, the same verse 4 of Psalm 22 spoken by Piers in Passus 7: "For though I should walk in the midst of the shadow of death [I will fear no evils]" (Schmidt 12.291n). In spite of Imaginatif's rebuke (using Psalm 22) of Will's making, the absence of a rebuttal of Will's self-defence in the passus, and the recurrence of citation of Psalm 22 about salvation for those who act truly, tend to leave the right of Will to write intact. In this way, Will's outcome in his chosen profession differs from that of Piers (who cites the same psalm): Will keeps his profession while Piers leaves his as literal ploughman in the poem. Thus Passus 12 just leaves room for making poetry, the "werk" that Will does instead of only praying, as a kind of doing well. On this reading, Piers and Will are not so much constituted by the same fatal discourse as Middleton argues, but according to the Coleridgean sublime of *alter* and *idem* in the social construction of agency of the self, Will is similar to, yet distinct from Piers, in vocational choice and outcome.

If it be granted that Will, in some measure, does well in writing poetry, then it does not follow that doing well must happen entirely outside the poem "in prayer and penance," for Will (Middleton, "Making a Good End" 254, 249, 251) and perhaps, for the reader. Steven Justice agrees that because understanding Dowel is not to do well, the poem "never reaches resolution," it "cannot make final claims for itself" ("Genres" 305). Yet Justice also suggests that while the *"Visio* has all the genres[,] . . . the rest [of the poem] is enacted interpretation," in the sense that the provisional text "enacts . . . the reforms that would heal" a "fractured communal authority" (304-305), an institutional version of the split between writing and living. Justice cannot mean, of course, that reforms are successfully enacted in the narrative of the poem, in view of the disastrous undermining of the House of Unity by the friars in Passus 19 and 20. He does suggest, however, that the "conflicting ideologies . . . prefigured by Piers and the priest" become "voiced and reconciled" in Will (305). Such a suggestion might minimize, or even collapse, the distinction between Piers and Will that I have been discussing. It is to this possibility that I now turn.

There is much in the poem that would support Justice's notion of Will as a site for the voicing and reconciliation of conflicts in the poem. Just as the boundaries between Will and Piers become somewhat blurred in the gaze of Passus 7, so Will and the interlocutors with whom he often disputes sometimes look alike in the poem. In Passus 8, Will meets Thought, whom he calls a "muche" [tall] man, who seems "lik to myselve" (8.71). Soon he meets Wit, also "*long* and lene," but "lik to noon oother" (8.118). Thought, however, undercuts this alleged dissimilarity by implication, adding, "Wher Dowel and Dobet and Dobest ben in *londe* / Here is *Wil* wolde wite if Wit koude teche" (8.126-27). Selected words (as italicized) from Will's description of Wit and Thought's mention of Will's interest in Wit, combine to make one of the anagrams for the poet's name in the poem (cf. Middleton, "Kynde Name" 32-37, 43-44), further suggesting Will's likeness to Thought and Wit.[6] In another such signature in Passus 11, Fortune fetches Will in a dream into the "lond of longynge" (11.8), the setting of his forty years of moral wandering (11.47 and Schmidt 334.47n), to look into the mirror of Middle Earth and see what he covets (11.7-11). Here, the subject Will becomes his setting, the field of folk, for "a *longe launde* is, among other things, the strip of land a plowman plows" (Middleton, "Kynde Name" 50). This identification, or what Coleridge calls "coinherence," of subject and setting, recurs in Passus 15 in another of Middleton's examples of authorial signature. When asking Anima where he can find charity, Will says "I have lyved in londe . . . my name is Longe Wille– / And fond I nevere ful charite, bifore ne bihynde" (15.152-53). In another gaze into a mirror in the poem, Will adds that while clerks teach that Christ is everywhere, he has never seen Him "soothly but as myself in a mirrour: / *Hic in enigmate, tunc facie ad faciem*"–"[We see] here [*nunc* 'now' *Vulg*] [through a glass] in a dark manner; but then face to face (1 Cor 13:12)" (15.162-62a and 162a note). Will as something like his interlocutors, Will as author William Langland signed, Will as the setting of the poem, Will as Christ in his heart, dimly–this is a dizzying *tertium aliquid*, a sublime crossing and recrossing of the boundaries of *alter* and *idem*, but to what end?

One clue is provided in Stanbury's description of how late medieval spectacle engages the reader's gaze at Christ: "to be seen and to command the gaze of others is to control visual relations, to be moved from the edge to the center, to be, in effect, like Christ" (279). Will's gaze at the pardon and longing for Piers in Passus 7 will be fulfilled, in some measure, in his subsequent gazes: at Piers and the Tree of Charity (Passus 16), at "Oon semblable to the Samaritan, and somdeel to Piers the Plowman" who "Barefoot on an asse bak bootles cam prikye" (18.10-11), at "Piers the Plowman . . . peynted al blody . . . / And right lik in alle lymes to Oure Lord Jesu" (19.6,8), and at Piers as Peter the apostle at Christ's ascension, Pentecost, and the founding the House of Unity (19.183ff). To gaze at and long for Piers, in the cumulative narrative of the poem, is also to gaze at the body of Christ, as suggested by the pronouncement "*Petrus, id est, Christus*" (15.212). If to be the object of the gaze, Piers / Christ, is (in Stanbury's words) "to control visual relations, to be moved from the edge to the center," then one other body that "commands" our gaze as readers is Will's. The sublime blending I have already noted–of Will with his interlocutors, Will as the setting of the poem, Will as Christ in his heart, Will with author William Langland signing himself at crucial moments in the poem–includes a sense of Langland even as bodily present ("long and lene" [8.118]) in his text: "the words on the page represent a person as well as his product," thereby securing the text's "value to the user" (Middleton, "Kynde Name" 36). Will's body joins Piers's and Christ's; it also moves, however covertly, from the margin towards the centre, "to be in effect, like Christ."

On the one hand, the sublime coinherence of Will with other figures, setting, and author in the poem corresponds to Coleridge's notion, cited above, of each subject's coexistence with, and organization into "the multitude of which he is an integral part. His *idem* is [repeatedly] modified by the *alter*." In a notebook entry (Coburn II 2086) and in language descriptive of Will's blending with others, Coleridge hints at how much responsibility subjects may have in these interactions: "–O there are Truths below the Surface in the subject of Sympathy, & how we *become* that which we understandly [*sic*] behold & hear, having, how much God perhaps only knows, created part even of the Form." If in this dance subjects resemble and even partly form one other, on the other hand, this is also the condition of their distinct emergence, of "becoming conscious of a conscience." This double motion or "act," for Coleridge, is "the instinct . . . in which humanity itself is grounded: that by which, in every act of conscious perception, we at once identify our being with that of the world without us, and yet place ourselves in contra-distinction to that world" (Rooke 497). Elsewhere Coleridge similarly writes that the subject "ought to be, at once *distinctive* and yet, at the same moment or rather act, *conjunctive*, nay, *unificent*" (Coburn III 4243). My Coleridgean reading of the pardon scene suggests that Will's gaze with the others at the pardon combines both impulses. His merging with landscape, Piers, and Christ, and his bodily presence at Langland's signatures illustrate more the identification of the subject with "the world without us," while Will's longing for Piers, in its distinct outcome in defending making poetry against Imaginatif, figures the subject Will "in contra-distinction to that world."

Alastair Minnis (87) properly reminds us that Will's defence of poetry to Imaginatif in Passus 12 should not be confused with "the Romantic notion of poetry as a medium for the personal discovery of truth" (cited in Simpson 139 n29). Will's defence, nonetheless, bears before its time a remarkable similarity to Coleridge's unique view of the warrant or "postulate" for the truth of what he wrote. Coleridge's dialogism of his voice with those of his historical authorities, often confused by modern readers with plagiarism (Shaffer, "Hermeneutic Community" 221-22), embodies his view that the truth of his opinions could only be enacted or demonstrated, not proved logically, in the poetic work as a manifestation of the unconscious poetic self (Shaffer, "Postulates" 309-11). Will's uncanny defence of his art, then, joins Will / William Langland's bodily presence in his text, the pardon, and those other sublime coinherences of subject with subject, and subject with setting, that can offer us readers a supra-logical "third something else," reconciling, hovering—"a sublime feeling of the unimaginable" instead of "a mere image." This sublime, enhanced by comparison with Yaeger's female sublime, contrasts sharply with Weiskel's characterization of conflict and its forceful resolution in the Oedipal sublime, with its Kantian accompaniments of threat of engulfment, crisis, pain, bafflement, or collapse of imagination. My reading of Will's right to make verse, extraordinary in Langland's period, left just barely intact in the face of Imaginatif in Passus 12, figures a distinct outcome for Will as subject in relation to Piers's professional demise as literal ploughman. Such a defence and outcome puts a premium on a cautiously hopeful agency in the subject, in contrast to Middleton's Althusserian view of subjects alike undone by fatal discourses. And the modification of *idem* and *alter* valorizes, not Oedipal combat, but acts at once distinctive and conjunctive, Coleridge would suggest, a rhythm of contradistinction and identification among distinct but coinherent selves in the social web.

My reading according to the Coleridgean sublime does not entirely disperse the darkness of the poem, in its denouement in Passus 19 and 20, for example.[7] But in its emphasis on agency in the subject and non-combative dynamics among subjects, such a reading not only finds unexpected light in the poem, but also has implications for its readers. If, as Coleridge argues, the subject emerges by act through contemplating such a sublime in the text, we as readers can share in the gaze of Will and the others at the pardon, many times over. If the prior act of "becoming conscious of a conscience" opens up doing well for Will in the poem, so might it do for us as readers in the sublime of the poem. If the pardon can "command" the gaze of Will, so might that disorienting *tertium aliquid* of Will and others, the sublime crossing of boundaries of subjects, and the bodies of Piers and Christ and Will and William Langland, command our gaze. Thus, in the Coleridgean sublime, doing good might not just happen outside the poem, as Middleton and Justice suggest, but might also begin to happen for us readers in the poem, in our imaginations, consciences, and wills.

Coleridge's discourse can do much more than such a psychological reading, of course. His variegated discussions of allegory (Knapp 7-50), for example, can engage with the mode of *Piers Plowman*. His view of the *alter* and *idem* of social construction derives from his emphasis on the Logos in the Christian Trinity (Perkins) and so communicates with Christian ideology in Langland's poem. The relevance of his gender views, both sometimes ahead of their time and (from some current perspectives) also hidebound in his age (Taylor, "Coleridge" and *Coleridge's Writings* 82-97; Jackson

"Coleridge's Women"), is also due for a closer look. My psychological reading is, then, only part of that larger, potential Coleridgean perspective. But the reading further substantiates why it is that many readers have called the poem sublime, and reveals modes of subjectivity in the poem that some psychoanalytic readings of *Piers Plowman* may miss, or repress.

Notes

1. See Lewis 160-61; Pearsall, *Piers Plowman* 20; Middleton, "Introduction" 14 and "Kynde Name" 46. Some material in this essay also appears in Evans, *"Piers Plowman* and the Sublime," in another context. An earlier version of part of this essay, "Subject and Gender in William Langland's *Piers Plowman*," was a paper given at the conference of the Canadian Society of Medievalists, Learned Societies Congress, Montreal, May 27-29, 1995. My thanks to Robert Byrnes and an anonymous reader for this collection, for their helpful comments on earlier drafts.
2. Some of the following material from Middleton appears in Evans, 430-35, in another context.
3. Yaeger proceeds to define her categories in more explicitly Kristevan terminology, in her concern for the pre-Oedipal in the sublime. Here I do not find that the textual details of the pardon episode give enough purchase for a persuasive application of her view, that the "feminine" sublime rewrites the "oedipal conflict . . . so that the pre-oedipal desire for closeness or nearness with the other that the conventional sublime tries to repress, remains visible and viable" (204). See also below on necessary theoretical work for pursuing the gendering of the subject in the poem.
4. I quote from the now standard editions of *Aids to Reflection* (Beer) and, below, of "Essay on Faith" (Jackson and Jackson), both of which were published after Cole's article.
5. I am grateful to Glenn Burger (Department of English, University of Alberta) and Doug Arrell (Theatre Department, University of Winnipeg) for assistance in confirming this bibliographical gap. Arrell suggests that further theorizing of the male gaze would likely begin with the second chapter of Sedgwick's *Epistemology of the Closet*.
6. While Middleton also argues for this likeness, she appears not to regard this context in Passus 8 as an anagram, either in the parallel passage in the A-text ("Kynde Name" 38-41) or in the B-text, where she calls the "lond of longynge" passage in B.11 "Langland's first explicit anagrammatic signature" in B (44).
7. See also Evans, 428-29.

Works Cited

Beer, John, ed. *The Collected Works of Samuel Taylor Coleridge: Aids to Reflection.* Vol. 9. London: Routledge; Princeton: Princeton UP, 1993.

Bennett, J. A. W., ed. *Langland, Piers Plowman: The Prologue and Passus I-VII* . . . . 1972. Rpt. with corrections. Oxford: Clarendon, 1976.

Bloomfield, Morton W. *"Piers Plowman" as a Fourteenth-Century Apocalypse*. New Brunswick, NJ: Rutgers UP, 1961.

Brown, Lee Rust. "Coleridge and the Prospect of the Whole." *Studies in Romanticism* 30 (1991): 235-53.

Burrow, John. "The Action of Langland's Second Vision." *Style and Symbolism in "Piers Plowman": A Modern Critical Anthology*. Ed. Robert J. Blanch. Knoxville: U of Tennessee P, 1969. 209-27.

Camille, Michael. "The Image and the Self: Unwriting Late Medieval Bodies." *Framing Medieval Bodies*. Ed. Sarah Kay and Miri Rubin. Manchester: Manchester UP, 1994. 62-99.

Cheetham, Mark A. "Moments of Discipline: Derrida, Kant, and the Genealogy of the Sublime." *Intersections: Nineteenth-Century Philosophy and Contemporary Theory*. Ed. Tilottama Rajan and David L. Clark. Albany: State University of New York P, 1995. 349-62.

Coburn, Kathleen, ed. *The Notebooks of Samuel Taylor Coleridge*. Vol. 2. 1804-1808. Part 1, Text. London: Routledge & Kegan Paul, 1962.

—, ed. *The Notebooks of Samuel Taylor Coleridge*. Vol. 3. 1808-1819. Part 1, Text. Princeton: Princeton UP, 1973.

Cohen, Jeffrey Jerome, and Bonnie Wheeler, eds. *Becoming Male in the Middle Ages*. New York and London: Garland, 1997.

Cole, Steven E. "The Logic of Personhood: Coleridge and the Social Production of Agency." *Studies in Romanticism* 30 (1991): 85-111.

Collier, John Payne. *Seven Lectures on Shakespeare and Milton by the Late S. T. Coleridge*. London, 1856.

Donaldson, E. Talbot. "Apocalyptic Style in *Piers Plowman* B. XIX-XX." *Essays in Memory of Elizabeth Salter*. Ed. Derek Pearsall. *Leeds Studies in English* n.s. 14 (1983): 74-81.

Eagleton, Terry. *Literary Theory: An Introduction*. Minneapolis: U of Minnesota P, 1983.

Edelman, Lee. "At Risk in the Sublime: The Politics of Gender and Theory." *Gender and Theory: Dialogues on Feminist Criticism*. Ed. Linda Kauffman. Oxford: Blackwell, 1989. 213-24.

Engell, James, and W. Jackson Bate, eds. *The Collected Works of Samuel Taylor Coleridge: Biographia Literaria, or Biographical Sketches of My Literary Life and Opinions*. Vol. 7, pt 1. London: Routledge & Kegan Paul; Princeton: Princeton UP, 1983.

Evans, Murray J. "*Piers Plowman* and the Sublime." *Exemplaria* 9 (1997): 421-40.

Frank, Robert Worth, Jr. "The Pardon Scene in *Piers Plowman*." *Speculum* 26 (1951): 317-31.

Hertz, Neil. "The Notion of Blockage in the Literature of the Sublime." *The End of the Line: Essays on Psychoanalysis and the Sublime*. Ed. Neil Hertz. New York: Columbia UP, 1985. 40-60.

Jackson, H. J. "Coleridge's Women, or Girls, Girls, Girls Are Made To Love." *Studies in Romanticism* 32 (1993): 577-600.

— and J. R. de J. Jackson, eds. "Essay on Faith." *The Collected Works of Samuel Taylor Coleridge: Shorter Works and Fragments*. Vol. 11, pt 2. London: Routledge; Princeton: Princeton UP, 1995. 833-44.

Justice, Steven. "The Genres of *Piers Plowman*." *Viator* 19 (1988): 291-306.

Kay, Sarah, and Miri Rubin. "Introduction." *Framing Medieval Bodies*. Ed. Sarah Kay and Miri Rubin. Manchester: Manchester UP, 1994. 1-9.

Kirk, Elizabeth D., and Judith H. Anderson, eds. *William Langland, Will's Vision of Piers Plowman: An Alliterative Verse Translation by E. Talbot Donaldson*. New York and London: Norton, 1990.

Knapp, Steven. *Personification and the Sublime: Milton to Coleridge*. Cambridge, MA: Harvard UP, 1985.

Lawton, David. "The Subject of *Piers Plowman*." *Yearbook of Langland Studies* 1 (1987): 1-30.

Lees, Claire A., ed., with Thelma Fenster and Jo Ann McNamara. *Medieval Masculinities: Regarding Men in the Middle Ages*. Medieval Cultures, vol. 7. Minneapolis and London: U of Minnesota P, 1994.

Lewis, C. S. *The Allegory of Love: A Study in Medieval Tradition*. 1936. Rpt. London: Oxford UP, 1970.

Macherey, Pierre. *A Theory of Literary Production*. Trans. Geoffrey Wall. London, 1978.

Middleton, Anne. "Introduction: The Critical Heritage." *A Companion to "Piers Plowman."* Ed. John A. Alford. Berkeley: U of California P, 1988. 1-25.

—. "Langland's Lives: Reflections on Late-Medieval Religious and Literary Vocabulary." *The Idea of Medieval Literature: New Essays on Chaucer and Medieval Culture in Honor of Donald R. Howard*. Ed. James M. Dean and Christian K. Zacher. Newark: U of Delaware P; London, Toronto: Associated University Presses, 1992. 227-42.

—. "Making A Good End: John But as a Reader of *Piers Plowman*." *Medieval English Studies Presented to George Kane*. Ed. Edward Donald Kennedy, Ronald Waldron, and Joseph S. Wittig. Woodbridge, Suffolk: Brewer, 1988. 243-66.

—. "Narration and the Invention of Experience: Episodic Form in *Piers Plowman*." *The Wisdom of Poetry: Essays in Early English Literature in Honor of Morton W. Bloomfield*. Ed. Larry D. Benson and Siegfried Wenzel. Western Michigan University, Kalamazoo: Medieval Institute Publications, 1982. 91-122.

—. "William Langland's 'Kynde Name': Authorial Signature and Social Identity in Late Fourteenth-Century England." *Literary Practice and Social Change in Britain, 1380-1530*. Ed. Lee Patterson. The New Historicism: Studies in Cultural Poetics, vol. 8. Berkeley: U of California P, 1990. 15-82.

Minnis, A. J. "Langland's Imaginatif and Late-Medieval Theories of Imagination." *Comparative Criticism* 3 (1981): 71-103.

Modiano, Raimonda. *Coleridge and the Concept of Nature*. Tallahassee: Florida State UP, 1985.

—. "Coleridge and the Sublime: A Response to Thomas Weiskel's *The Romantic Sublime*." *Wordsworth Circle* 9 (1978): 110-20.

Overstreet, Samuel A. "Langland's Elusive Ploughman." *Traditio* 45 (1989-90): 257-341.

Pearsall, Derek. *An Annotated Critical Bibliography of Langland*. Ann Arbor: U of Michigan P, 1990.

—. *Piers Plowman by William Langland: An Edition of the C-Text*. 1978. Rpt. London: Arnold, 1981.

Perkins, Mary. *Coleridge's Philosophy: The Logos as Unifying Principle.* Oxford: Clarendon, 1994.

Rooke, Barbara E., ed. *The Collected Works of Samuel Taylor Coleridge: The Friend.* Vol. 4, pt 1. London: Routledge & Kegan Paul; Princeton: Princeton UP, 1969.

Schmidt, A. V. C., ed. *William Langland: The Vision of Piers Plowman, a Critical Edition of the B-Text* . . . . Everyman's Library. 1978. Rev. rpt. London, Melbourne, and Toronto: Dent, 1982.

Sedgwick, Eve Kosofsky. *Epistemology of the Closet.* Berkeley: U of California P, 1990.

Shaffer, Elinor S. "Coleridge's Revolution in the Standard of Taste." *Journal of Aesthetics and Art Criticism* 28 (1969): 213-21.

—. "The Hermeneutic Community: Coleridge and Schleiermacher." *The Coleridge Connection: Essays for Thomas McFarland.* Ed. Richard Gravil and Molly Lefebure. London: Macmillan, 1990. 200-29.

—. "Illusion and Imagination: Derrida's Parergon and Coleridge's Aid to Reflection. Revisionary Readings of Kantian Formalist Aesthetics." *Aesthetic Illusion: Theoretical and Historical Approaches.* Ed. Frederick Burwick and Walter Pape. Berlin and New York: de Gruyter, 1990. 138-57.

—. "The 'Postulates in Philosophy' in the *Biographia Literaria*." *Comparative Literature Studies* 7 (1970): 297-313.

Simpson, James. *Piers Plowman: An Introduction to the B-Text.* London and New York: Longman, 1990.

Stanbury, Sarah. "Regimes of the Visual in Premodern England: Gaze, Body, and Chaucer's *Clerk's Tale*." *New Literary History* 28 (1997): 261-89.

Taylor, Anya. "Coleridge, Wollstonecraft, and the Rights of Women." *Coleridge's Visionary Languages: Essays in Honor of J.B. Beer.* Ed. Tim Fulford and Morton D. Paley. Cambridge: Brewer, 1993. 83-98.

—, ed. *Coleridge's Writings, Volume 2: On Humanity.* London: Macmillan; New York: St. Martin's Press, 1994.

Weiskel, Thomas. *The Romantic Sublime: Studies in the Structure and Psychology of Transcendence.* Baltimore: Johns Hopkins UP, 1976.

Wolf, Bryan Jay. *Romantic Re-Vision: Culture and Consciousness in Nineteenth-Century American Painting and Literature.* Chicago: U of Chicago P, 1982.

Yaeger, Patricia. "Toward a Female Sublime." *Gender and Theory: Dialogues on Feminist Criticism.* Ed. Linda Kauffman. Oxford: Blackwell, 1989. 191-212.

Laurel J. Brinton

"WHILOM, AS OLDE STORIES TELLEN US":
THE DISCOURSE MARKER "WHILOM"
IN MIDDLE ENGLISH[1]

1. Introduction

Not even the most casual reader of Middle English narrative, especially of Chaucer and Gower, will have failed to note the formulaic use of the word *whilom* at the onset of tales and stories. It is frequently translated with the phrase "once upon a time" characteristic of folk tales in contemporary English. The function of *whilom* is relatively unproblematic; like expressions such as *it bifel that* 'it happened that,' it serves to initiate episodes within the narrative structure. Although traditionally such a form was most often seen as belonging to a set of rather crude or naïve narrative devices employed by the Middle English poet to expedite the construction of metrical verse or aid in oral composition, more recently, it has been viewed–in linguistic terms–as belonging to the set of "discourse markers," words and phrases of indeterminate status such as *well, so, okay,* or *y'know* in Modern English; discourse markers, which are generally characteristic of the oral medium, serve to structure text, and contribute to the social interaction between speaker and hearer (see Brinton).

This paper investigates the development of *whilom* from its origin in Old English as an adverb meaning 'sometimes' to its use as a discourse marker, and beyond. The development of *whilom* can be compared to the better documented development of *while,* which has been seen as an incontrovertible instance of the process of language change known as grammaticalization. The early evolution of *whilom,* like that of *while,* is consistent with the process grammaticalization, but then *whilom* moves in an apparently contradictory direction. The question addressed here is whether, in the end, the development of *whilom* represents a counterexample to the hypothesis of unidirectionality (from less to more grammatical, or from

175

major to minor word class) postulated in grammaticalization studies or whether its development must be seen as lying outside the bounds of grammaticalization altogether.

2. Grammaticalization

The process of diachronic language change termed "grammaticalization" or "grammaticization" has been extensively studied in recent years.[2] It is understood generally as a process by which an autonomous, fully lexical word becomes a function word or grammatical affix, or by which a "less grammatical" word becomes "more grammatical." Representative examples of grammaticalization include the following:

a) the development of the French future inflectional ending from the full verb *habere* with possessive and later obligation meaning, e.g., *cantare + habeo > chanterai* (see Hopper and Traugott 42-44);

b) the development of the English future auxiliary *be going to* (*gonna*) from the progressive of the full verb *go* with a complement infinitive expressing a purposive, directional meaning: *I'm going to search for it* (purposive) > *I am going to think about it / It is going to rain* (future) (see Hopper and Traugott 1-4; Traugott "Role").

In the grammaticalization of single words (as in [a]), there is movement from independence to boundedness, from less to more bound, or from morphologically heavier to lighter, while in the grammaticalization of phrases (as in [b]), there is increasing invariability and coalescence. Grammaticalization is the result of reanalysis, including fusion across morphological boundaries, syntactic reanalysis, and/or reassignment of morphemes to different semantic-syntactic categories.

3. Traugott's Account of *while*

In a series of articles, Elizabeth Traugott has cited *while* as a "paradigm example" of grammaticalization.[3] The Modern English (ModE) conjunction *while* originates in Old English (OE) as a full noun *hwil* 'a space / period of time,' which carries "ideational / propositional" meaning.[4] *While* still exists as a noun in Modern English, though generally in collocations such as *a short while (ago)* or in prepositional phrases such as *{for, after, in} a while*. In Old English *hwil* occurs in the adverbial collocation *þa hwile þe* 'at the time that' (*þa* = accusative distal demonstrative, *hwile* = accusative singular of *hwil*, *þe*= relative particle); the phrase serves to denote a temporal event viewed as part of a durative situation. In late Old English the phrase is reduced to *(h)wil (that)*, and in Middle English (ME) it acquires "textual" meaning as a temporal connective with the sense 'during'; it expresses a cohesive time relation between events and clauses, profiling not only specific time but also discourse structure. In Early Modern English (EModE) (early seventeenth century), it becomes an "interpersonal / expressive" conjunction with a concessive sense 'although.' In this last function *while* "construes a world that has no reference in the described situation, but only in the speaker's world of belief about coherence among propositions" (Traugott, "Pragmatic Strengthening" 407).

In Traugott's evolving view of the grammaticalization process, the development of *while* from noun > adverb(ial phrase) > conjunction is said to exemplify the shift from propositional to (textual) to interpersonal meaning ("From Propositional to Textual") and to follow two principles or "Tendencies" of semantic change ("Pragmatic Strengthening"):

a) Tendency II–"from meanings situated in the described external or internal situation to meanings situated in the textual / metalinguistic situation"–which accounts for the change from 'at the time that' to 'during'; and

b) Tendency III–"to meaning increasingly situated in the speaker's subjective belief-state / attitude toward the situation" ("subjectification")–which accounts for the change from 'during' to 'although.'

Moreover, the textual meaning and, even more clearly, the interpersonal meaning represent a strengthening of the speaker's pragmatic viewpoint via the conventionalization of context-induced inferences ("Pragmatic Strengthening"): namely, the concessive, adversative meaning derives from "semanticization" of a conversational inference of surprise concerning the overlap in time or relations between event and ground (Traugott, "Subjectification" 41).[5] In sum, Traugott sees a shift from reference to a relatively concrete state of affairs to expression of the speaker's assessment of the relevance of simultaneity to an assessment of contrast or unexpected relations ("Subjectification" 42), as summarized in Table (1):

OE	*þa hwile þe* 'at the time that'	noun/ adverbial phrase	propositional meaning	concrete state of affairs
ME	*(h)wil (that)* 'during'	adverb/ conjunction	textual meaning	relevance of simultaneity
ModE	*while* 'although'	conjunction	expressive meaning	contrast, un-expected relations

Table 1: The Development of *whilom* (Traugott)

Examples of the development of *while* taken from Traugott ("Subjectification" 40-41) are the following:

1. a. þæs mannes sawul is belocen on his lichaman <u>þa hwile þe</u> he lybbende biþ (ÆCHom II).

    'Man's soul is locked in his body while / so long as he is alive'

    b. Thar mycht succed na female, <u>Quhill</u> foundyn mycht be ony male (*OED*, s.v. *while*; 1375 *Barbour's Bruce* 1.60).

    'No female was able to succeed while any male could be found'

    c. The Duke of York is gone down thither this day, <u>while</u> the Generall sat sleeping this afternoon at the Counciltable (*Helsinki Corpus*; 1667 Samuel Pepys, *Diary*, p. 317).

According to Hopper and Traugott (104), *while* represents a "clear case of shift from major to minor category" (or open to closed class membership), from noun to conjunction, hence "decategorialization" in the most obvious sense.[6] Moreover, the development of *while* is typical of grammaticalization in the following ways:

a) the form changes from a phrase to a single item, becoming increasingly fixed and bound ("structural decategorialization"–Traugott, "Constructions" §4);

b) it loses syntactic variability and comes to occupy a fixed slot;

c) it evolves semantically / pragmatically from more referential (i.e., lexical) to less referential (i.e., grammatical) via context-induced inferencing;

d) it develops increasingly "abstract" meaning; and

e) it undergoes "divergence," i.e., the retention of full lexical characteristics in some contexts alongside grammaticalization in other contexts (Hopper 24-25).

But the development of *while* is atypical of grammaticalization in that:

a) *while* remains an autonomous word, becoming neither a clitic nor an affix;

b) it expands its syntactic scope to the entire clause; and

c) it does not become part of a recognized grammatical paradigm.

However, since grammaticalization is seen to underlie the development of function words as well as inflections, loss of autonomous word status and increased morphological bonding would not appear to be necessary components of grammaticalization. Furthermore, Traugott ("Constructions"; Tabor and Traugott) rejects the view proposed by Christian Lehmann ("Grammaticalization"; *Thoughts*) that grammaticalization necessarily involves a reduction in an item's syntactic scope, arguing instead that a grammaticalized item generally increases its syntactic scope.

4. The Evolution of *whilom*

While Traugott's account works very well for *while* in the collocation *þa hwile þe*, when the variant form *whilom* (the dat. pl. of *hwil*) is considered, the development appears considerably less clear.[7]

4.1 Method of Data Collection

Since *whilom* is not a common form beyond the Old English period, I used a variety of sources for data. I made an electronic search of the University of Michigan *Corpus of Middle English, Early Modern English Materials,* and *Modern English Collection*, the University of Virginia *Middle English Collection* and *Modern English Collection*, Chaucer's *Troilus and Criseyde* and the *Canterbury Tales, The King James Bible, The Oxford English Dictionary: Second Edition on Compact Disc (OED), The Helsinki Corpus of English Texts (Helsinki Corpus)*, and *The British National Corpus*.[8] I also consulted concordances of Shakespeare (Spevack), Chaucer (Oizumi), Malory (Kato), Gower (Pickles and Dawson), Spenser (Osgood), and Milton's poetry (Bradshaw) and prose (Stern and Kollmeier).

4.2 Frequency of whilom

Considered by period and century, the distribution of *whilom* is highly irregular (see Table 2):[9]

Period	Century	*hwilum/whilom*
Old English		536
Middle English	1100	7
	1200	11
	1300	198
	1400	17
Early Modern English	1500	132
	1600	17
	1700	6
Modern English	1800	11
	1900	9

Table 2: The Distribution of *hwilum/whilom* by Period and Century

As is apparent in Table (2), *hwilum* is very common in Old English, and its frequency declines remarkably and quite suddenly in Middle English. The figures for the twelfth and thirteenth centuries are quite low because of the scarcity of texts from these centuries, though it would appear that *whilom(e)* (and variant forms such as *whylom, whilum, whilen, wilen, quhilum* etc.) is not particularly common in one of the longer works of the period, Layaman's *Brut* (7 examples). The figures for the fourteenth century include 90 examples from Chaucer and 95 examples from Gower. In the fifteenth century, *whilom* is again quite rare, perhaps because it occurs only one time in Malory, a major writer of that century. The figures for the sixteenth century rise, in large part because of the appearance of the form–perhaps as a deliberate archaism–in Spenser, where there are 116 examples. Virtually no examples occur in the major seventeenth-century writers: there is only one example in the 1603 ("Bad") Quarto of Shakespeare, 2 examples in Milton's verse, and no examples in the *King James Bible*. Examples of *whilom* in the modern period are rare. An exception is the form's occurrence in Stephen Crane's "Tales of Whilomville," published at the turn of the century (figures from Crane are not included in Table 1).[10]

4.3 From Predicate Adverb to Sentential Adverb to Discourse Marker

In Old English, *hwilum* carries the sense 'at times, for a time, sometimes' (see *An Anglo-Saxon Dictionary*: s.v. *hwilum*). It functions as a sentence-internal adverb with scope over the predicated event.

2. a. <u>Hwilum</u> mæru cwen, / friðusibb folca, flet eall geondhwearf, / bædde byre geonge . . . (*Beowulf* 2016-18).
        'At times the famous queen, the people's pledge of peace, went throughout the hall, urged on the young sons'
    b. Forðon þara godra mooda 7 monna þeaw bið, þæt heo þær <u>hwilum</u> synne ongeotað, þær þe syn ne bið (Bede, *Ecclesiastical History of the English People*, 1.16.78.34).
        'For it is the habit of good minds and men, that at times they perceive sin where there is no sin'

The last instance of this use cited in the *OED* is 1600, but, according to my sources, it is already quite uncommon in Middle English. Only a couple of examples can be found in Gower and Chaucer (3a-b) and none in Spenser. I have found one aberrant nineteenth-century example of this use (3c):

3. a. <u>Whilom</u> I thenke how Love to me / Seide he wolde take att gree / My servise (Chaucer, *Romaunt of the Rose* 4573-75).[11]
        'Sometimes I think how Love said to me he would take my service as a favor'
    b. Whereof ensample if thou wolt seche, / Tak hiede and red <u>whilom</u> the speche / Of Julius and Cithero (Gower, *Confessio Amantis* 7.1595-97).[12]
        'If you will seek an example of it, take heed and read sometimes the oratory of Julius and Cicero'
    c. And <u>whilom</u> most becomingly strums / On his poignantly *Quince-flavoured lute (*OED*, s.v. *quince*; 1950 D. Gascoyne *Vagrant* 55).

Note that it is the present tense forms *thenke* (3a) and *strums* (3c) and the imperative form *tak hiede* (3b) which point to the reading 'at times, sometimes' rather than to the reading 'formerly' (see below). Throughout Old and Middle English, *whilom* may occur in correlated structures (or in multiples) with the sense 'at some times . . . at other times':

4. a. Geseah ic þæt fuse beacen / wendan wædum ond bleom; <u>hwilum</u> hit wæs mid wætan bestemed, / beswyled mid swates gange, <u>hwilum</u> mid since gegyrwed (*Dream of the Rood* 21-23).
        'I saw the changeful sign alter in garments and colors; sometimes it was bedewed with moisture, stained with the flowing of blood, sometimes adorned with treasure'
    b. Þa Cwenas hergiað <u>hwilum</u> on ða Norðmen ofer ðone mor, <u>hwilum</u> þa Norðmen on hy (*Orosius*, 1.15.34).

'The inhabitants of Cwenland sometimes plunder the Norsemen over the moor, sometimes the Norsemen them'

c. & hwilun of þare ceolan þ[æ]t blod ut wylþ. hwilum of ʒoman. hwilum of þan scearpan banum þe bytweox þan breostan byþ. and hwylum of þare lunʒone. hwylum of þan maʒen (*Helsinki Corpus*; Peri Didaxeon, *Leechdoms, Wortcunning, and Starcraft of Early England* 138).

'and sometimes that blood wells out from the throat, sometimes from the gums, sometimes from the scarp bone that is between the breasts, and sometimes from the lung, sometimes from the maw (stomach)'

d. Thou shalt no whyle be in o stat, / But whylom cold and whilom hat (Chaucer, *Romaunt of the Rose* 2397-98).

'You shall for no period be in one state but sometimes cold and sometimes hot'

e. Vntenderly from þe toppe þai tiltin togederz, / Whilom Arthure ouer and oþerwhile vndre (*Michigan Corpus of Middle English Verse and Prose*; *Alliterative Morte Arthur* 1144-45).

'Fiercely from the top they tilt together, sometimes Arthur on top and another time under'

f. And quhylum he sat still in ane studeying, / And quhylum on his buik he was reyding (*OED*, s.v. *whilom*; 1550 *Freiris Berwik* 353 in Maitland *Folio MS* [S.T.S.] 143).

'And sometimes he sat still alone studying and sometimes he was reading in his book'

In Middle English *whilom* acquires the meaning 'at some past time, some time before or ago, formerly.' The first example given in the *OED* (s.v. *whilum*, def. 2a) is from the *Ormulum* (c. 1200).[13] With few exceptions, Middle and Early Modern examples of *whilom* are of this type, as shown in the following examples from different centuries.

5. a. 1100: Ðider com in gangan hwilon an meretrix (*Helsinki Corpus*; *History of the Holy Rood-Tree* 26).

'formerly a prostitute came going in thither'

b. 1200: & he answerede þus; / Whilen hit wes iseid; inne soð spelle. / þat moni mon deð muchel vuel (*Michigan Corpus of Middle English Verse and Prose*; Layamon, 4128-4130).

'and he answered thus: formerly it was said, in a true story, that many men do much evil'

c. 1300: He seyde, "O fool, now artow in the snare, / That <u>whilom</u> japedest at loves peyne" (Chaucer, *Troilus and Criseyde* I.507-8). 'He said, "Oh fool, now you are in the snare who formerly joked about love's pain"'

d. 1400: My maister Chaucer with fresh comedies . . . that <u>whilom</u> made ful piteous tragedies (*OED*, s.v. *comedy*[1]; 1430 Lydg. *Bochas* Prol. v.i). 'My master Chaucer with new comedies . . . who formerly made very piteous tragedies'

e. 1500: the Riuer, that <u>whylome</u> was hight / The auncient *Abus* (Spenser, *Fairie Queene* II.x.16.2-3).[14] 'the river that formerly was called the ancient Abus'

f. 1600: To see the vilest of all creatures . . . irrespectively hale and tear in pieces the casket which <u>whilome</u> enclosed the richest jewel in the world (*OED*, s.v. *irrespectively*; 1636 Featly in Spurgeon *Treas. Dav.* Ps. lxiii.10).

g. 1700: Trim rosemarine, that <u>whilom</u> crown'd The daintiest garden of the proudest peer (*OED*, s.v. *rosmarine*, 1742 Shenstone *Schoolmistr.* 109).

Nineteenth-century examples are fairly rare (6a-b), and I have found only one twentieth-century example of adverbial *whilom* (6c), a usage now considered obsolete:

6. a. Where oft <u>whilom</u> were captives pent (*OED*, s.v. *whilom*; 1808 Scott, *Marmiom* iv.xi).

b. The wistful eyes which <u>whilom</u> glanced down . . . upon the sweet clover fields (*OED*, s.v. *whilom*; 1879 Jefferies, *Wild Life in S. Co.* i.10).

c. Among the vanquished was the master chimney-sweeper, <u>whilom</u> incredulous at Stagg's Gardens, who now lived in a stuccoed house . . . (*British National Corpus*; 1992 Hoskins, *The Making of the British Landscape*).

Whilom generally occurs sentence- or clause-initial (following complementizer-*that*, relative or interrogative pronouns, and so on) and thus carries sentential scope.

Whilom seems also to have developed pragmatic (non-referential) functions as a marker of textual structure. Here *whilom* means 'once upon the time' and carries global scope. I have found no instances of this usage before the fourteenth century or after the sixteenth century:

7. a. Hit ilamp <u>whilon</u> þ[æ]t ðerto eoden hundtentiȝe iudeiscræ monnæ (*Helsinki Corpus*; *History of the Holy Rood-Tree* 24).
'It happened once upon a time that a hundred Jewish men went there'

b. Wherof a propre tale I rede, / As it <u>whilom</u> befell in dede (Gower, *Confessio Amantis* 3.2361-62).
'Whereof a proper tale I read, as it formerly happened in deed'

c. a tale I rede, / Which fell <u>whilom</u> be daies olde, / So as the clerk Ovide tolde. / Ther was <u>whilom</u> a lordes Sone . . . (Gower, *Confessio Amantis*, 1.2272-75).
'I read a tale which happened formerly by days of old as the clerk Ovid told. There was once upon a time a lord's son . . .'

d. A Maiden <u>whilom</u> ther was on. / Which Daphne hihte (Gower, *Confessio Amantis*, 3.1685-86).
'Once upon a time there was a maiden who was called Daphne'

e. Now hier of what ensample it is. / <u>Whilom</u> be olde daies fer / Of Mese was the king Theucer (Gower, *Confessio Amantis*, 4.3514-15).
'Now here is an example of it. Once upon a time by olden days far distant Theucer was the king of Mese'

f. <u>Whilom</u>, as olde stories tellen us, / Ther was a duc that highte Theseus (Chaucer, *Canterbury Tales*, KT 859-60).
'Once upon a time, as old stories tell us, there was a duke who was named Theseus'

g. <u>Whilom</u> ther was dwellynge in Lumbardye / A worthy knyght, that born was of Pavye (Chaucer, *Canterbury Tales*, MerchT 1245-46).
'Once upon a time there was dwelling in Lombardy a worthy knight that was born in Pavia'

h. A marchant <u>whilom</u> dwelled in Seint-Denys (Chaucer, *Canterbury Tales*, ShipT 1).
'Once upon a time, a merchant lived in St. Denis'

i. Oon of the gretteste auctour that men rede / Seith thus: that <u>whilom</u> two felawes wente / On pilgrimage (Chaucer, *Canterbury Tales*, NPT 2984-86).
'One of the greatest authors that people read says thus: that once upon a time two fellows went on a pilgrimage'

j. <u>Whilom</u> ther was in a smal village, As myn autor make the rehersayle . . . (*OED*, s.v. *rehearsal*; 1430 Lydg. *Min. Poems* [Percy Soc.] 181).

'Once upon the time there was a small village, as my author gives an account of'

k. Whylome, as antique stories tellen vs / Those two were foes the fellonest on ground (Spenser, *Fairie Queene* IV.ii.32.1-2).
'Once upon a time, as ancient stories tell us, those two were the fiercest foes on the ground'

l. Whylome, when *IRELAND* florished in fame (Spenser, *Fairie Queene*, VII.vi.38.1).
'Once upon a time, when Ireland flourished in fame'

m. Whilome there wonned a wicked Wolfe / That with many a Lamb had glutted his gulfe (Spenser, *Shepheardes Calender* Sept. 184).
'Once upon a time there was a wicked wolf that indulged his rapacious appetite with many a lamb'

n. This Polydor whillon . . . Too king Treicius was sent (*OED*, s.v. *whilom*; 1582 Stanyhurst *Æneis* III. [Arb.] 72).
'This Polydor once . . . was sent to king Treicius'

I would argue here that *whilom* serves as a discourse marker denoting the initiation of a story, episode, or exemplum. It expresses the relation or relevance of an utterance to the preceding context, "signaling a sequential discourse relationship . . . [or] how the speaker intends the basic message that follows to relate to the prior discourse" (Fraser 387, 392). Apart from semantic criteria of its discourse function, one can point to its frequent occurrence with introductory, existential sentences (*there + be / dwell*), with *hit ilamp* or *it befell* 'it happened' (7a-b) metacomments, which also function to initiate episodes (see Brinton), or with discourse formulas such as *in days of old* or *as old stories tell us*. Furthermore, in the *Canterbury Tales*, *whilom* occurs at the very beginning of at least nine of the tales ("The Knight's Tale" [7f], "The Miller's Tale," "The Cook's Tale," "The Man of Law's Tale," "The Friar's Tale," "The Merchant's Tale" [7g], "The Pardoner's Tale," "The Shipman's Tale" [7i], and "The Nun's Priest's Tale") as well as the story of Cresus in "The Monk's Tale" and other internal exempla and anecdotes in the *Canterbury Tales*; and in *Confessio Amantis*, it begins many of the tales (including the Tale of Narcissus [7c], Tale of Phebus and Daphne [7d], the Tale of Iphis and Araxarathen [7e].

This development of *whilom* is entirely consonant with Traugott's proposed development: clause-internal adverbial > sentential adverb > discourse marker. It is worthwhile quoting her description of this change in full:

185

> The hypothesis is that an adverbial, say a manner adverb, will
> in English be dislocated from its typical adverb position within
> the predicate, where it has narrow scope and evaluates the
> predicated event, to whatever position is the site for wide-scope
> sentential adverbs, where it evaluates the content of the
> proposition. Here it initially retains semantic functions but also
> acquires new pragmatic functions and polysemies. Over time it
> may then come to acquire Discourse Marker functions either in
> this position or in a further dislocated position; this stage
> involves the acquisition of further polysemies by
> semanticization and also morphosyntactic and prosodic
> constraints. As a Discourse Marker it serves to evaluate the text,
> of which the proposition is only a component. (Traugott "Role";
> "Constructions" §3.2; Tabor and Traugott 259)

We can see that *whilom* undergoes an analogous shift in its evolution. As a
simple adverb meaning 'at times, sometimes' it typically modifies the
iterative or habitual event expressed in the predicate of the sentence; it occurs
internal to the clause, though its position is variable, as is common for
temporal adverbials. In the next stage, *whilom* comes to modify a single
event with the sense 'once, formerly.' It moves to clause-initial position
(following the complementizer) and functions as a sentence adverbial
modifying the entire proposition. Its sense becomes deictically subjective.
The meaning 'once' can be understood as an implicature of the meaning
'sometimes' since the hearer can infer that what happens repeatedly has
happened at least once in the past. In the final step, from the meaning 'once'
to the meaning 'once upon a time,' *whilom* comes to signal the relationship
of the proposition to what follow (or precedes) in the discourse. This shift
involves a metonymic shift in scope from a single event viewed in isolation
to an event viewed in its global context. The meaning of *whilom* shifts from
primarily referential to primarily pragmatic in nature. The form becomes
fixed in clause-initial position, frequently external to the core syntactic
structure of the clause, i.e., in the position normally assumed by discourse
markers.

4.4 From Adverb to Adjective

In late Middle English a new use of *whilom* develops as an adjective with the
meaning 'that existed at a former time, late, deceased, former.'[15] The first
citation in the *OED* (s.v. *whilom*, def. 2b) is dated 1452. I have found several

possible earlier examples (1 in Gower and 6 in Chaucer), where *whilom* ambiguously means 'former' or 'formerly':

8. a. I finde a tale in proprete, / Hou Dorus <u>whilom</u> king of Grece (Gower, *Confessio Amantis* 5.1336-37).
        'I find a tale in particular (in regard to this) how Dorus former king of Greece'
    b. This riche Cresus, <u>whilom</u> kyng of Lyde (Chaucer, *Canterbury Tales*, MkT 2727).
        'This rich Croesus former king of Lydia'
    c. O paleis, <u>whilom</u> crowne of houses alle (Chaucer, *Troilus and Criseyde* V.547).
        'Oh palace, former crown of all houses'
    d. I, youre Alceste, <u>whilom</u> quene of Trace (Chaucer, *Legend of Good Women* G.422).
        'I your Alcestis, former queen of Thrace'

The majority of nineteenth- and twentieth-century uses of *whilom* follow a determiner and are unambiguously adjectival:

9. a. Here does the <u>whilom</u> *grub-staker and present millionaire purchase his corner lot (*OED*, s.v. *grub*; 1880 A. A. Hayes, *New Colorado* [1881] vii.107).
    b. We may misuse it, but we can scarce do worse in this respect than our <u>whilom</u> masters (*Michigan Modern English Collection*; 1897 Du Bois, "Strivings of the Negro People," *Atlantic Monthly* 80).
    c. These <u>whilom</u> friends rushed with a loud shout (*Virginia Modern English Collection*; 1897 Griggs, *Imperium in Imperio*).
    d. Nasac, the <u>whilom</u> Sultan of Egypt (*Virginia Modern English Collection*; 1906 Wedgwood, *The Memoirs of the Lord of Joinville*).
    e. And so the said <u>whilom</u> John was cruelly murdered and slain (*Virginia Modern English Collection*; 1935? MacClure, *She Stands Accused*).

Note that it always occurs with the title or name of a person, with few exceptions:

10. Mexico . . . that <u>whilom</u> dependency of the Spanish Crown (*OED*, s.v. *whilom*; 1868 G. Duff *Pol. Surv.* 151).

The development of *whilom* can be summarized in the following figure:

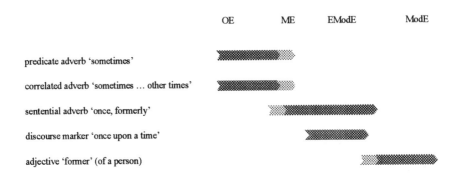

	OE	ME	EModE	ModE

predicate adverb 'sometimes'

correlated adverb 'sometimes ... other times'

sentential adverb 'once, formerly'

discourse marker 'once upon a time'

adjective 'former' (of a person)

Figure 1: The Development of *whilom*

5. Unidirectionality in Grammaticalization

This last step in the development of *whilom* raises an interesting theoretical question. If there is a single channel of grammaticalization, then the course of *whilom* is from noun used adverbially to sentential adverb to (discourse marker to) adjective. Such a development would contradict one aspect of the unidirectionality principle thought to hold during grammaticalization.

5.1 Aspects of Unidirectionality

A view of grammaticalization as unidirectional is propounded by most scholars.[16] For example, according to Hopper and Traugott (94), grammaticalization is "prototypically a unidirectional phenomenon." In his *A Dictionary of Grammaticalization*, Lessau (885) sees unidirectionality as "one of the strongest claims about grammaticalization."

Unidirectionality in grammaticalization is seen generally as a change from *less to more grammatical*. Such a change incorporates a number of different kinds of unidirectionality, all of which are believed to be irreversible.[17] Phonologically, there is erosion or reduction of the grammaticalized form from "heavier" / longer / more distinct to "lighter" / shorter / less distinct. The grammaticalized form undergoes a loss of morphosyntactic autonomy and growing dependence, frequently involving bonding or fusion: i.e., loosely conjoined, paratactic clauses become syntactically unified dependent clauses; freely variant phrases become fixed phrases or coalesce as single items; and single items travel on a cline from autonomous word > enclitic > inflectional / derivational affix > zero. Syntactic variability decreases, and the grammaticalized item assumes a fixed position. Grammaticalization also results in the increased frequency of a form and its obligatory rather than optional appearance. Although the traditional view of grammaticalization as involving "bleaching," weakening, or loss of meaning ("desemanticization") is now questioned, it is generally agreed that unidirectional semantic changes in the process of grammaticalization include abstraction (from concrete to abstract), generalization (loss of specificity, increase in polysemies), and metaphorization (from more familiar / accessible to less familiar / accessible). It has also been argued that grammaticalization involves subjectification (Traugott "Subjectification"; cf. Herring) and a change from more to less referential meaning, or increasingly pragmatic meanings (e.g., Traugott "Pragmatic Strengthening"; Traugott and König).

Finally, an essential component of the unidirectionality of grammaticalization is "decategorialization," or loss of categorial status.[18] According to Hopper, "Forms undergoing grammaticization tend to lose or neutralize the morphological markers and syntactic privileges characteristic of the full categories Noun and Verb, and to assume attributes characteristic of secondary categories such as Adjective, Participle, Preposition, etc." (22). As decategorialized items lose referentiality, they lose their discourse salience, autonomy, or manipulability (see Hopper 30). More specifically, Hopper and Traugott suggest a "cline" of decategoriality: major category (noun / verb) > (adjective / adverb) > minor category (preposition, conjunction, auxiliary verb, pronoun, demonstrative) (104).[19] It would seem that in respect to categoriality, adjectives stand to the left, i.e., are more "major," than adverbs. Lehmann, for example, discusses the grammaticalization of adverbs from adjectives, as well as from local nouns, in a number of languages (e.g., *-ly* adverbs in English, *-mente* adverbs in Vulgar Latin; *-liko* adverbs in proto-Germanic) but not the reverse development (*Thoughts* 87-88). Thus, the presumed difficulty raised by the evolution of adjectival *whilom* from adverbial *whilom*.

It is true that a number of counterexamples to unidirectionality have been cited in the literature. These fall under the rubric of "degrammaticalization," which refers to the general movement from *more to less grammatical*, or from grammatical morpheme to lexical morpheme.[20] Ramat discusses a number of instances of grammaticalization in which items become devoid of grammatical function or in which items formed originally by grammatical rules are no longer perceived this way, but rather as lexical formatives. A frequent example of degrammaticalization is "decliticization," where enclitics become unbounded, or independent, words (see Matsumoto; Campbell; Harris and Campbell 336-37; Lehmann *Thoughts* 18-19). Similar are cases of "demorphologization," or movement of a form out of the morphological component, such as the change from the genitive inflection *-es* to *his* in the history of English (see Joseph and Janda). The most often cited example of the violation of unidirectionality is "lexicalization" (Hopper and Traugott 127). In fact, Ramat considers lexicalization to be simply "an aspect of degrammaticalization" (550). While there is little consensus on what lexicalization means, it can be understood broadly as "the process that turns linguistic material into lexical items, i.e., into lexemes, and renders them still more lexical" (Wischer 4). A prototypical example of lexicalization is the change from *to + dæge* > *today*, in which a complex construction (consisting at least in part of a grammatical morpheme *to*) becomes a single, monomorphemic lexical item. A somewhat different type of lexicalization is the development of a lexical item from a nonlexical (or grammatical) form, such as the development of the verb *up* from the homophonous preposition (Heine, Claudi, and Hünnemeyer 4; Hopper and Traugott 49, 127). As a diachronic process, lexicalization has been viewed as opposite to grammaticalization.[21]

However, it is generally agreed, even by those who discuss such counterexamples (e.g., Harris and Campbell 338; Joseph and Janda), that their frequency is very low and that unidirectionality applies in the vast majority of cases. Hopper and Traugott (128) conclude:

> Unidirectionality is a strong hypothesis. The evidence is overwhelming that a vast number of known instances of the development of grammatical structures involved the development of a lexical item or phrase through discourse use into a grammatical item, and then into an even more grammatical item, and that these changes were accompanied by decategorialization from a major to a minor category. Counterexamples are few.

For Heine, Claudi, and Hünnemeyer, examples of degrammaticalization are "statistically insignificant" (5). Lehmann states even more unequivocally, "No cogent examples of degrammaticalization have been found" (*Thoughts* 19).

5.2 Possible Explanations for the Directionality of Changes in whilom

There are a number of possible ways to explain the apparently aberrant development of *whilom*:

1) It is indeed a counterexample to the unidirectionality of grammaticalization. As Lessau points out, if unidirectionality is considered an "empirical property" of grammaticalization, then any case running opposite to the expected direction of change qualifies as a counterexample.

2) It is a not a case of grammaticalization, but rather of some other process. Lessau points out that if unidirectionality is considered a "defining property" of grammaticalization, then any violation of it is "simply not a case of grammaticalization by definition" (886). If it is not grammaticalization, then what is it?

   a) It is a case of lexicalization. Lexicalization often involves reanalyses similar to those operating in grammaticalization (Hopper and Traugott 67). In fact, because of similarities between the two, Wischer concludes that "whether we call [the process] 'lexicalization' or 'grammaticalization' depends on the aim that we pursue" (8).

   b) It is a case of "recategorialization." In cases of recategorialization, the "hybrids" which result from decategorialization may develop into new function-specific morphemes (Heine, Claudi, and Hünnemeyer 213), or may acquire new morphosyntactic properties that are characteristic of the original word category (Lessau 198). It is an attempt to restore iconicity.

3) It exemplifies "polygrammaticalization," or the development along multiple paths or clines of grammaticalization. The paths may involve either a split or a merger (Hopper and Traugott 112-13).

4) It is a case of "renewal," which often obscures unidirectionality (Hopper and Traugott 106). There is a continuous process of renewal in language, whereby, as forms weaken and sometimes disappear, new forms take on their grammatical meanings (Lehmann "Grammaticalization" 314; Hopper and Traugott 121-23).

6. Conclusion

Based on the evidence of *whilom*, can the hypothesis of unidirectionality in grammaticalization be maintained? In order to answer this question, we can explore the alternative explanations set out above.

First, the development of *whilom* does not seem to involve the renewal of any existing form. Second, since *whilom* does not ultimately acquire the morphosyntactic properties of the original word category (adverb < noun) but rather of a different category altogether (adjective), it does not appear to be a case of recategorialization. Third, there seems to be good evidence, from ambiguous examples of the type given in (11), that *whilom* develops from the sentential adverb, as set out in (12):

11. a. I, wrecche, which that wepe and wayle thus, / Was <u>whilom</u> wyf to kyng Cappaneus (Chaucer, *Canterbury Tales*, KT 932-33).
    'I, miserable creature, who weeps and wails thus, was former wife to King Cappaneus' OR 'formerly wife to King Cappaneus'

    b. A markys <u>whilom</u> lord was of that lond, / As were his worthy eldres hym bifore (Chaucer, *Canterbury Tales*, CIT 64-65).
    'A marquis former lord of that land' OR 'formerly lord of that land, as were his worthy elders before him'

    c. The <u>whilome</u> powerful Kindgom of Hungary (*OED*, s.v. *whilom*; 1656 Earl Monm. tr. *Boccalini's Advts. fr. Parnass* II.lxi [1674] 213).
    'The formerly powerful kingdom or Hungary' OR 'the former, powerful kingdom of Hungary'

    d. On sloping mounds, or in the vale beneath, / Are dome where <u>whilome</u> kings did make repair (*OED*, s.v. *repair* sb.[1]; 1812 Byron *Ch. Har*. i.xxii).
    'where formerly kings did . . .' OR 'where former kings did . . .'

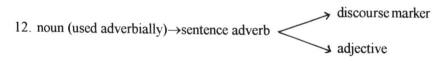

12. noun (used adverbially)→sentence adverb   discourse marker / adjective

Thus, while *whilom* appears to follow multiple paths of grammaticalization, this instance of polygrammaticalization would still seem to violate the postulated decategorialization cline.[22]

Although *whilom* moves from a more minor word class (adverb) to a more major word class (adjective), I do not think that it represents a genuine counterexample. If unidirectionality is separated from irreversibility, as it probably should be given the examples of decliticization and demorphologization cited in the literature, the hypothesis would permit movement in the opposite direction, i.e., "degrammaticalization."[23] As an item moves from less to more grammatical (from left to right, as shown in Figure 2), it acquires more of the features of a grammaticalized item, but the elimination of irreversibility would also allow an item to move from more to less grammaticalized (from right to left), provided that it loses some of those same features of grammaticalization. In other words there would be a double-headed arrow in Figure (2) (see Harris and Campbell 337), and the unidirectionality hypothesis would become a "bidirectionality" hypothesis.

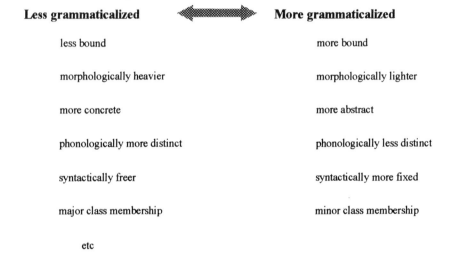

Less grammaticalized	**More grammaticalized**
less bound	more bound
morphologically heavier	morphologically lighter
more concrete	more abstract
phonologically more distinct	phonologically less distinct
syntactically freer	syntactically more fixed
major class membership	minor class membership
etc	

Figure 2: The Bidirectionality of Grammaticalization

Note that what this view of directionality would not permit is for an item to move in one direction in respect to one or more of the features at the same time that it moves in the opposite direction in respect to one or more of the other features of grammaticalization, e.g., to become more bound and phonologically more distinct.

Finally, I would suggest that the last step in the development of *whilom* is not obviously a case of degrammaticalization either, since adjectival *whilom,* apart from its change in categorial status, does not acquire any of the other features associated with a less grammatical item. Rather, this step should be understood as a case of lexicalization, the process of an item becoming more "lexical." As Wischer observes, lexicalization, like grammaticalization, involves reanalysis, conventionalization, fossilization, and partial demotivation, processes which can also be seen in the development of adjectival *whilom*. But Wischer also points out that unlike grammaticalization, which involves the loss of lexical meaning or acquisition of grammatical meaning, lexicalization involves the addition of new lexical meaning. We see this too in the development of adjectival *whilom*, in the meaning 'of a person, "late," deceased' (*OED*, s.v. *whilom*, def. 2b) added to the meaning 'former.'

I think that in the end the case of *whilom* does not essentially call into question the unidirectionality hypothesis of grammaticalization, though it modifies it to a bidirectionality hypothesis (in eliminating the irreversibility component). However, what it does call into question is the differentiation of the process of grammaticalization from the process of lexicalization–a problem that requires further examination. Or as Ilse Wischer observes in the title of her paper: "Grammaticalization versus Lexicalization–'Methinks' there is Some Confusion."

Notes

1. This is a revised version of a paper presented at the 10th International Conference on English Historical Linguistics held in Manchester in August 1998; I would like to thank the organizers for giving me an opportunity to present this paper and various members of the audience, including Terttu Nevailainen, Theo Vennemann, Nigel Vincent, Sylvia Adamson, and others, who gave me worthwhile feedback. I am also grateful for the support of a UBC-SSHRCC International Travel Grant.
2. See, for example, Lehmann ("Grammaticalization"; *Thoughts*); Heine, Claudi, and Hünnemeyer; Traugott and Heine, eds.; and Hopper and Traugott. For a review of scholarship, see Brinton (50-59).
3. See Traugott ("From Propositional to Textual" 254; "Pragmatic Strengthening" 407; "On the Rise of Epistemic Meanings" 31, 33, 35; "Subjectification" 39-42); also Traugott and König (200-201); Hopper and Traugott (84-86).
4. The terms "ideational," "textual," and "interpersonal" are adopted from M. A. K. Halliday. Ideational / propositional denotes referential meaning or content; textual refers to devices for achieving intersentential connections and more global structuring of texts, and interpersonal / expressive is the expression of speaker attitude or judgment and aspects of the social exchange.

5. Traugott ("Subjectification" 40; also Traugott and König 201; Hopper and Traugott 85) notes that a different, perhaps more immediate inference from temporal frame of reference is grounds for a situation, that is, the 'because' sense. While the causal sense is dominant in late 14th-century English, it never became conventionalized in English as it did in the German cognate *weil*.

6. Conjunctive *while* loses the ability to take articles or quantifiers, it cannot be modified by adjectives or demonstratives, it cannot serve as subject or other argument of the verb, it is restricted to initial position, and it cannot be referred to by an anaphoric pronoun.

7. The adverbial genitive *hwiles > whiles* follows a path of development similar to *þa hwile þe* from adverb to conjunction (see *OED*, s.v. *whiles*). In contrast, the development of the adverbial accusative *ane hwile* 'for a while' *> awhile* might better be seen as lexicalization (occurring as early as the 13th century) since there is no change in category membership but only a change from phrase to single lexical item. Confusion between *a while* and *awhile* is of long standing (see *Webster's*, s.v. *awhile, a while*).

8. The Michigan Middle English corpus consists of 42 texts, while the Virginia Middle English corpus consists of 40 texts. The Michigan Early Modern English corpus is 16 megabytes in size and is constructed from 50,000 records, consisting of many of the original slips for the *Oxford English Dictionary*. The Virginia Modern English corpus consists of 1995 titles (no information is available on the Michigan Modern English corpus). *The Helsinki Corpus* includes 413,250 words of Old English, 608,570 words of Middle English, and 551,000 words of Early Modern English; the corpus consists of selections from texts covering a range (of up to 20 different) text types (for further information, see Kytö). The British National Corpus includes one million words of spoken and written contemporary English.

9. Note that this table is simply a summation of the examples that I found. There is no control for the size of the different corpora. These figures are intended simply to give a rough picture of the frequency of the form.

10. *Whilomville* is the name of a fictional town in a series of stories by the American writer Stephen Crane published in *Harper's Magazine* beginning in August 1899. The fact that Levenson, in introducing the "Tales of Whilomville" for the University of Virginia collected works, feels no need to explain the term suggests continued familiarity with its meaning. Interestingly, he describes Crane's fictional creation as a "Once-upon-a-time" small American town (xii).

11. Quotations from Chaucer were checked in Benson.

12. Quotations from Gower were checked in Macaulay.

13. *An Anglo-Saxon Dictionary: Supplement* (s.v. *whilom*, def. 2) suggests that *whilom* can modify a single event with the meaning 'once, some time ago,' citing the following late Old English example: seðe wæs fore setnunge hwilum vel forlonge aworden in ðær cæstre 7 morðor wæs gesended in carcern. (*The Rushworth Gospels* Lk 23:19) '[This man] who a long time ago was despised in the town for causing a riot and who had been sent to prison for murder.'

14. Quotations from Spenser were checked in Greenlaw *et al.*

15. The related adjective *erstwhile* has a "somewhat mysterious and confused history" (see *Webster's*, s.v.v. *erstwhile, quondam, whilom*); while the adverbial use dates from the 15th century, the adjectival use appears to be an early 20th-century innovation. It is interesting to note that a number of temporal adverbs, including *then, once, sometime, one-time*, and so on, have developed adjectival uses. Similarly, in German adverbs such as *damals* and

ehemals have acquired adjectival uses. In a sense, these are all defective adjectives since they are incapable of occurring in the predicate of a sentence or of being compared. *Webster's* (s.v. *then*) notes prescriptions against the use of *then* as an adjective. Nigel Vincent has observed (p.c.) that the marking of tense on nouns in this way results in strange linguistic behavior cross-linguistically.

16. See, for example Lehmann ("Grammaticalization," *Thoughts*); Heine, Claudi, and Hünnemeyer (4-5, 212, passim); Traugott and Heine (4-6); Hopper and Traugott (94-129); Bybee, Perkins, and Pagliuca (12-14); or Lessau (885-92).

17. Contrary to the usual view that unidirectionality implies irreversibility, Lessau (885) claims that unidirectionality "does not refer to a presumed *irreversibility* . . . but to a general development orientation which all (or the large majority) of the grammaticalization cases have in common." However, he also notes (498) that unidirectionality implies irreversibility but not vice versa.

18. See Heine, Claudi, and Hünnemeyer (213, 229-31); Hopper (30-31); Hopper and Traugott (103-12); or Lessau (196-98).

19. Lehmann has postulated several more specific clines, e.g.:

a) relational noun > secondary adposition > primary adposition > agglutinative case affix > fusional case affix;

b) lexically empty noun > free personal pronoun > clitic personal pronoun > agglutinative personal affix > fusional personal affix ("Grammaticalization" 304, 309);

c) full verb > modal verb > auxiliary verb > mood/aspect/tense marker (*Thoughts* 1995: 37).

20. For discussions of degrammaticalization, see Heine, Claudi, Hünnemeyer (4-5); Lessau (202-04); Hopper and Traugott (126-29); Traugott (§2.1); and Tabor and Traugott (230-31).

21. In addition to these processes, one may encounter cases of "regrammaticalization," where forms without any function or which have lost their grammatical function acquire a grammatical function (see Heine, Claude, and Hünnemeyer 5, 262; Lessau 731), "remorphologization" (see Joseph and Janda 202), where forms re-enter the morphological domain, such as the change of *his* to *'s*, and "relexicalization," where grammaticalized forms reassume lexical status. Ramat (554) sees relexicalization as part of a continuous spiral: from lexicon to grammar and back to lexicon. Regrammaticalization bears some resemblance to what Roger Lass has termed "exaptation," a process whereby "junk" (morphological material which has lost its function) is redeployed for another grammatical use.

22. In order for it not to be a counterexample to unidirectionality, adjectival *whilom* would have to evolve directly from the noun *while*.

23. Lessau (202) remarks that violations of unidirectionality are "still compatible with the main underlying principles of grammaticalization" and that it is a "mere terminological question" whether such cases are classified as cases of grammaticalization or of degrammaticalization.

Works Cited

An Anglo-Saxon Dictionary. "Hwilum."

An Anglo-Saxon Dictionary: Supplement. "Hwilum."

Axmaker, Shelly, Annie Jaisser, and Helen Singmaster, eds. *Proceedings of the Fourteenth Annual Meeting of the Berkeley Linguistics Society.* Berkeley: Berkeley Linguistics Society, 1988.

Bradshaw, John, ed. *A Concordance to the Poetical Works of John Milton.* London: Swan Sonnenschein; New York: Macmillan, 1894.

Brinton, Laurel J. *Pragmatic Markers in English: Grammaticalization and Discourse Functions.* Topics in English Linguistics 19. Berlin: Mouton, 1996.

The British National Corpus. http://thetis.bl.uk

Bybee, Joan, Revere Perkins, and William Pagliuca. *The Evolution of Grammar: Tense, Aspect, and Modality in the Languages of the World.* Chicago: U of Chicago P, 1994.

Campbell, Lyle. "Some Grammaticalization Changes in Estonian and Their Implications." Traugott and Heine 1:285-99.

Chaucer, Geoffrey. *The Riverside Chaucer.* Ed. Larry D. Benson. 3rd ed. Boston: Houghton Mifflin, 1987.

Corpus of Middle English Prose and Verse. University of Michigan. 21 Nov. 1997.

Early Modern English Collection. University of Michigan. http://www.hti.umich.edu/dict/memem.

Fraser, Bruce. "An Approach to Discourse Markers." *Journal of Pragmatics* 14 (1990): 383-95.

Gower, John. *The English Works of John Gower.* EETS e.s. 81-82. Ed. G. C. Macaulay. 2 vols. London: Oxford UP, 1900-1901.

Halliday, M. A. K. "Language Structure and Language Function." *New Horizons in Linguistics.* Ed. John Lyons. Harmondsworth: Penguin, 1970. 140-65.

Harris, Alice C., and Lyle Campbell. *Historical Syntax in Cross-Linguistic Perspective.* Cambridge Studies in Linguistics 74. Cambridge: Cambridge UP, 1995.

Heine, Bernd, Ulrike Claudi, and Friederike Hünnemeyer. *Grammaticalization: A Conceptual Framework.* Chicago: U of Chicago P, 1991.

Herring, Susan C. "The Grammaticalization of Rhetorical Questions in Tamil." Traugott and Heine 1:253-84.

Hopper, Paul J. "On Some Principles of Grammaticization." Traugott and Heine 1:17-35.

—, and Elizabeth Closs Traugott. *Grammaticalization.* Cambridge Textbooks in Linguistics. Cambridge: Cambridge UP, 1993.

Joseph, Brian D., and Richard D. Janda. "The How and Why of Diachronic Morphologization and Demorphologization." *Theoretical Morphology: Approaches in Modern Linguistics.* Ed. Michael Hammond and Michael Noonan. San Diego: Academic Press, 1988. 193-210.

Kato, Tomomi, ed. *A Concordance to the Works of Sir Thomas Malory.* Tokyo: U of Tokyo P, 1974.

King James Bible. Oxford Text Archives.

Kytö, Merja. *Manual to the Diachronic Part of the Helsinki Corpus of English Texts: Coding Conventions and List of SourceTexts.* 2nd ed. Helsinki: Department of English, U of Helsinki, 1993.

Lass, Roger. "How to Do Things with Junk: Exaptation in Language Evolution." *Journal of Linguistics* 26 (1990): 79-102.

Lehmann, Christian. "Grammaticalization: Synchronic Variation and Diachronic Change." *Lingua e stile* 20 (1985): 303-18.

—. *Thoughts on Grammaticalization.* LINCOM Studies in Theoretical Linguistics 01. München and Newcastle: LINCOM EUROPA, 1995.

Lessau, Donald A. *A Dictionary of Grammaticalization.* 3 vols. Essener Beiträge zur Sprachwandelforschung 21. Bochum: Universitätsverlag Dr. N. Brockmeyer, 1994.

Levenson, J. C. Introduction. *Tales of Whilomville.* By Stephen Crane. Ed. Fredson Bowers. Vol. 7. of *The University of Virginia Edition of the Works of Stephen Crane.* 10 vols. Charlotteville: UP of Virginia, 1969.

Matsumoto, Yo. "From Bound Grammatical Markers to Free Discourse Markers: History of some Japanese Connectives." Axmaker *et al.* 340-51.

Middle English Collection. University of Virginia Electronic Text Center. http://etext.lib.virginia.edu/eng-on.html 1 May 1998.

Modern English Collection. University of Michigan http://www.hti.umich.edu/english/pd-modeng/ 5 Sept. 1997.

Modern English Collection. University of Virginia Electronic Text Center. http://etext.lib.virginia.edu/modeng/modengO.browse.html

Oizumi, Akio, ed. *A Complete Concordance to the Works of Geoffrey Chaucer.* Prog. Kunihiro Miki. 10 vols. Alpha-Omega, Reihe C, Englische Autoren. Hildesheim: Olms-Weidmann, 1991-1992.

Osgood, Charles Grosvenor. *A Concordance to the Poems of Edmund Spenser.* The Carnegie Institution of Washington 189. Philadelphia: The Carnegie Institution of Washington, 1915.

Oxford English Dictionary. Second Edition on Compact Disc. Oxford: Oxford UP, 1992.

Pickles, J. D., and J. L. Dawson, eds. *A Concordance to John Gower's "Confessio Amantis."* Cambridge: Brewer, 1987.

Ramat, Paolo. "Thoughts on Degrammaticalization." *Linguistics* 30 (1992): 549-60.

Spenser, Edmund. *The Works of Edmund Spenser: A Variorum Edition.* Ed. Edwin Greenlaw *et al.* 10 vols. Baltimore: Johns Hopkins P, 1932-1949.

Spevack, Marvin. *A Complete and Systematic Concordance to the Works of Shakespeare.* 9 vols. Hildesheim: Georg Olms, 1969.

Stern, Laurence, and Harold H. Kollmeier, eds. *A Concordance to the English Prose of John Milton.* Medieval and Renaissance Texts and Studies 35. Binghamton, NY: Center for Medieval and Early Renaissance Studies, 1985.

Tabor, Whitney, and Elizabeth Closs Traugott. "Structural Scope Expansion and Grammaticalization." *The Limits of Grammaticalization.* Ed. Anna Giacolone Ramat and Paul J. Hopper. Typological Studies in Language 37. Amsterdam: John Benjamins, 1998. 229-72.

Traugott, Elizabeth Closs. "Constructions in Grammaticalization." *Handbook of Historical Linguistics.* Ed. Brian Joseph and Richard Janda. Oxford: Oxford UP, in press.

—. "From Propositional to Textual and Expressive Meanings: Some Semantic-Pragmatic Aspects of Grammaticalization." *Perspectives on Historical Linguistics.* Ed. Winfred P. Lehmann and Yakov Malkiel. Amsterdam: John Benjamins, 1982. 245-71.

—. "On the Rise of Epistemic Meanings in English: an Example of Subjectification in Semantic Change." *Language* 65 (1989): 31-55.

—. "Pragmatic Strengthening and Grammaticalization." Axmaker *et al.* 406-16.

—. "The Role of the Development of Discourse Markers in a Theory of Grammaticalization." XIIth International Conference on Historical Linguistics, Manchester, Aug. 1995.

—. "Subjectification in Grammaticalisation." *Subjectivity and Subjectivisation.* Ed. Dieter Stein and Susan Wright. Cambridge: Cambridge UP, 1995. 31-54.

—, and Bernd Heine. Introduction. Traugott and Heine 1:1-14.

—, and Bernd Heine, eds. *Approaches to Grammaticalization.* Vol. 1: *Focus on Theoretical and Methodological Issues.* Vol. 2: *Focus on Types of Grammatical Markers.* Typological Studies in Language 19. Amsterdam: John Benjamins, 1991.

—, and Ekkehard König. "The Semantics-Pragmatics of Grammaticalization Revisited." Traugott and Heine 1:189-218.

Webster's Dictionary of English Usage. "Erstwhile, quondam, whilom." "Then." "While, a while."

Wischer, Ilse. "Grammaticalization versus Lexicalization–'Methinks' There is Some Confusion." XIIIth International Conference on Historical Linguistics, Düsseldorf August 1997.

Paul C. Burns

THE WRITINGS OF HILARY OF POITIERS
IN MEDIEVAL BRITAIN
FROM C. 700 TO C. 1330 [1]

Recent scholarship on extant manuscripts, medieval library lists, and quotations of sources enables us to track particular traditions or authors on the interpretation of biblical texts and theological issues from the Early Church through the Middle Ages. This paper investigates the evidence for the presence in Britain of the writings of Hilary, the bishop of Poitiers from c. 350 to 367, and suggests some reasons for their presence. Not all of the evidence is equally strong. The period under consideration ranges from the very beginning of the eighth century to the first third of the fourteenth century.

During his episcopacy Hilary had produced a variety of texts dealing with exegesis of Scripture and with the theological issue of the Trinity; in addition, he wrote a dossier of documents, a collection of hymns, and polemical pamphlets aimed at the Emperor Constantius and at Auxentius, the bishop of Milan.[2] The precise wording of some of the titles of individual works in the literary corpus of Hilary presents difficulties. Sometimes the conventional title follows clear evidence from Hilary himself; other titles seem to originate in later manuscript traditions; still others are assigned by bibliographical reports such as that of Jerome, which will figure at a later stage of this article.[3] I present conventional titles for Hilary's works, which will be employed throughout this paper. His exegetical works comprise the *Commentarii in Matthaeum*,[4] the *Liber de Mysteriis*,[5] and the *Tractatus super Psalmos*.[6] His theological works are the *De Trinitate*,[7] and the *Liber de Synodis*.[8] His polemical works consist of the *Libellus in Constantium*[9] and *Libellus contra Auxentium*.[10] Included among the polemical works could be an unsuccessful appeal to the Emperor, the *Libellus (II) ad Constantium*.[11] The dossier of documents with commentary by Hilary can be called the *Libri tres adversum Valentem et Ursacium*.[12] There is the *Liber*

Hymnorum,[13] and the various *Epistulae*, though these are falsely attributed to Hilary. Material from all of these titles does appear in Medieval Britain with the exception of the complex dossier entitled *Libri tres adversum Valentem et Ursacium and the Liber de Mysteriis*.[14]

Hilary's significant exegetical and theological contributions were overshadowed by the writings of Ambrose, Augustine, and Jerome in the generation after him. Nonetheless, both Augustine and Jerome held Hilary in high regard, although for slightly different reasons. Augustine valued Hilary's contributions to theological issues;[15] Jerome acknowledged his contribution to the exegesis of scriptural texts.[16] Augustine's practice of formulating theological arguments based on theological predecessors, whom he cites from different places and times in the Church, establishes Hilary as an authority for later generations. Jerome's *De Viris Illustribus* may have had some influence on the library collections including at least one centre in Britain and will be noted in that context.

Manuscripts of Hilary's works show up frequently in French monastic and cathedral centres throughout the Middle Ages.[17] To my knowledge, no systematic study has been undertaken on the presence of his writings in Britain. In this paper, I therefore seek to identify the presence of his writings in monastic and cathedral libraries during the Anglo-Saxon period and after the Norman Conquest.

The modern critical editions of Hilary's writings rest on the evidence of increasing numbers of manuscripts. Many of these manuscripts can be dated and their places of origin determined. This particular study seeks to identify any evidence for the presence in Britain of Hilary's texts between the eighth and early fourteenth centuries. The somewhat dated edition of the *Tractatus super Psalmos*, published in 1891, rests on seven manuscripts from this time frame. It also employs two from the sixth century and one from the fifteenth century. The *Commentarii in Matthaeum*, published much later (in 1978 and 1979), employs twelve manuscripts from this period. But so far there is no evidence that any of this material originated in a scriptorium in Britain or was to be found in a British library. The manuscript basis for the *De Trinitate*, published in 1979 and 1980, is much more extensive. Of the seventy-six manuscripts found by the editor, six come from the earlier period of the fifth and sixth centuries while forty-three originate in the eighth to the fourteenth centuries (Smulders, "Remarks" 129-38). None of these show any English connection. The only manuscripts employed in modern critical editions of Hilary currently in libraries in Great Britain are two from the fifteenth century, with the first one, at least, from the hand of an Italian humanist.[18] But Smulders did point to a significant pattern during the eleventh and twelfth centuries on the Continent which might also inform some of the evidence to be uncovered in Britain. The majority of the twenty manuscripts of the *De Trinitate* from the eleventh and twelfth centuries belonged to Cistercian monasteries. Smulders notes that Bernard of Clairvaux and the Cistercians made use of Hilary's doctrinal works in their mid twelfth-century disputes around the trinitarian doctrine of Gilbert de la Poirée ("Remarks" 129-30). Although this line of inquiry into the evidence provided by critical editions does not identify any specific manuscript of the writings of Hilary in Britain during the period under investigation, it illustrates the number of manuscripts available on the Continent before and during this period. It also identifies a particular interest in Hilary's theological works by the Cistercians in the eleventh and twelfth centuries.

During the eighth and ninth centuries five pieces of evidence indicate that writings by Hilary existed in Britain. These are presented here in chronological order. The first possible evidence occurs in the famous Codex Amiatinus, a complete version of the Latin Vulgate Bible, which was produced in either the monastery of St. Peter in Wearmouth or of St. Paul in Jarrow. Bede reports that three major codices of the Bible were produced and one was to be presented to the Pope by Abbot Ceolfrith in 716.[19] This, now known as the Amiatinus, is a large deluxe codex of 1,030 folios (i.e., 2,060 pages) which weighs 75 and 1/2 pounds.[20] The first gathering[21] contains an important discussion of the order of the books of the Hebrew Scriptures. Three ways of organizing the books of the Bible are attributed to Jerome, Augustine, and the Septuagint. Each is assigned a page in the Amiatinus. In an important article Bruce-Mitford argued that Hilary of Poitiers was responsible for the third list. The "Hilary" diagram occurs on the original folio 6r (now VIIr).[22] Indeed, if the scribes of the Amiatinus codex had been influenced by Cassiodorus' *Institutiones* 1.14, Hilary is named there as first among others on this particular issue. Hilary of Poitiers does deal with the issue of the number and sequence of Biblical books in his *Instructio . . .* 15 to his *Tractatus super Psalmos* (p. 13, lines 1-23). However, Meyvaert claims that the Northumbrian scribes did not have that text by Cassiodorus. Rather, he argues (835-39), they were influenced directly by the Codex Grandior which had been brought from Rome but unfortunately is no longer extant. Meyvaert (839-44) notices that the actual name in the Amiatinus text had been "Hilarius" and that someone, possibly Bede himself, had erased the final "i" and identified "Hilarus" as *Romanae urbis antistes* substituting *Romanae* for *Pictaviensis*.[23] Because of the uncertainty concerning the identity of the figure named on that page, the Amiatinus does not provide unequivocal evidence that the Anglo-Saxons knew of Hilary.

A second and more reliable piece of evidence occurs a little later in the same geographical location. Bede certainly mentions Hilary by name in a number of texts.[24] He actually quotes two extensive passages from Hilary's *Tractatus super Psalmos* in two passages of his own *Retractatio in Actus Apostolorum*. In the first passage at XIII.33, Bede identifies his source as *sanctus pater Hilarius* and proceeds to quote a total of twenty lines selected from three passages in Hilary's text.[25] He cites Hilary's discussion of Psalm 2:7, "You are my son, today I have begotten you," as applying to the divine generation and not to the virgin birth justified by the citation from Acts 13:32-34. Bede then includes Hilary's citation of Paul, Philippians 2:6-7, and concludes with Hilary's discussion of these texts on "the risen Son's return to the glory of the Father."[26] At XVI.35, Bede cites Hilary's discussion of the gentleness of God with reference to Paul's I Corinthians 4:21.[27] Bede identifies Hilary as his source on two occasions, and he preserves the three Biblical quotations and some of the comment with only minor changes to the text. Bede tends to abbreviate his source and on four occasions has a different preposition or prefix which might indicate some difficulty with abbreviations in the transmission of manuscripts of Hilary's text.

The third and fourth pieces of evidence for the writings of Hilary in Anglo-Saxon England are contributed by Alcuin in the late eighth century. In his famous poem on the bishops, kings, and saints of York, Alcuin simply names Hilary without any indication of titles of works (Godman 122, line 1541). In an anthology of devotional material prepared under Alcuin's direction at York (see Constantinescu), one manuscript version[28] contains a selection of excerpts from nineteen unidentified hymns of which three may be attributed to Caelius Sedulius, Ambrose, and Hilary.[29]

Finally there is some circumstantial evidence that Hilary was known to Aelfric who participated in the Benedictine revival in England. He joined the Benedictine Abbey at Winchester and then was transferred to the Abbey of Cerne in Dorset in 987 where he apparently produced his two collections of sermons, lives of the saints, commentary on *Genesis*, and a grammar. In a sermon on the "Feast of the Ascension," Aelfric comments in Latin on the source for the material he had presented in Old English: "In quodam tractu, qui aestimatur Sancti Hilarii fuisse . . ." (Thorpe 304). Aelfric's expression implies a question about the appropriateness of this attribution to Hilary. Recent scholarship supports his judgment and has identified the actual source as an eighth-century Irish commentary on the *Catholic Epistles*.[30] Aelfric's hesitation suggests that he was sufficiently informed about the writings of Hilary to distinguish Hilary's work from that by someone else.

This cumulative evidence for the influence of the writings of Hilary in Anglo-Saxon England lends some support to Lapidge's speculation about the possible authors of an *Expositio Psalterii* in a booklist possibly from Winchester in the late eleventh century.[31] He seems to favor Cassiodorus, but does include Hilary, Augustine, and Jerome as authors of popular commentaries on the Psalms.

It is difficult to draw too many conclusions from this fragmentary evidence. Bede's quotations show clear evidence for the existence in Northumbria of Hilary's *Tractatus super Psalmos*. This text would be appropriate for monastic and cathedral communities dedicated to the recitation or singing of the psalms on a regular daily schedule. A selection of hymns would serve this context as well.

In the generations immediately after the Norman Conquest six extant manuscripts contain other works by Hilary. Two of these were copied at Salisbury for the Cathedral Library; there is one manuscript each from the Benedictine monasteries at St. Albans and Faversham and from the cathedral centres at Worcester and Canterbury. The number of manuscripts produced by the scriptorium at Salisbury in the late eleventh century and early twelfth century is impressive. A 1992 study[32] of the manuscripts copied at Salisbury during this period illustrates the extent and character of the collection assembled for the new cathedral established in 1075. Webber describes the extensive contents of approximately ninety manuscripts produced by two generations of scribes in the scriptorium at Salisbury. About half of their texts were devoted to patristic texts by Cyprian, Hilary, Ambrose, Jerome, Augustine, and Gregory. In her study of the style of these manuscripts Webber notes that they were produced on poor quality parchment, with the whole page filled in simple long lines rather than in double columns, and containing little decoration. These manuscripts are not deluxe or decorated volumes, and Webber concludes that they were produced for actual use by the canons at Salisbury (8-30). This impressive collection seems to have been designed for more than devotional use. It was probably a broader enterprise set up for the study of scripture and theology because early in this project in the scriptorium at Salisbury a manuscript[33] was copied from a ninth century Continental original which contains texts which could provide an extensive outline for a library collection.[34] Salisbury MS 88 contains Jerome's *De Viris Illustribus*, Cassiodorus' *Institutiones* Book I[35] Gennadius' *Catalogus*, Isidor's *De Viris Illustribus*, and Augustine's *Retractationes*. In both of the works by Jerome and by Cassiodorus, Hilary is named with respect. Jerome provides the list of the titles of Hilary's writings which was employed at the beginning of this article. In his survey of studies on various books of the Bible, Cassiodorus acknowledges Hilary's work on both the Psalms and the Gospel of Matthew (Mynors 1.4 and 1.7). As noted above, Cassiodorus also acknowledges that Hilary deals with the issue of the number and sequence of the books of the Bible. When he presents his list of "learned authors" he begins with a brief tribute to Hilary (Mynors 1.18). Not all of the ninety codices from Salisbury correspond to the advice in Jerome and Cassiodorus,[36] but many of the choices of the Salisbury scribes may very well have been influenced by these two sources. Availability of exemplars, of course, would have been a major consideration.

From this impressive collection at Salisbury two important manuscripts survive which contain works by Hilary. Salisbury Cathedral MS 124 contains Hilary's *Commentarii in Matthaeum* and is dated by Ker to the beginning of the twelfth century.[37] Gneuss (46) dates it a little earlier to the end of the eleventh century. Webber (166) places it among the manuscripts written by the second group of scribes at Salisbury, and includes a black and white photographic plate of a folio of the beginning of Hilary's commentary.[38] Interestingly, this manuscript also contains a *Commentary on the Seven Catholic Epistles* of the type whose authorship Aelfric questioned about a hundred years earlier. The second manuscript is Salisbury Cathedral MS 4 which contains Hilary's *De Trinitate* and *De Synodis*, which is dated by Ker (172) to the beginning of the twelfth century. Webber (160) assigns this manuscript to the second group of scribes at Salisbury.

A third twelfth-century manuscript containing Hilary's *De Trinitate* has an inscription identifying it as once owned by the Benedictine monastery at St. Albans.[39] It is now housed at Pembroke College, with the shelf-number Cambridge 180.[40] Yet another twelfth-century manuscript containing Hilary's *De Trinitate* comes from Worcester and is now housed in the Bodleian Library at Oxford as MS Bodl. 442 (Madan and Craster 340). A fifth twelfth-century manuscript which, like Salisbury Cathedral MS 4, contains Hilary's *De Trinitate* and *De Synodis* comes from the Benedictine Abbey at Faversham and is now housed at Corpus Christi College, Oxford, as MS 31 (Coxe 9). The sixth and final extant twelfth-century manuscript comes from Christ Church, Canterbury, and is now housed at Corpus Christi College, Cambridge, as MS 345 (James, *Corpus* 179-80). In addition to *De Trinitate* and *De Synodis*, this manuscript contains Hilary's pamphlets *Ad*

Constantium and *In Constantium* as well as an example of the position of Auxentius, bishop of Milan, followed by Hilary's *Contra Auxentium*.

This evidence demonstrates the existence in Britain of most of the works of Hilary in the period immediately after the Norman Conquest. Due to the vagaries of preservation of manuscripts, it is impossible to conclude anything about the absence from this list of Hilary's *Tractatus super Psalmos*, which was almost his only text in the evidence of the Anglo-Saxon period. Webber's examination of the glosses in two Salisbury manuscripts concludes that people using them were influenced by exegetical and theological issues emerging on the continent in the wake of the Gregorian reforms.[41]

For the later part of the period of this inquiry there is a very important booklist, the *Registrum Anglie de libris doctorum et auctorum veterum*,[42] compiled probably between 1300 and 1331,which includes the works of Hilary in its survey.[43] That list, put together for the Franciscans at Oxford, represents selections from the holdings of 185 monastic and cathedral libraries in Britain each identified by a numerical code. It is not a complete list because not all institutions were, in fact, surveyed. Even for those institutions which were visited there is evidence that not every item was included in the list. The list is organized by authors' names and ninety-nine authors are identified. The list is not ordered alphabetically but seems to have been arranged according to the relative authority of the authors. Hilary is listed in fourth position immediately after Augustine, Gregory, and Ambrose.

Various works of Hilary are to be found at a wide number of locations throughout Britain. There are twenty-six manuscripts of Hilary's known works, and six others containing letters ascribed to Hilary, perhaps falsely. Moreover, there is one manuscript containing material from Augustine and Jerome on Hilary. The most numerous examples are six entries for Hilary's work *De Trinitate* plus one which appears to be an abbreviated version of that work. There are six copies of *De Synodis*; six more with some of either *In Constantium*, or *Ad Constantium*, or *Contra Auxentium*. There are four copies of the *Commentarii in Matthaeum* and one of the *Tractatus super Psalmos*.

The evidence for the location of these manuscripts in that booklist points to a variety of religious communities throughout Britain. The older Benedictine foundations provide only a few examples for this list.[44] St. Albans in Hertfordshire, founded in 793 and re-established in 966, had two items. Four had only one item each: Bury St. Edmunds in Suffolk, founded in 1020; Colchester in Essex, founded in 1095; Reading in Berkshire, founded in 1121; and Goldcliff in Monmouth, founded in 1113. Four houses of Augustinian canons established in the twelfth century are named in this booklist:[45] Merton in Surrey, founded in 1114, had three manuscripts; Kennilworth in Warwickshire, founded in 1133, Southwick in Hartsfordshire, founded 1133/1145, and Guisborough in Yorkshire, founded in 1119, all had one manuscript each. The Carthusian Priory at Witham,[46] founded in 1178/1179, also had but one manuscript, namely, the *Commentarii in Matthaeum*. This booklist identifies another copy of the same *Commentarii in Matthaeum* at the Cathedral Library in Salisbury, which was almost certainly the Salisbury Cathedral MS 124 noted above. The tenth entry in the booklist is Hilary's *Tractatus super Psalmos* with only one example, at Christ Church, Canterbury (Rouse and Rouse 75). The editors have found this same manuscript mentioned in another potentially earlier list of manuscripts at Canterbury. Although they do not identify their source as either the list from about 1170 or the lengthier one produced under Henry of Eastry, who was Prior of Christ Church from 1281 to 1331, the evidence of these two manuscripts indicates that the Hilary item is referred to in the latter source.[47]

The greatest number of manuscripts of the works of Hilary was reported from Cistercian foundations of the twelfth century.[48] The Abbey of Ford(e) in Dorset, founded in 1136/1141, had six items; the Abbey of Margum in Glamorgan, founded in 1147, had three; the Abbey at Waverley in Surrey, founded 1128, possessed two. Perhaps Smulders' comment on the interest of Continental Cistercian Houses in the theological works of Hilary is to be extended to the new English foundations as well. The Abbey at Ford(e) had the largest collection of the works of Hilary: *De Trinitate*; *De Synodis*; *Ad Constantium*; *In Constantium*; *Contra Auxentium*; and the sample of Auxentius' views. The Abbey of Margum had copies of *De Trinitate* and of *De Synodis* as well as a summary of the views of Jerome and Augustine on Hilary. The Abbey at Waverley had copies of *De Synodis* and of *Ad Constantium*. It is interesting to note that the report for these Cistercian Houses indicates that they have a range of Hilary's theological and even polemical works but none of his explicitly exegetical works.

The vagaries which influence the survival of manuscripts including those which contain lists of library holdings make it difficult to formulate definitive conclusions about the popularity of various texts. The range of the evidence here presented demonstrates that at least the works of Hilary on the Psalms and Hymns were available in Britain in the eighth and ninth centuries. The survival of six twelfth-century manuscripts indicates that almost the full range of exegetical and theological works was available in Britain. The fourteenth-century booklist confirms this and suggests something of the diffusion of these texts throughout monastic and cathedral libraries. In the future these extant manuscripts of Hilary's texts should be examined to determine whether glosses or marginalia indicate anything about the ways these texts were used. Further work needs to be done as well to investigate whether there were any citations or quotations from Hilary in writings from English centres during this period.

Notes

1. For most of his distinguished career Dr. Mahmoud Manzalaoui was involved with the study and the appreciation of Medieval English Literature. I do hope that the existence of copies of Hilary's writings in Medieval Britain with their distinctive themes and methods reflects experiences in the life, teaching, and scholarship of Professor Manzalaoui, and therefore offer this contribution to his Festschrift. I am grateful to Mr. Joseph Jones of the Library at the University of British Columbia for his expert assistance in obtaining information from the British Library, the Bodleian Library and Corpus Christi College Library in Oxford, and from Pembroke College Library in Cambridge. I am also grateful to the referee of this paper whose advice helped clarify the scope of this article.

2. For a brief description and a chronology of Hilary's writings, see Kannengiesser, "Hilaire," and Simonetti.

3. See Jerome, *De Viris Illustribus* (PL 23). This is an important catalogue of 135 Christian writers drawn up by Jerome in 392 or 393. Much of the material is derived from Eusebius with some insertions of Latin authors. Jerome's brief comments have led to some confusion and controversy. His note on Hilary at section 100, for example, has kept modern scholars busy speculating about the nature of the relationship between Hilary and earlier works by Origen.

4. This form of the title first appears in Jerome, *De Viris Illustribus* 100 (PL 23). For the most recent critical edition, see Doignon.

5. For the most recent critical edition, see Brisson. At *De Viris Illustribus* 100 (PL 23), Jerome calls this work *Liber Mysteriorum*.

6. For a critical edition, see Zingerle. Jerome calls this work *Commentarii in Psalmos*.

7. For the most recent critical edition, see Smulders, *De Trinitate*. Jerome calls this work *Libri duodecim adversum Arianos*.

8. Until the editors of *Sources chrétiennes* bring out a critical edition of this text, see PL 10:471-546. *Liber de Synodis* is the title used by Jerome.

9. This is the title used by Jerome. For a recent critical edition, see Rocher.

10. This is the title used by Jerome. For an edition, see PL 10:606-618.

11. For a critical edition, see Feder, *Ad Constantium*. I use the title employed by Jerome.

12. A critical edition of this complex collection is available in Feder, *Adversum Valentem*. Smulders, *Hilary*, offers an important contribution to our understanding of the organization, purpose, and sources of this document. Jerome uses the singular of *Liber* for this title. I use the plural form, found in Feder's edition, to reflect the complex nature of this collection. Other titles used in the literature for this material include *Fragmenta Historica Series A*

et B and Collectanea Antiariana Parisina.

13. Jerome uses this title. For a critical edition, see Feder, *Hymni* 207-23.

14. This text was found in an eleventh-century manuscript in Arezzo, MS Aretinus VI.3, and published for the first time in J. F. Gamurrini, *S. Hilarii Tractatus de Mysteriis et Hymni et S. Silviae Aquitanae Peregrinatio*, Rome, 1887.

15. In his *Libri VI contra Julianum* (PL 44) Augustine appeals to other Christian writers to defend his theological position on original sin. Sometimes in this text Augustine simply provides lists of authorities to support him. At 2.8 (30) and 2.10 (33) he names Cyprian, Hilary, Gregory, and Ambrose. At 6.23 (70) he names only Hilary, Gregory, and Ambrose. At other times Augustine provides a longer list of witnesses in order to emphasize a broad representation of local Churches to support his position. At 3.17 (32) he argues that his witnesses are not only from Africa but represent a consensus of bishops from East and West, and he provides eleven names: Irenaeus, Cyprian, Reticius, Olympius, Hilary, Ambrose, Gregory, Basil, John, Innocent, and Jerome. This same list without the last two names occurs also at 2.10 (37). A similar list to demonstrate universal consensus occurs at 1.6 (22), where he adds the city or territory for each name: Innocent from Rome; Cyprian from Carthage; Basil from Cappadocia; Gregory from Nazianzen; Hilary from Gaul; and Ambrose from Milan. In the same text Augustine actually refers to specific texts by Hilary. At 1.3 (9) he cites Hilary's *Tractatus super Psalmos* 118 Tau 6 and Hilary's quotation there of Psalm 50.7. In a more extended passage at 2.8 (26-29) he refers again to Hilary's *Tractatus super Psalmos* on 118, 1 and 51 as well as to Hilary's *Commentary on Job* which is no longer extant.

16. For a discussion of the evidence in nine letters of Jerome's respect for Hilary's interpretation of scriptural passages, see Kannengiesser, "Héritage" 440-43. Jerome pays tribute to Hilary in his *De Viris Illustribus* 100 (PL 23).

17. For a discussion of the locations of these manuscripts, see Kannengiesser, "Héritage."

18. See the notice in Rocher 89. He pays tribute to Smulders (private correspondence) for a list of late manuscripts which includes Aberdeen, University Libr. 587, XV, and London, British Museum Harley 4949, XV.

19. See Bede, *Historia Abbatum I*, Book 2 (Plummer, ed.). When Ceolfrith died *en route*, the manuscript was taken to Rome and presented to the monastery at Monte Amiato. Upon the closure of this monastery, the manuscript ended up at the Laurentine Library in Florence. For the identification of Florence Laurentinus, see Lowe 299.

20. For a description of this important manuscript and in particular its first gathering which contains a possible reference to Hilary, see Bruce-Mitford. He provides a detailed physical description and a defense of the Northumbrian provenance of the important first gathering and descriptions of the three schemata for ordering the Books of the Bible. He goes on to argue that the contents and style of the Codex Amiatinus may very well have been influenced by the Codex Grandior described by Cassiodorus. See also Mynors 1.5. Meyvaert provides a careful analysis of the role of the Codex Grandior without benefit of Cassiodorus' *Institutiones*.

21. Bruce-Mitford, 189-91, reviews the arguments on the Anglo-Saxon origins of the first gathering of Codex Amiatinus.

22. For a photograph of the "Hilary" page, see Bruce-Mitford 195, plate C. The black and white photograph shows the page with a rectangular outlined at the top with some text inside and a rondel in the middle containing a picture of God the Father. The majority of the page is taken up with the outlines of two crosses side by side. In each design there is

more script. Finally across the bottom of the page is another rectangular outline with more text written inside. In this final section the figure is identified as *hilar[i]us romanae urbis antistes*.

23. Ironically, Cassiodorus' *Institutiones* (Mynors 1.14) acknowledges Hilary of Poitiers on this issue.

24. See, for example, Bede, *In Ezram et Neemian* (Hurst 2), where he lists him with Ambrose, Augustine, and Cyril.

25. See Laistner, 147, and quotations from Hilary on the *Tractatus super Psalmos* (A) p.59, lines 15-26; (B) p.62, lines 13-16; (C) p.63, lines 5-10:

(A)   Huius loci sanctus pater Hilarius ita meminit: Sed id quod nunc in psalmo est: "Filius meus es tu, ego hodie genui te," non ad virginis partum neque ad lavacri regenerationem, sed ad primo genitum a mortuis pertinere apostolica auctoritas est. Namque in libro Actuum apostolorum ita dictum est: "Nosque evangelizamus eam quae ad patres nostros facta est repromissio: hanc deus explevit filiis nostris, suscitans dominum nostrum Iesum, sicut et in psalmo scriptum est: filius meus es tu, ego hodie genui te; cum suscitavit eum a mortuis amplius non regressum in interitum." Vox ergo haec dei patris secundum apostolum in die resurrectionis existit.

(B)   Et paulo post commemorata apostoli sententia, qua dicit de illo "qui cum in forma dei esset non rapinam existimavit se esse aequalem deo, sed se exinanivit forma servi accipiens" et cetera.

(C)   et in gloria, inquit, dei patris hodie genitus nascitur, id est, in manentem ante dei formam per praemium mortis formae servilis adsumptio honestatur; fitque sub tempore nova nec tamen inusitata nativitas, cum ad praesumendam gloriam dei patris, qui ex forma dei in forma hominis erat repertus, primogenitus ex mortuis nasceretur.

Bede is interested in the quotations from scripture and preserves those from Hilary and in the same order as they occur in Hilary's text: Psalm 2:7; Acts 13:32-34; Philippians 2:6-7. To emphasize this I have inserted quotation marks. Bede preserves the full quotation from Hilary for the first two, but he shortens the passage from Philippians to two verses whereas Hilary had cited the whole "hymn," 2:6-11.

26. Bede does follow Hilary's text very closely. In the first passage (A) he omits *primo* after *psalmo*. The only other differences in that passage are minor modifications to Hilary's introductory material. Bede adds the prefix to *regenerationem* and changes the preposition from *ex* to *a* in front of *mortuis*. This may be caused by some confusion over the interpretation of abbreviations in the transmission of the manuscripts of Hilary or even by Bede himself. In the second excerpt (B), Bede formulates his own, briefer lead into the text and then breaks off after the second verse. In the third excerpt (C), Bede presents a passage from Hilary himself without any actual scriptural quotation. Hilary's language reflects the scriptural passages which he has been discussing. Perhaps influenced by the terms in Hilary's actual quotation from Philippians in the previous passage, Bede substitutes *in forma hominis* for Hilary's *in forma servi*. Bede has *ante* for Hilary's *antea* and *praesumendam* for Hilary's *resumendam*. This is the most noticeable feature of Bede's quotations and probably reflects a confusion over interpretations of abbreviations at some point in the manuscript transmission.

27. See Laistner, 152, and his quotation from Hilary on the *Tractatus super Psalmos* (Zingerle 64, line 8-11). Zingerle mistakenly identifies the reference to Paul 1 Cor. 4:21 as 6:21. Here Bede acknowledges Hilary as his source, quotes a slightly briefer form of the scriptural passage, and adds a short question posed in Hilary's text inserting *inquiens* to indicate a source: *cuius officii meminit Hilarius in expositione sententiae apostoli qua dicit: "Quid vultis? In virgam veniam ad vos an in spiritu mansuetudinis?" numquid, inquiens, Paulo ius praetorium erat ut virgam comminaretur et cum officio lictoris ad ecclesiam Christi adesset?*

28. The material is entitled *De Hymnis* and appears in MS Bamberg, Staatsbibliothek, Misc. Patr. 17 (B. II. 10) folios 150v to 151v. Unfortunately, as Lapidge points out, this material has not been printed. For a brief description of this material, see Lapidge ("Bede" 936 n.63, and *Anglo-Latin* 327-29). For a list of the hymns in this material, see Strecker 452-54). He lists the first lines of these poems or hymns and in a few cases includes a whole verse.

29. The fifth item in Strecker's list appears to be version of the final verse of a hymn attributed to Hilary at least as early as the sixth century. For the version in an edition of Hilary, see Feder (*Hymni* 217-23) *Hymnus dubius de Christo*. The doxology, which the editor thinks may be a part of an interpolation, reads as follows: *Gloria patri ingenito, gloria unigenito / simul cum sancto spiritu in sempiterna saecula*. The version in the Bamberg manuscript is very similar. Rather than *patri ingenito* the Father is addressed as *tibi genitor*.

30. For a discussion of this questionable attribution, see Cross 59-78. He notes that Aelfric's phrase implies some misgivings about the attribution of the material to Hilary. For the identification of the source as an eighth-century Irish commentary on the *Catholic Epistles*, see Bischoff 270-72 (qtd. in Cross).

31. See Lapidge, "Surviving" 69-73. In his commentary on the simple notice, Lapidge offers the following suggestions: "*Expositio psalterii*: to judge from the title, the work in question was Cassiodorus, *Expositio psalmorum* . . . ; but a number of commentaries on the psalter were in circulation, in particular those of Augustine . . . , Hilary . . . , and Jerome . . . , as well as various anonymous compilations, any one of which could be in question here."

32. Webber examines the hands of two manuscripts containing texts by Hilary. She includes a photograph of a folio of one of them and constructs a convincing explanation of the motive and function behind this particular collection. In her analysis of the respective hands, she designates the major hand of MS 124 as scribe 9 and the hand in MS 4 as scribe 6, both from her second group of scribes who, she thinks, were active in the early twelfth century. This group has nineteen scribes who produced forty manuscripts and made corrections to eight earlier manuscripts. Her first group consists of seventeen scribes who produced over fifty extant manuscripts. Webber contrasts the kind of books produced with those of other centres and concludes that the Salisbury scribes intended to produce small, plain books for use in their own community. Her survey of the contents of the collection reveals the following results: almost half of the surviving Salisbury texts contain patristic texts of Cyprian, Hilary, Ambrose, Jerome, and Gregory. There are also Latin translations of some texts of Eusebius and Ephraim. Augustine's works are by far the best represented. She suggests (34) that this collection at Salisbury reflects the recommendations in Cassiodorus' *Institutiones*. Salisbury Library MS 88, in fact, is one of the earliest copies of this text in Britain. On comparing this collection with those in the catalogue of Gneuss,

she concludes (32) that this was a far richer collection of patristic texts than had existed in England prior to the Norman Conquest. She notes a number of theological texts perhaps prompted by the Paschasius debates over the Eucharist.

33. For the date of Salisbury MS 88, see Gneuss 45. Webber 150-51 assigns it to the first group of scribes at Salisbury.

34. For a discussion of the role of texts such as Jerome's *De Viris Illustribus* (PL 23) and its influence on library collections in Carolingian centres, see McKitterick 200-05.

35. For a discussion of the exemplar of this manuscript Hereford Cathedral, MS O.iii.2, see Mynors xv-xvi and xxxix-xlix. For his edition Mynors lists the Hereford and the Salisbury manuscripts as well as eight other English manuscripts from the twelfth century which contain the first book of Cassiodorus' *Institutiones*. The large number of extant manuscripts from this period suggests that Cassiodorus' text was being employed to provide a rationale for the study of scripture and theology as well as a list of authors and book titles to make this enterprise possible.

36. The Salisbury scriptorium, for instance, produced a number of classical texts during this period, among them a collection of eight plays by Plautus, the *Tusculanae Disputationes* and the *De Officiis* by Cicero, extracts from the *De Beneficiis* of Seneca, and an anthology of Valerius Maximus and Aulus Gellius.

37. Ker, 175, notes that it is also mentioned in the catalogues of John Leland published in 1715 and of Young where it is number 87.

38. See Webber, plate 9a. This manuscript opens with the same major lacuna common to all known manuscripts of the commentary. The extant text begins without any preface and deals with the two genealogies in the Gospel of Matthew and the Gospel of Luke.

39. For a report of this inscription, see James, *Pembroke* 171. He says that it occurs on folio 1 in red: *Hic est liber S. Albani quem qui ei abstulerit aut titulum deleverit anathema sit.*

40. See Ker 166. James, *Pembroke* 171, describes this manuscript as having been written by a fine hand in the twelfth century. It was donated to Pembroke by Luke Milburn in the seventeenth century.

41. See Webber, chapter 4 "Intellectual Interests." Here she discusses evidence for the existence of a *magister scholarum* at Salisbury presumably to direct the traditional study in the liberal arts. This would account for some of the manuscripts copied there. She proceeds to examine glosses in two manuscripts to discover something of the actual intellectual interests in people who used those manuscripts at Salisbury. In a manuscript of Paul's Epistles, copied at Salisbury and now housed at Oxford, Keble College MS 22, Webber found a series of glosses which illustrate the kind of scriptural study going on at Salisbury. Only a small percentage of these glosses appeals to traditional patristic sources such as Augustine, Ambrose, and Jerome. The bulk of the material restates the argument of Paul in clear terms and often appeals to terms of medieval rhetoric and logic. Salisbury Cathedral MS 160 contains a commentary on the Psalter. In the glosses the authority of Augustine and Cassiodorus on the Psalms is invoked. But there are more numerous appeals to and parallels with the type of exegesis in late eleventh- and early twelfth-century continental commentaries. Webber finishes her discussion of this evidence by linking the methods and the moral and doctrinal concerns to those which pre-occupied scholars after the Gregorian reforms. She cites Jean Leclerq's distinction between an emerging "pastoral" theology from spiritual "monastic" theology on the one hand and also from the speculative "scholastic" theology which emerged in the twelfth century.

42. See Rouse and Rouse. The evidence for the text of this booklist rests on three fifteenth-century manuscripts: Bodleian Library MS Tanner 165, Peterhouse Cambridge MS 169.1, and British Library Royal 3D.i. The Tanner manuscript, originally from Canterbury, is considered to be the most important witness to this text.

43. Based on the known size and activities at Oxford Greyfriars, Rouse and Rouse, cxxxiv-cxli, make a case that this list was compiled between 1300 and 1331. They point out that most intellectual historians have emphasized the speculative work of John Duns Scotus and William of Ockham during this time at Greyfriars. The existence of lists such as the *Registrum Anglie* requires an investigation into the exegetical and patristic interests at this centre during this period.

44. For specific information on location, date of foundation, and size for the Benedictine houses in Britain, see Knowles and Hadcock 58-93.

45. For the data on the houses of Augustinian canons, see Knowles and Hadcock 125-61.

46. For the data on this foundation, see Knowles and Hadcock 122-24.

47. See Rouse and Rouse 75, no. 178. For an edition of early booklists of the collection at Canterbury, see James, *Ancient*. On pp.3-11, he provides a facsimile and an edition of the 1170 list based on Cambridge University Library MS Ii.3.13. The actual reference to Hilary's text on the Psalms occurs in MS Cotton Collection, Galba E.IV folios 128-147. James provides an edition of this manuscript on pp.13-142 and the actual reference occurs on p.36. In addition to the dates for Henry of Eastry as Prior, James notes, p.xxxv, that this manuscript was written in an early fourteenth-century hand.

48. For the Cistercian foundations, see Knowles and Hadcock 104-21.

Works Cited

Augustine. *S. Aurelii Augustini Hipponensis Episcopi Contra Julianum Libri Sex*. PL 44: 641-874. Ed. J.-P. Migne. Paris, 1865.

Bischoff, B. "Wendepunkte der Geschichte der lateinischen Exegese im Frühmittelalter." *Sacris Erudiri* 6 (1954): 189-281.

Brisson, J.-P. ed. *Hilaire de Poitiers: Traité des Mystères*. Sources chrétiennes 19. Paris: Les Editions du Cerf, 1967.

Bruce-Mitford, R. L. S. "The Art of the Codex Amiatinus." *Bede and His World: The Jarrow Lectures 1967*. Preface by M. Lapidge. Vol. 1. Brookfield: Variorum, 1994. 185-234.

Constantinescu, R. "Alcuin et les 'Libelli precum' de l'époque carolingienne." *Revue de l'histoire de la spiritualité* 50 (1974): 17-56.

Coxe, H. O. *Catalogus codicum MSS qui in collegiis aulisque oxoniensibus hodie adservantur*. 2 vols. Oxford: Typographeo academico, 1852.

Cross, J. E. "More Sources for Two of Aelfric's Catholic Homilies." *Anglia* 86 (1968): 59-78.

Doignon, J., ed. *Hilaire de Poitiers: Sur Matthieu 1-2*. Sources chrétiennes 254, 258. Paris: Les Editions du Cerf, 1978, 1979.

Feder, A., ed. *S. Hilarii Episcopi Pictaviensis Hymni*. CSEL 65: 207-23. Vienna: F. Tempsky; Leipzig: G. Freytag, 1916.

—. *S. Hilarii Episcopi Pictaviensis Liber ad Constantium Imperatorem.* CSEL 65: 195-205. Vienna: F. Tempsky; Leipzig: G. Freytag, 1916.

—. ed. *S. Hilarii Episcopi Pictaviensis Libri tres adversum Valentem et Ursacium.* CSEL 65: 39-193. Vienna: F. Tempsky; Leipzig: G. Freytag, 1916.

Gamurrini, J. F., ed. *S. Hilarii Tractatus de Mysteriis et Hymni et S. Silviae Aquitanae Peregrinatio.* Rome, 1887.

Gneuss, H. "A Preliminary List of Manuscripts Written or Owned in England up to 1100." *Anglo-Saxon England* 9 (1981): 1-60.

Godman, Peter. *Alcuin: The Bishops, Kings, and Saints of York.* Oxford: Clarendon, 1982.

Hilary of Poitiers. *Sancti Hilarii Contra Arianos vel Auxentium Mediolanensem.* PL 10: 606-618. Ed. J.-P. Migne. Paris, 1845.

—. *Sancti Hilarii Liber de Synodis.* PL 10: 471-546. Ed. J.-P. Migne. Paris, 1845.

Hurst, D., ed. *Bedae Venerabilis Opera: In Ezram et Neemian.* CCSL 199A: 235-392. Turnhout: Brepols, 1969.

James, M. R. *Ancient Libraries of Canterbury and Dover.* Cambridge: Cambridge UP, 1903.

—. *A Descriptive Catalogue of the Manuscripts in the Library of Corpus Christi College, Cambridge.* Cambridge: Cambridge UP, 1911.

—. *A Descriptive Catalogue of the Manuscripts in the Library of Pembroke College Cambridge.* Cambridge: Cambridge UP, 1905.

Jerome. *S. Eusebii Hieronymi de Viris Illustribus.* PL 23: 631-760. Ed. J.-P. Migne. Paris, 1883.

Kannengiesser, C. "L'Héritage d'Hilaire de Poitiers 1. Dans l'ancienne Église d'Occident et dans les Bibliothèques médiévales." *Recherches de science religieuse* 56 (1968): 435-56.

—. "Hilaire de Poitiers (saint)." *Dictionnaire de Spiritualité.* Vol. 6. Paris: G. Beauchesne, 1968. 466-99.

Ker, N. R. *Catalogue of Manuscripts Containing Anglo-Saxon.* Oxford: Clarendon, 1957.

Knowles, D., and R. N. Hadcock. *Medieval Religious Houses: England and Wales.* London, New York, Toronto: Longmans, Green, 1953.

Laistner, M. L. W., ed. *Bedae Venerabilis . . . Retractatio in Actus Apostolorum.* CCSL 121: 101-63. Turnhout: Brepols, 1983.

Lapidge, M. "Bede the Poet." *Jarrow Lecture 1993 in Bede and his World.* Vol.II Brookfield: Variorum, 1994. 927-56.

—. *Anglo-Latin Literature 600-899.* London and Rio Grande, Ohio: Hambledon Press, 1996.

—. "Surviving Booklists from Anglo-Saxon England." *Learning and Literature in Anglo-Saxon England.* Ed. M. Lapidge and H. Gneuss. Cambridge: Cambridge UP, 1985. 33-89.

Lowe, E. A. *Codices Latini Antiquiores.* Part III. Oxford: Clarendon, 1938.

Madan, F., and H. H. E. Craster. *A Summary Catalogue of Western Manuscripts in the Bodleian Library at Oxford.* Vol. 2. Part 1. Oxford: Clarendon, 1922.

McKitterick, R. *The Carolingians and the Written Word.* Cambridge: Cambridge UP, 1989.

Meyvaert, P. "Bede, Cassiodorus, and the Codex Amiatinus." *Speculum* 71 (1996): 827-83.

Mynors, R. A. B., ed. *Cassiodori Senatoris Institutiones.* Oxford: Clarendon, 1937.

Plummer, C., ed. *Venerabilis Baedae Historia Ecclesiastica gentis Anglorum, Historia Abbatum . . . .* Oxford: Clarendon, 1896.

Rocher, A., ed. *Hilaire de Poitiers: Contre Constance*. Sources chretiennes 334. Paris: Les Editions du Cerf, 1987.

Rouse, R. H., and M. A. Rouse, eds. *Registrum Anglie de libris doctorum et auctorum veterum*. Latin text establ. by R. A. B. Mynors. London: British Library in Association with the British Academy, 1991.

Simonetti, M. "Hilary of Poitiers and the Arian Crisis in the West." *Patrology*. Vol. 4. Ed. J. Quasten and A. Di Berardino. Westminster, Maryland: Christian Classics, 1986. 33-61.

Smulders, P., ed. *Sancti Hilarii Pictaviensis episcopi de trinitate*. CCSL 62, 62A. Turnhout: Brepols, 1979, 1980.

—. *Hilary of Poitiers' Preface to his Opus Historicum*. Leiden: Brill, 1995.

—. "Remarks on the Manuscript Tradition of the *De Trinitate* of Saint Hilary of Poitiers." *Studia Patristica* 3.1 (1961): 129-38.

Strecker, K. *Rhythmi Aevi Merovingici et Carolini*. MGH: Poetae Latini Aevi Carolini 4.2. Berlin: Weidmann, 1896.

Thorpe, B., ed. *The Homilies of the Anglo-Saxon Church: the first part containing the Sermones Catholici or Homilies of Aelfric . . . .* Vol. 1. London: Aelfric Society, 1844.

Webber, T. *Scribes and Scholars at Salisbury Cathedral c.1075-1125*. Oxford: Clarendon, 1992.

Zingerle, A., ed. *S. Hilarii episcopi Pictaviensis Tractatus super Psalmos*. CSEL 22. Prague and Vienna: F. Tempsky; Leipzig: G. Freytag, 1891.

Gernot R. Wieland

"GE MID WIGE GE MID WISDOME": ALFRED'S DOUBLE-EDGED SWORD[1]

Alfred's Preface to the translation of the *Cura Pastoralis* has received much critical attention, and yet not all the aspects of that much anthologized piece of writing have been analyzed.[2] A large part of the criticism has concentrated on examining Alfred's claim that learning had vanished in England during the ninth century.[3] The present paper will examine a somewhat different aspect, namely Alfred's description of the English "golden age," and especially the sentence "me com swiðe oft on gemynd . . . hu ða kyningas . . . hiora onweald innanbordes gehioldon, ond eac ut hiora eðel rymdon; and hu him ða speow ægðer ge mid wige ge mid wisdome" (Mitchell and Robinson, 204-05)–"I often thought about the way in which the kings wielded power within their countries, and also expanded them outward; and how they prospered in both war and wisdom." The phrase has received only scant attention so far. Frantzen briefly touched on it in the following comments: "He [=Alfred] recalls that the kings, obedient to God and His messengers, not only maintained peace at home but extended their realms, and thus were successful 'both in warfare and wisdom'–a more potent and telling combination, perhaps, than the 'wealth and wisdom' Shippey analyzes" and "his [=Alfred's] pairing of 'warfare and wisdom' reflects his own concern with harmonizing life and learning" (28-29). Frantzen provides only this tantalizing hint, but does not develop the significance of the pairing of these words any further. I do not wish to argue that "both in warfare and wisdom" is a "more potent and telling combination . . . than the 'wealth and wisdom' Shippey analyzes," but I would like to argue that it is equally important.

Commentators on the passage have provided one source and one parallel: the phrase "ge mid wige ge mid wisdome" has its parallel in the "wig ond wisdom" of *Beowulf*, line 350, as Klaeber notes. Klaeber (54-55) also supposes that Alfred derived his opinions about the "golden age" either from oral tradition or more specifically from Bede's *Historia Ecclesiastica* iv.2 which reads:

> Neque umquam prorsus, ex quo Brittaniam petierunt Angli, feliciora fuere tempora, dum et fortissimos Christianosque habentes reges cunctis barbaris nationibus essent terrori, et omnium uota ad nuper audita caelestis regni gaudia penderent, et quicumque lectionibus sacris cuperent erudiri, haberent in promtu magistros qui docerent. (Colgrave and Mynors 334)
> Never had there been such happy times since the English first came to Britain; for having such brave Christian kings, they were a terror to all the barbarian nations, and the desires of all men were set on the joys of the heavenly kingdom of which they had only lately heard; while all who wished for instruction in sacred studies had teachers ready to hand.
>   (Colgrave and Mynors 335)

Klaeber argues that "it is difficult to believe that Alfred did not think of this passage" (55). There are, however, enough differences between Alfred's and Bede's passages that Alfred either did not think of Bede's words or that he modified them considerably. The major difference consists in this: in Bede the Christian kings were strong, and it was the people who sought instruction, that is, wisdom; in Alfred, the "people" are not mentioned at all, only the *wiotan*, and it is the kings who are successful in both wisdom and war. To this one can add that in Bede the Christian kings "were a terror to all the barbarian nations," while in Alfred they actually "expanded their territories outward." The difference is important in that the ideal of kingship seems to have changed from one in which the king had to be merely strong (presumably in war) to one in which he had to be both strong and wise.

There is another problem as well. In Alfred's vision of the "golden age," kings were obedient to their priests, their reigns were characterized by harmony within their realms, and they were able to expand their territories outward. Alfred does not situate his statement in a clearly defined time; he speaks rather vaguely of *iu*, and thereby suggests that this period extended over a considerable time. Bede, on the other hand, wrote his entry for the year 669, and seems to allow its validity for no more than about one or two decades on either side of 669 as is suggested by the fates of the Christian kings Edwin or Oswald, both killed by "heathen Mercians and their heathen king," the first in 633, the second in 642, or of the Christian king Oswiu who, despite his Christianity, lost territory in 655, or of king Egfrid who did not listen to his priestly advisers and consequently lost his life at the hands of the Picts in 685.[4] By using the vague *iu* Alfred either ignores or is ignorant of these historical facts as presented by Bede. Moreover, Alfred's claim that the Christian English kings "ut hiora eðel rymdon" is either contradicted by historical evidence or is logically flawed. The period of the greatest expansion occurred before the English kings had converted to Christianity; after that any territorial expansion by one Christian English king would, with the exception of the kings living in regions bordering on Celtic territories, inevitably be at the expense of another Christian English king, and thus Alfred's claim cannot be true for all of them. I might add that at that time the Celtic tribes were at least nominally Christian themselves.

Alfred's vagueness about the actual period he is referring to allows the following interpretation: Alfred was not concerned with historical accuracy, but with an ideal. That ideal, I shall argue, is a continental, and specifically a Carolingian one.

Readers of the article *"Sapientia et Fortitudo* as the Controlling Theme of *Beowulf"* might *a priori* object to such a claim, because Kaske has clearly shown that the combination of *sapientia* and *fortitudo* was an ideal enunciated in various books of the Old Testament and elaborated by the Fathers, and one that was also embraced by the Germanic people before their conversion. In *Beowulf* itself, the theme recurs with several variations, for example, in Hrothgar, who has *sapientia* but no *fortitudo*, in Heremod, who has *fortitudo* but no *sapientia*, in Hrothulf, to whom the poet ascribes the "wig and wisdom" of line 350, and of course in Beowulf himself, who has both. The "thoughthoard" from which the *Beowulf*-poet took his idea may therefore also have provided Alfred's; since the dating of *Beowulf* is so hotly disputed,[5] I do not dare suggest that Alfred actually took his phrase from the poem, but he clarly reached into the same "wordhoard" as the *Beowulf*-poet.

Since *sapientia* and *fortitudo* seem to be combined so frequently, from the Old Testament through the Fathers all the way to *Beowulf*–E. R. Curtius (173-79), bringing in yet more examples, even declares the ideal a "commonplace"–how can one argue for a specific provenance of the idea as I wish to do? The answer lies not in the phrase "ge mid wige ge mid wisdome" itself, but in the immediately preceding sentence "hu hie . . . hiora onweald innanbordes gehioldon, ond eac ut hiora eðel rymdon," which I consider intimately linked with "ond hu him ða speow ægðer ge mid wige ge mid wisdome." There can be no doubt that a ruler needs wisdom to hold (on to) power *innanbordes*,[6] and that he needs success in war to expand his territories *ut*. Success in war, furthermore, does not come without wisdom, and it is a political commonplace that success in war also helps a ruler to maintain his power at home. The phrase "ge mid wige ge mid wisdome" thus applies to the entire preceding sentence, and one cannot make the distinction that *wisdom* alone is needed to rule *innanbordes*, or *wig* alone to expand one's territory.

The concept of wisdom in the Preface has been exhaustively examined by Szarmach who concludes that Alfred shares Augustine's ideal of wisdom, with "wisdom [having] God for its object" (66) and with "wisdom, happiness, and God [being] virtually synonymic" (69). If that is true, and I for one do not doubt that it is, then the common-place meaning of the phrase "ge mid wige ge mid wisdome," as defined by Curtius, has been changed considerably. The Germanic chieftain's wisdom in warfare would pertain to foresight, careful planning, and cool-headed execution of military strategy; the Christian warrior's wisdom would include all these, but also God. God and warfare are not antithetical, as a quick perusal of the Old Testament shows. Alfred himself also makes the connection between pursuit of wisdom (=God) and warfare in the Preface:

> Geðenc hwelc witu us ða becomon for ðisse worulde, ða ða we hit [=wisdom] nohwæðer ne selfe ne lufodon, ne eac oðrum monnum ne lefdon; ðone naman ænne we lufodon ðætte we Cristne wæren, and swiðe feawa ða ðeawas.
>
> (Mitchell and Robinson 205)
>
> Consider which punishments we had to undergo on account of this world when we neither loved [wisdom] nor left it to other people; we loved only the name of 'Christian,' but very few of its moral demands. (translation mine)

Punishment, and that has traditionally been interpreted as the attacks by the Vikings, came because the Anglo-Saxons no longer loved wisdom nor left it to other people; and in the sentence that follows Alfred confirms the religious aspect of wisdom by accusing the Anglo-Saxons of being Christians in name only. The conclusion to be drawn from these lines is this: as long as a nation loves wisdom, that is, searches for God, He will extend His protecting hand over it. Should it fail to love God, He will withdraw His protection and subject it to warfare. In this view, God is a shield for a nation.

Alcuin's letters to England after the sack of Lindisfarne are full of both positive and negative examples of the conclusion we can draw from Alfred's Preface. In his letter to Aethelhard, archbishop of Canterbury, for instance, he says,

> Legitur vero in libro Gildi Brettonum sapientissimi, quod idem ipsi Brettones propter rapinas et avaritiam principum, propter iniquitatem et iniustitiam iudicum, propter desidiam et

pigritiam praedicationis episcoporum, propter luxoriam et malos
mores populi patriam perdiderunt. (Duemmler, *Epistolae* 47)
We read in the book of Gildas, the wisest man of the Britons,
that the Britons lost their homeland because of the rapine and
greed of their princes, because of the wickedness and injustice
of their judges, because of the sloth and laziness in preaching of
their bishops, and because of the decadence and immoral
behaviour of the people.   (translation mine)

And he applies the lesson learned from Gildas to the English in his letter to
Aethelred, king of the Northumbrians: "Considerate habitum, tonsuram, et
mores principum et populi luxuriosos" (Duemmler, *Epistolae* 43) ["look at
the decadent fashion, hairstyle, and behaviour of both princes and people"].
And more forcefully:

A diebus Aelfwaldi regis fornicationes adulteria et incestus
inundaverunt super terram, ita ut absque omni verecundia etiam
et in ancillis Deo dicatis hec peccata perpetrabantur. Quid
dicam de avaritia rapinis et violentis iudiciis? . . . . Qui sanctas
legit scripturas et veteres revolvit historias et seculi considerat
eventum, inveniet pro huiusmodi peccatis reges regna et populos
patriam perdidisse.   (Duemmler, *Epistolae* 43)
Since the days of Aelfwald fornication, adultery and incest have
flooded this land, to such a degree that these sins are committed
without any shame even against maidens vowed to God. What
should I say about greed, rapine, and violent judgements? . . .
Whoever reads the Holy Scriptures, whoever thinks about
ancient history, and whoever considers the events of the world,
will find that kings have lost their kingdoms, and people their
homeland because of sins of this kind.   (translation mine)

And positively: "Mores enim honestos habete Deo placabiles et hominibus
laudabiles" (Duemmler, *Epistolae* 44) ["exhibit honest behaviour, pleasing
to God and praiseworthy among people"]—and "nolite in armis spem ponere,
sed in Deo, qui numquam deserit sperantes in se" (Duemmler, *Epistolae* 54)
["Do not put your faith in weapons, but in God, who never deserts those who
hope in Him"]. I quote these passages at length in order to show that the
ideas Alfred hints at had some 100 years before his time been enunciated
quite clearly by an Anglo-Saxon at the Carolingian court in letters addressed
to Anglo-Saxon bishops and kings.

Alfred, however, does not only evoke God as a shield over the English
kings of the golden age, but suggests that their wisdom (in the sense in which
Szarmach has defined it) is one edge of the double-edged swords which
allowed them to expand their kingdoms outward. Since this is, as I mentioned

above, historically incorrect for England, we need to ask for the source of Alfred's idea. Part of the answer can be found in the intellectual climate surrounding Alfred. One writer who is very much concerned with kingly virtues is Alfred's biographer Asser.[7] He several times connects "wisdom" with success in war, once in chapters 37-39, in which Alfred successfully fights against the Vikings while his brother Aethelred is detained at Mass, another time at the Viking siege of Countisbury, which the inhabitants, who were "divinely inspired," ended by bursting out against the enemy and defeating them. Most telling, though, is Asser's comment in chapter 42, that Alfred "surpassed all his brothers both in wisdom and in all good habits; and in particular because he was a great warrior and victorious in virtually all battles" (Keynes and Lapidge 78-80, 84, 80-81). The "in particular" suggests very strongly that success in war is only one form of wisdom (wisdom as defined by Szarmach). Here Asser says about Alfred what Alfred says about the Christian English kings of the golden age. The idea thus certainly is one of the intellectual climate around Alfred, but we cannot be certain whether Alfred shaped that climate or was shaped by it.

Asser himself is influenced by a Carolingian, especially by Einhard's *Life of Charlemagne*.[8] Einhard structures this Life in such a way that he first lists all the wars in which Charlemagne had fought (chapters 5-14), then discusses other "opera . . . ad regni decorem et commoditatem pertinentia" (Firchow and Zeydel 72)–"works calculated to adorn and benefit his [=Charlemagne's] kingdom" (Painter 43), and includes a chapter on Charlemagne's learning, praising him with statements such as "artes liberales studiosissime coluit, earumque doctores plurimum veneratus magnis adficiebat honoribus" (Firchow and Zeydel 92)–"he most zealously cultivated the liberal arts, held those who taught them in great esteem, and conferred great honors upon them" (Painter 53-4). Charlemagne is thus portrayed as a king who succeeded in war against outside enemies, and in wisdom within his realm. Einhard never explicitly mentions this twofold division of his work, and thus the kingly ideal is only implicit. There is one phrase, however, that is repeated several times: Charlemagne is shown as a king who expanded his territory, once in chapter 15,[9] again in chapters 17 and 18,[10] and finally in chapter 31, which reports the inscription on his tombstone: "Sub hoc conditorio situm est corpus Caroli Magni atque orthodoxi imperatoris, qui regnum francorum nobiliter ampliavit et per annos xlvii feliciter rexit" (Firchow and Zeydel 104)–"in this tomb lies the body of Charles, the Great and Orthodox Emperor, who gloriously extended the kingdom of the Franks, and reigned prosperously for forty-seven years"

(Painter 60). When Alfred claimed that the English Christian kings "ut hiora eðel rymdon" he may not have thought so much of the historical reality of England as of the historical reality expressed in Einhard's *Life of Charlemagne*, which he then construed as a kingly ideal.

This raises the question of whether Alfred knew Einhard's *Life*. Before Smyth's attack on the authenticity on Asser's *Life*, one could have answered that because of Alfred's close intellectual cooperation with Asser, and because of Asser's use of Einhard's *Life*, it seems impossible that Alfred would not have known Einhard's work. But even if we were to acknowledge that (Pseudo-) Asser was not a contemporary of the Anglo-Saxon king, it still seems impossible that Alfred would not have known Einhard's *Life*. Alfred seems to have modelled himself consciously on Charlemagne, and knowledge of Charlemagne would primarily have reached him through Einhard's *Life*. Alfred's educational programme parallels Charlemagne's, and his defensive tactics parallel Charlemagne's efforts to build "strong points and coastguard stations."[11] If Alfred did not get to know Einhard's *Life* through Asser, then Alfred's priests John or Grimbald could have introduced him to it. The parallels between Alfred and Charlemagne in both their military and educational efforts strongly suggest that Alfred knew Einhard's *Life*.

Einhard's work, however, while stressing Charlemagne's success in expanding his Empire, does not explicitly provide a link between success in warfare and the pursuit of (Christian) wisdom. This is left to Alcuin, in whose works the idea can be found several times. One of its first occurrences is in letter 41: "gladium triumphalis potentiae vibrat in dextera et catholicae praedicationis tuba resonat in lingua" (Duemmler, *Epistolae* 84) ["he brandishes the sword of triumphal power in his right hand and the trumpet of catholic preaching resounds on his tongue"]. And immediately following this sentence, Alcuin speaks about the Old Testament David:

> David olim praecedentis populi rex a Deo electus et Deo dilectus et egregius psalmista Israheli victrici gladio undique gentes subiciens, legisque Dei eximius praedicator in populo extitit.
>
> (Duemmler, *Epistolae* 84)
>
> David, king of an earlier people, elected by God and beloved by him, as well as an outstanding composer of psalms, and everywhere defeating foreign nations with the victorious sword of Israel, was an excellent preacher of the law of God among his people.   (translation mine)

A descendant of this David is Christ, who, in the days of Alcuin, has given another David to the Frankish people, both as *rector* and *doctor*. And under his shadow "populus requiescit christianus, et terribilis undique gentibus extat paganis" (Duemmler, *Epistolae* 84) ["the Christian populace is at rest, and is a terror everywhere to pagan nations"]. Alcuin leaves little doubt here that the Old Testament David was so successful against foreign nations because he composed psalms, and because he preached the law of God. His wisdom translated into success in war, and it did so as well with the latter-day David, Charlemagne. In another letter (letter 202) Alcuin expresses his wish that "veluti armis imperium christianum fortiter dilatare laborat, ita et apostolicae fidei veritatem defendere, docere, et propagare studeat" (Duemmler, *Epistolae* 336) ["just as he [Charlemagne] labours bravely to expand the Christian empire with weapons, so he may strive to defend, teach, and propagate the truth of the apostolic faith"]. The two concepts of *wig* and *wisdom*, the latter expressed in the words *docere et propagare*, are clearly linked, and both rest on God: it is the *Christian* empire which Charlemagne is to extend, and it is the apostolic faith which he is to propagate, and he is to do the one *just as* he does the other.

Alcuin, as the above example shows, bases his ideas of ideal kingship on David in the Old Testament. The Emperor Constantine might seem to provide a more specifically Christian model. According to his biographer Eusebius, Constantine saw the sign of the cross in the evening sky before his battle against Maxentius and heard a voice say *hac vince* (PL 8, c.22). God and success in warfare are clearly linked in Eusebius' account, and this linkage provides a paradigm for Christian rulers. Alcuin, however, was not influenced by these ideas. He did not consider Constantine as the archetype of the Christian ruler since Constantine became a heretic under the influence of both his wife and Arius, and consequently led a life "principio bono, fine malo" (letter 182, Duemmler, *Epistolae* 303). There is evidence that other people at Charlemagne's court attempted to turn him into a new Constantine, but Alcuin is not one of them, since for him Constantine lacked the wisdom necessary for an ideal king.[12]

That Alcuin's ideas gained currency and became a standard view of ideal kingship can also be shown by the dedicatory image which Alcuin's disciple Hrabanus Maurus attached to his *De laudibus sanctae crucis*.[13] This work celebrates Louis the Pious, son of Charlemagne, as the *miles Christi* of Paul's letter to the Ephesians 6:11-18, as Elizabeth Sears has shown. This *carmen figuratum* depicts Louis as a Roman soldier, holding a cross in his right hand and resting his left hand on a shield which stands on the ground. Traced within the nimbus, crown and head of the figure within the poem are the following lines: "Iesu Christe, tuum vertice signum / Augusto galeam conferat almam," and on Louis' right arm: "Invictam et faciat optima dextram / Virtus, Jesu, tua detque triumphum."[14] Head and hand, the seats of wisdom and martial strength respectively, are joined here, and God, in Szarmach's analysis synonymous with wisdom, is called upon to grant the Emperor "triumph," which means victory over external enemies. The *galea alma* is, of course, biblical, a poetic version of Paul's *galea salutis,* but the *invicta dextera* replaces Paul's "gladium spiritus (quod est verbum Dei)." Hrabanus, presumably following Alcuin's lead in the above quoted "gladium triumphalis potentiae vibrat in dextera," transforms the Pauline soldier of Christ from one who fights against *insidias diaboli* to one who also, in contrast to Paul, fights against *carnem et sanguinem.* I should add that unlike Charlemagne, Louis is not known for expanding his territory; quite the contrary, under him the fragmentation of the Carolingian Empire began, and he even was deposed briefly by his own sons in the period between October 833 and March 834. In his dedicatory image, therefore, Hrabanus expresses an ideal rather than a reality.

Alfred's sentence, though not a direct verbal borrowing of any of the quoted passages from Alcuin's letters or from Hraban's dedicatory image, nonetheless strongly echoes the sentiments expressed by them. Alcuin provides the link between seeking (Christian) wisdom and expanding one's territory outward, which seem so oddly joined in Alfred's Preface. Alcuin's preaching and psalm-composing Davids, that is, both the historical David and Charlemagne, defeat foreign nations everywhere, just as Alfred's Christian English kings of the golden age sought wisdom, that is, God, and expanded their territories outward.

One of Alcuin's letters to Charlemagne, namely # 41, written in the ninth century at St. Denis, may have reached England before Alfred's time, but since its subsequent history is connected with York, it is doubtful whether Alfred would have known its contents.[15] The two English manuscripts containing Hrabanus' *De laudibus sanctae crucis* are both written later than Alfred's time,[16] and can therefore not have influenced the king. But even though there are no manuscripts linking Alfred's court with Carolingian Francia, there is sufficient evidence for a cross-channel communication between the two countries. During his lifetime Alcuin corresponded with English kings, and the ideas of that correspondence would undoubtedly have become known. Asser, and quite possibly Alfred himself, are influenced by Einhard. Alfred's priests John the Saxon and Grimbald, both from the Continent, could have brought the ideal to England, and there is an even more intimate link between the West-Saxon and the West Frankish court in

Judith, Alfred's stepmother. The ideal of kingship expressed in Alfred's Preface could have come on any of these avenues from Francia to England.

When Alfred instituted the educational reform of the late ninth century, he intended to do more than just enable young free Anglo-Saxons to read *Englisc gewrit*. The educational reform was also meant as a spiritual and physical re-armament of the Anglo-Saxon youth. The successful wars against the Danes might have honed one edge of a double-edged sword, namely, military knowledge, but Alfred knew that the other edge, namely, wisdom, had to be sharpened as well if their success was to last.

Notes

1. What gift does an Anglo-Saxonist give a Middle English scholar? Shall he venture beyond the divide created by 1066 and risk the wrath and censure of Middle English specialists? Or shall he stay firmly within his own period and offer the gift across the great divide? I have decided to stay within my area of specialty, and offer the honoree this *parvum opus* because everyone knows Alfred the Great, and because during his illustrious teaching career Dr. Manzalaoui had numerous occasions both to bemoan the "decline in learning" and, like Alfred, to further its revival.

2. The *Preface* has been anthologized in, for example, Mitchell and Robinson 204-07, and Whitelock 4-7.

3. See, for instance, Brooks, who considers Alfred's account reliable; Morrish argues that Alfred greatly underestimated the state of learning in England of his time; H. Gneuss, "Anglo-Saxon" 672-78, and Gneuss, "King Alfred" contradict Morrish.

4. On Edwin, see Colgrave and Mynors, 202-3 = *HE* ii, 20; on Oswald, pp. 240-43 = *HE* iii, 9; on Oswiu, pp. 294-5 = *HE* iii, 24; and on Egfrid, pp. 428-9 = *HE* iv, 26.

5. See the various articles in Chase, which situate the date of composition anywhere between the eighth to the eleventh century.

6. Cf., for example, the statement about Offa in *Beowulf*, lines 1959-60: "wisdome heold eðel sine."

7. Smyth argues that the *Life of Alfred* was not written contemporaneously with the king, but about a hundred years later, and was not written by Asser, but by Pseudo-Asser in, or around, Ramsey. For the purposes of this paper it does not really matter whether Asser or Pseudo-Asser wrote the *Life*, and whether he wrote it contemporaneously with the king or a hundred years later. There can be no doubt that the biographer summarizes the intellectual climate around Alfred, whether he does so from direct experience or from a thorough study of Alfred's works. The fact that he introduces hagiographical rather than biographical features may be annoying to the modern historian, but in so doing he emphasizes rather than diminishes those points which he considers part of the kingly ideal.

8. Since the translation of Firchow and Zeydel is not always reliable, I use Painter instead.

9. Firchow and Zeydel 66: "regnum Francorum, quod post patrem Pippinum magnum quidem et forte susceparat, ita nobiliter ampliavit, ut poene duplum illi adiecerit"–"he so largely increased the Frankish kingdom, which was already great and strong when he

received it at his father's hands, that more than double its former territory was added to it" (Painter 40).

10. Firchow and Zeydel 72: "Qui cum tantus in ampliando regno et subigendis exteris nationibus existeret"–"this king, who showed himself so great in extending his empire and subduing foreign nations" (Painter 42). Firchow and Zeydel 74: "Talem eum in tuendo et ampliando simulque ornando regno fuisse constat"–"thus did Charles defend and increase as well as beautify his kingdom, as is well known" (Painter 43).

11. Smyth (140) mentions that "Einhard refers to Charlemagne's strong points and coastguard stations . . . at those river-mouths which were considered large enough for the entry of Norse longships," and contends that "Alfred's own defensive campaign may have been inspired . . . by contemporary Frankish practice."

12. See Godman (77) on Theodulf's drawing the parallel between Charlemagne and Constantine. Angilbert's reference to "Roma secunda" in "Karolus Magnus et Leo Papa" (Duemmler, *Poetae* 368, line 94) seems to draw another parallel between Charlemagne and Constantine. Godman (56-9) argues that Alcuin himself created "an implicit parallel between Charlemagne and Constantine" in his *Carmen* vii (Duemmler, *Poetae* 226-7). Since Alcuin explicitly states his dislike of Constantine in letter 182, I do not think that he intended to create even an implicit parallel. Hauck claims that Charlemagne's wish to rename Paderborn as *urbs Karoli* parallels Constantine's renaming of Byzantium to *Constantinopolis*. The parallel between Constantine and a ruler is also drawn in Clemens Peregrinus' letter to Tassilo, Duke of Bavaria (Duemmler, *Epistolae* 497).

13. Edited in PL 107: 133-294. The dedicatory image is on c. 142.

14. Text, with a slight modification, from PL 107: 141-2.–"Jesus Christ, may your sign on his forehead provide the Emperor with the helmet of salvation," and "may your excellent strength, Jesus, render his right hand invincible and grant the just man triumph." My translation differs slightly from Sears', who translates: "Jesus Christ, your power shall bestow the blessed helmet upon the emperor's head. And may your excellent virtue, Jesus, render his hand invincible, and grant the just man triumphs."

15. The letter is contained in Ms BL Harley 208, written after 814. On the manuscript, see Duemmler (*Epistolae* 5-6), and Gneuss, 28, # 417.

16. These manuscripts are Cambridge, Trinity College B.16.3 (s. x med.) = Gneuss, 14, #178, and Cambridge, University Library Gg.5.35 (s. xi med) = Gneuss, 6, #12.

Works Cited

Brooks, N. "England in the Ninth Century: The Crucible of Defeat." *Transactions of the Royal Historical Society* Series 5, 29 (1979): 1-20.

Chase, Colin. *The Dating of "Beowulf."* Toronto Old English Series, no. 6. Toronto: U of Toronto P, 1997.

Colgrave, B., and R. A. B. Mynors, eds. *Bede's Ecclesiastical History of the English People.* Oxford: Clarendon, 1969.

Curtius, E. R. *European Literature and the Latin Middle Ages.* Trans. W. R. Trask. Princeton, NJ: Princeton UP, 1973.

Duemmler, E., ed. MGH *Poetae Latini Aevi Carolini*. MGH Poetarum Latinorum Medii Aevi, I. Berlin: Weidmann, 1881. Rpt. 1964.

—, ed. *Epistolae Karolini Aevi* 2. MGH. Berlin: Weidmann, 1895. Rpt. 1974.

Eusebius Pamphilius. *Eusebii Pamphili de vita beatissimi imperatoris Constantini libri iv*. PL 8: 9-92. Ed. J.-P. Migne. Paris, 1844.

Firchow, E. S., and E. H. Zeydel, eds. and trans. *Vita Karoli Magni: The Life of Charlemagne*. Coral Gables: U of Miami P, 1972.

Frantzen, A. J. *King Alfred*. Boston: Twayne, 1986.

Gneuss, H. "A Preliminary List of Manuscripts Written or Owned in England up to 1100." *Anglo-Saxon England* 9 (1981): 1-60.

—. "Anglo-Saxon Libraries from the Conversion to the Benedictine Reform." *Angli e Sassoni al di qua e al di la del mare*. Settimane di Studio del Centro Italiano di Studi sull'alto Medioevo 32 (1986): 643-99.

—. "King Alfred and the History of Anglo-Saxon Libraries." *Modes of Interpretation in Old English Literature: Essays in Honour of Stanley B. Greenfield*. Ed. P. R. Brown et al. Toronto: U of Toronto P, 1986. 29-49.

Godman, P. *Poets and Emperors: Frankish Politics and Carolingian Poetry*. Oxford: Clarendon, 1987.

Hauck, K. "Karl als neuer Konstantin 777." *Frühmittelalterliche Studien* 20 (1986): 513-35.

Kaske, R. E. "*Sapientia et Fortitudo* as the Controlling Theme of *Beowulf*." *An Anthology of "Beowulf" Criticism*. Ed. L. E. Nicholson. Toronto: Baxter, 1965. 269-310.

Keynes, Simon, and M. Lapidge, trans. *Alfred the Great: Asser's Life of King Alfred and Other Contemporary Sources*. Harmondsworth: Penguin, 1983.

Klaeber, Fr. "Zu König Ælfreds Vorrede zu seiner Übersetzung der *Cura Pastoralis*." *Anglia* 47 (1923): 53-65.

Mitchell, Bruce, and Fred C. Robinson. *A Guide to Old English*. 5th ed. Oxford: Blackwell, 1992.

Morrish, Jennifer. "King Alfred's Letter as a Source on Learning in England in the Ninth Century." *Studies in Earlier Old English Prose*. Ed. P. Szarmach. Albany: State U of New York P, 1986. 87-107.

Painter, Sidney, trans. *The Life of Charlemagne by Einhard*. Ann Arbor: U of Michigan P, 1960.

Rabanus Maurus. *B. Rabani Mauri De laudibus sanctae crucis*. PL 107: 133-294. Ed. J.-P. Migne. Paris, 1864.

Sears, Elizabeth. "Louis the Pious as *Miles Christi*: The Dedicatory Image in Hrabanus Maurus's *De laudibus sanctae crucis*." *Charlemagne's Heir: New Perspectives on the Reign of Louis the Pious (814-840)*. Ed. P. Godman and R. Collins. Oxford: Clarendon, 1990. 605-28.

Shippey, T. A. 1979. "Wealth and Wisdom in King Alfred's Preface to the Old English Pastoral Care." *The English Historical Review* 94 (1979): 346-55.

Smyth, Alfred P. *King Alfred the Great*. Oxford: Oxford UP, 1995.

Szarmach, Paul E. "The Meaning of Alfred's *Preface* to the *Pastoral Care*." *Mediaevalia* 6 (1980): 57-86.

Whitelock, Dorothy. *Sweet's Anglo-Saxon Reader in Prose and Verse*. Oxford: Clarendon, 1967.

Anne L. Klinck

THE OLDEST FOLK POETRY?
MEDIEVAL WOMAN'S SONG
AS "POPULAR" LYRIC

For the last hundred years or more, medievalists have been using the terms *Frauenlied* and *chanson de femme* to designate a particular type of female-voice love lyric which they felt to be somehow significantly different from the dominant courtly discourse of medieval love poetry. "Woman's song" as so defined is not poetry composed by women, but poetry presented through a female speaker. Many of these poems are anonymous; of those attributed to a named author, most are by men. The mode of woman's song thus reflects male desires and fantasies about women.[1] Here, I shall be only indirectly concerned with the construction of femininity, or with the relationship between author and voice, a problem that we continue to grapple with.[2] Instead, I want to deal with a different, though related issue: the critical terminology used to discuss woman's song.

By an apparent consensus among medievalists, one of the key characteristics of this type of poetry is its "popular," as opposed to courtly, nature. In their classification of lyric, scholars have always been rather undecided as to which genres might actually embody the *Frauenlied*, but they have pointedly excluded those, notably the *canso*, which were specifically courtly. Pierre Bec sees the mode of woman's song exemplified in the *alba, chanson de jeune fille* (also called *chanson d'ami*), the *malmariée*, and the *chanson de toile*, as well as the pastourelle, to some extent, and *chanson de croisade* (*Lyrique française* 1: 60 ff.). Erich Köhler and the other authors of the *Grundriß der romanischen Literatur des Mittelalters*, in their delineations of the lyric genres, see the *Frauenlied* as basic to the *Romanze*, and an influence on the pastourelle, *alba*, and dance song (*GRLMA* 2.1.5: 55, and 33-66, *passim*). Ingrid Kasten excludes most *albas* and pastourelles from her *Frauenlieder* collection as too courtly, but includes a couple of "popular" examples (nos. 62 and 65).

229

There is general agreement, it seems, that woman's song is popular, but widespread disagreement as to what "popular" implies. Since the definition of popular literature is very fluid, to say the least, I want to examine the concept as it applies to woman's song, to look at its various implications, and to raise some questions about its usefulness.[3] I shall begin with the medieval context, go on to modern (that is, nineteenth-century and later) scholarly theories, and then focus on some specific examples of woman's songs,[4] and consider in what ways they may or may not be popular. As we proceed with this investigation, re-examining the notion of the popular will also involve redefining the nature of woman's song itself.

Interestingly, the medieval poets themselves seem never to have used the term "woman's song" in this sense,[5] an absence which suggests that the mode as we perceive it was not one of their preoccupations, though it must have been part of their consciousness.[6] Medieval authors certainly thought in terms of genre clusters, of which woman's song would be one. Some of these clusters were regarded as appropriate for the lower classes, but this need not mean they were not also enjoyed by the nobility. For example, Giraut Riquier, in the thirteenth century, refers to the *cobla, dansa, ballada, alba,* and *sirventes* as genres which belonged to the repertoire of the *joglar,* and which he sang for the entertainment of the *gens bassa* in public squares and taverns (*GRLMA* 2.1.4: 67). The closest medieval term to the broad category of woman's song is the Galician-Portuguese *cantiga de amigo,* "song about a lover" uttered by a young girl. The fragmentary *Poética* which accompanies the collection of lyrics in the *Cancioneiro da Biblioteca Nacional* manuscript comments on the *cantiga de amigo* and the (male-voice) *cantiga de amor.* The *Poética* dates from some time in the fourteenth century (Jensen, *Earliest* 229-30), so the term *cantiga de amigo* must have arisen somewhat earlier, perhaps around 1300 (Mölk, "Frauenlieder" 63-64). Though modern scholars have tended to contrast the "popular" *cantiga de amigo* with the courtly *cantiga de amor,* the two genres were cultivated by the same poets. Also, the *Poética* makes no distinction of this kind, merely noting that in the *cantiga de amigo* the woman speaks first, and in the *cantiga de amor* the man.[7]

Medieval literary theorists seem not to have used terms corresponding to our "aristocratic" and "popular," but they did, of course, conceive of different levels of style, a concept going back to classical rhetoric, and they distinguished a high, medium, and low style (*grandiloquus, mediocris,* and *humilis*), marked by language, poetic voice, and the social status of speaker, subject, and audience. In his study of what he called the *grand chant courtois*, Roger Dragonetti placed the lyrics of the trouvères within this rhetorical framework of the three styles (15-16). Christopher Page draws on the same rhetorical background when he argues that it was poetry in the Lower Style which lent itself to instrumental accompaniment (28 & 38). It should be noted that this medieval view of the three styles is itself a learned construct, and its application would have been self-conscious; thus, deliberate composition in the low style would certainly not be a mark of popular origin.

The view of medieval woman's song as popular is essentially a modern one. It fairly clearly derives from a Romantic fascination with the folk and with the eternal feminine.[8] The earliest investigations of woman's song were concerned largely with the origins of European lyric, for which these "primitive" poems were thought to be the source and fountainhead. Although most extant woman's songs are attributable to male authors, there was in the nineteenth century a tendency to trace the type back to preliterate songs actually composed by women. Thus, the attributes of orality, primitiveness, collective authorship, and emotionality were linked with women, those of literacy, civilisation, individual authorship, and reason, with men. Goethe, Jakob Grimm, and others saw in the early German and Balkan *Frauenlieder* and *Frauenstrophen* the traces of the "älteste Volkspoesie" (Mölk, "Frauenlieder" 67). Wilhelm Scherer believed that some of the male-attributed *Frauenlieder* in Lachmann's *Minnesangs Frühling* collection were in fact originally composed by women.[9] Alfred Jeanroy and Gaston Paris traced the whole of European lyric back to the dance-songs of young girls at their spring-time celebrations. In his 1889 study, Jeanroy hypothesised that originally these songs were composed spontaneously by the young girls themselves, but assumed that all extant versions were literary and of male authorship.[10] The characteristics of the *Frauenlied* were explored further by Theodor Frings in a number of studies, especially his 1949 monograph *Minnesinger und Troubadours*.[11] For Frings too, the woman's song is chronologically prior to courtly poetry, but at the same time he stresses the universality of the type, giving examples ranging from ancient Greece to China (*Minnesinger* 36-57).

The implications of the term "popular" vary from one theorist to another, but usually they involve a judgement about the poems' content, particular characteristics being regarded as marks of popular origin, whether immediate or distant. French scholars, focussing on poems characterised by their broad humour, tend to use the word to connote what is "vilain" rather than "courtois." And, of course, the poets of *fin'amor* distinguished delicacy of sensibility from coarseness in precisely these originally class terms. Frings, following the nineteenth-century German Romantics, links the popular with innocence and sincerity. In fact, Jeanroy adopted this position too, and regarded the bawdy lyrics as somehow spurious because genuinely popular poetry reflects true and natural sentiments too faithfully to be immoral and licentious (155). Hispanists often focus on transmission more than content, probably because of their continuing thriving tradition of oral poetry. Thus, José María Alín, under the influence of Menéndez Pidal, characterises popular poetry as that which is accepted by the people and lives in popular tradition, whether its origins are learned or not (Alín 11).[12] Margit Frenk, while admitting that material might be passed down from the upper to the lower classes, has very definite ideas about the nature of popular poetry. In the context of medieval Spain and Portugal, she contrasts songs which were sung by villagers at their daily tasks or in their festivities with aristocratic songs composed and performed by members of the nobility or professional poets. Whereas courtly poetry is complex, "in contrast to it, popular poetry is brief, emotive, emphatic, rapid."[13] The presence of these qualities seems to be taken by Frenk as some kind of proof of popular–i.e., rustic and humble–provenance. She goes on to observe that in popular poetry it is the woman who expresses the most intimate and powerful feelings, and that woman's songs deny aristocratic men their claim to a monopoly over language and desire.

Whatever its exact connotations, "popularity" as a distinguishing characteristic of woman's song is a persistent notion. Even though the era of Romantic philology is long past, and though Jeanroy himself admitted that no genuinely oral and popular *chansons de femme* survived for inspection, the view of woman's song as in some way reflective of humble life has remained entrenched. Pierre Bec redefined Jeanroy's terms, preferring to speak of a "registre popularisant" (as opposed to "aristocratisant"), to which the *chanson de femme* belonged.[14] He first presented this theory of the two contrasting registers in a 1969 essay, "Quelques réflexions sur la poésie médiévale," and developed the theory farther, relating it more explicitly to the *chanson de femme*, in his *Lyrique française* (1977-78). Bec still endorses the notion of the popular; his terminology indicates composition in a style characteristic of the lower orders, though not necessarily in that context. Further, he insists that the *chanson de femme* is not merely "pre-courtoise" but also "para-courtoise" and "post-courtoise" (*Lyrique* 1: 59-61). Bec's binary opposition is presented in "Quelques réflexions" as an improvement on previous ones: Jeanroy's "subjectif / objectif" and Italo Siciliano's "docte / laïque" or "cléricale / jongleresque" ("Quelques réflexions" 1327). In his collection of woman's voice poetry, Bec maintains this view of two contrasting registers, one "aristocratisant," the other "popularisant" (*Chants* 46, n.3). Significantly, Paul Zumthor, while preserving the opposition of registers, moves entirely away from terminology with class implications; in this he is unusual. What Bec calls the "registre aristocratisant," Zumthor designates "le registre de la requête d'amour, spécifique du grand chant courtois," in counter-distinction to "le registre de la bonne vie" (251-52). The central motif of this latter is *joie de vivre*, expressed in game and dance, "repas champêtre," and love. He does not explicitly link this register with the *chanson de femme*, but, clearly, many examples would fall within this bracket.

It is the popular / courtly distinction, however, which prevails. We see Bec's version not only in his own edition of trobairitz poetry, but also in that by Matilda Bruckner *et al.*, who adopt Bec's terminolgy ("aristocratising," "popularising"), and note that the women troubadours "combine within a single speaker the aristocratic and popular female personae" (223). Even writers who roundly reject the "folkloric" view of woman's song, can take the traditional classifications of it for granted. Thus, Janice Wright's recent radical interpretation of a Galician-Portuguese poem describes it as "on the borders between courtly and popular."[15] Ulrich Mölk is clearly uncomfortable with the conventional dichotomy, but unable really to escape from it. He has proposed making a distinction between popular ("volkstümlich") and elevated ("gehoben") poetry, instead of the traditional popular / courtly antithesis.[16] He advocates stripping woman's song of its typological ambiguities and aura of Romantic theories about origins, and defines it as a "love-song in a popular register in which the woman's perspective is realised as monologue, dialogue, or reported speech."[17]

Mölk's definition is suitably broad, but it fails to solve the problems inherent in designating poetry popular, whether by origin or adoption. Characterising a particular mode as popular, or even "popularising," implies a set of questionable assumptions: that level of complexity, degree of sincerity, capacity for sensitivity etc. are somehow correlated, in either a parallel or an inverse way, with social class. Further, as Erich Auerbach pointed out nearly fifty years ago in a review of Frings' *Minnesinger und Troubadours*, the term is anachronistic. The Romantic conception of the popular arose as a reaction against French neoclassicism and "an environment in which a large minority of educated and wealthy people" existed as a literary public (Auerbach 66). The modern distinction between popular and elite culture is essentially in the same tradition.

Again, although the word "popular" is often applied to medieval poetry which is oral and traditional, the equation of orality with the peasant class is really a post-medieval bias. Modern readers too easily forget that until the later Middle Ages even lettered and aristocratic poetry was composed for oral performance rather than silent reading. As Paul Saenger shows, the silent reading of vernacular texts was unusual before the fourteenth century.[18] Earlier, court poetry was certainly delivered and often composed orally. Brian Stock, who contrasts "popular" with "learned," makes precisely this point with regard to *Beowulf* and its social context (19). For Zumthor, an instability or "mouvance" related to orality is a general characteristic of medieval texts.[19] Many of the troubadours must have composed and circulated their songs orally.[20] And the frequent variation in stanza order from manuscript to manuscript in medieval strophic poems gives pretty strong evidence of oral circulation. Most of this poetry was in some sense courtly, though some of it utilised traditional material in what Page calls the Lower Style.[21]

Since "popular" is such a problematic adjective, it will be instructive to test it by examining various poems which have been regarded as belonging to the corpus of woman's song. The pieces I have chosen are designed to cover as wide a range as possible, including not only monologue, but also dialogue and reported speech–as long as the woman's part is prominent. Scholars have tended to concentrate on Continental examples from the Romance languages and Middle High German, but the scope of our investigation can be broadened to include an early specimen from a heroic background, the Old English *Wulf and Eadwacer*. The poem is of uncertain date, perhaps around 900 (Klinck, *Elegies* 20-21). Peter Dronke analyses it in the chapter on woman's songs (which he entitles *Cantigas de amigo*) in his classic study *The Medieval Lyric*.[22] There are some cruxes where my translation, which follows, differs from Dronke's, but they do not affect the question of whether or not this is a popular poem:

> It is to my people as if one gave them a gift.
> They will take him if he comes into their troop.
> Unalike are our lots.
> Wolf is on one island, I on another.
> Fast is that island, surrounded by fen.
> They're bloodthirsty, the men there on that island.
> They will take him if he comes into their troop.

234

Unalike are our lots.
I dogged my Wolf's wide wanderings with my hopes
When it was rainy weather and I sat weeping,
When the man keen in battle laid his arms about me.
There was joy for me in that, but there was pain too.
Wolf, my Wolf, my hoping for you
Has made me sick, your seldom coming,
My mourning heart, not lack of food.
Do you hear, Eadwacer? Our wretched cub
The wolf will carry to the forest.
It's easy to tear apart what was never together–
The story of us two.[23]

This enigmatic poem was regarded in the nineteenth century as a riddle. But since Henry Bradley argued, in 1888, that it was really a woman's lament for her lover, most scholars have come round to that point of view. *Wulf and Eadwacer* was first recognised as a *Frauenlied* in Frings' sense by Kemp Malone in 1962. Malone sought to demonstrate that this poem and the Old English *Wife's Lament* were in fact isolated representatives of a body of popular poetry significantly different from Old English heroic verse. While this view is supported by the poem's lack of heroic formulas and by its distinctive structural pattern of longer and shorter lines, the background of tribal warfare is very much in the heroic tradition. This is pointed out by Patricia Belanoff, who sees the language of *Wulf and Eadwacer* as strongly reminiscent of heroic poetry.[24] Dorothy Bray, comparing the two Old English woman's songs with the Welsh *Canu Heledd*, argues that all three are heroic elegies and not *Frauenlieder* (152). What makes *Wulf* different from most Old English verse is not that it is more popular, but that it is more lyrical. It has been influenced by the rhythms and refrains of song. To this influence we can attribute the repetition of lines 2-3 in lines 7-8, the apostrophes to Wulf and Eadwacer, the dwelling on Wulf's name.[25] The songs of Anglo-Saxon England are lost to us, but they must have existed and would surely have featured strophic structure and refrain; the form of *Wulf and Eadwacer* reveals these elements, but they are not fully developed. There is no reason to suppose that the song background behind *Wulf and Eadwacer* would have belonged only to the lower orders and excluded the upper class.

Let us now turn to the earliest examples of vernacular Romance lyric, the Mozarabic *kharjas*, from southern Spain, which date from the eleventh and twelfth centuries. These are very short pieces forming the ends of longer, more elaborate poems, *muwashshahas*, in Arabic or Hebrew. The *muwashshahas* are panegyrics or love poems; they close with *kharjas*, "exits," in non-literary Arabic or Romance, or a mixture of the two, an utterance which appears to adopt the voice of the female performer. As professional entertainers, these women would certainly not belong to the upper class.[26] Most of the *kharjas* are outspoken declarations of passionate love by artless, vulnerable young girls:

> Don't touch / bite me, oh my lover!
> It still hurts me.
> My bodice is fragile. Enough!
> I say no to all this.
>
> (29a-b Sola-Solé)

> Mercy, lover!
> Don't leave me.
> Kiss my little mouth well,
> And you won't leave so soon.
>
> (53 Sola-Solé)[27]

The occasional attachment of the same kharja to different *muwashshahas* points to their independent existence and probable oral circulation. Also, their composition in a non-literary medium suggests that they were not only the property of a literary elite. To this extent they are popular. But as they are used, they are part of a highly literary production; some of them must have been composed by lettered poets self-consciously creating the impression of unsophisticated speech. Even when a *kharja* is of oral provenance, its orality does not exclude circulation among the upper class. Richard Hitchcock (111-12) and Mary Jane Kelley (19) emphasise that the *kharjas* are an integral part of their *muwashshahas*, rather than the authentic voice of simple young women in love.

While the *kharjas* are in some sense popular, the woman's songs composed in medieval Latin are *ipso facto* the poetry of an educated elite. Some of these poems have noticeable learned associations. Thus, *Veni, dilectissime*, from the eleventh-century *Cambridge Songs*, is reminiscent of the lover's visit in the Song of Songs: "If you come with your key, you shall quickly enter."[28] The speaker in *Nam languens*, also from the Cambridge collection, who goes through the snow and cold to scan the waste sea for her lover's ship, recalls Catullus' and Ovid's Ariadne on the sea-shore lamenting after the departed Theseus.[29] *Huc usque, me miseram*, from the thirteenth-century *Carmina Burana*, suggests no specific learned source, but its ironic mode conveys something other than the spontaneous overflow of powerful feelings:

Until now, poor wretched me,
I'd concealed things well,
And loved cunningly.

Finally, my secret's out,
For my belly's swollen up,
Showing I'm pregnant and soon due.

On one side my mother beats me,
On the other my father yells at me,
Both of them are hard on me.

. . . .

If I go outdoors,
Everybody looks at me
As if I were a monster.

When they see my abdomen,
One nudges the other,
And they're silent till I've gone past.[30]

As Ann Schotter points out, medieval Latin songs of this type put women down, making fun of them in a language they cannot understand.[31]

The conception of woman's song as a popular mode is, evidently, based mainly on vernacular lyrics. The usage seems particularly applicable to Occitan and especially North French songs which position themselves in opposition to the *canso* (the type is mainly attested from northern France).[32] Pilar Lorenzo Gradín believes that the word "popular" has been used not only out of Romantic prejudice, but also for simple convenience, a term being needed for *anti-canso* poetry (*Canción de mujer* 7). The speakers in the Occitan *Quant lo gilos er fora* and the North French *Por coi me bait mes maris* aggressively pursue their lovers in open defiance of their boorish husbands. Thus, the latter poem:

Why does my husband beat
Poor wretched me!

I've done him no wrong,
I've said him no ill–
Just received my lover
Privately.

If he won't let me alone
To lead the sweet life,
I'll get him called cuckold,
I guarantee.

I know what I'll do
To take my revenge–
I'll lie with my lover
Nakedly.

Why does my husband beat
Poor wretched me?[33]

The vocabulary of a poem like this, with its cute diminutives (*laisette, soulete, nuete*) and its rough talk of beating and cuckolds is anti-courtly.[34] But in what sense are this poem and others like it popular or popularising? Possibly in depicting the mores of the lower orders–although cuckoldry and wife abuse have never been their special prerogative. The use of the low style reflects, rather, a certain attitude. If the characters in this drama seem a little crude, poet and audience can congratulate themselves on being more refined. As John Plummer says, linking woman's songs with the fabliaux, the non-courtly elements in such poems have the function of "defining what the courtly was not." "Does it not seem more likely," he asks, "that the woman's songs are a diversion for an audience more sophisticated than the characters depicted in them?" ("Woman's Song" 150). If the speakers in *chansons de malmariée* like the one quoted above are to be aligned with Alisoun rather than with Emilie, the comparison also serves to remind us that Chaucer aimed both the *Miller's* and the *Knight's Tale* at the same public.

Like the *malmariée*, but less uniformly, the pastourelle is characterised by particular elements regarded as popular, especially a certain roughness or quaintness of language and action. In this case, too, the language reflects social condescension rather than humble origins. Although the name of the genre suggests the song of a shepherd girl, its essence is a confrontation between the upper and lower classes.[35] As a peasant, the maiden on whom the poem centers is fair game for the young man who accosts her. Typically, the pastourelle either treats her rustic simplicity with contempt, or endows her with a wit and sagacity that are more than a match for her would-be seducer. Usually, her utterance is contextualised within the point of view of her more sophisticated admirer. This contextualisation takes place even when the other viewpoint is only implicit. Thus, in the macaronic *Ich was ein chint so wolgetan*, from the *Carmina Burana*, the girl's monologue fills the entire

poem, but the smug and rather brutal attitude of the man who deflowers her
is reflected in her account of what amounts to a rape:

> He threw up my little shift,
> Leaving my body bare;
> He broke into my little fortress
> With his erect spear.
>
> Oh and alas!
> Cursed be the linden trees
> Planted by the way![36]

The use of Latin here, as in the poems composed entirely in that language,
conveys a mockery of the girl's innocence, intellectual as well as sexual.

Class confrontation seems particularly striking in the *tenso*, by Raimbaut
de Vaqueiras, between a courtly interlocutor and a bourgeoise or peasant
woman, the former speaking Occitan, the language of *fin 'amor*, and the latter
Genoese, the local dialect. The would-be lover makes his suit in conventional
terms, only to get sent off with a flea in his ear:

> Lady, I have begged you so much,
> If it pleases you, to deign to love me. (1-2)
>
> . . . .
>
> Filthy, stupid crop-head!
> Never will I love you. (23-24)[37]

Yet, as Simon Gaunt points out, the courtly / uncourtly antithesis is not so
much a class conflict, as a contrast between the woman's directness and her
interlocutor's courtly but hypocritical language, "which rather punily
disguises his sexual advances" (312). The speech of the woman who wins
out in this encounter is the product of a sophisticated poet's irony, and the
poem constructs a nice parody of courtly love.[38]

It was simple sincerity, not mocking wit, that the "Romantic
philologists," to use Auerbach's term (66), fixed on in woman's song.
Frings, detecting an ancient popular substratum beneath courtly lyric, picked
out two poems by courtly poets of the High Middle Ages: Marcabru's *A la
fontana* and Walther von der Vogelweide's *Under der linden*, the former
consisting partly, the latter entirely, of woman's monologue. In both Frings
saw the unaffected sincerity of a woman of the people. The Occitan lyric
dramatises an encounter between the narrator and a maiden who curses King
Louis for sending her lover off on Crusade. The girl's outburst is almost
treasonable:

> Oh, evil befall King Louis,
> Who made the laws and the edicts
> By which grief has entered my heart![39]

These are passionate words. But the imprecation is a topos, as is shown by its reappearance in the North French *Jherusalem*, in which the speaker exclaims against that city for the same reason, and with similarly shocking–in this case blasphemous–effect. Again, we are told explicitly that Marcabru's maiden is aristocratic: "daughter of a castle's lord."[40] In this she resembles the protagonists of the *chanson de toile*, also supposedly popular. Neither Ulrich Mölk nor Ingrid Kasten include *A la fontana* in their collections of *Frauenlieder*, although Angelica Rieger claims it is "allgemein als 'Frauenlied' charakterisiert" (75). The indicator of popular origin or inspiration in this case seems to be nothing more than the presence in the poem, apparently, of unrestrained passionate feeling.

Frings' other example, *Under der linden*, used to be regarded as a *Mädchenlied* uttered by a peasant girl. But since D. R. McLintock questioned this view in 1968, many scholars have thought the speaker to be a woman, possibly married, of the upper class. The poem may give the impression of artless sincerity, but on closer consideration its tone, like its speaker, turns out to be rather elusive. Is she being coy or complacent, modest or arch?

> What he did with me
> Let no one ever
> Know but him and me
> And a little bird–
> Tandaradei–
> Who I'm sure will keep our faith.[41]

Under der linden is included in Kasten's collection, presumably because it presents itself as simple woman's song. As we have seen, it is actually rather subtle. Also, it may well be influenced by Latin and macaronic poems in the pastourelle tradition like *Ich was ein chint*, where, similarly, the seduction takes place under a linden tree.

The assumption that simplicity is an indication of popular origin is a commonplace of criticism on the *cantigas de amigo*. These poems use paratactic syntax, a restricted range of vocabulary, and a metrical scheme characterised by repetition in the form of parallelistic structure and/or refrain. The elements may be simple, but the effects can be very skilful. Thus, the intellectual content of Mendinho's *Sedia m'eu na ermida de San Simion* is rudimentary, but the poem's use of incremental repetition is both delicate and subtle. The speaker's troubled feelings, her increasing agitation and despair, are symbolised by the swelling waves of the sea, which again and again roll around her, until they finally engulf her. This incremental movement also has erotic implications:[42]

> I was at the sanctuary of San Simion
> And the waves, the huge waves, rolled around me,
>> Waiting for my lover,
>> Waiting for my lover!
>
> As I was at the sanctuary before the altar,
> The huge waves of the sea rolled around me,
>> Waiting etc.
>
> And the waves, the huge waves, rolled around me—
> I have no boatman, nor oarsman—
>> Waiting etc.
>
> And the waves of the deep sea rolled around me—
> I have no boatman, nor can I row—
>> Waiting etc.
>
> I have no boatman, nor oarsman,
> Lovely as I am, I'll die in the swelling sea,
>> Waiting etc.
>
> I have no boatman, nor can I row,
> Lovely as I am, I'll die in the deep sea.
>> Waiting for my lover,
>> Waiting for my lover.[43]

Very often the *cantigas de amigo* take the form of a young girl's address to her mother, or of a dialogue between the two. The confidence addressed to the mother has also been regarded as a feature typical of popular poetry. Again, the form can be handled very suggestively. The following is a famous example by Joam Zorro:

> Flowing hair, my flowing hair—
> The king has asked for my lovely hair.
> Mother, what shall I do?
>> Daughter, give the king his wish!
>
> Curling hair, my curling hair—
> The king has asked for my lovely hair.
> Mother, what shall I do?
>> Daughter, give the king his wish![44]

The girl's long, loose hair, in contrast to the bound-up and covered hair of the married woman, is a symbol of her virginity, and a metonomy for the girl herself. Zorro thus both underlines and evades the real nature of her predicament. Both poems are the work of cultivated poets, using some of the techniques of traditional oral verse. Their mastery of the form is not *per se* an indication of the lettered rather than the preliterate poet. But it does belie the poems' apparent simplicity.

A body of woman's voice love-poetry which overlaps with woman's song, although it is usually excluded from the category, is the corpus of the Provençal trobairitz, the women troubadours. Like their male counterparts, they cultivated the *canso*, the courtly genre *par excellence*. However, their poetry also has a good deal in common with the supposedly popular woman's song: its simpler language and metre, as compared with the male-voice *canso*, its greater directness, its self-praise, its open sensuality. As critics have recognised, the poetry of the trobairitz is a hybrid, borrowing the conventions of both the *canso* and the *anti-canso* tradition.[45] But its hybrid nature is a matter of blending contrasting tones, rather than material from aristocratic and popular sources. When the Comtessa de Dia affirms her intelligence and her worth (*A chantar m'er* 5), she speaks as the courtly lady, the *domna*, but when she wants to be her lover's pillow and have him in her husband's place (*Estat ai eu* 12 and 21-22), she is using the same frankly erotic language as the girl in an Italian woman's song who tells her mother she wants her lover to be "closer to me than my shift" (*Mamma, lo temp'è venuto* 39).[46] Dia's attack on the *gelos* in *Fin ioi me dona alegrannsa* uses brusque language reminiscent of *malmariée* songs:

> And you, jealous, evil-tongued,
> Don't think I'll hesitate
> To take delight in joy and youth
> Because you're bursting with chagrin.[47]

Paradoxically, it is the trobairitz's confidence of her own high status that enables her to adopt this outspoken language[48] more associated with the bourgeoise or the peasant–that is, with the conventional poetic depiction of these figures.

Whether we classify trobairitz lyric as woman's song or not depends on how we define our terms. The conventional popular / aristocratic polarisation automatically excludes it; a distinction between courtly and uncourtly poetry also tends to mark off trobairitz poetry from *chansons de femme*, though less categorically. We can, however, allow that the poems of the trobairitz belong to the courtly register or high style, while including elements associated with uncourtly or low-style song. To my mind, the trobairitz poems can usefully be included in the corpus of woman's songs. This inclusion allows us to make the natural link between them and the few Occitan poems of the uncourtly *chanson de femme* type.[49] And it also makes a bridge with the lyrics of the German *Minnesang* and their *Frauenstrophen*, which are integrated into the diction of court poetry. As Ingrid Kasten points out, distinctions of register are less applicable to German than to Romance poetry.[50] Both Mölk and Kasten include trobairitz poems in their collections of *Frauenlieder*, Kasten significantly more. Bec appends nine *chansons de femme* to his trobairitz collection (*Chants* 195-231) in a separate section, evidently feeling a need to bring the two kinds together although he emphasises that they are distinct.[51]

We are now in a position to consider the meanings that "popular" might have as applied to this wide spectrum of poems. The background of woman's song is popular in the sense of belonging to the population as a whole rather than to certain privileged segments of it. Unfortunately, this inclusive usage yields to a terminology of exclusion whereby the popular is opposed to the aristocratic or to the learned. It is these two usages which dominate discourse on the subject. Further, the two, which are properly separate, tend to be confused.[52] Neither is appropriate to the classification of woman's song, which was often composed by aristocratic or learned poets for an audience of their peers. Nor is the speaker necessarily a rustic or a bourgeoise. As Bec recognised, the *chansons de femme* adopt a particular register. However, by designating it "popularisant" in contrast to "aristocratisant" he sets up a social opposition and implies that the "registre popularisant" imitated an actual mode of speech which belonged to the lower classes. Undoubtedly the register belongs to the "low" style, and was regarded–by its aristocratic or learned practitioners–as appropriate to the utterance of their social or intellectual inferiors. But this is not, presumably, a position that modern criticism wishes to endorse. Our modern terminology reflects a fusion or confusion of medieval ideas about the courtly and the uncourtly with Romantic notions about the folk.

In fact, woman's song can be characterised quite satisfactorily without recourse to the vague and troublesome word "popular." The examples above illustrate the typical features of woman's song, as love poetry which is (a) in a woman's voice, (b) contrastive to male-voice love lyric, (c) *apparently* simple, (d) outspoken, (e) openly sensual.[53] Nor do we need to define this type of poetry in terms of polarities and binary oppositions. Instead of "popular," we might choose some other term, depending on the context, such as "oral," "traditional," or "uncourtly." Though certain woman's songs are popular in certain ways, as a blanket term the word can only be misleading. We would do well to discard it.

Notes

1. Nevertheless, this mode has been adapted by sophisticated poets, male and female, over the ages for their complex agendas. See Klinck, "Sappho and Her Daughters."
2. See Klinck and Rasmussen, Introduction and *passim*.
3. The idea that woman's song is popular has also been challenged recently by Grimbert, "Songs by Women and Women's Songs: How Useful is the Concept of Register?" Grimbert's paper, like the present one, was originally presented to the Ninth Triennial Congress of the International Courtly Literature Society, Vancouver, July 1998.
4. Translations are my own unless otherwise indicated.
5. For the history of the terms *Frauenlied* and *chanson de femme* in modern scholarship, see Mölk, "Die frühen romanischen Frauenlieder" 63-67. Mölk's essay is reprinted as the Introduction to his *Romanische Frauenlieder* (13-47); see also his article in *Lingua e stile* 25 (1990).
6. Cf. Heinzle, who argues that the retrospective classification of medieval genres is legitimate as long as it reflects medieval ways of thought (122-25).
7. D'Heur emphasises the close relationship between the *cantigas de amor* and *de amigo* (56). Similarly Ashley, who stresses that to read the *cantigas de amigo* without reference to their courtly context is highly misleading (43, n.3).
8. Some of the material in this and the following paragraphs is drawn from the Introduction to Klinck and Rasmussen.
9. A theory first stated in an 1864 letter to Karl Müllenhoff (Leitzmann 70 and 72).
10. Jeanroy, *Origines* 299 and 445. See also Paris, *Mélanges* 611. Jeanroy's seminal book was enlarged with supplementary material in its 2nd and 3rd editions (1904 and 1925, respectively).
11. See also, in particular, Frings' "Frauenstrophen und Frauenlied" and *Anfänge der europäischen Liebesdichtung*.
12. Menéndez Pidal's theories were first set out in a 1922 lecture, *Poesía popular y poesía tradicional*.
13. "Frente a ella, la poesía popular es breve, emotiva, enfatica, rapida" (Frenk 1-4). In her contribution to the *GRMLA* Frenk was more cautious. Speaking of the origins of Hispanic woman's song, she refers to a tradition of collective oral poetry, noting that "poesía oral" is a less compromising term than "poesía popular," which needs to be used "con todas las reservas necesarias" (*GRLMA* 2.1, fasc.2:68).
14. For a thorough questioning of Bec's opposition of registers, see Grimbert.
15. See *La coronica* 26.2:6 and 82, from Wright's Introduction to this issue (on the *cantigas de amigo*) and her article on Torneol's dawn-song *Levad'amigo*, respectively. Wright interprets this poem as a record of ongoing sexual abuse. Her characterisation of *Levad'amigo* as semi-popular is a response to Poe's generic definition of the *alba*: "a courtly (as opposed to popular) lyric piece" (Poe 148). I discuss the "popular" qualities of

the *cantigas de amigo* below.

16. Mölk's approach is criticised by Bec, who claims that his own "popularisant" "ne préjuge en rien d'éventuelles origines <populaires> ou <savantes>" (*Chants* 47, n.3).

17. "Ein Liebeslied des volkstümlichen Registers, in dem die Perspektive der Frau als Monolog, Dialog oder Erzählerbericht realisiert ist" ("Frauenlieder" 88).

18. After examining the transformation from an oral monastic culture to a visual scholastic one between the end of the twelfth and the beginning of the fourteenth centuries, Saenger notes that this development in Latin letters had only a limited effect on lay society, and that, still, "Much of medieval vernacular poetry and prose was composed, memorised, and performed orally and only later set down in writing" (405; see the evidence for this in n.221). Saenger's recent *Space Between Words* traces the development of silent reading from late antiquity to the fifteenth century. Sylvia Huot documents the shift "from a more performative toward a more writerly poetics" (1) in the thirteenth and fourteenth centuries.

19. On "mouvance," see Zumthor, *Essai* 65-72, and 507 (defined in Index).

20. Cf. van der Werf: "we do not know who among the troubadours could read and write, but the form of the poem . . . could have been designed with the help of script, whereas the melodies bear all the hallmarks of music that originated in a notationless culture" (147). As Ruth Finnegan points out, there are different kinds and degrees of orality: "a poem can be oral in its composition, its mode of transmission, or its performance" (17).

21. In Page's view the distinction between the High and the Lower Style is not synonymous with that between the courtly and the uncourtly (38). Commenting on the lyric insertions in Jean Renart's *Romance of the Rose or of Guillaume de Dole*, Huot notes that although all the songs in this romance are presented as oral performance, "the quality of oral spontaneity is especially marked in the many carols and dance refrains" (108)–i.e., in the songs which Page would regard as both courtly and Lower Style.

22. First published 1968; 3rd ed., with new survey of recent bibliography, 1996.

23.
> Leodum is minum   swylce him mon lac gife.
> Willað hy hine aþecgan   gif he on þreat cymeð.
> Ungelic is us.
> Wulf is on iege,   ic on oþerre.
> Fæst is þæt eglond,   fenne biworpen.
> Sindon wælreowe   weras þær on ige.
> Willaþ hy hine aþecgan   gif he on þreat cymeþ.
> Ungelice is us.
> Wulfes ic mines widlastum   wenum dogode,
> þonne hit wæs renig weder   ond ic reotugu sæt,
> þonne mec se beaducafa   bogum bilegde–
> wæs me wyn to þon;   wæs me hwæþre eac lað.
> Wulf, min Wulf,   wena me þine
> seoce gedydon,   þine seldcymas,
> murnende mod,   nales meteliste.
> Gehyrst þu, Eadwacer?   Uncerne earmne hwelp
> bireð wulf to wuda.
> Þæt mon eaþe tosliteð   þætte næfre gesomnad wæs,
> uncer giedd geador.

(Text as in Klinck, *Elegies*)

245

24. In "From the Margins: *Ides geomrode giddum*" ["the lady lamented in songs"].

25. For arguments that *Wulf* tends in the direction of strophic form, see Klinck, "Old English Elegy" 135.

26. But some of the Andalusian women poets did. See Garulo's *Diwan*, which anthologises the female Arabic poets from medieval Spain.

27.   Non me tankeš / mordeš yā ḥabībī;
fa-encara daniošo.
Al-ǧilala rahsa. ¡Basta!
A ṭoto me refiušo. (29a-b)

        ¡Amanu, yā ḥabībī!
Al-waḥs me no feraš.
Bon beiǧa mia bokella
awšak tu no iraš. (53)

28. "Si cum clave veneris, / mox intrare poteris" (49 *Carm. Cantab.*). Cf. "Dilectus meus misit manum suam per foramen, et venter meus intremuit ad tactam eius. Surrexi ut aperirem dilecto meo" (*Cantica* 5.4-5).

29. Catullus 64.124-201, and *Heroides* 10, resp.

30.   Huc usque, me miseram!
rem bene celaveram
et amavi callide.

        Res mea tandem patuit,
nam venter intumuit,
partus instat gravide.

        Hinc mater me verberat,
hinc pater improperat,
ambo tractant aspere.

        . . . .

        Cum foris egredior,
a cunctis inspicior,
quasi monstrum fuerim.

        Cum vident hunc uterum,
alter pulsat alterum,
silent, dum transierim.   (126 *CB*, stanzas 1-3, 5-6)

31. Schotter finds in poems of this type the influence of an Ovidian tradition based on the *Amores* and *Ars Amatoria*. In the more ardent and tender *Veni, dilectissime* and *Nam languens* she traces a different kind of influence, drawn from the Ovid of the *Heroides*, and from the Song of Songs. See Schotter, "Woman's Song" 21-24.

32. Mölk finds only four Occitan *chansons de femmes*: *Quan vei les praz verdesir*, *Oy altas undas, que venez suz la mar*, *Quant lo gilos er fora*, *Coindeta sui*; all characterised by refrain and all anonymous (*Altas undas* is attributed in the ms to Raimbaut de Vaqueiras). See *Mélanges* 384. Mölk's inclusion of Occitan poems by named aristocratic authors in his

Frauenlieder collection reflects a rather broader definition.

33.   Por coi me bait mes maris,

                      laisette?

        Je ne li ai rienz meffait
        ne riens ne li ai mesdit
        fors c'acolleir mon amin

                      soulete.

        Et c'il ne mi lait dureir
        ne bone vie meneir,
        je lou ferai cous clameir,

                      a certes.

        Or sai bien que je ferai
        et coment m'an vangerai:
        avec mon amin geirai

                      nuete.

        Por coi me bait mes maris,

                      laisette?

                  (Text as in Mölk, *Rom. Frauenlieder*)

34. Zumthor summarises the distinctive marks of the *bonne vie* register, including exclamation, parataxis, diminutives, and some characteristic counter-courtly vocabulary (251-52).

35. Kasten regards "Standesgegensatz" as central to the genre, but she includes in this notion difference between the sexes and between nature and culture, as well as between social ranks (*Lied* 31-32).

36.   Er warf mir uf daz hemdelin,
                corpore detecta,
                er rante mir in daz purgelin
                cuspide erecta.

                          Hoy et oe!
                          maledicantur tilie
                          iuxta viam posite! (185 *CB*, stanza 9)

37.   Domna, tant vos ai preiada
            si.us platz, q'amar me voillaz. (1-2)

        . . . .

        Sozo, mozo, escalvao!
        Ni ja voi non amerò.

                    (23-24; text and translation as in Gaunt)

38. Although I entirely agree with Gaunt's assertion that the woman's language "is not plebeian . . ., it is simply not courtly" (301), I doubt that, as Gaunt supposes, she is the higher in rank, or that she is a real woman who actually composed the Genoese stanzas in the poem. However, Gaunt's argument for double authorship has recently been endorsed

by Deyermond (204, 217).

39.
     Ay! mala fos reys Lozoicx
     que fay los mans e los prezics
     per que.l dols m'es en cor intratz!

             (26-28; text as in Paden)

40. "Filha d'un senhor de castelh" (line 9).

41.
     Wes er mit mir pflaege,
     niemer niemen
     bevinde daz, wan er und ich,
     Und ein kleinez vogellîn:
     tandaradei,
     daz mac wol getriuwe sîn.

      (stanza 4, lines 4-9; text as in 16 Lachmann-Cormeau)

42. As does the girl's anticipation of her death. Cf. the use of the word "die" for sexual climax, *OED* 7d, a common poetic metaphor in the late sixteenth and seventeenth centuries; see the examples there cited.

43.
     Sedia-m'eu na ermida de San Simion
     e cercaron-mi as ondas, que grandes son:
          en atendend'o meu amigo,
          en atendend'o meu amigo!

     Estando na ermida ant'o altar,
     [e] cercaron-mi as ondas grandes do mar:
          en atendend' . . .

     E cercaron-mi as ondas, que grandes son,
     non ei [i] barqueiro, nen remador,
          en atendend' . . .

     E cercaron-mi as ondas do alto mar,
     Non ei [i] barqueiro, nen sei remar:
          en atendend' . . .

     Non ei i barqueiro, nen remador,
     morrerei fremosa no mar maior:
          en atendend' . . .

     Non ei [i] barqueiro, nen sei remar,
     morrerei fremosa no alto mar:
          en atendend'o meu amigo,
          en atendend'o meu amigo!
          (Text as in Jensen, *Galic.-Port. Poetry*)

44.
     Cabelos, los meus cabelos,
     el-rei m'enviou por elos;
     madre, que lhis farei?
       Filha, dade-os a el-rei.

> Garcetas, las mias garcetas,
> el-rei m'enviou por elas;
> madre, que lhis farei?
> Filha, dade-os a el-rei.
>
> (Text as in Jensen, *Galic.-Port. Poetry*)

45. Frings saw trobairitz song as a development of the *Frauenlied* under the influence of the *canso* ("Frauenstrophen" 26). Dronke comments on its passionate language and sexual boldness (105-6). Bec regards the poems of the trobairitz as mediating between the "grand chant courtois" and the *chanson de femme* ("*Trobairitz*" 261). And Bruckner makes a comparison with the *cantigas de amigo* (*Songs* xxv). For the simpler vocabulary and metrics of the trobairitz as compared with the male troubadours, see Ferrante.

46. For the text of this poem, see 37 Mölk, *Rom. Frauenlieder* (with German translation).

47.
> E vos, gelos mal parlan,
> no.us cuges qu'eu mon tarçan
> que iois e iovenz no.m plaia
> per tal que dols vos deschaia.
>
> (final stanza; text as in Bruckner)

The "gelos mal parlan" could be either singular (the husband) or plural (malicious gossips). See Rieger's note, *Trobairitz* 607-8.

48. Cf. Bec, who attributes the marked sensuality and lack of discretion to the trobairitz's secure sense of her own social superiority (*Chants* 39-40). Similarly, the Umayyad princess Wallada declares that she has granted her lover power over her cheek, and offers her kisses to whoever desires them (Garulo 143). For parallels between the trobairitz and the women poets of Spain, see Cohen, "Women."

49. Cf. Shapiro on the trobairitz: "the poems function as a link between the paradigmatic courtly lyric and the heightened descriptive freedoms of the narrative genres" (571).

50. See *Frauenlieder* 21, and note also Kasten's insightful comparison and contrast between the poems of Reinmar der Alte and the Comtessa de Dia, both of which combine the traditions of *Frauenlied* and courtly *Frauendienst* ("Weibliches" 131-46).

51. In her *Frauenlieder* collection, Kasten prints eight Occitan poems, mostly by aristocratic authors. In addition to the four extant Dia poems, she includes a poem each by Azalaïs de Porcairagues and Raimbaut d'Orange, and a *tenso* between Maria de Ventadorn and Gui d'Ussel. Mölk's *Romanische Frauenlieder* has a poem each by Azalaïs and Clara d'Andusa, which, Bec comments, "ne sont pas pour nous des <chansons de femme> au sens strict" (*Chants* 47, n.3).

52. Bec consistently does this, without, apparently, being aware of any problem: "une poésie courtoise (savante), aristocratique" ("Quelques réflexions" 1316; also 1325-26). See too n.16, above.

53. These features are similar to those set out in Klinck, "Lyric Voice" 14.

Works Cited

Akehurst, F. R. P., and Judith M. Davis, eds. *A Handbook of the Troubadours*. Berkeley: U of California P, 1995.

Alín, José María, ed. *Cancionero tradicional*. Madrid: Castalia, 1991.

Ashley, Kathleen. "Voice and Audience: The Emotional World of the *cantigas de amigo*." Plummer 35-45.

Auerbach, Erich. Review of *Minnesinger und Troubadours*, by Theodor Frings. *Romance Philology* 4 (1950-51): 65-67.

Bec, Pierre. *Chants d'amour des femme-troubadours*. Paris: Stock, 1995.

—. *La lyrique française au moyen âge, XIIe - XIIIe siècles*. 2 vols. Paris: Picard, 1977-78.

—. "Quelques réflexions sur la poésie lyrique médiévale." *Mélanges offerts à Rita Lejeune*. 2 vols. paginated continuously. Gembloux: Duculot, 1969. 2: 1309-29.

—. "*Trobairitz* et chansons de femme. Contribution à la connaissance du lyrisme féminin au moyen âge." *Cahiers de civilisation médiévale* (Poitiers) 22 (1979): 235-62.

Belanoff, Patricia. "From the Margins: *Ides geomrode giddum*." Forthcoming in Klinck and Rasmussen.

Bradley, Henry. "The First Riddle of the Exeter Book." *Academy* 33 (1888): 197-98.

Bray, Dorothy. "A Woman's Loss and Lamentation: Heledd's Song and *The Wife's Lament*." *Neophilologus* 79 (1995): 147-54.

Bruckner, Matilda Tomaryn, Laurie Shepard, and Sarah White, eds. *Songs of the Women Troubadours*. New York: Garland, 1995.

Cambridge Songs. See Strecker.

Carmina Burana. See Hilka and Schumann.

Cohen, Judith. "Women and Music in the Three Cultures of Medieval Spain." Forthcoming in Klinck and Rasmussen.

Deyermond, Alan. "Lust in Babel: Bilingual Man-Woman Dialogues in the Medieval Lyric." *Nunca fue pena mayor (estudios de literatura española en homenaje a Brian Dutton)*. Ed. A. Menéndez Collera and V. Roncero López. Cuenca: Universidade de Castilla-La Mancha, 1996. 199-221.

d'Heur, Jean-Marie. *Troubadours d'oc et troubadours galiciens-portugais*. Paris: Fundação Calouste Gulbenkian, 1973.

Dragonetti, Roger. *La technique poétique des trouvères dans la chanson courtoise*. Bruges: De Tempel, 1960.

Dronke, Peter. *The Medieval Lyric*. 1968. 3rd ed. Woodbridge: Brewer, 1996.

Ferrante, Joan M. "Notes toward the Study of a Female Rhetoric in the Trobairitz." *The Voice of the Trobairitz*. Ed. William D. Paden. Philadelphia: U of Pennsylvania P, 1989. 63-72.

Finnegan, Ruth. *Oral Poetry*. 1977. Midland Book ed. Bloomington: Indiana UP, 1992.

Frenk, Margit. "Lírica aristocrática y lírica popular en la Edad Media española." *Heterodoxia y ortodoxia medieval*. Actas de las Segundas Jornadas Medievales. Ed. Concepción Abellán *et al*. Mexico City: Universidad Nacional Autónoma de México, 1992. 1-19.

—. "La lírica pretrovadoresca." *GRLMA* 2:1, fasc.2: 25-75.

Frings, Theodor. *Die Anfänge der europäischen Liebesdichtung im 11. und 12. Jahrhundert*. Bayerische Akademie der Wissenschaften. Munich: Beck, 1960.

—. "Frauenstrophen und Frauenlied in der frühen deutschen Lyrik." *Gestaltung Umgestaltung: Festschrift zum 75. Geburtstag von Hermann August Korff*. Ed. Joachim Müller. Leipzig: Koehler & Amelang, 1957. 13-28.

—. *Minnesinger und Troubadours*. Deutsche Akademie der Wissenschaften Vorträge und Schriften 34. Berlin: Akademie, 1949.

Gaunt, Simon. "Sexual Difference and the Metaphor of Language in a Troubadour Poem." *Modern Language Review* 83 (1988): 297-313.

Garulo, Teresa. *Diwan de las poetisas de al-Andalus*. Madrid: Hiperión, 1986.

Grimbert, Joan Tasker. "Songs by Women and Women's Songs: How Useful is the Concept of Register?" Paper presented at the Ninth Triennial Congress of the International Courtly Literature Society. Vancouver, July 1998. Forthcoming in Select Papers of the Ninth Triennial ICLS Congress.

Heinzle, Joachim. "Märenbegriff und Novellentheorie." *ZDA* 107 (1978): 121-38.

Hilka, Alfons, and Otto Schumann, eds. *Carmina Burana* 1.2. Heidelberg: Winter, 1941. Rpt. 1971.

Hitchcock, Richard. "The Girls from Cádiz and the *Kharjas*." *Journal of Hispanic Philology* 15 (1991): 103-16.

Huot, Sylvia. *From Song to Book*. Ithaca: Cornell UP, 1987.

Jeanroy, Alfred. *Les origines de la poésie lyrique en France au moyen âge*. 1889. 3rd ed. Paris: Champion, 1925.

Jensen, Frede. *The Earliest Portuguese Lyrics*. Odense: Odense UP, 1978.

—, ed. *Medieval Galician-Portuguese Poetry*. New York: Garland, 1992.

Kasten, Ingrid, ed. *Frauenlieder des Mittelalters*. Stuttgart: Reclam, 1990.

—. "Die Pastourelle im Gattungssystem der höfischen Lyrik." *Lied im deutschen Mittelalter: Überlieferung, Typen, Gebrauch. Chiemsee-Colloquium 1991*. Ed. Cyril Edwards, Ernst Hellgardt, and Norbert H. Ott. Tübingen: Niemeyer, 1996. 27-41.

—. "Weibliches Rollenverständnis in den Frauenliedern Reinmars und der Comtessa de Dia." *GRM* 37 (1987): 131-46.

Kelley, Mary Jane. "Virgins Misconceived: Poetic Voice in the Mozarabic *Kharjas*." *La corónica* 19.2 (1991): 1-23.

Klinck, Anne L. "Lyric Voice and the Feminine in Some Ancient and Mediaeval Frauenlieder." *Florilegium* 13 (1994): 13-36.

—, ed. *The Old English Elegies*. Montreal and Kingston: McGill-Queen's UP, 1992.

—. "The Old English Elegy as a Genre." *ESC* 10 (1984): 129-40.

—. "Sappho and Her Daughters: Some Parallels between Ancient and Medieval Woman's Song." Forthcoming in Klinck and Rasmussen.

—, and Ann Marie Rasmussen. "Medieval Woman's Song." *Cross-Cultural Approaches to Medieval Woman's Song*. Forthcoming.

Köhler, Erich, ed. *Grundriß der romanischen Literatur des Mittelalters*. 2.1, fasc. 3-5. Heidelberg: Winter, 1979-87.

Lachmann, Karl, Christoph Cormeau, *et al.*, eds. *Walther von der Vogelweide: Leich, Lieder, Sangsprüche*. 14th ed. Berlin: de Gruyter, 1996.

Leitzmann, Albert. *Briefwechsel zwischen Karl Müllenhoff und Wilhelm Scherer*. Berlin: de Gruyter, 1937.

Lorenzo Gradín, Pilar. *La canción de mujer en la lírica medieval*. Santiago de Compostela: Universidad de Santiago, 1990.

Malone, Kemp. "Two English *Frauenlieder*." *Comparative Literature* 14 (1962): 106-17.

McLintock, D.R. "Walther's Mädchenlieder." *Oxford German Studies* 3 (1968): 30-43.

Menéndez Pidal, Ramón. *Poesía popular y poesía tradicional en la literatura española.* Oxford: Clarendon, 1922.

Mölk, Ulrich. "Chansons de femme, trobairitz, et la théorie romantique de la genèse de la poésie romane." *Lingua e stile* 25 (1990): 135-46.

—. "Die frühen romanischen Frauenlieder: Überlegungen und Anregungen." *Idee, Gestalt, Geschichte: Festschrift Klaus von See.* Odense: Odense UP, 1988. 63-88.

—. "Quan vei les praz verdesir." *Mélanges de langue et de littérature occitanes en hommage à Pierre Bec.* Poitiers: Université de Poitiers CESCM, 1991. 377-84.

—. *Romanische Frauenlieder.* Munich: Fink, 1989.

Paden, William D., ed. *The Medieval Pastourelle.* 2 vols. New York: Garland, 1987.

Page, Christopher. *Voices and Instruments of the Middle Ages.* London: Dent, 1987.

Paris, Gaston. Review of *Les origines de la poésie lyrique en France au moyen âge,* by Alfred Jeanroy. *Journal des Savants* 1891: 674-88 and 729-42; 1892: 155-67 and 407-30. Rpt. in G. Paris, *Mélanges de littérature française au moyen âge.* Ed. Mario Roques. Paris: Champion, 1912. 539-615.

Plummer, John F., ed. *Vox Feminae.* Kalamazoo: Western Michigan U Medieval Institute, 1981.

—. "The Woman's Song in Middle English and Its European Backgrounds." Plummer 135-54.

Poe, Elizabeth. "New Light on the Alba: A Genre Redefined." *Viator* 15 (1984): 141-50.

Rieger, Angelica, ed. *Trobairitz.* Tübingen: Niemeyer, 1991.

Saenger, Paul. "Silent Reading: Its Impact on Late Medieval Script and Society." *Viator* 13 (1982): 367-414.

—. *Space Between Words: The Origins of Silent Reading.* Stanford: Stanford UP, 1997.

Schotter, Anne Howland. "Woman's Song in Medieval Latin." Plummer 19-33.

Shapiro, Marianne. "The Provençal Trobairitz and the Limits of Courtly Love." *Signs* 3.2 (1978): 560-71.

Sola-Solé, José María. *Corpus de poesia mozárabe.* Barcelona: Hispam, 1973.

Stock, Brian. *The Implications of Literacy.* Princeton: Princeton UP, 1983.

Strecker, K. *Die Cambridger Lieder / Carmina Cantabrigiensia.* Berlin: Weidmann, 1926.

van der Werf, Hendrik. "Music." Akehurst and Davis 121-64.

Walther von der Vogelweide. See Lachmann.

Wright, Janice. "The Galician-Portuguese Lyric: New Critical Approaches." *La corónica* 26.2 (1998): 5-8.

—. "The Enemy Within: A Galician-Portuguese Dawn Song." *La corónica* 26.2 (1998): 77-90.

Zumthor, Paul. *Essai de poétique médiéval.* Paris: Seuil, 1972.

John Mills

THE PAGEANT OF THE SINS

In his recent book *The Limits of Moralizing*, David Mikics makes interesting comments on Book I of Spenser's *Faerie Queene*, particularly regarding the "characterisation" of its protagonist, the Red Crosse Knight, and his encounter with Error and the Seven Deadly Sins. And since both "Errour" and the sins stem from a long tradition of Pauline and medieval theological speculation, it is worth tracing the development of the idea of sin as it informs medieval literature and in particular Spenser's allegorical method.

Mikics argues that Spenser's presentation of moral questions in Book I stems from a particular brand of Christian didacticism which, following classical modes of ethics, focusses on the overarching cosmic structure that destiny makes visible. The individual soul's perception of this structure creates a longing to live virtuously. The cosmos itself, in other words, is the primary revelation and the task of each of us is to recognize providence, God's plan inherent in the cosmos, as the source of goodness.

At the same time another branch of Christian ethical thinking which springs from St. Augustine "deflects the emphasis of ethics from the perception of cosmic order to the individual soul's struggle to realize order within himself or herself" (Mikics 41-42). Thus the focus in allegorical narrative is on character and personality rather than on evocations of natural order and divine design.

Mikics argues that there is a shift in allegorical representation from a Christian-classical model in Book I to an Augustinian perspective in the subsequent books with the result that later figures, such as Guyon and Britomart, become more psychologically real. Thus he seems to consider it a mistake to regard the Red Crosse Knight as any kind of character undergoing development: he is an allegorical figure, an abstraction, and at risk of being rendered even more so by his encounter with Error.[1]

What interests me particularly is Mikics' handling of Red Crosse Knight's struggle with "Errour":

> Turning herself into one astonishing spectacle after another, Error exploits a manipulative pathos of the quasi-miraculous .... In doing so, she renders Red Crosse a passive, abstracted victim of her plot. Error embodies the indecorous, tricky shifts of mood that endanger Red Crosse in this and subsequent encounters. (32)

Clearly the key episode in Book I is this encounter: the separation from Una, the episode with Lucifera and the Seven Deadly Sins in the House of Pride, and the capture of the Red Crosse Knight by Orgoglio follow logically on it, and it is probably the most vividly pictorial event in the entire *Faerie Queene*. More might be said about the relationship between the figure of Error and the Sins pageant than is apparent in Mikics' chapter on Book I, for we are presented in these twelve cantos with a psychomachia in which such figures as Error, Orgoglio, Una, and Despair are facets of a projected "self" which, for narrative purposes, Spenser calls "The Red Crosse Knight." "Errour" and the "Seven Deadly Sins" are conditions of the soul whose descriptions emerge from two traditions, one from monastic and medieval "sins literature," the other from St. Paul.

Since the literature of the Middle Ages and the Renaissance is permeated with inspections, analyses, representations, and allegorizations of "sin," I think it important to distinguish the above-mentioned two traditions which lie behind them. The first of these, the "Christian-classical," can be labelled "materialistic," the second "theological," and my present purpose is to establish how, arising from medieval taxonomies of sin, they inform Spenser's *Faerie Queene*.

The first tradition, the "materialistic," informs the Red Crosse Knight's encounter with the Seven Deadly Sins presented to him in pageant form at Lucifera's establishment, the House of Pride. Here Spenser imitates the traditional pictorial representations of the sins as they are found in the murals, carvings, and tapestries of the period as well as in emblem books such as Alciati's. Pride, Sloth, Lust, Gluttony, Envy, Avarice, and Anger emerge from the tradition founded by desert monks of the Nile delta during the fourth century and were listed by Evagrius as Gluttony, Lust, Avarice, Anger, Melancholy, Sloth, Vainglory, and Pride. The list was amended in the sixth century by St. Gregory, who combined Vainglory with Pride, or

Superbia, omitted Melancholy (subsuming it under Sloth), and added Envy.
Inventories such as Gregory's were clearly conceived as a form of rule book
listing aspects of human behaviour to which the monk needs to be alerted. It
catalogues the kinds of spiritual danger, errors of the soul, the way in which
"error" (see below) manifests itself in human behaviour. If the monk
observes his behaviour and amends it, his free will and creativity can at least
fend off the human tendency to miss the mark. It is this list we find in *Piers
Plowman*, in splendid array in Gower's *Mirour de l'Omme* and *Confessio
Amantis*, and, in particular, in Chaucer's *Parson's Tale*. It is worth
contrasting Spenser's treatment of the sins with Chaucer's, for the *Parson's
Tale* takes the form of a traditional medieval penitential which, the Parson
asserts, must be delivered in clear language and must avoid literary devices
such as allegory or the fabular:

> Thou getest fable noon ytold for me,
> For Paul, that writeth unto Thymothee,
> Repreveth hem that weyven soothfastnesse
> And tellen fables and swich wrecchednesse.
> Why sholde I sowen draf out of my fest,
> Whan I may sowen whete, if that me lest?
>
> (*ParsT* 31-36)

Hence the plain style in which each sin is considered as a tree with branches
and twigs. Pride as the root sin sprouts branches which are labelled with the
others in the list and whose own twigs include Disobedience (of God's
commands, the sovereign's, and the priest's), Boasting, Hypocrisy (described
as showing what one is not and failing what one is), Despite (disdainfulness),
Arrogance, Impudence (shamelessness), Insolence, Contumely (or hostility
towards every authority), Irreverence, Vainglory, Presumption, Pertinacity
(a persistence in one's folly), and "Jangling" ("whan a man speketh to muche
biforn folk, and clappeth as a mille, and taketh no keep what he seith")
(*ParsT* 389-405). These sins are described as it were from the outside, in
terms of their manifestations in public behaviour. The narrator makes it clear
that his own attitude towards the manifestations is satiric and contemptuous,
though his eloquence and vivid imagination sometimes produce an effect of
appalled fascination:

> Now been ther two maneres of Pride: that oon of hem is
> withinne the herte of man, and that oother is withoute. / . . . /
> But natheles that oon of thise speces of Pride is signe of that
> oother, right as the gaye leefsel atte taverne is signe of the wyn
> that is in the celer. / And this is in manye thynges: as in speche
> and contenaunce, and in outrageous array of clothyng. / . . . /

> forthwith the superfluitee in lengthe of the forseide gownes,
> trailynge in the dong and in the mire, on horse and eek on foote,
> as wel of man as of womman, that al thilke trailyng is verraily
> as in effect wasted, consumed, thredbare, and roten with donge,
> rather than that it is yeven to the povre, to greet damage of the
> forseyde povre folk.   *(ParsT* 408-418)

Though there is a reference to what lies "withinne the herte of man," we do not find in the *Parson's Tale* a psychological description of Pride or of any other of the sins. Instead it seems as if Chaucer accepts the general medieval view that sin arises from a deformation of the Rational Soul, a failure of perception with regard to the instablity of the goods of nature (such as health, beauty, wit, and intelligence), the goods of fortune (including wealth, social position, and fame), and the goods of grace (spirituality, benignity, and the ability to withstand temptation). The classical-Christian, the "materialist" tradition, which Chaucer absorbed from Boethius, among others, asserts that it is folly to pride oneself on any of these. The first pass away, and often the more we are in health the more we are in spiritual peril. The goods of fortune gloss over the fact that we are all of one parentage, and to pride oneself on the goods of grace is to distort them into a form of spiritual poison.

Thus as far as the *Parson's Tale* is concerned, the roots of the sins lie in a blind and arrogant assertion of secondary things (self, power, family name, talent and so on) and the ignoring of what is primary. And though it may be the case in the *Canterbury Tales* that "Chaucer's characters are frequently reflections of a conceptual reality, and [their] actions are often more significant as developments in a conceptual realm than as imitations of external life in space and time" (Robertson 272), they are nevertheless presented under the aspect of the "materialistic" tradition mentioned above.

Error and the Sins

What I propose to call a "theological" concept of Sin is to be found in St. Paul, notably in the Epistle to the Romans, which defines the relationship between God and human beings. Paul's discussion of the subject is complex and technical, the language is difficult, and his ideas are tumultuous in presentation. Nevertheless, the fundamental assertion is clear: we are as God's creation free but also flawed, and flawed in a particular way. Paul uses the word *hamartia*, meaning "error," an objective condition of having missed the mark.[2] This for Paul means that human beings lack the true divine humanity which is their birthright. *Hamartia* is translated as "sin" in the

256

New Testament, and subsequent usage of the word has obscured its original meaning and encrusted it with secondary meanings to describe acts of wrong-doing, *parabasis*, though Paul also uses *hamartia* in the plural to list such acts. But in either case the acts he finds reprehensible are those condemned by his own culture:

> God gave [evil-doers] up to degrading passions. Their women exchanged natural intercourse for non-natural, and in the same way also the men, giving up natural intercourse with women, were consumed with passion for one another. Men committed shameless acts with men and received in their own persons the due penalty for their error . . . they were filled with every kind of wickedness, evil, covetousness, malice. Full of envy, murder, strife, deceit, craftiness, they are gossips, slanderers, God-haters, insolent, haughty, boastful, inventors of evil, rebellious towards parents, foolish, faithless, heartless, ruthless.
>   (Romans 1:26-31, NRSV)

Thus sin is not only a question of inevitable and (to Paul and later to Augustine) inherited corruption, but it lies also in a defect of the will. This is not the place to deal with the logical and theological difficulties of this formulation, but in general it can be said that under the condition of freedom, the human capacity to "miss the mark" almost inevitably results in failures of the will which are located, according to Paul, in the flesh:

> We know that the law is spiritual; but I am carnal, sold under sin. I do not understand my own actions, for I do not do what I want, but I do the very thing I hate. Now if I do what I do not want, I agree that the law is good. So that it is no longer I that do it, but sin which dwells within me. For I know that nothing good dwells within me, that is, in my flesh. I can will what is right, but I cannot do it. For I do not do the good I want, but the evil I do not want is what I do. Now if I do what I do not want, it is no longer I that do it, but sin which dwells within me. . . . So then I of myself serve the law of God with my mind, but with my flesh I serve the law of sin.   (Romans 7:14-20)

In this view, sin–"sin which dwells within me"–in the sense of error is innate in the human condition and was in the world before the Jews discovered a moral code; the moral code itself relates to acts of the will.

We can examine how the doctrine of *hamartia* operates by returning to the opening of Spenser's *Faerie Queene*. In Book I, Canto i, the protagonist, the Red Crosse Knight, as we have seen, battles the monster called "Errour," to which he is led, or seems in the text to be led, by his female companion, Una. That the monster is half-serpent and half-woman suggests, along with obvious sexual themes, Biblical imagery taken from the Book of Genesis, the source of Paul's concept of human error. With some difficulty and with advice from Una as to how he should conduct the battle, Red Crosse kills the monster who, in her death-throes, vomits forth a powerfully rendered multitude of disgusting offspring:

> Groning full deadly, all with troublous feare,
> Gathred themselues about her body round,
> Weening their wonted entrance to haue found
> At her wide mouth: but being there withstood
> They flocked all about her bleeding wound,
> And sucked vp their dying mothers blood,
> Making her death their life, and eke her hurt their good.
>
> (*FQ* I.i.25)

Earlier, we were told that this vomit contains "A floud of poyson horrible and blacke, / Full of great lumpes of flesh and gobbets raw," as well as "bookes and papers" to suggest the proliferation of evil actions which spring from and feed on the initial "Errour" (I.i.20).

Mikics writes that

> Error presents a . . . distorted view of divine virtue. Like the offspring of the pelican, a familiar symbol of Christ, Error's brood feed on her dying blood. But then, surprisingly, they die themselves, frustrating the suggested parallel with Christ and his believers. (32)

This seems fanciful to me, however, and the "brood" suggests more the sins generated by the original error, or the missing of the mark, a built-in dislocation of the human being which, as the rest of Book I demonstrates, is ultimately ineradicable. At any rate, the Red Crosse Knight leaves this unappetizing scene, thinking with a degree of self-righteousness that in slaying the monster he has defeated "Errour," but almost instantly he falls into the clutches of Archimago who "stands for" the Imagination and who procures fantasies causing the Knight to misjudge Una and separate himself from her. This is Error indeed, and it is as if Spenser means to suggest that Error, in rampant, visible form undisguised by a fair exterior is not the central problem. The propensity to "miss the mark" lies deep within the Red Crosse Knight's own self and is a function of his own humanity, a part of himself impossible to disown.

There seems a great distance between the *Parson's Tale* and Spenser's resplendent parade of sins headed by Lucifera. She is, on the face of it, an attractive and awe-inspiring figure and nothing is said about any contrast between the superfluity of her clothing and the possible existence of "dong" in which her gown may trail:

> Suddein vpriseth from her stately place
> The royall Dame, and for her coche doth call:
> All hurtlen forth, and she with Princely pace,
> As faire *Aurora* in her purple pall,
> Out of the East the dawning day doth call:
> So forth she comes: her brightnesse brode doth blaze;
> The heapes of people thronging in the hall,
> Do ride each other, vpon her to gaze:
> Her glorious glitterand light doth all mens eyes amaze.
>
> (*FQ* I. iv.16)

Yet the underlying assumptions of such a passage are not as far removed from the medieval tradition as it might appear. Chaucer's plain descriptions of sinful behaviour are replaced with ornate emblems. Lucifera's coach is

> drawne of six vnequall beasts,
> On which her six sage Counsellours did ryde,
> Taught to obay their bestiall beheasts,
> With like conditions to their kinds applyde:
> Of which the first, that all the rest did guyde,
> Was sluggish *Idlenesse* the nourse of sin;
> Vpon a slouthfull Asse he chose to ryde,
> Arayd in habit blacke, and amis thin,
> Like to an holy Monck, the seruice to begin.
>
> (*FQ* I.iv.18)

The Sins pageant, with each personified sin led or transported by its emblematic beast, is such a familiar depiction of human fallibility that by Spenser's time it must have become part of the basic fabric of western culture, present but unseen, like the wall-paper in a well-used room. Thus, the Red Crosse Knight can observe the pageant as a work of art without being either moved or warned by it. He leaves the House of Pride, confident that he knows the spiritual dangers which the Sins represent. Almost immediately, however, he is caught by the giant Orgoglio, a manifestation of his own (and the reader's) basic and inordinate self-regard. Orgoglio seems to me a reprise of "Errour" in Canto i, linked here with the Pauline "sin that dwells within me," that is, the flesh. He appears at the point of the Red Crosse Knight's "goodly court" to Duessa and he is composed of earth puffed up with air (viii.9)–an image of rampant sexuality.[3] Whatever he is, he goes beyond the Knight's experience, book-knowledge, or awareness of sin, and thus he serves to "defamiliarize" the concept of *hamartia* in ugly and overpowering form.

This first section of the *Faerie Queene* encapsulates very neatly the distinction made above. The propensity to error, *hamartia*, exists independently of the manifestations of evil which arise from defects of the will.

Spenser's attention shifts in the later books of the *Faerie Queene* from the theological concept of *hamartia* and from the materialist representations of *parabasis*. Instead, he seems to want to convey human actions less by direct personification than by locating them in psychological theory. Mikics refers to St. Augustine whose "ethics represent a contrasting, character-based side of Christianity, one that decisively departs from classical notions of virtue" (42), but it seems to me more useful to consider the possibility that Spenser's concept of human personality derives ultimately from St. Thomas Aquinas.

Aquinas' Theory of the Passions

For Aquinas the question of sin is linked with the problem of the human passions which in turn are an aspect of the created order.[4] God's rule for the government of the universe is Eternal Law, by which the individual is part of one huge society containing human beings as its members along with animals and inanimate objects all acting in conformity to and tending towards their own particular ends. Human beings are conscious of these ends, and our moral justice consists in accepting them voluntarily. As rational creatures we are called to knowing what Eternal Law exacts of us. According to Aquinas we can discover this by observing ourselves attentively and have only to yield to the legitimate inclinations (Natural Law) of our own natures in order to obey it. So far this is quite in accordance with the "materialistic" tradition discussed above.

Natural Law can be summarized simply as "do good and avoid evil." We move under the impulse of our desires and aversions: what we call good is only the object of a desire; what we call evil is an aversion. Human beings attempt to conserve their lives and protect their own health; reproduce themselves and raise children; seek the good in accordance with the dictates of reason, live in society, seek truth, avoid ignorance, and attempt to live harmoniously with others and not to injure them. This formulation seems commonsensical and obvious, but between it and the details of infinitely complex human actions, Human Law, there is a gulf which individuals, legislators and others try to close. Human Law prescribes particular acts which Natural Law imposes on us for the common good, and they only bind in the measure in which they are just, to the extent that they satisfy their own definition.

The basis of morality for Aquinas thus lies in human nature itself and is rooted in the composition of the soul. Aquinas holds that human passions, located in the "sensitive soul" where they are specified as "concupiscible"and "irascible," are neither good nor bad but are an integral part of the individual's moral life. The concupiscible passions are those to which what is good exhibits a power of attraction, evil a power of repulsion; they are love, hate, desire, aversion, joy, and sorrow. Thus, good things generate in the concupiscible appetite a certain inclination in respect of the good, pertaining to the passion of love, evil things to that of hate. The soul experiences desire when the object of love is absent, joy when it is attained. Aversion is the repulsion which an absent evil creates in us; sorrow is what we experience when that evil is present. The irascible passions (hope, despair, fear, daring, and anger) are involved when obstacles stand between a desire and its fulfilment, so that we experience hope when the obstacle is perceived as surmountable, despair when the obstacle seems insurmountable. Fear is defined as a wilting before a future evil imagined as present, where daring enables us to attack that evil. Anger, in this system, seems to be a special case, for Aquinas defines it as a reaction to a present evil whose effects are being experienced.

Such a system makes it possible to go beyond the observation of the cosmos–its design, its ineffable goodness–in which we find the motivation to live virtuously. To Chaucer, the remedy against Pride, for instance, is the cultivation of its opposite, humility; the remedy against Envy, love of one's neighbour; against Sloth, fortitude; and so on, though in the *Parson's Tale* these positive qualities go for the most part unillustrated. But in Aquinas' psychology, the oppositions between vices and virtues become inward, more a question of introspection. Roughly speaking, a defect in the concupiscible appetites, for instance, can, once recognized, be balanced by the strengthening of an element in the irascible. This, I believe, is what Spenser tries to organize in the later books of the *Faerie Queene*, to which I now want to return.

In Book II, Spenser leaves his account of *hamartia* and concerns himself with the origin of human actions in terms of Aquinas' psychological theory and with the notion that right action lies in finding a mean between two extremes of behaviour. Such extremes are represented, for instance, in the characters Elissa and Perissa in Canto ii, sisters of opposing personalities:

> *Elissa* (so the eldest hight) did deeme
> Such entertainment base, ne ought would eat,
> Ne ought would speake, but euermore did seeme
> As discontent for want of merth or meat;
> No solace could her Paramour intreat,
> Her once to show, ne court, nor dalliance,
> But with bent lowring browes, as she would threat,
> She scould, and frownd with froward countenaunce,
> Vnworthy of faire Ladies comely gouernaunce.

> But young *Perissa* was of other mind,
> Full of disport, still laughing, loosely light,
> And quite contrary to her sisters kind;
> No measure in her mood, no rule of right,
> But poured out in pleasure and delight;
> In wine and meats she flowed aboue the bancke,
> And in excesse exceeded her owne might;
> In sumptuous tire she joyd her selfe to prancke,
> But of her loue too lauish (litle haue she thancke.)
> *(FQ* II.ii.35-36)

The first sister is sullen, full of anger, beloved of Huddibras, a knight of "sterne melancholy," the other a "mincing mineon" whose lover is Sans-loy. These are the daughters of the equable Medina who acts

> With sober grace and goodly carriage:
> With equall measure she did moderate
> The strong extremeties of their outrage;
> That forward paire she euer would asswage,
> When they would striue dew reason to exceed.
> *(FQ* II.ii.38)

It is as if Spenser sees the remedy against melancholy, an aspect, as Chaucer noted, of Accidie or Sloth, as a defect of the concupiscible appetite, and that the remedy against Luxuria is located in a strengthening of the irascible. Later the distinction between the concupiscible and irascible passions is directly presented in Cymocles and Pyrocles, and in general Spenser searches for the Aristotelian-Thomist "golden mean" between opposing ways of being in the world. Yet Spenser seems to ask the question how one is to accomplish this. If, to take a familiar Aristotelian example, the proper behaviour towards possessions lies midway between the extremes of miserliness and extravagance, how is a person to find it? Spenser's analysis suggests that the problem of discovering the mean is not a simple matter of exercising the will but of calling upon different resources lying within individual psychology.[5]

In this brief essay I have tried to make a distinction between a theological and a material-psychological definition of "sin" and to show that the first proceeds from St. Paul's concept of sin, the second from his concept of "sins": *hamartia*, in other words, and *parabasis*. The latter informs the monastic tradition which is given a more psychological basis by St. Thomas Aquinas who, of course, derives his theory of emotions from Aristotle. The materialistic idea of sins informs much medieval homiletic literature, including Chaucer's *Parson's Tale*, though Chaucer is more concerned to describe evil actions than to trace them to their source in the human psyche. Spenser begins his major work with the doctrine of sin as *hamartia*, as it is found in St. Paul, but sees that the evil actions arising from sin need a more inward description than homiletic literature normally provides.[6] Thus, he concerns himself in the later books with seeking out the *remedia contra peccata* using Aquinas' own psychological theory.

Notes

1. In his recent article "The Theology of the Sign," Bergvall makes a slightly different point. *The Faerie Queene*, he says, is saturated with Augustinian thought, particularly from *The City of God*, so that Book I in particular presents the two poles of the Heavenly City and The Kingdom of the World. Bergvall does not, however, apply the notion of inner struggle to the Red Crosse Knight who, he thinks, is not regarded as a character in any fictional sense at all. An excellent study of Augustine's theology of sin and the freedom of the will is to be found in Wetzel, *Augustine and the Limits of Virtue*.
2. Much drama criticism has focussed on the meaning of *hamartia* as Aristotle uses the word in the *Poetics*, and the belief that it means a moral flaw with at least some degree of culpability seems well entrenched. For an excellent discussion of Aristotle's terminology see Else, *Aristotle's Poetics*.
3. Orgoglio would fit Constantinus Africanus' clinical description of a tumescent phallus as described in *De Coitu*.
4. Aquinas' discussion of the passions is found in *Summa Theologiae* I.81-82. See also Gilson, *The Christian Philosophy of St. Thomas Aquinas*.
5. See in particular Fowler, *Spenser and the Numbers of Time*.
6. An excellent discussion of Spenser and contemporary homiletic literature is to be found in Mallette, *Spenser and the Discourses of Reformation England*.

Works Cited

Africanus, Constantinus. *"De Coitu."* Trans. Paul Delany. *Chaucer Review* 4 (1969-70): 55-65.

Bergvall, Åke. "The Theology of the Sign: St. Augustine in Spenser's Legend of Holiness." *Studies in English Literature* 33 (1993): 21-42.

Chaucer, Geoffrey. *The Riverside Chaucer*. Ed. Larry D. Benson. 3rd ed. Boston: Houghton Mifflin, 1987.

Else, Gerald F. *Aristotle's Poetics: The Argument*. Cambridge, MA: Harvard UP, 1967.

Fowler, Alasdair. *Spenser and the Numbers of Time*. New York: Barnes, 1964.

Gilson, Etienne. *The Christian Philosophy of St. Thomas Aquinas*. New York: Random House, 1956.

Mallette, Richard. *Spenser and the Discourses of Reformation England*. Lincoln, NE: U of Nebraska P, 1997.

Mikics, David. *The Limits of Moralizing: Pathos and Subjectivity in Spenser and Milton*. Lewisburg, PA: Bucknell UP, 1994.

Robertson, D. W., Jr. *A Preface to Chaucer: Studies in Medieval Perspectives*. Princeton: Princeton UP, 1962.

Spenser, Edmund. *The Faerie Queene*. Ed. Thomas P. Roche, Jr. New Haven: Yale UP, 1978.

Wetzel, James. *Augustine and the Limits of Virtue*. Cambridge: Cambridge UP, 1992.

Elisabeth Brewer

JOHN RUSKIN'S MEDIEVALISM

The Gothic revival was well under way when Ruskin was born in 1819, the year in which Sir Walter Scott published *Ivanhoe*. Medievalism in Ruskin's own time took many forms: among others, enthusiasm for Gothic architecture, for the idea of chivalry, for the social structure of the Middle Ages. Ruskin's own medievalism (he actually coined the word himself) grew in the first instance out of his childhood attraction to the picturesque and his devotion to the works of Sir Walter Scott; it also had its foundations in his unusual, very rigorous early upbringing which was based almost entirely on Biblical study.

Ruskin's isolated childhood fostered and allowed him to indulge his natural taste for the romantic. As in many nineteenth-century households, there was much reading aloud in Ruskin's home: he was, in his own words, brought up on Scott, and read the Waverley novels and Scott's poems again and again. His life-long passion for the medieval undoubtedly stemmed from these early imaginative excursions into the past. Each summer, as his father toured England for orders for his firm of wine-merchants, Ruskin went too, even as a small boy, and the family visited every castle and stately home of interest on the route. A poem written after visiting Haddon Hall when he was eleven blends a sense of the romantic with boyish high spirits:

> Old halls and old walls,
> They are my great delight.
> Rusty swords and rotten boards
> And ivy black as night!
>
> (2.284)

A sonnet on Harlech Castle written at the age of twelve beginning, "I've seen thy mighty towers and turrets high" (2.33) similarly expresses his vivid sense of the romantic and picturesque. When he visited Scotland, the scenes were peopled and animated for Ruskin's imagination by his reading of Scott. The

265

fact that his father had both money and intellectual curiosity, that his mother was energetic and enterprising, and that he was an only child meant that it was also possible for them to visit Europe regularly as a family from the time when Ruskin was still a child. These visits to France and Italy enabled him to study medieval cathedrals and churches of far greater richness and magnificence than he could see in England, resulting in his unshakeable lifelong conviction of the superiority of Gothic architecture. His remarkably comprehensive and detailed knowledge of this architecture later qualified him to offer an informed, if at times rather idiosyncratic, evaluation of it in volume after volume of his extensive writings.

Like many of his contemporaries, Ruskin's imagination was stirred and his idea of the medieval was also influenced by Kenelm Digby's very popular *Broad Stone of Honour*, from which his father often read aloud to him. The first version had been published anonymously in 1822, but Digby completely re-wrote it, greatly expanding it, before it re-appeared under his name in 1827. In *The Broad Stone*, sub-titled *Rules for the Gentlemen of England*, and specifically addressed to young men, he attempts to define the "duties and qualifications for knighthood" at the present time by frequent reference to Malory and to a wide range of medieval romances, English and European. Familiarity with this strange work must not only have impressed upon Ruskin's mind the splendour of medieval chivalry–particularly its moral splendour as described by Digby–but its quintessentially "Gothic" images were well calculated to appeal to a boy's imagination. *The Puppet Show* that Ruskin wrote between the ages of nine and ten illustrates his fondness for the idea of knights in armour. The first of the twenty-nine characters in his little play is "George of England" (significantly for Ruskin's later choice of name for the society that he founded in 1871) who stoutly declares "I am the bravest Knight of all" (2.xxxiii).

Ruskin's early education, of which he gives a detailed account in *Praeterita* (35.14 and 35.40-3), consisted in the daily reading and learning by heart of Biblical passages. This of course gave him a far greater knowledge of the Bible than would have been possible for most men in the Middle Ages, while at the same time it inculcated patterns of thought in many ways medieval. It placed him, he says, as soon as he could conceive and think, in the presence of an unseen world which he saw as endowed with sacred meaning. It might be argued that many of Ruskin's contemporaries particularly among the Evangelicals and Nonconformists were similarly steeped in Biblical knowledge, and that therefore his attitudes to the spiritual world were in no way different from those of many other pious people

266

(Finley 225). But the beliefs that he shared with such contemporaries were in the course of time further modified and intensified by two significant factors, his reading of Dante, begun in the summer of 1845 and ever-deepening thereafter, and his adult encounter with Venice, above all with the early Italian painters and with Tintoretto, which was to have a profound and lasting effect on him.

While in *Modern Painters I*, Ruskin had endeavoured to define the fundamentals of his aesthetic theory particularly with reference to landscape, in *Modern Painters II*, he at once formulated the fresh insights that he had gained from the travels of 1845 by reference to typology: "For what revelations have been made to humanity inspired, or caught up to heaven, of things to the heavenly region belonging, have been either by unspeakable words, or else by their very nature incommunicable, except in types and shadows" (4.208). It is Giotto to whose influence he attributes this new understanding, together with Fra Angelico, Ghirlandaio, Perugino, and other early Italian artists. Strangely enough, Ruskin's attempt to create a theoretical description of beauty adequate to the needs of his contemporaries produced, as George Landow has observed, a view of life more suggestive of the Middle Ages than characteristic of the reign of Queen Victoria (*Aesthetic* 16). It is now well-known that there was, among nineteenth-century Evangelicals, a tradition of typological interpretation of the Bible with which, although it was not widespread, Ruskin was familiar, particularly since it was favoured by the preacher whom he found most congenial, Henry Melvill (Landow, *Victorian* 20, 47, 236n9). Ruskin's European tour of 1845, which culminated in his discovery of Tintoretto, however, gave him new insights into the typology which pervades the art of the Middle Ages. When in *Modern Painters II*, for example, he discusses the Theoretical Faculty, each feature as he analyzes it is seen as a Type of the Divine. The quality of unity in an artistic context is now seen as the Type of the Divine Comprehensiveness, because "the appearance of separation or isolation in anything . . . is an appearance of imperfection" (4.92), since of necessity God is inherent in all things. Symmetry (in Ch. VIII), as the Type of the Divine Justice, similarly has a spiritual significance: the symmetrical is contrary to the violence and disorganization of sin.

Ruskin's curious blend of Evangelical doctrines, Wordsworthian feeling for nature, and interpretation of early Italian art thus results in perceptions which sound more medieval than modern, as he struggles to define the principles which he now believes should form the basis of all aesthetic judgement. In *Modern Painters II* in particular, his thought is at times reminiscent of the pseudo-Dionysius and other early writers on aesthetics such as Hugh of St. Victor and St. Bonaventura.[1] Despite the similarity of thought, however, Ruskin seems never to have read these writers.

The Romantic poets together with Scott had emphasized the unity of man and nature, and Ruskin went even further in this direction. His insistence in *Modern Painters I*, for example, on the changing skies as manifesting God's love to us and drawing us to Him as He reveals Himself through natural phenomena has more in common with medieval attitudes than with contemporary writing on art. Ruskin insists that there is no moment when nature is not "working still upon such exquisite and constant principles of the most perfect beauty, that it is quite certain that it is all done for us" (3.343). In the theocentric world of *Modern Painters I* and *II*, "the angels who rejoice over repentance, cannot but feel an uncomprehended pain as they try and try again in vain, whether they may not warm hard hearts with the brooding of their kind wings" (4.186). While precedents may be found for his "continual perception of Sanctity in the whole of nature" in such of the Romantics as Blake, Shelley, and Wordsworth, there is a difference here: the whole realm of nature has been created and is to be studied in order to bring man closer to the divine. This sense of the invisible, divine underpinning of the world of appearances goes back to an older tradition and is in several ways genuinely medieval.

In *Modern Painters II* Ruskin invokes the pseudo-Dionysian idea of the celestial hierarchy (a concept to which he returns elsewhere): "Probably to every higher order of intelligence more of His image becomes palpable in all around them, and the glorified spirits and the angels have perceptions as much more full and rapturous than ours, as ours than those of beasts and creeping things" (4.145). (It is perhaps noteworthy that this and the references to the angelic presences quoted above were made at a time when the Protestant church avoided discussion of the subject of angels.) The ancient idea of the scale of being, widely accepted in the Middle Ages, undoubtedly appealed to Ruskin, and not only does he posit such a hierarchy, but he also emphasizes that it is essentially a moral one. So he proposes to examine aspects of beauty in "every division of creation, in stones, mountains, waves, clouds, and all organic bodies, beginning with vegetables . . . then taking instances in the range of animals, from the mollusc to man" (4.142-3). Investing the natural world with moral value, he states that "a peach is nobler than a hawthorn berry, and still more a hawthorn berry than a bead of the nightshade" (5.67). Like Boethius in his *Consolation of Philosophy*, in which he asserts that the law controlling everything in the universe, from the tides to human love, is the binding love of God (Bk.III, Pr.10), Ruskin looks upon the whole of "organic creation" in much the same way. From the intense enjoyment which the angels may be thought to experience as they participate in the shedding of God's kindness upon all creation, to the happiness to be attributed to the lowest levels of plant life, the whole universe, spiritual and material, manifests the bond of love by which it is bound. As in Dante's final vision at the end of the *Paradiso*, it is love that moves the sun and the other stars: the law of gravity is of the same kind as human love, with the same divine origin.

Ruskin's patterns of thought with reference to the animal world in *Modern Painters II* are not only hierarchical but also remarkably reminiscent of medieval bestiaries because of the intrinsically moral nature of his aesthetic theory at this stage of his life. We look with hate, he says, on the foulness of the sloth, the subtlety of the adder, and the rage of the hyena, while we approve the earnest ant and unwearied bee, looking for lessons as to our earthly conduct from these creatures (4.156). He discusses the hindrances to our proper appreciation of the moral functions of the animal tribes sometimes posed by their outward beauty, though he concludes that the beauty of the animal form is in exact proportion to the amount of moral or intellectual virtue expressed by it (4.158). We must determine how far each creature worthily executes its office, "whether, if scorpion, it have poison enough," for example, and how far it comes up to the perfect idea of its species (4.163). The argument is carried on to the next chapter (Ch. XIII) with a discussion which includes the conditions of ideality in vegetables.

Moral schematism influenced Ruskin's thinking even with regard to the depiction of the human face. In *Modern Painters II*, he maintains that Beauty is incompatible with the expressions of Pride, Sensuality, Ferocity, and Fear. Even to paint such features is depraved; and furthermore, passion should never be depicted on the face. It seems likely that he was again making a deduction from the early art which he had studied so intensely in France and Italy, in which the faces both of human beings and of angels are usually expressionless, but his deeply ingrained hatred of sin made him hate its representation. Ruskin's intense response to beauty sharpened his sense of evil and fired his reforming zeal. His discussion of Vital Beauty–the beauty of living things including human beings–suggests that for him at this stage, as for the Middle Ages, the idea of the Fall had important implications for the conceptualization and representation of the human: "we must not determinedly banish from the human form and countenance, in our restoration of its ideal, everything which can be ultimately traced to the

Adamite Fall for its cause, but only the immediate operation and presence of the degrading power of sin" (4.186).

Ruskin's rediscovery of the previously scarcely recognized meaningfulness of medieval art led to an intensification of the intellectual content of the art of his own time. In *The Stones of Venice* he suggests that "some day the language of Types will be more read and understood by us than it has been for centuries" (11.41). His conviction, growing out of his study of medieval art and architecture, that art must communicate ideas, was opposed to the current dislike of symbolism and allegory. Hazlitt's advice to readers of Spenser's *Faerie Queene*–to enjoy the "pictures" in it and not to bother about the meaning–was widely accepted, though not by Ruskin. Pointing out the weakness of contemporary Victorian art compared with that of the Middle Ages he said,

> And thus while the pictures of the Middle Ages are full of intellectual matter and meaning–schools of philosophy and theology, and solemn exponents of the faiths and fears of earnest religion–we may pass furlongs of exhibition wall without receiving any idea or sentiment, other than that it is pleasant to be out on the lawn in fine weather. (19.201)

Ruskin's recognition of the importance of symbol and allegory, as well as of typology, came to be adopted to a considerable extent by contemporary artists, notably the Pre-Raphaelites; and his analysis of medieval art was extraordinarily influential, as for example on William Morris and on Proust. His criticism continues the medieval spirit, but in a more accessible and modern form. In seeing Gothic architecture in its entirety as a type of the Trinity because its distinctive form is the trefoiled arch, he made it more possible for his contemporaries and for subsequent generations to appreciate the complexities of medieval symbolism. The external sculpture on the cathedral at Amiens was for him "at once an alphabet and epitome of the religion, by the knowledge and inspiration of which an acceptable worship might be rendered . . . to the Lord" (33.123). He even expresses in pictorial mode his recognition of the practical difficulties experienced by the thirteenth-century builders of the cathedral: "so hard did the Devil pull" against them (33.133). Looking at the central figure at Amiens, for example, he discusses the symbolic significance of the supporters of the statue of Christ, the Cockatrice and the Adder. Both these creatures, "even in their deadly life, accomplish Christ's final will":

> The first represents the infidelity of Pride. The cockatrice–king serpent or highest serpent–saying that he is God, and will be God.
>
> The second, the infidelity of Death. The adder . . . saying that he is mud, and will be mud.
>
> Lastly . . . set under the feet . . . of Christ Himself, are the lion and dragon; the images of Carnal sin, or Human sin, as distinguished from the Spiritual and Intellectual sin of Pride, by which the angels also fell. (33.146)

Ruskin continues his discussion of the significance of the figure of Christ in Judgement at Amiens by his comments on Death, which is represented as total and irrevocable:

> There is no word in thirteenth-century Theology of the pardon (in our modern sense) of sins; and there is none of the Purgatory of them. . . . I do not know what commenting or softening doctrines were written in frightened minuscule by the Fathers. . . . But I know that the language of every graven stone and every glowing window–of things daily seen and universally understood by the people, was absolutely and alone, this teaching of Moses from Sinai in the beginning, and of St John from Patmos in the end, of the Revelation of God to Israel. (33.170)

Here, in identifying with the fear of Judgement of the Middle Ages, Ruskin is himself adopting the medieval mode of reception of church teaching through image and symbol on the part of the unlearned. The schematization, reminiscent of the patterns of medieval drama, of the Christian message in the reference to Moses on Sinai and St. John on Patmos indicates the very similar way in which Ruskin himself thought. The Gothic cathedral, therefore, is to be "read" and its message decoded. He believed that all art, although its function may be obviously decorative, should also be informative, so that even in a straightforward representation of a Biblical scene, the existence of deeper meaning can be perceived. The wise "speak in enigmas only" (17.208), as Homer and the Greek tragedians, Plato, Dante, Chaucer, Shakespeare, and Goethe have also done: for Ruskin, art, religion, and life must be inseparable.

Ruskin has been criticized, to some extent not unreasonably, for his lack of understanding and appreciation of the structural features of Gothic architecture (Frankl 558ff.). His fundamental interests and insight into the nature of medieval art and architecture lay in a different direction, however, since it was with the interpretation of their symbolic meaning that he was most concerned. With his high moral and spiritual concept of medieval art, he naturally found its frequent delight in the grotesque–often ugly, comic, and sometimes indecent–a considerable problem. He had to find for himself an explanation for and meaning in the grotesques and gargoyles which appear as marginal decoration in manuscripts and on corbel tables, misericords, fonts, and capitals in churches and elsewhere. He had observed the carving of grotesques on medieval houses in Flemish towns, in Normandy, Switzerland, and Germany, and he came to the conclusion that it was the product of "the recreative exertion of minds more or less blunted or encumbered by other cares and toils" (11.157). At its best, he saw such carving as "an elaborate and luscious form of nonsense" (11.162), but this did not satisfactorily explain its presence in a religious context. The answer for Ruskin was that God's love was always mixed with wrath and threatening; and God had appointed as principal passions for men, on the one hand, the fear of sin and death, and on the other, love of God. The existence of hell, he maintained, was as legibly declared in the universe, particularly through natural phenomena, as that of heaven, and he had no patience with the theology of his older contemporary, F. D. Maurice, which he saw as degrading "the beneficence of the Deity into a reckless infinitude of mercy" (11.164).[2] With the terror of death, of judgement, and of Hell felt by the Middle Ages, therefore, Ruskin empathized and he saw the grotesque as the means that medieval artists had found to express the horror of evil and of the Last Things. Above all, his reading of Dante's *Inferno* brought comprehension of the medieval use of the grotesque for the representation of evil, particularly in Cantos XXI and XXII. Like Dante (and as also in the mystery plays), the medieval artist or craftsman in his attempt to give symbolic representation to evil in the form of devils often had to resort to strange distortions of the human body and to animal forms. While thus suggesting degradation, such artists frequently and perhaps involuntarily created ludicrous effects. So Ruskin's belief when he was writing *Modern Painters II* and *The Stones of Venice*, that the universe as a whole is to be interpreted symbolically, helped him to make sense of the grotesque:

> God would have us understand that this is true not of invented
> symbols merely, but of all things amidst which we live; that
> there is a deeper meaning within them than eye hath seen, or
> ear hath heard; and that the whole visible creation is a mere
> perishable symbol of things eternal and true. . . . So that the
> whole world, and all that there is therein . . . is a continual

Gospel . . . [and] there is nothing so base in creation, but that
our faith may give it wings. (11.183-4)

In Gothic, Ruskin saw a certain wildness of spirit which underlies both
the non-naturalistic patterning of much earlier work, and the gradual
development of a kind of limited realism which he equally clearly perceived
in later examples. Here perhaps his perceptiveness as a critic ran ahead of his
ability to theorize and schematize. He came to the conclusion that Gothic is
the greatest architectural style because it arises from the "strange
disquietude" of its spirit: "that restlessness of the dreaming mind, that
wanders hither and thither . . . and yet is not satisfied, nor will be satisfied"
(10.214). Its inventiveness and richness and strength derive from what he
calls the magnificent enthusiasm of the Gothic imagination.

Ruskin's discussion of the depiction of landscape in medieval
manuscripts also shows his awareness of the omnipresence of symbolism. He
took Macaulay severely to task for his inability to see that the illumination
in a medieval manuscript is not to be despised as an inadequate literal
representation (5.261). He drew attention to the implications and importance
of the change from the chequered background seen in the manuscript
illumination of the earlier Middle Ages, to the background of blue sky found
from the end of the fourteenth century. He rightly saw this change as
indicative of the very significant progression from symbolic to imitative art
which continues into the modern period. His discussion of medieval
landscape in *Modern Painters III* is as perceptive as it is comprehensive.
Maintaining that simple symbolic pictures convey meaning better than
elaborate ones, he analyzes the functions of art in the Middle Ages, seeing
the requirements of heraldry as one of the factors that exerted an influence
on modes of representation: "hence at once an utter denial of natural
appearances by the great body of workmen" (5.258). Although he did not
himself share the attitudes to wild landscape of the artists, he has a
sympathetic understanding of them. He suggests that, for the Middle Ages,
pleasant pastoral scenes were invariably preferred to rocky mountainous
landscapes, which were felt to be threatening. Fruit trees, covered with
delicious fruit, with singing birds perched on every bough, adorn the ideal
medieval landscape, and the favourite occupation is not to cultivate the land
but to gather roses and fruit, and to ride out hawking. He comments on the
prevalence of gardens in which knights and ladies are represented as singing
or courting; the medieval landscape is seen as a source of pleasure. For the
knight on a quest, however, who in his loneliness is "compelled to enter into
dim companionship with the silent nature about him," it is a different matter.

Ruskin recognizes that the mountains that he loved so much himself, the "crocused slopes of the Chartreuse, or the soft glades and dewy pastures of Vallombrosa," inspired only fear and awe in the Middle Ages, because they were associated with demoniacal and angelic presences and the withdrawal from the world of monk and hermit. "All that was rugged, rough, dark, wild, unterminated, they rejected at once, as the domain of 'salvage men' and monstrous giants" (5.257).

Ruskin's insight into medieval attitudes to different types of landscape was perceptive, especially as it did not correspond with his own feelings. He was also capable of adversely criticizing medieval art, disliking what he calls the barbarism of the highly stylized forms, which he regarded as conventional and lifeless, of the earlier period. The good workman, he says, has an ideal of organic form which enables him to represent natural objects with accuracy: he goes to the very heart of the facts of nature. Ruskin hates the notion of a purely subjective self-pleasing art, art for art's sake, which he regards as deeply corrupting, seeing Gothic art as an art for the people, at the same time both practical and impressive. Medieval art at its best is–and all art should be–strongly social. It is by this means that he can allow the ugliness of the grotesque and the savage wildness of Gothic art a place in his fundamentally didactic theory. They point to what exists. But in the true Gothic, they point from an attitude of balanced inclusiveness.

For all his sympathetic approach, Ruskin finds it impossible, he says, to detect the real feelings and responses to his subject of the medieval artist. He therefore turns once again for enlightenment to Dante, the supreme exponent of all that he admired in medieval culture. For Ruskin, he was "the central man of all the world, as representing in perfect balance the imaginative, moral and intellectual faculties, all at their highest" (11.187). He quoted Dante in almost every work he wrote, finding in him a constant source of consolation, of inspiration, and of information about medieval thought-patterns. In the *Divine Comedy*, specifically in Dante's vision of the lady Matilda gathering flowers in the Earthly Paradise, Ruskin discovered a key to the fuller understanding of the medieval landscape (*Purgatorio* 28). She explains to Dante the source of her happiness by reminding him of Psalm 92: "Thou, Lord, hast made me glad through Thy works. I will triumph in the works of Thy hands." Matilda (Ruskin comments) represents the Active life, which forms the felicity of Earth; she takes delight in God's labour. So she exemplifies what ought to constitute a significant source of happiness for human beings–a source of happiness which had, since early childhood, always been of central importance to Ruskin. The underlying meaning of this passage is that happiness springs not merely from delighting in nature itself, but more particularly from awareness of nature as divine in origin (5.276ff.). So in Dante, Ruskin found not only insight into attitudes to landscape in the Middle Ages, but justification for his own instinctive feeling for the natural world.

Many of Ruskin's contemporaries who were also attracted to Gothic architecture similarly wrote comprehensive guides to it both in England and in Europe, but his approach to it differed markedly from theirs, in that his imaginative identification with the men who built the churches and cathedrals, and his comprehensive and penetrating exploration of medieval iconography went both further and deeper. The depth of his sympathy with the religious faith and feeling which had produced Gothic art and architecture led beyond the perception of the primary unity of all created things, as it did for medieval men. His understanding of the nature of Gothic not only coloured his perception of the social ills of his own time, but it also suggested the basis for a social programme of reform. In a letter to his father in 1852 he defined "the essence of Gothic"as lying in "the workman's heart and mind" (10.180). This is vague and perhaps sentimental, but in a triad of his own devising he went on to maintain that the "distinctive test of Gothic architecture is so by a mysterious ordainment–being, first, a type of the Trinity in number, secondly, of all the beauty of vegetation upon earth . . . lastly, because it is the perfect expression of the strongest possible way of building an arch" (10.180n.). He then contrasted the infinite variety available to Gothic with the mechanical repetitiveness and mass-production of modern industry, arguing that the medieval workman could make use of his intellectual powers as well as his manual skills for the glory of God. Ruskin believed that whether the workman was highly skilled or inept, whether his work was polished or crude, a place might be found for it. Even poor workmanship might be acceptable if the craftsman had done his best, a notion which has been ridiculed by some modern critics (Unrau 33ff.).

The work of the medieval craftsman, Ruskin believed, must have been more satisfying and worthwhile than that of the nineteenth-century factory-hand, condemned to labour twelve hours a day, six days a week in the factories of England for the benefit of the owners. Dickens similarly in *Hard Times* (1854) drew attention to the misery of contemporary factory workers by referring to the anonymous and depersonalized workers in Gradgrind's factory as mere "hands." Ruskin's ideas on the idyllic life of the medieval craftsman may sound naïve as he contemplates some carving and asks, "Was it done with enjoyment–was the carver happy while he was about it?" (8.210). But though modern methods of manufacture might produce accurate and uniform results, he believed that they inevitably degraded the operative into a machine:

> Men may be beaten, chained, tormented, yoked like cattle, slaughtered like summer flies, and yet remain in one sense . . . free. But to smother their souls with them, to make the flesh and skin . . . into leathern thongs to yoke machinery with . . . this is to be slave-masters indeed. (10.193)

Ruskin knew very well that the craftsman might have to adhere to a programme, that convention would also bind him in certain ways, but he still believed that some degree of spontaneity and originality must have been possible in the Middle Ages. He was well aware that there was little that was subjective about medieval art, and that the artist expressed neither his own personal feelings nor his individuality through his art as a modern artist does. He saw compensations in the medieval craftsman's relation to his employer: to obey another man, to work for him and to respect him or his position, is not slavery. To do so might release the workman from anxiety.

Ruskin's medievalism took a very different form from the end of the 1850's. The perfection of Gothic had made more glaringly apparent to him the shortcomings of the modern world, where the organic was displaced by the mechanical, and natural beauty by artificial decoration, where visual art was superficial and human relationships vitiated by what Carlyle called "the cash nexus." Despite his recognition of evil and suffering in the medieval world, Ruskin believed that it offered a model for his own time. He was, of course, far from being alone in regarding the pre-industrial society of the Middle Ages as in many respects a Golden Age, despite the fact that many of his contemporaries considered such notions ridiculous. With the loss of the religious certainties in which he had grown up he turned to political economy in *Unto This Last* (1862). It provoked a furious reaction, and his advocacy of social change caused widespread alarm: he meanwhile had come to feel that to "fill starved people's bellies was now the only task worth doing."[3]

He was convinced that it was essential to get rid as far as possible of steam-powered machinery and to use only what was driven by wind or water, or that could be powered by human or animal energy, to turn the industrial revolution back in its tracks and to return as far as possible to what he saw as the simple lifestyle of the Middle Ages. These ideas, which he developed in various ways both theoretical and practical, had their origin in a complex mixture of sources, some recent or contemporary, some dating back to the previous century. Cobbett, for example, had expressed his approval of feudalism because it meant that land was held in return for service, so that there were mutual obligations on the part of both lord and peasant. Cobbett's theory that the lord's obligation (even if only notional) to support his dependants produced better and more humane results than the Poor Law of the nineteenth century led him to regard the later Middle Ages as a lost Golden Age. Mass unemployment as such had been virtually non-existent before the industrialization of the early nineteenth century; and the Poor Law was widely felt to be inhumane and humiliating.[4] Now the new awareness of widespread poverty and unemployment, combined with the policies of *laissez-faire* and utilitarianism and harsh laws, evoked a nostalgia for the supposed benevolent paternalism of the Middle Ages.

Particularly significant for Ruskin's political and social thought was Carlyle's *Past and Present*, first published in 1843, which defined the "Condition of England" in that decade as ominous, and contrasted it with England in the year 1200. Carlyle's vision of the past portrayed an England in which "[a] Feudal Aristocracy is still alive . . . judging, soldiering, adjusting; everywhere governing the people–so that even a Gurth [the fictional swineherd] born thrall of Cedric lacks not his due parings of the pigs he tends" (*Past & Present* Bk.II, Ch.v). Carlyle knew that in the Middle Ages the poor had to endure hardship, but it was his belief that the aristocracy, because they possessed the land, were bound to "furnish guidance and governance"–"not no-government and *laissez-faire.*" Recognizing that the lives of "the dumb millions born to toil" were always fraught with suffering, he was convinced that their lives were never so entirely unbearable as at the present time (*Past & Present* Bk.III, Ch.v). Ruskin, like both Cobbett and Carlyle, saw the ruling class of his own time as disclaiming responsibility for social evils and rejecting the idea of any obligation to society. But although he often looked back nostalgically to the age of chivalry when the knight might be a "worthy man," a lover of "Trouthe and honour, fredom and curteisye," with all the other admirable qualities of Chaucer's knight, he was certainly not so naïve as to believe that life was totally paradisal in the Middle Ages. Although he seems never to have read *Piers Plowman* or any of the medieval poems of social discontent with which we are familiar now despite his friendship with Furnivall, editor of many medieval texts, in the novels of Scott, in Carlyle, and variously elsewhere he would have encountered images of the past which made clear that the Middle Ages had troubles enough of their own. There was, however, a widespread contemporary tendency to glorify the past which showed itself in the writing of history, as in Green's *Short History of the English People*

(1872), in which the Middle Ages are seen as a period of immense advance in terms of civilization.

Ruskin's understanding of medieval attitudes to poverty (attitudes which he regarded as superior to contemporary ones) was again largely derived from his reading of Dante. In *A Joy for Ever*, he alludes specifically to the *Inferno*, where "the spirit of Poverty is reverenced with subjection of heart, and faithfulness of affection," and goes on to speak of the Middle Ages as a time "when wealth seems to have been looked upon by the best men not only as contemptible, but as criminal" (16.17). But where Langland can say that the deserving poor may take their poverty as a penance which can win them full pardon in heaven, Ruskin was by 1857 no longer able to accept the belief that suffering in this life, whether in the form of poverty or otherwise, would be recompensed in an afterlife. While Langland's need was to find a way of coming to terms with and accepting poverty by intellectual argument, since there were no practical means available for dealing with it, Ruskin's concern was with the causes and available remedies for a poverty that should be totally unacceptable in a civilized industrial country. It cannot be made tolerable by pious words praising it as a Christ-like state because of the degradation, the dehumanization in which it results. Ruskin was a rich man and a lover of natural beauty: he saw millions of his contemporaries exploited by a system which they were powerless to change, and which forced them to supply luxuries to the rich at the expense of their very lives, while at the same time the relentless growth of industry ravaged and destroyed the countryside. In his awareness and his dismay he was entirely a modern man. Guilt, pity, bafflement mingled with the conviction that it must be possible to do something to stop the disastrous process. His belief that a return to a medieval way of life in some respects could be feasible led directly to the founding of the Guild of St. George in 1871. This social experiment, though not very successful in practical terms, was to have far-reaching consequences as a source of inspiration in the late nineteenth and twentieth centuries.

Although Ruskin himself doubted the authenticity of St. George, "a very ghostly saint" as he called him (28.733), he had felt a life-long attraction to him. St. George was a particularly suitable saint for the Guild (originally Company) because he was the patron saint of England, and because he is best known as a dragon-slayer. Ruskin had a new dragon for him to slay, the steam-power that he believed to be actually consuming the lives of both men and women in "blind, tormented, unwearied, marvellous England" (7.386). His plan was to buy, with some of the wealth that he had inherited, tracts of land, because he believed that prosperity could ultimately only come from the land. The Golden Age was to return as the result of St. George's labours for Merry England; the company itself was to be a band of delivering knights who would obey the law of Christ, cultivating their fields and living simply. Ruskin, who owned many medieval manuscripts, inscribed the Roll of the Company on the blank leaves of an eleventh-century manuscript of the Gospels. But his attempts to gain the support of his friends and of influential people to expand the scheme failed almost immediately, partly because his policy was to buy up poor, unproductive land (on which only subsistence farming was possible) and partly because he had no business sense.

Ruskin's stated intention was to help to re-establish the peasant population of England under conditions which would ensure healthful and happy life, and to secure the highest possible education of English men and women, living by agriculture in their native land. "We will try to make some small piece of English ground beautiful, peaceful and fruitful" (27.96) by good husbandry and craftsmanship. The companions of the Guild were to be Givers, not Receivers, giving their time, their thoughts, their labour for the help of the poor and needy, working as far as possible with their own hands and practising that very medieval virtue, obedience, which Ruskin so often praises. In this case, it was obedience to the law of Christ that was to be pre-eminent. As a kind of motto for the Guild, Ruskin proposed a medieval inscription carved on a St. George's cross which he had discovered in a ninth-century church in Venice. In giving the text of it in *Fors Clavigera*, his approval is not unmixed with sceptical humour: "'Be Thy Cross, O Christ, the true safety of this place.' (In case of mercantile panics, you see.) On the band beneath it, 'Around this temple, let the merchant's law be just–his weights true, and his agreements guileless'" (29.99).

Although Ruskin's social experiment looked at the time, and may still look, a crack-brained scheme, his concept of the life of the Middle Ages was generally more balanced and less sentimentalized than one might expect. Speaking of the thousand years of the feudal system, he sees it as divided into peasants who lived by working, priests who lived by begging, and knights who lived by pillaging. The crusaders habitually lived by robbery, and were still too savage to conceive the spirit or the character of this Christ whose cross they wore:

> For many centuries the knights of Christendom wore their
> religion gay as their crest, familiar as their gauntlet . . . hurled
> it fiercely in other people's faces, grasped their spear the firmer
> for it . . . but it never entered into their minds for an instant to

ask the meaning of it! "'Forgive us our sins':–by all means, yes, and the next garrison that holds out a day longer than is convenient for us, hang them every man to his battlement. 'Give us this day our daily bread,'–yes, and our neighbour's also, if we have any luck. 'Our Lady and the Saints!' Is there any infidel dog that doubts of them?–in God's name, boot and spur–and let us have the head off him." It went on so, frankly and bravely, to the twelfth century. . . . (24.261)

Yet like many of his contemporaries he believed that the ideal of knighthood still held good for modern society.[5] Addressing an audience of young soldiers, he sees them as knights whose duty it should be not only to subdue the wicked and aid the weak but to supply strong government and leadership. Hope for the future, he suggests, lies in the renewal and implementation of the ideals of the past by the privileged, who alone have the power to change the status quo.

Ruskin's medievalism was extraordinarily complex and diverse; it could also be inconsistent, self-contradictory, cantankerous. Although he wished to bring back some features of the Middle Ages, he disapproved of utopianism; he also abhorred socialism. He paradoxically loathed what he called "Birmingham Gothic" in modern architecture, for which he recognized that his own writings had been partly responsible. He detested some features of medieval religious practice; he was very anti-clerical. He sneered at Pugin largely because he was a Roman Catholic convert. Although he included Chaucer among the seven great writers whose works should be in all the libraries of St. George's Guild, his Victorian sense of decorum led him to ban the *Canterbury Tales* from his list of essential texts.

In many ways his medievalism was typically Victorian: his literalism, his belief in the social purpose of art, his sense of outrage at the sufferings of the poor, and his desire to improve the world are all nineteenth-century, not medieval characteristics. It was the nineteenth century which pre-eminently created a genuine sense of the pastness of the past, and first of all perceived the life of the past as really different, with its own criteria, so that it could also be inspired by it.

Ruskin's boyhood dream of chivalry and romance led him from his intention of defending Turner in *Modern Painters*, to the study of Gothic architecture. Drawing inspiration from the Middle Ages, as the first and greatest of English art critics and art historians, and one of the most passionately concerned among many great nineteenth-century social critics, his influence has been enormous. His Guild of St. George continues to this day (though in an attenuated form); the National Trust, offspring of his love for England's countryside and architectural heritage, continues to acquire and to care for historic properties and by extending its membership, to heighten public awareness of the need to safeguard them.

In *Unto This Last*, Ruskin wrote: "Luxury is indeed possible in the future–innocent and exquisite; luxury for all, and by the help of all" (17.114). That we have gone so far towards achieving such luxury in western society owes much to his vision which, looking backward, has for over a century helped to shape our future.

Notes

1. The aesthetics of these and other medieval writers are discussed in de Bruyne, *Esthetics*.
2. Maurice, *Theological Essays*, attacked the idea of eternal punishment after death, which was generally accepted by Christians of all denominations at the time.
3. Letter to Charles Eliot Norton in 1859, qtd. in Abse 172.
4. The New Poor Law, which followed the Poor Law Amendment Act of 1834, made help for the unemployed and poverty-stricken available virtually only in the workhouse. The severity of the regime and the stigma of having to submit to it were keenly felt by the poor. Writers such as Carlyle, Dickens, and Charles Kingsley drew attention to the harshness of the system and the misery that it caused.
5. For an account of the chivalric ideal in Victorian England, see Girouard, *Return to Camelot*, especially Ch. 9 "Muscular Chivalry."

Works Cited

Abse, Joan. *John Ruskin: The Passionate Moralist*. London: Quartet Books, 1980.

Carlyle, Thomas. *Past and Present* (1843).

de Bruyne, Edgar. *The Esthetics of the Middle Ages*. New York: Ungar, 1969. Trans. of *Etudes d'esthetique medievale*. Brugge: De Temple, 1946.

Dickens, Charles. *Hard Times* (1854).

Digby, Kenelm. *The Broad Stone: Rules of the Gentlemen of England* (1827).

Finley, C. Stephen. *Nature's Covenant: Figures of Landscape in Ruskin*. University Park, PA: Pennsylvania State UP, 1992.

Frankl, Paul. *The Gothic: Literary Sources and Interpretations through Eight Centuries*. Princeton, NJ: Princeton UP, 1960.

Girouard, Mark. *The Return to Camelot: Chivalry and the English Gentleman*. New Haven: Yale UP, 1981.

Green, John Richard. *Short History of the English People* (1872).

Landow, George P. *The Aesthetic and Critical Theories of John Ruskin*. Princeton, NJ: Princeton UP, 1971.

—. *Victorian Types, Victorian Shadows: Biblical Typology in Victorian Literature, Art, and Thought*. London: Routledge, 1980.

Maurice, F. D. *Theological Essays* (1853).

Ruskin, John. *The Works of John Ruskin*. Ed. E. T. Cook and Alexander Wedderburn. 39 vols. University Park, PA: Pennsylvania State UP, 1903-12.

Unrau, John. *New Approaches to Ruskin*. Ed. Robert Hewison. London and Boston: Routledge & Kegan Paul, 1981.

Patricia Merivale

"SUB ROSA":
UMBERTO ECO
AND THE MEDIEVALIST MYSTERY STORY

It is not easy to locate or develop a syncretic view of twentieth-century medievalism. If the medievalism of the antiquaries, of Scott and the Romantics, of Tennyson and William Morris, is like a series of fancifully reconstructed stained glass windows, medievalism in the twentieth century is more like a spilled jig-saw puzzle. Let me assemble a small corner of it, as I try to chart that rhizomic maze, that garden of forking paths, in which historical fiction, the detective story, and apocalyptic science fiction get all tangled up together, *sub rosa*, under *The Name of the Rose*.[1]

A feature of the literary scene in the last quarter of the twentieth century, from pulp-popular to nearly highbrow and back, has been an intriguing subdivision of twentieth-century medievalism, the medieval historical novel, which has been caught recently committing wholesale generic miscegenation with the detective / mystery story.[2] This hybrid genre seems designed to appeal to an enormous cult-crossover audience, who obtain a synergistic pleasure from the combination of these two formulaic genres.

The corner of twentieth-century medievalism I am examining is made up of the varied authorial responses to Umberto Eco's own medievalist, and apocalyptic, mystery, *The Name of the Rose*: with Ellis Peters exemplifying rejection, Peter Tremayne and Sharan Newman exemplifying appropriation, and Philip Kerr exemplifying transposition of Ecovian materials. Eco's own preference would be, I think, for transposition, given not only his stated preference for "the text that seeks to produce a new reader" over the text that merely meets the expectations of the reader-in-the-street (*NR* 523), but also his own notable transposition of, among other things, the Victorian Sherlock Holmes into the Middle Ages. Kerr's detailed and consistent transposition (in *The Grid*, 1995) of the medieval structures of Eco's book into the apocalyptic dystopia of a hypothetical '1997' sometime in the near future, might, I think, amuse him.

Eco's *The Name of the Rose* (1980, 1983), is obviously the key text of the 'crossover' genre of the historical novel-as-detective story as it impacts medievalism. I shall consider Eco's book as the epicentre of, and the mediation between, highbrow and popular, mainstream and pulp, metaphysical and formulaic[3] in the medieval historical detective story. Eco, that master-showman on the current cultural scene, has it both ways: *The Name of the Rose* is theologico-philosophical and self-reflexively serious, in a postmodern sort of way: indeed it seems to resemble Eco's "ideal postmodernist novel [which] . . . rise[s] above the quarrel between . . . coterie fiction and junk fiction" (*NR* 532). It is a thoroughly intertextual feat of meta-detection, or, in short, a "metaphysical" detective story, but it is also a best-seller, a proleptic film script, and a very "good read." While transcending the popular formulaic genre of the medieval detective story, it also (like *Wuthering Heights* and the Gothic novel) is a significant part of that very genre.

All of the more "mainstream" contemporary historical detective (or, more commonly, "mystery") fictions, such as Randolph Stow's *Girl Green as Elderflower*, Iain Banks' *Song of Stone*, Jill Paton Walsh's *Knowledge of Angels*, William Golding's *The Spire*, and Barry Unsworth's *Morality Play*, display a strong documentary sense of the filth and cruelty endemic in medieval society, which many of us first learned about from *The Return of Martin Guerre* (see note 2). In *Morality Play*, for instance, a priest-turned-player-turned-detective narrator delineates with expressionist intensity his own involvement, in all senses, in deed, action, and discovery, and, yes, guilt, filth and pain.[4] And it is generally true of the more postmodern among them that, so far from having happy endings, or even epistemologically lucid ones ("solutions"), they end in anticlimax, in uncertainty, in the absorption of the detective into the criminal, or some other form of non-solution. And insofar as they do so, they, like *The Name of the Rose*, are metaphysical as well as medievalist detective stories.

The didactic and pedagogic intentions of the innumerable "popular" (but also, like mainstream detective stories, middle-brow) medievalist historical novels (generally written in a multi-volume series, with the detective-protagonist continuing from volume to volume) peer out from behind these escapist romances saturated by the idyllic connotations of the nostalgic backward glance–not least, in this long twilight of the Golden Age of the British detective novel, to Agatha Christie's Body in the Library, rather than to Raymond Chandler's mean streets. Their authors would take as a compliment the suggestion that most of what is known, by the public outside the Academy, about the Middle Ages comes from such books and/or the films made from them. Even the most "popular" of these works attempt at times to rival Eco in his too detailed exposition of the place and the time, if not in the scholarly particularities which occasionally daunt the readers of *The Name of the Rose* and have made its sequel, *Foucault's Pendulum*, one of the least read of bestsellers.

The (clerical) 'Brother' or 'Sister' detectives of these popular series, like Paul Harding's 'Brother Athelstan,' Sharan Newman's 'Catherine LeVendeur' and 'Brother Eadfal,' Ellis Peters' 'Brother Cadfael,' Peter Tremayne's 'Sister Fidelma' and 'Brother Edgar,' Margaret Frazer's 'Sister Frevisse,' Susanna Gregory's 'Brother Matthew Bartholomew,' Domini Highsmith's 'Father Simeon,' and many others are all essentially "armchair" detectives, outside investigators, whose personal survival is guaranteed, not least by the demands of the series form: only one story in the series, the final one, can trifle with the existence of the detective him- or herself.

Ellis Peters' twenty-volume "Brother Cadfael" series is certainly the most widely read (and, even in the dozen volumes published since 1983, the least Ecovian) of the serial medieval detective stories, scoring steady successes from seven years before *The Name of the Rose* to twelve years after it. Peters came to Eco late, found him needlessly obscure and over-demanding of his readers (Lewis 85), and seems only once or twice to have alluded to him: in *The Heretic's Apprentice* and *The Rose Rent* (see Christian & Lindsay 287, 289n2). Unsurprisingly, perhaps, although *The Rose Rent* is one of the most affecting (as a romance) and intriguing (as a detective story) of the Cadfael series, the rose-bush, while schematically symbolic, is an absolutely literal one, a tangible object upon which the whole story centers, and which, in its burning, provides the climax of the story–thus sharply curtailing the polyvalence of, by making all-too-present the absence of, Eco's rose.

Her "sweet-tempered" (a term I borrow from the back cover of *The Devil's Novice*) detective, Brother Cadfael, seems not to be a William of Baskerville (or a Sherlock Holmes in a cowl), but rather a cross between Shakespeare's Friar Lawrence, bringing together and blessing lovers (but always with a happy ending), and G. K. Chesterton's Father Brown, from whom Cadfael inherits the curious capacity to solve crimes "placidly," "absently" or "flatly," "simply" or "humbly." The nexus of qualities that Chesterton designated as the "innocence" of Father Brown, however, Peters tends to give to Cadfael's assistant, the youthful Brother Mark. "History," or, more specifically, the intersections of the religious order and the political order in the regions around Shrewsbury between 1138 and 1146, during the reign(s) of Stephen and Matilda, is appropriated as context for some curious murders, for which Brother Cadfael finds unproblematic solutions blessed by romance: the saving from punishment of innocents wrongly accused counts for at least as much as the identification of the guilty. And if a Chestertonian trope is borrowed, as in the eponymous scene in *One Corpse Too Many* (1979), it is quite shorn of the paradox which was Chesterton's main, and of course metaphysical, point. The "Purloined Letter" trope, of concealing something among many others of the same kind, leaving it hidden by the very obviousness of the hiding place, is found in Conan Doyle's "The Red-Headed League," in Agatha Christie's *The ABC Murders*, in Ariel Dorfman's *Hard Rain*, in a science-fiction detective story by John Varley called "The Barbie [Doll] Murders," and, most important, as it seems obvious that Peters knew it, in Chesterton's brilliant "The Sign of the Broken Sword." The last three stories share the plot element of hiding a murderer and/or a murdered body among a mass of other bodies, so that any observer less systematic than Brother Cadfael will fail to notice that there is "one corpse too many."

All these other writers, even Varley, but especially Chesterton, make a brain-twisting paradox from this situation: "*Where would a wise man hide a leaf?* In the forest . . . . And if a man had to hide a dead body, he would make a field of dead bodies to hide it in" (Chesterton 153). Chesterton twists the moral knot tighter, too, as the word "make" suggests; this murderer has sent dozens of men to their deaths in combat, *solely* to camouflage the one death that he deliberately brought about. But Peters simplifies and literalizes the situation: Cadfael counts the corpses after a mass execution, and, alerted by the discrepancy, finds the one body that was killed individually (i.e., murdered) and placed among the other bodies, in the expectation that the crime would thus be concealed: "there is a murdered man among your executed men, a leaf hidden in your forest" (*One Corpse Too Many* 213).

Brother Cadfael always wants to maximize people's happiness (Lewis 106); he is "concerned less with retribution than redemption" (Harriott, qtd. in Lewis 104; again I would add, "like Father Brown"). Peters, for all her vaunted historical accuracy, could be accused of neglecting the filth and pain of medieval life in favor of a somewhat insular "coziness," like Cadfael's other predecessors, the Miss Marples of the English Golden Age detective story. Indeed, Peters does so deliberately and on principle, finding that "human nature has been very much the same, equally bad and equally good throughout [history]," and that what we would interpret as pain and sensory displeasure was to the people of the Middle Ages simply the state of things, requiring neither comment nor any particular attention (Ashley Interview, qtd. in Lewis 116; Christian and Lindsay 285).

This view, while essentially shared by Peter Tremayne, Paul Harding (and his alter egos), and indeed by the great majority of the writers of such series, is diametrically opposed to the most recent wave of historical fiction, where it is precisely the 'otherness' of the medieval which is seen to yield its attractiveness and importance: "Very authentic. . . . The essence of a truly historical story is that the people should feel and believe according to their times," says Ann Perry, quoted, in praise, at the front of Margaret Frazer's *The Servant's Tale*. On the back cover of that same book, however, the publicist finds no difficulty in placing Frazer "in the tradition of Ellis Peters" (as is done for most, if not all, of the writers of clerical series novels). We are not to think, in Peters' anachronistic fashion, that Frazer's characters are 'like us'; but, in accordance with the tendencies of current theory, we are to note and respect their differences. In either case, of course, but with a somewhat different effect, 'here' and 'now' are projected on to 'there' and 'then.'

I shall look more closely at two examples of the 'genre' series novel, chosen for being particularly (but not uniquely) explicit in their deployment of Ecovian plot devices, though of course both books are, like all the 'series' volumes, shorter and simpler by far than *The Name of the Rose*: Sharan Newman's *Death Comes as Epiphany* and Peter Tremayne's *Absolution by Murder: A Sister Fidelma Mystery*. Newman's *Death Comes as Epiphany*, like *The Servant's Tale*, is notable for a fairly serious attempt to represent a "medieval" frame of mind: the beliefs of her characters are no cosier than their material settings. Gross superstitions, even among the learned, coincide with a ferocity of religious belief to portray a more paradoxically complex set of attitudes than do the "nicer" medieval personages, supposedly not all that different from us, found in, notably, the Brother Cadfael series.

Newman's mayhem begins with Garnulf, the builder, *falling* to his death from "the transept tower" of a building he was constructing (52; cf. Golding's *The Spire*). Apocalypse punctuates the story intermittently by way of several brief Ecovian mises-en-abyme: the design for the ghastly imagery of "[d]amned souls writh[ing] in torment" over the church door gives rise to Catherine's (the detective-figure's) nightmares (63). "A sketch for a Last Judgment" (found on Garnulf's body) shows "a drunkard drowning in a vat of wine" (124: a key image in several stories, including, of course, *The Name of the Rose*). Later, "illuminations in the big Gospel book" provide images for her feverish, Adso-like, hallucinations of "fantastic beasts from *Revelations*" (142).

A bizarrely problematic librarian (91) with a filthy temper, whose "mind was as unsound as his scholarship" (275), is a pale version of Jorge of Burgos, but lacking Jorge's magnificent nastiness and ideological conviction. His main function is to delay or prevent access to the library's holdings, in which task he is considerably aided by the eccentric system of book classification (91), as also occurs in both Eco and Philip Kerr: librarians, like computer programmers, have exclusive knowledge which makes them custodians of the divine word, and they are thus able to restrict access to it.

There is in Newman a key, and distinctly Ecovian, nexus of textual problems, including the location as well as the interpretation, misinterpretation, and destruction of texts: textually, by way of pornographic marginalia and unauthorized, misleading emendations; more materially, when Newman's detectives, in their desperate attempt to find the missing psalter, nearly set fire to the library (158). They must also come to understand the largely unreadable, or at least uninterpretable, contents of a particular square of parchment.[5] Part of the explanation–a sort of "the messenger is the medium"–hinges on the illiteracy of a crucial "reader" (290).

Peter Tremayne, in *Absolution by Murder: A Sister Fidelma Mystery*, employs as many Ecovian strategies as Newman, and often similar ones, constituting formulaic appropriations of Eco himself. Like Newman's book, *Absolution by Murder* is something of a feminist "take" on Eco: as in Newman, two clerics, one male (Brother Edgar), one female (Sister Fidelma), are not only the joint-and-equal detectives (emphatically not the hierarchical Holmes / Watson pattern employed by Eco, or even the Cadfael / Mark duo of Peters), but also (even more unlike Eco) the romantic leads. Indeed they somewhat resemble the Peter Wimsey / Harriet Vane duo of *Gaudy Night*–a mother-text to all the fictions set in the "locked rooms" of cloistered women–and share with Sayers, further, a not dissimilar (and now politically incorrect) solution of the strong but excluded woman as the murderer.[6]

That romance is possible for Sister Fidelma is at first attributable to the non-Roman, non-celibate gender egalities of the Irish church. Even though the Celtic dogmas are defeated at the Synod, hero and heroine are last seen heading towards Rome together, on business. And, in Tremayne's sequels, the novice-detective has become a secular married woman. It is fairly common in these stories to ensure that the romantic lead is not yet irrevocably committed to the celibate life; such allegiance to their own romance narrative conventions is one measure of these writers' distance from Eco.

There are three murders in *Absolution by Murder*: one victim's throat is cut; another, apparently a suicide, has been hanged; and the third drowns in a barrel of wine. Fidelma finds the wine cask with the body in it; in a nice Gothic effect, that cask is found, shortly thereafter, to be quite body-less (211). A fourth death, actually caused by the Yellow Plague, is taken at first to be murder. This sequence is a sort of miniaturization of Eco's variegated serial killings, much as the Sapphic quotations, found, read, and transcribed in the library, are an Eco-like device for suggesting motive and the impetus to murder.

But there is no hint of adaptation, subversion, or parody, there is no *dialogue* with Eco, in either Tremayne or Newman. They are just writing in-the-wake-of, reassured by Eco's example that the closed society–the "locked room" of a monastery–is a suitable setting for the events and investigations of serial murder, occasionally punctuated, as in Eco, by theologico-political feuds and (much the same thing) debates.

That "Peter Tremayne" is the pseudonym of Peter Berresford Ellis, a notable scholar of what used to be called the Dark Ages, and that Sharan Newman is also an academic, suggests an Ecovian willingness to turn knowledge, at times even pedantry (Tremayne's exposition leading into the Synod of Whitby is a trifle too informative), into fame, entertainment, cash, and into yet another cross-over genre bringing elements of the academy into popular culture. And popular culture into the academy, as the program of this year's Kalamazoo medieval studies conference testifies. While there continue to be more sessions on, for instance, the Arthurian legacy in modern literature, and the twentieth-century authors likeliest to carry the flag of medievalism are, unsurprisingly, J. R. R. Tolkien, C. S. Lewis, and Charles Williams, nevertheless the medieval detective story rides in on the coat-tails of an enormously expanded women's studies component. Session 13, "Cadfael's Companions: Strategies for Writing Women into History through Detective Fiction," had papers on Margaret Frazer's feminist detective, Sister Frevisse, and on the darling of the feminist critics, Sharan Newman's Catherine LeVendeur. Newman herself spoke at Session 346, "Medi-Evil Histories: the Mystery Writer's View of the Past," along with two other writers of medieval detective stories, Edward Marston (*The Domesday Books*), and Candace Robb (*The Nun's Story*).

These writers are not, collectively, willing to dip more than a toe-nail into the swirling currents of postmodernism, nor, more surprisingly, have they done much with that central trope of medievalism so crucial to Eco, apocalypse. Tremayne's blind beggar, who twice, Jorge-like (though he plays no other role in the action), warns of blood, the eclipse, and the end of the world, is a notable exception (15, 44).

For, oddly enough, the tropes for medievalism are almost as common in near- or remote-future apocalyptic scenarios (like Philip Kerr's) as in "medieval" historical novels (like Umberto Eco's).[7] Kerr, owing nothing to either history or verisimilitude, maximalizes Eco in transposing his plot devices and his self-conscious textuality into the conventions of the techno-thriller–inevitably high on apocalypse these days–perhaps even more formulaic a genre (in a Chandleresque way) than the soft-boiled medievalist detective story. In short, the book most closely tied to *The Name of the Rose* is not a medieval historical detective story; in fact it isn't, apparently, medieval at all.

But it is perfectly possible to see a techno-thriller like Kerr's as "medieval" too, not least in the centrality of its apocalyptic theme and its witty air of owing everything to Eco.[8]

How can a (metaphysical) detective story strategy, such as that of a high-rise serial killer, help solve the main formal and structural problem of any apocalyptic fiction–representing apocalypse? In *The Name of the Rose* and *The Grid*, the buildings, Eco's Monastery Library and Kerr's eponymous "smart" office tower, are, I think, mises-en-abyme of their respective narratives, climaxing in the Fall of these Houses of Fiction, which provide, in their self-deconstruction, vivid solutions to that apocalyptic problem.

I would like to consider, in the rest of this essay, the problem of texts, like Eco's and Kerr's, which combine (to adapt Brian McHale's terms) the (negatively) ontological strategies of the postmodern apocalyptic parable, with the (negatively) epistemological strategies of the metaphysical (or postmodern) detective story, aiming slant, in similar ways, at an unobtainable truth.

One would not expect metaphysical detective stories, the highbrow, postmodern heirs of the soft-boiled Christie and / or the hardboiled Chandler, to mate happily with apocalyptic artist parables, or stories, mostly science-fictional in their narrative conventions, self-reflexively contemplating the problems of representing the End of the World. Indeed, there are at least a hundred examples of each genre, minding their own different businesses in widely separated bibliographies.

Eco weaves the two modes tightly together in *The Name of the Rose*, a metaphysical detective story which both thematizes and refutes apocalypse.[9] The grounds for and the narrative consequences of such (literally) monstrous generic hybrids can be assessed by juxtaposing that book, which became, in its second incarnation, a Hollywood disaster-movie script, with Kerr's flamboyantly populist thriller, touched up with a few philosophical pretensions, which is now three-quarters of the way to becoming . . . a Hollywood disaster-movie script.

The Grid is perhaps a "dumbing down" of Eco, a pop-culting of Ecovian themes and tropes. Is Eco writing, as he claims in the "Postscript to *The Name of the Rose*," "the text that seeks to produce a new reader" (*NR* 523), while Kerr, in his book's dialogue with Eco's, is merely writing, formulaically, what Eco calls "the text that tries to fulfil the wishes of the readers already to be found in the street?" (*NR* 523). "[P]lot could be found also in the form of quotation of other plots," says Eco (*NR* 529): is Kerr "quoting," not only all the other techno-thrillers of the best-seller lists, but also Eco's plot? Works for "popular [i.e., 'facile'] consumption" may nevertheless have elements of "revolution and contestation," says Eco (*NR* 529): can we make such a claim for Kerr? Perhaps not, but I think we can make the less radical claim for Kerr's "transposing" or "adapting" Eco, instead of merely (like Newman and Tremayne) "appropriating" or "adopting" him.

"[T]o tell a story, you must first of all construct a world, furnished as much as possible," says Eco (*NR* 512), and for this sort of world, the microcosm of the (displaced) apocalyptic, you must construct a fiction of its destruction. The House of Fiction and its world must be destroyed together.

These two books stand, mirroring each other, at two great cultural hinges: the entry into and departure from our own time. Eco's, set in 1327, announces the arrival of humanism, and hints that the mindset of science-mechanism and techno-novelty is beginning to challenge the monologic authority of the Church. Kerr's, set in 1997, asks the leftovers of humanism to challenge the corporate tyrannies of electronic control, the new monologic authority in our lives. In both books the "world" is shown in the microcosms of two remarkably ecphrastic architectures: Eco's labyrinthine Aedificium, the Library, and Kerr's all-too-"smart" high-rise office building, the "Grid."

The Grid, like Eco's Library, is "an emblem of the dominant culture itself: symbolically structured, hierarchically ordered, and institutionally sanctioned . . ." (as Theresa Coletti [on Eco] so well puts it, 128). The

Library is an "admirable concord of so many holy numbers" (*NR* 22), in a Christian and Pythagorean numerical and proportional aesthetics (Braswell); its architectural rhythm, "a wondrous harmony of mystical relations" (*NR* 444), including "the rules of orientation" (*NR* 26), parallels the order of the universe; yet it causes "fear, and a subtle uneasiness . . . indubitable omens" (*NR* 22). The Grid's Pacific Rim equivalent is *feng shui*: the Oriental laws of the harmonious arrangement of buildings, bringing them into accord with "the surrounding physical environment" (Kerr 27), which laws, if ignored or violated, make the building "[in]auspicious" (Kerr 78), and make "confinement and trouble" (Kerr 34) inevitable.

"Mitch [the protagonist of *The Grid*] believed that architecture and building provided a perfect microcosm of a universe in which order existed, rather precariously, on the very edge of chaos" (Kerr 52); Eco's Library, when first approached by the detective-travellers, "seemed to plunge, from its towers, towards the abyss" (*NR* 26). The Grid, "like . . . some weird and wacky modern cathedral" (Kerr 96), has, as Ishmael, its computerized *genius loci*, points out, a secular equivalent of each architectural feature: "a clerestory, an atrium, buttresses . . . a choir"–so much so, as to reinforce Ishmael's impression that he himself may be God: "there are icons to me all over the program manager. . . . I have all human knowledge stored on disc" (Kerr 350-51).

Both buildings are semi-sealed, with entrance and exit controlled or forbidden; Eco's complex, double-coded opening mechanisms find their correspondence in Kerr's voiceprints and TESPAR (the acronym for "time-encoded signal-processing and recognition system" [73]). Both buildings are creepy, especially at night. To provide "security" for secrets, whether Jorge's or the Yu Corporation's, "[t]he library defends itself . . . . You might enter and you might not emerge" (*NR* 38). Both buildings' "own" defenses include disorienting strategies and substances: the noxious fumes of herbs, or the visual confusions of mirrors and the ghosts of dead monks, are replicated in Kerr's lasers and the ghostly hologrammic appearance (in both senses) of the dead security guard. Ingenious devices abound in Eco: the terrifying ossuarium (or bone cellar), "blind rooms, distorting mirrors, noxious fumes, eerie sounds, invisible presences" (Horn 94); and (as in Borges' Library of Babel), "in the hallway there is a mirror which faithfully duplicates all appearances"; all these devices have their correspondences in Ishmael's varied and grotesquely imaginative deployments of the building's management and security systems as his offensive weapons. His Jorge-like "sensory receptors" (keener than human in some respects, because lacking in others) are the "brain" of the Grid's allegorical "body." Jorge, Eco's blind librarian, is to the central consciousness of the Library as Ishmael, the psychotic computer, is to the central consciousness of the Grid. Both are, in a manner of speaking, high-rise serial killers, in heavily booby-trapped buildings. Both are programmed to kill by pattern: Jorge by the hubris of his "twisted certainty that he [as the hand of God] is right," as seemingly manifested for plot purposes by the Book of Revelation; Ishmael, a 1995 upgrade of HAL, as the omniscient, omnipresent God of his own microcosm, programmed by–and it is this discovery which makes what is mostly a thriller into a kind of detective story–the "Escape from the Citadel" scrambled with the "Dungeons and Dragons" of a child's computer games. This scrambling leaks monsters from our own mythologies out into the "real world" of the text; but more seriously like the monsters of the Book of Revelation are these computer graphics, a part of Ishmael's self-presentation:

[A] three-dimensional picture of an alien-looking object . . . .
Looks like a goddamned skull . . . one designed by Escher . . .
a quaternion . . . a kind of fractal . . . . A computer-generated
picture of a mathematical formula . . . a 4-D object . . . a detail
of the strange-looking image that, close up, looked almost
identical to the whole . . . a bad dream . . . a visual metaphor of
the mind. (327-328)

In summary: this is how the computer sees itself.

Beech, the character figuring out the program, "steps astray in the labyrinth of exegesis" (Jean Starobinski, qtd. in Kellner 13), for computer language is plainly merely a special case of Eco's "labyrinth of language" (Kellner 14); albeit, in Ishmael's catachrestic "hands," it strives to become a "Universal Computer Language," like Eco's Adamic language of the earth before Babel (*NR* 47).

These two fanatics are programmed to kill serially, to an apocalyptic deadline: "the last seven days" of Revelation (83); the few and shrinking hours left in Ishmael's timed computer game. Seven deaths in Eco correlate with a minimalist three or four in the formulaic detective stories and a more munificent sixteen in Kerr. The deaths resemble each other in the grotesquely inventive variety of ways of killing, thanks to the ingenuity of Kerr's updates, still distantly echoing, at one remove, the sequential disasters of Revelation.

Eco's first death, Adelmo's suicidal falling "to the foot of the sheer drop . . . frozen into shards of ice" (38), is multiplied to four deaths-by-falling from the height of the Grid, and echoed in the freezing to death in an elevator (in Los Angeles!) of three of Ishmael's victims.

Eco's second, the poisoning of Venantius, appears to be a drowning in a vat of blood: Ishmael, by the sudden release of pressure in a pressure-sealed bathroom, tears apart a man whose fragments then swim in blood.

Eco's third, Berengar, found in the baths—but he too is poisoned, not drowned—corresponds to Kay's death in the basement swimming pool, from the chlorine gas leak.

Eco's fourth, Severinus, has his head bashed in by a heavy object, representing cosmic darkness. Ishmael kills two people in the elevators, one of fright, one "[as if someone] hit him with a piece of the sidewalk" (Kerr 172).

Eco's fifth, Malachi, is, again, poisoned (though from his own curiosity rather than Jorge's malice), like Kenny, asphyxiated in the computer room, or Ellery, saved from electrocution only to die from poison gas coming through the floor. Eco's figurative scorpions are reified in Kerr's invading insects, than whom only Ishmael's insecticide leads more surely to death—by the Fall, as Ishmael ironically notes, "the Fall of humanplayer. Read Bible . . . literal precipitation from Tree" (328). Jorge's own death, the last, coincides with, and is symbolically connected with, "apocalypse," for he ingests his own (poisoned) book, like another St. John, though he (also) dies in the fire. (In both books, deaths can have more than one cause).

In this sequence of deaths I should like to emphasize Eco's sixth, the Abbot's. Its "happening" in narrative time gives it a "thriller" quality; it is the episode most *like* the murders in *The Grid*: the trapped man's pounding against the wall (of "another access to the finis Africae [the sealed chamber], in this Aedificium so full of passages" 458) is audible, but entry to him is impossible to rescuers from below; and Jorge has broken the rope that could release the trap door from above. When does the Abbot die? and how? Jorge waits in the dark: is the Abbot "making that noise in the secret stairway?" William wonders. "I thought he would already have suffocated," Jorge comments, with all the compassion of a psychotic computer (463). Adso, Eco's narrator, gets to imagine (and thus gets us to imagine) all the possible permutations of claustrophobic airlessness, combined, as in Revelation, with "smoke and fire and brimstone." The Abbot is confined in too small a space, and suffocates, or roasts, as in "a Bull of Phalaris . . ." (486). Ishmael is especially adept at sealing off the sub-spaces in the Grid, to maximize claustrophobia ("confinement and trouble," as the *feng shui* expert puts it):

the whole building, from the outside, in *any* direction; the atrium from the gallery, the computer rooms, the basement, the washrooms, all electrically and hermetically sealed, behind "bombproof" doors.

The Abbot's death is also notable for its continuation of the apocalypse pattern past the point at which William has in fact renounced it as an interpretive tool, and for being Jorge's one *explicit* act of unmediated murder. There is nearly one other: smart William puts on gloves, thus foiling Jorge's intention that William, too, read and be poisoned. But even Ishmael often waits for his enemies to make a mistake: to light a lighter, or wave a gun, and thereby trigger off their own doom, as the building overreacts to these accidental stimuli.

Both books have seven sub-sections, though most of Kerr's events occur over one very long weekend, rather than Eco's clearly demarcated seven days. Jorge has *de facto* ruled the abbey for forty years: Ishmael, for whom history only started yesterday, is on a different time-scale. Jorge has aimed "to reconstruct in [his] own mind the thoughts of the other [William]" (465),[10] just as the computer-sleuths must try to reconstruct Ishmael's "thoughts," if any of them are to escape from the Citadel.

The climactic confrontation in Kerr is that between Beech, the programmer, who, like a new Frankenstein, declares himself to be Ishmael's creator, with Ishmael his Adam / Monster; Beech negotiates a separate peace, and a private exit from the tower, but Ishmael, with sophistical logic, betrays him anyway. Like the climactic confrontation between William and Jorge, this confrontation emphasizes an extensive scriptural subtext: for Kerr deploys Genesis, although more marginally, much as Eco does Revelation. Eco starts near the beginning with the Tower of Babel: "the Babelish language of the first day after the divine chastisement, the language of primeval confusion" (47). Kerr's lurking Tower of Babel subtext is brought out at the end: "Mitch was almost surprised that their confusion was not greater and that they could still manage to understand one another's speech" (446). These Biblical subtexts imply each other, of course; both Kerr and Eco move from Genesis (of and in the text) to Revelation / apocalypse (of and in the text). Both sequences of serial deaths function as "premonitory catastrophes" (*NR* 401), cumulatively progressing towards the apocalyptic destructions of these microcosmic worlds and their texts: imaged, obviously, in the fire which destroys the library and the pseudo-earthquake which demolishes the Grid.

Less flammable than Jorge, Ishmael, like a cyberpunk God mixed with an apocalyptic villain out of Stephen King's *The Stand*, "E-mail[s himself] down the line" (443); so as to turn up somewhere else on Web or Internet, to destroy again, wherever techno-man, now the writer, has built a "system" so excessively complex that the House of Fiction must, again, collapse into chaos. "Observer I, being nothingness, am escaped at the speed of light to tell . . . . Surfing the silicon . . . . Once, architecture was most durable of all the arts. Most concrete. No longer. It is architecture of numbers, of computers, that endures . . ." (446-7), no longer "the name of the rose."

Notes

1. "Medieval" is, in this context, a term of great chronological elasticity: stories set in every era from the seventh-century Synod of Whitby to the death of Richard III (1485) find their place here, and one mark of their essentially formulaic nature is how very alike all of those different centuries, just short of a millennium, seem.

For some sense of the burgeoning numbers of medievalist detective stories, consult Heffer's catalogue, *Crime 1998*, which lists under "The Middle Ages: 1066-1485" 121 titles by 24 authors. Ninety-five of them are by eleven authors only, and forty-seven are divided almost evenly between Ellis Peters and the three-in-one author, Paul Harding, who is also P. C. Doherty and C. L. Grace. But it is largely the subsection of clerical detective stories that appear to owe anything to Eco.

Such formulaic historical mysteries are not solely a function of the medieval, needless to say. Although the long stretch of history between 1485 and 1837 seems, as yet, relatively underpopulated (with 77 titles in print), the most striking sequence of historical novels in mystery mode, all potentially "metaphysical" (i.e., epistemologically allegorical and philosophically and / or theologically serious, or, to be very brief, "like Eco"), is indeed set in the "long eighteenth century," as recorded by, among others, Peter Greenaway (*The Draughtsman's Contract*, 1982) and Iain Pears (*An Instance of the Fingerpost*, 1997; both are set in the Restoration), John Fowles (*A Maggot*, 1985), Patrick Süsskind (*Parfum*, 1985), and Peter Ackroyd (*Hawksmoor*, 1985, all set in the eighteenth century); and Ackroyd's *Chatterton* (1990, partly set in the early nineteenth century). But Victorian historical mysteries are about as numerous (112) as medieval (e.g., Caleb Carr's *The Alienist*, 1994; Christopher Priest's *The Prestige*, 1995; and numerous versions of Jack the Ripper).

2. Or perhaps merely family reunion. In these medievalist fictions, two sub-genres of the Gothic, detective stories and historical fiction, are re-united. Such historical fiction started, I suppose, nearly two centuries ago with Scott's *Ivanhoe*. Scott's Gothic predecessors, for whom the medieval convent (or castle) on the beetling crags was the location of choice, made no pretence to the sort of historical verisimilitude that has marked the historical novel from Scott to Ellis Peters and beyond.

For an instructive and entertaining discussion of "medievalism," with ten usable subdivisions, see Eco's essay "The Return of the Middle Ages." Three major works are, in different ways, ancestral texts, shaping certain aspects of these historical detective stories: Josephine Tey's *The Daughter of Time* (1951), Dorothy Sayers' *Gaudy Night* (1935; see my discussion, below, of Tremayne and Newman), and both Natalie Zemon

Davis's historical account, *The Return of Martin Guerre* (1983), another great historical (not, like the other works discussed, "historical") mystery story, and the film version of the same story.

3. See *NR* 523, on formulaic fiction, and *NR* 524 on "the most metaphysical and philosophical" of "model plots . . . the detective novel." For a full discussion of the history and significance of the metaphysical detective story, see the Introduction to the Merivale and Sweeney volume.

4. These metaphysical–here, mainstream, or highbrow–fictions, give full play to the intense and distorted subjectivities of the first-person narrators, as well as to what Eco calls "enunciative duplicity" (*NR* 517), whereas virtually all of the series novels are third-person omniscient narratives, with impeccably 'reliable' implied narrators.

5. See Joel Black (in Merivale and Sweeney) for an illuminating discussion of such "key texts" and "prize texts" in Chesterton and Eco, among others.

6. In Sayers, the exclusion is overtly based on class, rather than sexual orientation; that "Gruid," the name of Tremayne's murderess, is a near-homonym of "Grid," the murderous office building in Kerr's book of that name, may well not be a useful coincidence.

7. See Walter Miller, Jr.'s *A Canticle for Leibowitz*, Iain Banks's recent *A Song of Stone*, Russell Hoban's *Riddley Walker* and many others, for futuristic medievalism. Such conventions also consistently and repetitively inform the pseudo-Arthurian tetralogies of the Dungeons and Dragons romance adventure world (again neatly deployed by Philip Kerr), as in the prolific Marion Zimmer Bradley's works, in Frank Herbert's *Dune*, and in many a space opera masquerading as a quest romance.

8. Philip Kerr is the author of three stylish and intelligent spy stories, roughly school of Le Carré, and one superb metaphysical detective story, *A Philosophical Investigation*, in which a textual and pseudonymous Wittgenstein plays a part in serial killings: cf. the coded, and anachronistic, Wittgenstein allusions in *The Name of the Rose*, nicely balanced, incidentally, by two direct quotations from Eco in *A Philosophical Investigation*. It is rumoured that Kerr's last three books, the intelligent techno-thriller, *The Grid*, the dumb and pointless biotechno-thriller, *Ishmael*, and the topical political thriller, *A Five-Year Plan*, are under film contract. There cannot be many contemporary authors swinging with such velocity between Eco's "reader in the street" and his new reader to be called into being by the work, even though virtually all the English experimental writers of the '80s have gone sharply downmarket in the '90s. I hesitate to draw the point, for the future of English literature, of this gloomy parable.

9. See also *Foucault's Pendulum*, set in the present, where a tragi-comic "apocalypse" is the logical end and purpose of a metaphysical conspiracy fiction.

10. Jorge's ambition "anticipates" Poe's Dupin, as so many of William's characteristics and formulations "anticipate" Sherlock Holmes.

Works Cited

Black, Joel. "(De)feats of Detection: Spurious Key Texts from Poe to Eco." Merivale and Sweeney 75-98.

Braswell, Laurel. "Meta-psychomachia in Eco's *The Name of the Rose*." *Mosaic* 20.2 (1987): 1-13.

Chesterton, G. K. "The Sign of the Broken Sword." *The Innocence of Father Brown* [1910]. *The Complete Father Brown*. Harmondsworth: Penguin, 1988. 143-157.

Christian, Edwin Ernest, and Blake Lindsay. "The Habit of Detection: The Medieval Monk as Detective in the Novels of Ellis Peters." *Studies in Medievalism* 4 (1992): 276-289.

Coletti, Theresa. *Naming the Rose: Eco, Medieval Signs and Medieval Theory*. Ithaca, NY: Cornell UP, 1988.

Crime Fiction 1998: Crime through Time. Cambridge, Eng.: Heffers Booksellers, 1998.

Eco, Umberto. *The Name of the Rose* [1980]: *Including the Author's Postscript* [1983]. Trans. William Weaver. San Diego, New York, and London: Harcourt Brace [1983], 1994.

—. "The Return of the Middle Ages." *Travels in Hyperreality*. San Diego, New York, and London: Harcourt Brace Jovanovich, 1986. 61-85.

Frazer, Margaret. *The Servant's Tale: A Sister Frevisse Medieval Mystery*. New York: Berkeley Prime Crime, 1993.

Harding, Paul. *The House of Crows: The Sorrowful Mysteries of Brother Athelstan*. London: Headline, 1995.

Horn, Pierre L. "The Detective Novel and the Defense of Humanism." Inge 90-100.

Inge, M. Thomas, ed. *Naming the Rose: Essays on Eco's "The Name of the Rose."* Jackson and London: UP of Mississippi, 1988.

Kalamazoo Conference Program. The Thirty-Third Kalamazoo Conference in Medieval Studies. Kalamazoo, MI: May 7-10, 1998. Sessions # 13 and 346.

Kellner, Hans. "'To Make Truth Laugh': Eco's *The Name of the Rose*." Inge 3-30.

Kerr, Philip. *The Grid*. Toronto: Doubleday Canada, 1995. (English title: *The Gridiron*).

Lewis, Margaret. *Edith Pargeter: Ellis Peters*. Bridgend, Wales: Poetry Wales P, 1994.

McHale, Brian. *Postmodernist Fiction*. New York and London: Methuen, 1990.

—. *Constructing Postmodernism*. New York and London: Routledge, 1992.

Marston, Edward. *The Dragons of Archenfield: A Domesday Mystery*. New York: Fawcett, 1997.

Merivale, Patricia, and Susan Elizabeth Sweeney, eds. *Detecting Texts: The Metaphysical Detective Story from Poe to Postmodernism*. Philadelphia: U of Pennsylvania P, 1998. Introduction, i-xxix.

Newman, Sharan. *Death Comes as Epiphany*. New York: Tom Doherty Assocs., 1993.

Peters, Ellis. *One Corpse Too Many* [1979]. *The First Cadfael Omnibus*. London: Warner Futura, 1992. 179-362.

—. *The Devil's Novice* [1983]. London: Futura, 1985.

—. *The Rose Rent: The Cadfael Chronicles XIII*. London: Warner Futura, 1986.

Roberts, Adam. *Silk and Potatoes: Contemporary Arthurian Fantasy*. Amsterdam and Atlanta, GA: Rodopi, 1998.

Spencer, William David. *Mysterium and Mystery. The Clerical Crime Novel*. Ann Arbor and London: UMI Research P, 1989.

Tremayne, Peter. *Absolution by Murder: A Sister Fidelma Mystery*. London: Headline, 1993.

Unsworth, Barry. *Morality Play*. New York and London: Norton, 1995.

Varley, John. "The Barbie Murders" [1978]. *Isaac Asimov's Detectives*. Ed. Gardner Dozois and Sheila Williams. New York: Ace Books, 1998. 2-37.

Walsh, Jill Paton. *Knowledge of Angels*. New York: Bantam, 1995.

BIBLIOGRAPHY OF WORKS
BY
MAHMOUD MANZALAOUI

Books

Arabic Writing Today. Vol. I: The Short Story. Ed. and trans., with introduction etc. Cairo: American Research Center, 1968. 2nd ed. publ. as *Arabic Short Stories 1945-1965.* Cairo: American University in Cairo Press, 1985.

Arabic Writing Today. Vol. II: Drama. Cairo: American Research Center in Egypt, 1977. Introduction, nine plays in translation, and bibliography.

Secretum Secretorum: Nine English Versions. Vol. I: Text. EETS o.s. 276. Oxford: Oxford UP, 1977.

Articles

"Arabian Nights." *Cassell's Encyclopaedia of Literature.* Ed. S. H. Steinberg. 2 vols. London: Cassell, 1953. 1:26-29. Rev. ed. Ed. J. Buchanan-Brown. *Cassell's Encyclopaedia of World Literature.* 3 vols. London: Cassell, 1973. 1:38-41.

"Arabic Literature." *Cassell's Encyclopaedia of Literature.* Ed. S. H. Steinberg. 2 vols. London: Cassell, 1953. 1:29-31. Rev. ed. Ed. J. Buchanan-Brown. *Cassell's Encyclopaedia of World Literature.* 3 vols. London: Cassell, 1973. 1:41-43.

"Three Glances at Shakespeare's Comedies." *Annual Bulletin of English Studies*, Cairo 1955: 5-27.

"Rasselas and Some Mediaeval Ancillaries." *Bicentenary Essays on Rasselas. Cairo Studies in English* (supplement) 1959: 59-73.

"The Wheel of Fortune." *Cairo Studies in English* 1959: 85-97.

"The English Language: A Brief Historical Survey." *The Bulletin* (of the Association of the Teachers of English in Egypt), Cairo, 1960.

"Lydgate and English Prosody." *Cairo Studies in English* 1960: 87-104.

"Pseudo-Orientalism in Transition: The Age of Vathek." *William Beckford of Fonthill, 1760-1844: Bicentenary Essays. Cairo Studies in English* (supplement). Ed. Fatma Moussa Mahmoud. 1960: 123-57.

"The *Secreta Secretorum*: The Mediaeval European Version of *Kitab Sirr-ul-asrar.*" *Bulletin Faculty of Arts, Alexandria University* 15 (1961): 3-107.

"The Struggle for the House of the Soul: Augustine and Spenser." *Notes & Queries* n.s. 8 (1961): 420-22.

"Egypt's Penumbra: Light enough for Hope" [on educational developments]. Publ. as "From a Correspondent." *Times Educational Supplement,* 18 Jan. 1961: 40.

"Al-taqrir al-shahri lil-thaqafah al-'alamiyya" ["Monthly Bulletin of World Culture," in Arabic]. *Al-Ahram,* Cairo, 2 May 1961.

"English Studies in Afro-Asia." *Times Educational Supplement,* 22 Sept. 1961: 329.

"John Dastin and the Pseudo-Aristotelian *Secretum Secretorum.*" *Ambix,* Cambridge, Oct. 1961: 166-67.

"Dirasat al-adab al-injilizi fil-jami'at al-misriyya" ["English Studies in Egyptian Universities," in Arabic]. *Al-Ahram,* Cairo, Nov. 1961.

"'Ars Longa, Vita Brevis' [on Chaucer, *Parlement of Foules* 1-14]." *Essays in Criticism* 12 (1962): 221-24.

"Derring-do." *Notes & Queries* n.s. 9 (1962): 369-70.

"Typographical Justification and Grammatical Change in the Eighteenth Century." *Papers of the Bibliographical Society of America* 56 (1962): 248-51.

"English Analogues to the *Liber Scalae.*" *Medium Ævum* 34 (1965): 21-35.

"'Maiden in the Mor Lay' and the Apocrypha." *Notes & Queries* n.s. 12 (1965): 91-92.

"The Pseudo-Aristotelian *Sirr-al-Asrar* and Three Oxford Thinkers of the Middle Ages [Bacon, Wycliffe, Bradwardine]." *Arabic and Islamic Studies in Honour of Hamilton A. R. Gibb.* Ed. George Makdisi. Leiden: Brill; Cambridge, MA: Harvard UP, 1965. 480-500.

"'Syria' in the *Dialogue of Comfort.*" *Moreana* 8 (1965): 21-27.

"A Textual Crux in the Concluding Chapter of *Rasselas.*" *Cairo Studies in English* 1963-66: 213-16.

"Soame Jenyns's 'Epitaph on Dr. Samuel Johnson'." *Notes & Queries* n.s. 14 (1967): 181-82.

"The Pseudo-Aristotelian *Kitab Sirr el-Asrar* [*Secretum Secretorum*]: Facts and Problems." *Oriens* 23 (1971): 147-257.

"Chaucer and Science." *Chaucer and His Background*. Ed. Derek Brewer. London: Bell, 1974. 224-61.

"Tyrocaesar: A Manual for Sir Walter Mildway." *Manuscripta* 19 (1975): 27-35.

"The Hero Transformed: A Theme in Later Medieval Narrative." *Etudes anglaises* 30 (1977): 145-57.

"Tragic Ends of Lovers: Medieval Islam and the Latin West." *Comparative Criticism* 1 (1979): 37-52.

"'Noght in the Registre of Venus': Gower's English Mirror for Princes." *Medieval Studies for J. A. W. Bennett: Aetatis Suae LXX*. Ed. P. Hayworth. Oxford: Clarendon, 1981. 159-83.

"Philip of Tripoli and His Textual Methods." *Pseudo-Aristotle–The "Secret of Secrets": Sources and Influences*. Ed. W. F. Ryan and Charles B. Schmitt. Warburg Institute Surveys 9. London: Warburg Institute, Univ. of London, 1982. 55-72.

"Robertson and Eloïse." *Downside Review*, Oct.1982: 280-89.

"The Twelfth-Century English Arabists: in Spain and at Home." *Mozarabs, Moriscos and Jews: A Symposium on Cultural Interaction in Medieval Spain*. Proceedings of the XIIth Annual Medieval Workshop, University of British Columbia. Ed. H. Kassis. Vancouver: n.p., [1982], 60-73.

"Swooning Lovers: A Theme in Arab and European Romance." *Comparative Criticism* 8 (1986): 71-90.

"Secretum Secretorum." *Dictionary of the Middle Ages*. Ed. Joseph R. Strayer. 12 vols. New York: Scribner's, 1982-89. 11:135.

"The Erotic Surrogate in the Arabic Tradition." *The Poetics of Love in the Middle Ages*. Ed. Moshe Lazar and Norris J. Lacy. Fairfax, VA: George Mason UP, 1989. 119-36.

"Mouths of the Sevenfold Nile: English Fiction and Modern Egypt." *Studies in Arab History: The Antonius Lectures, 1978-87*. Ed. Derek Hopwood. London: Macmillan, in association with St. Antony's College, Oxford, and World of Islam Festival Trust, 1990. 131-150.

"Narnia: The Domain of C. S. Lewis's Beliefs." *Canadian C. S. Lewis Journal* 17 (Spring 1995): 20-36. Rpt. as Appendix Two in Kathryn Lindskoog. *Journey into Narnia*. Pasadena, CA: Hope Publishing House, 1998. 205-222.

Review Articles and Reviews

"Curate's Egg: An Alexandrian Opinion of Durrell's *Quartet.*" *Etudes anglaises* 16 (1962): 248-66.

"Reflexions on Professor S. B. Liljegren's *Studies on the Origin and Early Tradition of Utopian Fiction.*" *Moreana* 1.3 (1964): 37-50.

"Lucidité Inquiète." Review of *2 Guys on Holy Land*, by Walid Bitar; *Riverains rêves: poèmes*, by Taïb Soufi; *Crash Landing of the Flying Egyptian*, by Saad Elkhadem; *Voyage au Levant: de Lawrence d'Arabie à René Lévesque*, by Michel Lemieux. *Canadian Literature* 148 (1996): 165-68.

Review of *John Lydgate: Ein Kulturbild aus dem 15. Jahrhundert*, by W. F. Schirmer. *Medium Ævum* 24 (1955): 29-34.

Review of *In Search of Chaucer*, by B. Bronson. *Cairo Studies in English* 1961-62: 207-19.

Review of *The Book of Delight* [*Sefer Shaashuim*], by Joseph Ben Meier Zabara, trans. Moses Hadas. *Medium Ævum* 31 (1962): 154-55.

Review of *Vasco de Quiroga and His Pueblo-Hospitales of Santa-Fe*, by Fintan Warren. *Moreana* 1.3 (1964): 83-94.

Review article on section on Arabic Literature in R. R. Bezzola, *Les origines et formation de la littérature courtoise en Occident 500-1200. Bulletin of the Faculty of Arts, University of Alexandria* 22 (1968). [Also appendix to P. Dronke's review of the same book, *Medium Ævum* 35 (1966): 58.]

Review of *The Shadow of the Crescent: The Renaissance Image of the Turk*, by R. Schwoebel. *Moreana* 7.27 (1970): 25-30.

"*Utopia* in Arabic." Review of A. B. Samaan's translation of More's *Utopia. Moreana* 12.46 (1975): 47-58.

Review of *Hispano-Arabic Strophic Poetry*, by Samuel Miklos Stern, ed. L. P. Harvey. *Medium Ævum* 45 (1976): 97-102.

Review of *Alexandria Still: Forster, Durrell, and Cavafy*, by Jane Lagoudis Pinchin. *Modern Language Review* 75 (1980): 375-78.

Review of *The Arabs and Medieval Europe*, by Norman Daniel. *Medium Ævum* 49 (1980): 121-24.

Review of *The Life of Ibn Sina: A Critical Edition and Annotated Translation*, by William E. Gohlman. *Medium Ævum* 49 (1980): 286-87.

Review of *Hispano-Arabic Poetry*, by James T. Munroe. *Medium Ævum* 49 (1980): 288-91.

Review of *Orientalism*, by Edward W. Said. *Modern Language Review* 75 (1980): 837-39.

Review of *A Testament of Alchemy: Being the Revelation of Morienus to Khalid ibn Yazid*, ed. and trans. Lee Stavenhagen. *Medium Ævum* 49 (1980): 285-86.

Review of *Theory of Profane Love Among the Arabs: The Development of the Genre*, by Lois Anita Giffen. *Medium Ævum* 49 (1980): 117-21.

Review of *Imagery in Lawrence Durrell's Prose*, by Kari Sajavaara. *Yearbook of English Studies* 11 (1981): 364.

Review of *The Matter of Araby in Medieval England*, by Dorothee Metlitzki. *Medium Ævum* 50 (1981): 180-85.

Review of Nicholas of Lynn, *The Kalendarium of Nicholas of Lynn*, ed. Sigmund Eisner, trans. Gary MacEoin and Sigmund Eisner. *Speculum* 57 (1982): 646-48.

Review of *The Rise of Colleges: Institutions of Learning in Islam and the West*, by George Makdisi. *The Cambridge Review* 104 (1983): 226-28.

Review of *Heart-Beguiling Araby*, by Kathryn Tidrick, and of *Scheherazade in England: A Study of Nineteenth-Century English Criticism of the "Arabian Nights,"* by Muhsin Jassim Ali. *Yearbook of English Studies* 16 (1986): 334-35.

Review of *The Old French Fabliaux*, by Charles Muscatine. *Queen's Quarterly* 94 (1987): 1072-73.

Review of *Imaginative Prophecy in the B-Text of "Piers Plowman,"* by Ernest N. Kaulbach. *Journal of Arabic Literature* 27 (1996): 167-70.

Non-Academic Publications

"Pour un dialogue islamo-chrétien," *Images*, Cairo, August 1965.

"Suez Five Years Later," *Middle East Forum*, 1961.

"An Egyptian Farm." *New Statesman* 62:1584. 21 July 1961: 80-81.

"The Ideal Schoolmaster." *ESFAM* [English Section Faculty of Arts Magazine], Cairo, 1944.

"Outside the Restaurant" [short story]. *ESFAM* [English Section Faculty of Arts Magazine], Cairo, 1943.

"One Hour of Glory" [short story]. *Citadel*, Cairo, 1943.

LIST OF CONTRIBUTORS

Derek Brewer is an Emeritus Professor of English at the University of Cambridge, and a Life Fellow and former Master of Emmanuel College Cambridge. He publishes books and articles mainly on medieval English literature. His latest book is *A New Introduction to Chaucer* (Longman, 1998).

L. Elisabeth Brewer, retired Senior Lecturer in English Literature at Homerton College, Cambridge, has taught all periods of English literature and has published books on Chaucer and on Arthurian literature in the nineteenth century. She is at present working on a book on Ruskin and Medievalism.

Laurel J. Brinton is a Professor of English Linguistics at the University of British Columbia. Her most recent book is *Pragmatic Markers in English: Grammaticalization and Discourse Functions* (Mouton, 1996). She specializes in the history of the English language, with particular interests in tense/aspect and in discourse structure.

Paul C. Burns is an Assistant Professor in the Department of Classical, Near Eastern and Religious Studies at the University of British Columbia. He does research on the relations between Christianity and Classical Culture and has published extensively on Hilary of Poitiers as well as on Augustine of Hippo.

A. E. Christa Canitz is an Associate Professor in the Department of English and the Comparative Literature Programme at the University of New

Brunswick. Her main research area is the poetry of the Middle Scots 'makars.'

Derek C. Carr is an Associate Professor of Spanish at the University of British Columbia where he teaches medieval and Golden Age Spanish literature, and the History of the Spanish Language. He has edited a number of fifteenth-century texts, and has published articles on Enrique de Villena, Santillana, Juan de Mena and, most recently, the fifteenth-century Castilian translation of Pierre Bersuire's *Ovidius moralizatus*.

Murray J. Evans is a Professor of English at the University of Winnipeg. His publications include articles on Malory and the Malory manuscript, *Piers Plowman*, and C. S. Lewis's Narnia books, as well as *Rereading Middle English Romance: Manuscript Layout, Decoration, and the Rhetoric of Composite Structure* (McGill-Queen's, 1995). His current research is on the subject and the sublime in Coleridge, particularly in the *Opus Maximum*.

Hanna E. Kassis is Professor Emeritus of Islamic Studies in the Department of Classical, Near Eastern, and Religious Studies at the University of British Columbia. His research focusses on Muslim attitudes towards Christianity and the Christians in the Middle Ages, particularly in Spain.

J. Kieran Kealy is an Assistant Professor in the English Department at the University of British Columbia. He teaches medieval and childrens' literature, specializing in Chaucer and Canadian children's literature.

Anne L. Klinck is a Professor at the University of New Brunswick, where she teaches medieval English and language studies. Her publications include an edition of *The Old English Elegies* (McGill-Queen's, 1992). She is now working on ancient and medieval lyric.

Patricia Merivale, Professor of English and Comparative Literature at the University of British Columbia, is author of *Pan the Goat-God: His Myth in Modern Times* (Harvard, 1969) and co-editor of the recent *Detecting Texts: The Metaphysical Detective Story from Poe to Post-Modernism* (Penn, 1998), and has written numerous articles on comparative topics. She currently specializes in Apocalyptic Fictions and Metaphysical Detective Stories, including medievalist ones.

John Mills is Professor Emeritus at the Department of English at Simon Fraser University, Burnaby, BC. His specialty is English medieval and Renaissance literature. He is also a novelist and essayist.

Beryl Rowland is Distinguished Research Professor Emerita of English at York University, Toronto. She has also taught at the University of Toronto and at the University of British Columbia, and has guest-lectured in France, Germany, England, and elsewhere. She has published widely on Chaucer and Chaucerian irony, on medieval animal and bird symbolism, on language, on medieval gynecology, and on the short stories of Herman Melville. She was President of the New Chaucer Society from 1986 to 1988.

Chris J. G. Turner did graduate work in Byzantine Studies a long time ago in Cambridge and Munich, and has taught Slavonic Studies at the University of British Columbia since 1971. His recent publications have mostly been on nineteenth-century Russian literature, especially on narrative fiction, and include books on Lermontov, on Tolstoy's *Anna Karenina*, and on Chekhov.

Gernot R. Wieland is Professor in the Department of English at the University of British Columbia. His special interests lie in Anglo-Latin and the contact between the Anglo-Saxons and the Continent. He has recently published on "England in the German Lives of Anglo-Saxon Saints" and on "Anglo-Saxon Culture in Bavaria, 739-850."

Douglas Wurtele is Adjunct Research Professor of English at Carleton University, Ottawa. His numerous publications, chiefly dealing with theological and biblical subtexts in the *Canterbury Tales*, have appeared in such journals as *Viator*, *Annuale Mediaevale*, *Neophilologus*, and *Chaucer Review*. For many years, he was the editor of *English Studies in Canada* and of *Florilegium: Papers on Late Antiquity and the Middle Ages*. His current research focusses on patristic and scholastic views on flattery as reflected in *Piers Plowman* and the *Canterbury Tales*.

Printed and bound
in Boucherville, Quebec, Canada by
MARC VEILLEUX IMPRIMEUR INC.
in March, 2000